OXFORD EARLY CHRISTI/

General Editors
Gillian Clark   Andrew L

THE OXFORD EARLY CHRISTIAN STUDIES series includes scholarly volumes on the thought and history of the early Christian centuries. Covering a wide range of Greek, Latin, and Oriental sources, the books are of interest to theologians, ancient historians, and specialists in the classical and Jewish worlds.

Origen and Scripture

The Contours of the Exegetical Life

PETER W. MARTENS

OXFORD
UNIVERSITY PRESS

OXFORD
UNIVERSITY PRESS

Great Clarendon Street, Oxford, OX2 6DP,

Oxford University Press is a department of the University of Oxford.
It furthers the University's objective of excellence in research, scholarship,
and education by publishing worldwide. Oxford is a registered trade mark of
Oxford University Press in the UK and in certain other countries

© Peter W. Martens 2012

The moral rights of the author have been asserted

First published 2012
First published in paperback 2014

Published in the United States of America by Oxford University Press
198 Madison Avenue, New York, NY 10016, United States of America

British Library Cataloguing in Publication Data
Data available

Library of Congress Cataloging in Publication Data
Data available

ISBN 978-0-19-963955-7 (Hbk)
ISBN 978-0-19-871756-0 (Pbk)

Table of Contents

Abbreviations

Note: Abbreviations for Origen's works are found in the bibliography.

ABD	*Anchor Bible Dictionary*
ACW	Ancient Christian Writers
ANF	*Ante-Nicene Fathers*
ATR	*Anglican Theological Review*
Aug	*Augustinianum*
BGl	*Beweis des Glaubens*
BLE	*Bulletin de littérature ecclésiastique*
CCG	Corpus Christianorum. Series Graeca
CCL	Corpus Christianorum. Series Latina
CF	*Collectanea Friburgensia*
CH	*Church History*
CPG	*Clavis Patrum Graecorum*
CSEL	Corpus Scriptorum Ecclesiasticorum Latinorum
DBS	*Dictionnaire de la Bible. Supplément*
DNP	*Der Neue Pauly: Enzyklopädie der Antike*
DS	*Dictionnaire de spiritualité ascétique et mystique, doctrine et histoire*
ECQ	*Eastern Churches Quarterly*
EnEC	*Encyclopedia of Early Christianity*, 2nd edn
EnECh	*Encyclopedia of the Early Church*
EThR	*Études théologique et religieuses*
FC	Fontes Christiani
FOTC	Fathers of the Church
GCS	Die griechischen christlichen Schriftsteller der ersten drei Jahrhunderte
GK	Görgemanns H. and H. Karpp. *Origenes. Vier Bücher von den Prinzipien*. 3rd edn (Darmstadt: Wissenschaftliche Buchgesellschaft, 1992)
GOTR	*Greek Orthodox Theological Review*
HTR	*Harvard Theological Review*
HWP	*Historisches Wörterbuch der Philosophie*
IKZ	*Internationale Kirchliche Zeitschrift*
JAC	*Jahrbuch für Antike und Christentum*

JBL	*Journal of Biblical Literature*
JECS	*Journal of Early Christian Studies*
JQR	*Jewish Quarterly Review*
JTS	*Journal of Theological Studies*
Lampe	*A Patristic Greek Lexicon*
LCL	Loeb Classical Library
LSJ	*Greek–English Lexicon*
LXX	*Septuagint*
MH	*Museum Helveticum*
MTZ	*Münchener theologische Zeitschrift*
NPNF	A Select Library of the Nicene and Post-Nicene Fathers of the Christian Church
NTS	*New Testament Studies*
OCD	*Oxford Classical Dictionary*
ODCC	*Oxford Dictionary of the Christian Church*, 3rd edn
OED	*Oxford English Dictionary*, 2nd edn
Orig I–IX	*Published proceedings from the Origen Colloquia*
PG	Patrologiae Cursus Completus: Series Graeca
PL	Patrologiae Cursus Completus: Series Latina
RAC	*Reallexicon für Antike und Christentum*
RB	*Revue Biblique*
REG	*Revue des études grecques*
RHE	*Revue d'histoire ecclésiastique*
RHPhR	*Revue d'histoire et de philosophie religieuses*
RHR	*Revue de l'histoire des religions*
RHT	*Revue d'histoire des texte*
RQ	*Römische Quartalschrift für christliche Altertumskunde*
RSE	*Revue des sciences ecclésiastiques*
RSR	*Recherches de Science Religieuse*
SC	Sources Chrétiennes
SP	*Studia Patristica*
ThQ	*Theologische Quartalschrift*
TLG	*Thesaurus Linguae Graecae*: Canon of Greek Authors and Works
TRE	*Theologische Realenenzyclopädie*
TS	*Theological Studies*
TU	Texte und Untersuchungen zur Geschichte der altchristlicher Literatur
VC	*Vigiliae christianae*

VetChr	*Vetera Christianorum*
ZAC	*Zeitschrift für Antikes Christentum*
ZKG	*Zeitschrift für Kirchengeschichte*
ZKTh	*Zeitschrift für katholische Theologie*
ZNW	*Zeitschrift für die Neutestamentliche Wissenschaft und die Kunde der Älteren Kirche*
ZPE	*Zeitschrift für Papyrologie und Epigraphik*
ZTK	*Zeitschrift für Theologie und Kirche*

Preface

Scriptural interpretation was an important form of scholarship for Christians in late antiquity. For no one does this claim ring more true than for Origen of Alexandria, one of the most prolific scholars of Scripture in early Christianity. While his approach to this collection of sacred writings has been fruitfully studied from several different perspectives, in this book I will examine it biographically: the focus is on his account of the scriptural interpreter, the animating center of the exegetical enterprise. In pursuing this largely neglected line of inquiry, I intend to disclose the contours of Origen's sweeping vision of scriptural exegesis as a way of life. For him, ideal interpreters were far more than philologists steeped in the skills and teachings conveyed by Greco-Roman education. Their profile also included a commitment to Christianity from which they gathered a spectrum of loyalties, guidelines, dispositions, relationships, and doctrines that tangibly shaped how they practiced and thought about their biblical scholarship. My central thesis in this book is that Origen contextualized interpreters—himself included—within the Christian drama of salvation. In examining this drama as it unfolded on Scripture's pages, ideal interpreters participated in it: biblical interpretation afforded these philologists an occasion through which to express various facets of their existing Christian commitment, as well as to receive divine resources for their continued journey in their faith. This study will explore the many ways in which Origen thought ideal scriptural interpreters embarked upon a way of life, indeed a way of salvation, culminating in the everlasting contemplation of God. This new and integrative thesis is offered primarily as a contribution to Origenian studies. But of course, in taking seriously how the discipline of scriptural interpretation was envisioned by one of its pioneering and most influential practitioners, this book also opens a window onto the immense panorama of exegetical practices and theories in the ancient world, and beyond.

I have had the pleasure of writing this manuscript, as well as teaching parts of it, at Yale Divinity School and St. Louis University, my current academic home. I thank the anonymous reviewers solicited by Oxford University Press, as well as my many students who have pushed me to expand (and at places truncate) my argument, and express myself with greater clarity. Kyle Schenkewitz and Sarah White both graciously read the entire manuscript in its final stages. Andrew Chronister, Peter and Elaine Martens, and Jordan Wood helped carefully correct the proofs. Thanks also to Thomas P. Scheck for granting me access to his translations of Origen's *Homilies on Numbers* and *Ezekiel* while both were still in manuscript form. This book is a substantial revision of my doctoral dissertation, "Origen on the Reading of Scripture" (University of Notre Dame, 2004). The beginnings of this project reach back to D. Jeffrey Bingham and David Balás, O.Cist., both of whom ably introduced me to the world of early Christian scriptural interpretation. I extend thanks to them, to Rowan Greer who first taught me Origen, as well as to the members of my dissertation committee, John Cavadini, Vittorio Hösle, Joseph Wawrykow, and my director, Brian E. Daley, S.J. Each provided valuable suggestions for the improvement of this work.

The University of Notre Dame's Presidential Fellowship supported the beginning and end of my doctoral research. Between those years I had the privilege of serving as a Summer Fellow for Byzantine Studies at Dumbarton Oaks (Washington, D.C.), a Fulbright Fellow at the University of Zurich, and a DAAD Fellow at the University of Heidelberg. I owe a debt of gratitude to each of these fellowship programs, institutions, and especially to Ingolf Dalferth and Christoph Markschies, both of whom oversaw my project while I researched overseas.

I dedicate this book to my wife, Rachel. She has joyfully accompanied me on the last phase of what is, I hope, only the beginning of my scholarly journey.

1

Introduction

TOPIC AND THESIS

Scriptural interpretation was a central scholarly practice among Christians in late antiquity. Among those versed in this form of scholarship, arguably none was as preeminent as Origen (*c*.185–254). For him, as for other early Christian exegetes, the discipline of biblical scholarship embraced, yet also transcended, the application of prevailing philological principles to Scripture. Biblical interpretation was an extraordinarily rich practice, as much an intellectual as a spiritual exercise. It was, in short, a way of life. Yet what did this life, as Origen understood it, look like? In this book I will answer this question by approaching the discipline of early Christian scriptural interpretation from a biographical perspective. The focus in this study will be on the scriptural interpreter, since it was this figure who animated, and indeed lived, this way of life.

Origen is a particularly suitable candidate for reassessing early Christian scriptural interpretation because he embodied the exegetical life to such a remarkable extent. Few commentators and homilists in the early church cultivated scholarship of the Christian Scriptures—the law, prophets, gospels, and apostolic writings—as exuberantly as he did. By training Origen was a philologist, a scholar of the Greek language and its literature.[1] His main biographer, Eusebius, tells us that after his conversion to a more dedicated form of Christianity in his early days in Alexandria, Origen embarked upon an ambitious course of scriptural study that would occupy him for the rest of his life.[2] Within the span of three decades of concentrated literary activity, most of which was spent in Caesarea Maritima, he became one of the most prolific authors of his generation, and indeed of all antiquity.[3] His surviving writings,

---

[1] Eusebius, HE 6.2.15; 6.19.7.

[2] Eusebius, HE 6.3.9.

[3] The best estimates attribute seventy-seven titles to him, comprising roughly eight hundred volumes (P. Nautin, *Origène: Sa vie et son oeuvre* [Paris: Beauchesne, 1977], 241–260, and followed by B. Neuschäfer, *Origenes als Philologe*, vol. 1 [Basel: Friedrich Reinhardt, 1987], 39). The original catalogue of Origen's works was listed in the third book of Eusebius' *Life of Pamphilus* which is, however, no longer extant (see Eusebius, HE 6.32.3 and Jerome, *Apology*

though notoriously lacunose, attest to his wide-ranging examination of his church's Scriptures. So do the reports of his ancient and modern readers. "He memorized the Scriptures, and he toiled day and night in the study of their meaning. He delivered more than a thousand homilies in church, and also published innumerable commentaries which he called 'tomes.' Who of us," Jerome asked, "can read everything he wrote? Who can fail to admire his enthusiasm for the Scriptures?"[4] Centuries later, Adolf von Harnack would echo Jerome's sentiment: "There has never been a theologian in the church who desired to be, and indeed was, so exclusively an interpreter of the Bible as Origen was."[5]

Given his achievement (and his pervasive influence), it does not surprise that modern historians have often considered Origen a paragon of ancient Christian scriptural interpretation.[6] Accordingly, his exegetical practice and theory have been the subject of dedicated exploration. Much of the territory has been carefully mapped, and parts of it many times over, though it is also the case that this famously large literature tends to follow well-worn paths. In my estimation it tends to cluster around four foci. One of the oldest approaches to Origen's biblical interpretation in the modern literature, reaching back to the seventeenth century, focuses on its procedural moment, explicating the principles of literary analysis that surface in his work. This

---

against Rufinus 2.22). Incomplete lists of Origen's writings are transmitted in Eusebius' *Ecclesiastical History* (at 6.24, 6.32, and 6.36) and Jerome's *Letter* 33. For an analysis of this important letter, see E. Klostermann, "Die Schriften des Origenes in Hieronymus' Brief an Paula," *Sitzungsberichte der königlich preussischen Akademie der Wissenschaften* 2 (1897): 855–870. The list is reconstructed by P. Nautin (*Origène*, 227–241) and conveniently presented in A. J. Carriker, *The Library of Eusebius of Caesarea* (Leiden: Brill, 2003), 242–243.

On the dating of Origen's works, see R. P. C. Hanson, *Origen's Doctrine of Tradition* (London: SPCK, 1954), 1–30; P. Nautin, *Origène*, 363–412; *Der Kommentar zum Evangelium nach Mattäus*, Part 3: *Die Kommentariorum Series*, intro., transl., and notes by H. J. Vogt (Stuttgart: Anton Hiersemann, 1993), 377–391.

For a list of Origen's works and their modern editions, see M. Geerard, ed., *Clavis Patrum Graecorum*, vol. 1 (Turnhout: Brepols, 1983), 141–186 (nr. 1410–1525). The modern critical editions of Origen's writings are found with few exceptions in the series "Die griechischen christlichen Schriftsteller der ersten Drei Jahrhunderte." See C. Markschies, "Origenes in Berlin und Heidelberg," *Adamantius: The International Journal of Origen and the Alexandrian Tradition* 8 (2002): 135–145, for a brief overview of the history, and future, of Origen's writings in this series. On occasion, I will cite from the editions in the *Sources chrétiennes* series, but only when these make substantive improvements on the GCS volumes. H. Görgemanns and H. Karpp author the critical edition of *On First Principles*. I will indicate where translations are my own; otherwise I follow existing English translations. For a full list of the editions and translations used (and their abbreviations), please see the bibliography.

[4] *Letter* 84.8/*Epistulae*, 2nd edn, ed. I. Hilberg, CSEL, vol. 55 (Venice: Verlag der Österreichischen Akademie der Wissenschaften, 1996), 130.22–131.3—transl. mine. For similar praise of Origen's industriousness, see *Letter* 33.

[5] A. von Harnack, *Der Kirchengeschichtliche Ertrag der Exegetischen Arbeiten des Origenes*, vol. 2, *Die Beiden Testaments mit Ausschluss des Hexateuchs und des Richterbuchs*, TU 42.4 (Leipzig: J. C. Hinrichs, 1919), II.4 A3.

[6] For brief remarks on Origen's influential exegetical legacy, see the discussion in the epilogue.

trajectory often attends to his use of allegory (undoubtedly since this stands in sharp contrast to much modern biblical scholarship). It also sometimes contextualizes his literary principles against their backdrop in Greco-Roman philology.[7] Another venerable path examines Origen's exegesis through the lens of a standard locus in modern Christian theology, the doctrine of Scripture. Here questions about his views of Scripture's divine and human authorship (i.e. inspiration), its message, and multiple senses shape the inquiry.[8] Another more recent perspective focuses upon the topical, asking how Origen understood such and such a scriptural text or theme.[9]

---

[7] P. D. Huet, *Origeniana: Tripartitum opus, quo Origenis narratur vita, doctrina excutitur, scripta recensentur* (Rouen: Ioannis Bertholini, 1668), 2.3.8; 2.2.13; 3.2.4 (reprinted in *PG* 17.634–1384); C. Delarue, *Origenis Opera Omnia*, vol. 2 (Paris: Vincent, 1733), i–xxv (reprinted in *PG* 12.30–42); J. A. Ernesti, *Disputatio historico-critica de Origene interpretationis librorum Sacrae Scripturae grammaticae auctore* (Leipzig: Ex Officina Langenhemiana, 1756); J. G. Rosenmüller, *Historia interpretationis librorum sacrorum in ecclesia christiana, inde ab Apostolorum aetate usque ad Origenem*, vol. 3 (Leipzig: Fleischer, 1807), 1–156; K. R. Hagenbach, *Observationes historico-hermeneuticae circa Origenis Adamanti methodum interpretandae Sacrae Scripturae* (Basel: A. Wieland, 1823); J. J. Bochinger, *De Origenis allegorica Scripturae Sacrae interpretatione: Dissertatio historico-theologica*, 3 parts (Strasbourg: F. G. Levrault, 1830); J. G. V. Engelhardt, *Bemerkungen über die Exegese des Origenes* (Erlangen: C. H. Kunstmann, 1836); E. R. Redepenning, *Origenes: Eine Darstellung seines Lebens und seiner Lehre* (Bonn: E. Weber, 1841–1846), 1:219–231; 2:156–212; C. Bigg, *The Christian Platonists of Alexandria: Being the Bampton Lectures of the Year 1886*, rev. edn (Oxford: Oxford University Press, 1913), 164–190; H. de Lubac, *Histoire et Esprit: L'Intelligence de l'Écriture d'après Origène* (Paris: Aubier, 1950), transl. A. E. Nash and J. Merriell, *History and Spirit: The Understanding of Scripture according to Origen* (San Francisco: Ignatius Press, 2007), 159–336; R. M. Grant, *The Letter and the Spirit* (London: SPCK, 1957), 93–104; W. Gruber, *Die Pneumatische Exegese bei den Alexandrinern: Ein Beitrag zur Noematik der Heiligen Schrift* (Graz: Akademische Druck- und Verlagsanstalt, 1957); R. P. C. Hanson, *Allegory and Event: A Study of the Sources and Significance of Origen's Interpretation of Scripture* (Richmond: John Knox Press, 1959; reprint with introduction by J. W. Trigg in Louisville: Westminster John Knox Press, 2002), 233–356; R. M. Grant, *The Earliest Lives of Jesus* (London: SPCK, 1961), 40–49; 50–78; R. Gögler, *Zur Theologie des Biblischen Wortes bei Origenes* (Dusseldorf: Patmos, 1963), 39–119; J. Pépin, *Mythe et Allégorie: Les origines grecques et les contestations judéo-chrétiennes* (Paris: Études Augustiniennes, 1976), 453ff; B. Neuschäfer, *Origenes als Philologe*; M. J. Edwards, *Origen Against Plato* (Aldershot: Ashgate, 2002), 123–158; A. Grafton and M. Williams, *Christianity and the Transformation of the Book: Origen, Eusebius, and the Library of Caesarea* (Cambridge, MA: Belknap Press, 2006), 22–132.

[8] See esp. A. Zöllig, *Die Inspirationslehre des Origenes: Ein Beitrag zur Dogmengeschichte* (Freiburg: Herder, 1902); H. de Lubac, *History and Spirit*, 190–222, 396–406; R. P. C. Hanson, *Allegory and Event*, 187–310; R. Gögler, *Zur Theologie des Biblischen Wortes bei Origenes*, 244–389; K. J. Torjesen, *Hermeneutical Procedure and Theological Method in Origen's Exegesis* (Berlin: W. de Gruyter, 1986), 108–124; E. A. Dively Lauro, *The Soul and the Spirit of Scripture within Origen's Exegesis* (Leiden: Brill, 2005).

[9] For example, M. F. Wiles, *The Spiritual Gospel: The Interpretation of the Fourth Gospel in the Early Church* (Cambridge: Cambridge University Press, 1960); J. Christopher King, *Origen on the Song of Songs as the Spirit of Scripture: The Bridegroom's Perfect Marriage-Song* (Oxford: Oxford University Press, 2005). This concern for the particular interpretations of Scripture is reflected prominently in two contemporary series, "The Church's Bible," ed. R. L. Wilken (Grand Rapids: Eerdmans, 2003) and "Ancient Christian Commentary on Scripture," ed. T. C. Oden (Downers Grove, IL: InterVarsity Press, 1998–).

Yet another approach attends to the instrumental character of interpretation, assessing how his exegesis implemented a particular concern or agenda.[10]

Each of these approaches, sometimes occurring within the same work, gives voice to a discernible facet of Origen's biblical interpretation. At the same time, none of them attends principally to his account of the interpreter. Missing in the literature is a detailed investigation of Origen's composite portrait of the ideal, and less than ideal, biblical scholar. Already in 1950, Henri de Lubac stumbled upon this lacuna. The figure of the scriptural interpreter had been examined neither in the traditional Origenian scholarship of his day, nor in his own monumental study of Origen's biblical scholarship, *Histoire et esprit*. It is remarkable to observe de Lubac come to a standstill over this belated realization in the penultimate chapter of his book. To grasp Origen's approach to biblical exegesis required far more than a study of how he viewed the object of his interpretation, Scripture. Yet this had been de Lubac's principal concern in his book: "we must abandon the point of view—which is too purely objective, too impersonal, and also too purely intellectual—that we have almost never ceased to maintain since the beginning of this study."[11] What was required was a complementary perspective on Origen's biblical interpretation that took the *personal subject*—the interpreter—seriously. After all, de Lubac remarked, Scripture for Origen was not a self-interpreting document, but rather words "addressed to someone from whom it awaits a response."[12] Neither de Lubac nor the subsequent

---

[10] Karen J. Torjesen's central insight is her insistence that Origen's scriptural interpretation facilitated in his audiences the soul's journey back to God (*Hermeneutical Procedure*, 70–107). Several scholars have accepted and developed Torjesen's persuasive thesis. For instance, F. M. Young in *Biblical Exegesis and the Formation of Christian Culture* (Cambridge: Cambridge University Press, 1997) emphasizes the function of biblical interpretation to help generate Christian ways of life (esp. 217–284, and citing Torjesen approvingly on 242). Also E. A. Dively Lauro's work, *The Soul and the Spirit of Scripture*, bears strong affinities to Torjesen's conclusions as she too contends that exegesis sought to lead the hearer to salvation (1–5, 26–31). Distinct from (and perhaps even opposing) this perspective, David Dawson contends that allegory in early Christianity was an instrument pressed into the service not of salvation but of cultural revision, where "readers secure for themselves and their communities social and cultural identity, authority, and power" (D. Dawson, *Allegorical Readers and Cultural Revision in Ancient Alexandria* [Berkeley: University of California Press, 1992], 2). This passage is cited approvingly in another major study on early Christian exegesis: E. A. Clark, *Reading Renunciation: Asceticism and Scripture in Early Christianity* (Princeton: Princeton University Press, 1999), 77–78. Note, however, Dawson's more recent book on Origen, *Christian Figural Reading and the Fashioning of Identity* (Berkeley: University of California Press, 2002) that shifts the focus by exploring the role of figural (nonliteral) readings of the Old Testament in the formation of Christian identity.

[11] H. de Lubac, *History and Spirit*, 346.

[12] Ibid., 347.

scholarship has comprehensively addressed this theme of the scriptural interpreter in Origen's writings.[13]

Yet it is an important theme. Besides charting a new course through the world of Origenian biblical scholarship, the topic of the interpreter opens two valuable perspectives. To begin with, this topic is inextricably autobiographical. The descriptions Origen offered of interpreters were not simply the ruminations of a detached spectator, but rather the reflections of someone who already lived the exegetical life. The philological practices he described he also pursued (or sought to pursue); the hermeneutical perspectives he advocated to would-be interpreters were not only proposals for others, but views Origen already espoused in his own pursuit of the ideal exegetical life. Rather than suppress this autobiographical dimension of our topic, I will quarry the various ancient sources that testify to his biblical scholarship. These sources will add vivid detail to his portrait of the interpreter. As it turns out, Origen's stated vision of the scriptural interpreter was also a deeply held personal vision, with continuities often surfacing between the exegetical life he narrated and the exegetical life he pursued. This topic also holds the key for unlocking Origen's panoramic vision of the entire exegetical enterprise. Most studies focus only on a peripheral aspect of this undertaking. As important as themes such as literal and allegorical exegesis or scriptural authorship are, they do not grasp the sweeping contours of the exegetical project as Origen understood it, since they do not grasp its central and organizing force: the interpreter. This figure was the heart of the exegetical enterprise, the one who mastered philological skills, applied them in very particular ways to the explication of Scripture and, in turn, addressed its message(s) to diverse audiences. It was this same figure, moreover, who entertained theological perspectives that informed this scholarship—perspectives about education, the Scriptures themselves, and, of course, perspectives about the underlying aims of biblical scholarship. In short, the interpreter of Scripture for Origen was both a practical and a theoretical agent, the effective, animating center out of which radiated the activities and viewpoints associated with biblical exegesis. Since this figure was the focal point of the exegetical craft, research on this theme presents a distinctive challenge. The traditional scholarly foci noted above do not squarely address the interpreter, though they certainly touch upon elements of the exegetical life relevant to this figure. It is critical, thus, not to disregard the traditional approaches to Origen's biblical scholarship, but rather to seek to integrate and reorient their concerns around his account of the interpreter. At the same time, research on this figure offers a unique opportunity. Precisely because the interpreter enlivened and gave shape to the

---

[13] For a fine entrée into this theme, see R. Heine's fine essay, "Reading the Bible with Origen," in *The Bible in Greek Christian Antiquity*, ed. and transl. P. M. Blowers (Notre Dame: University of Notre Dame Press, 1997): 131–148.

entire discipline of biblical scholarship, attending to Origen's portrait of this figure positions us better than the other traditional scholarly trajectories for discerning his sweeping and integrative vision of scriptural exegesis as a way of life.

What, then, was Origen's portrait of the scriptural interpreter? It might be tempting to answer this question by contending that this figure, ideally construed, was simply a scholar deeply formed, and informed, by Greco-Roman scholarship, philology in particular. As such, an answer would require only an outline of this interpreter's education and how it was utilized to explicate Scripture. Indeed, scholarly competence was an indelible feature of Origen's profile of the ideal scriptural scholar. Yet as I will also contend in this study, such an answer is glaringly incomplete, if not distorting, as it fails to capture the richness of his portrait of this figure. For Origen, ideal interpreters were more than scholars. Their profile also included a commitment to Christianity from which they gathered a spectrum of loyalties, guidelines, dispositions, relationships, and doctrines that tangibly shaped how they practiced and thought about their biblical scholarship. The exercise of biblical interpretation was as much a scholarly as it was a spiritual practice.

In this book I will demonstrate that Origen contextualized the interpreter of Scripture—scholarly commitments included—within the Christian drama of salvation. By examining this drama as it was inscribed on Scripture's pages, ideal interpreters also participated in it. We can think of this participation transpiring in two distinct yet interrelated ways. On the one hand, biblical interpretation afforded Christian philologists an occasion through which to express various facets of their existing Christian commitment. The dispositions, loyalties and doctrines encouraged by their faith also colored their scriptural exegesis. On the other hand, inquiry into Scripture's saving message was one of the privileged means by which these interpreters received divine resources for their continued journey in the faith. In this study, then, I will advance a new and integrative thesis about the contours of the ancient exegetical life as Origen understood it, and as best we can gather, also practiced it. For him, the ideal scriptural interpreter was someone who embarked not simply upon a scholarly journey, but, more ambitiously, upon a way of life, indeed a way of salvation, that culminated in the vision of God.

LITERATURE REVIEW

Given the vastness of the scholarship on Origen's biblical exegesis and hermeneutics, it is neither feasible nor advisable to aim for a comprehensive survey. Yet before turning to a more detailed outline of my argument, it will be helpful to review a handful of the more prominent books in the literature. In what follows I will demarcate my project from the four wide-ranging studies authored by H. de Lubac, R. P. C. Hanson, K. J. Torjesen, and B. Neuschäfer. These works have arguably shaped the scholarly discussion more than any other literature during the past sixty years.

H. de Lubac's *Histoire et esprit: L'Intelligence de l'Écriture d'après Origène* (1950) and R. P. C. Hanson's *Allegory and Event: A Study of the Sources and Significance of Origen's Interpretation of Scripture* (1959) are the two most comprehensive examinations of Origen's biblical scholarship to date. Both these studies were animated by the same evaluative concern: whether Origen's biblical exegesis, particularly its divisive allegorical moment, was in any way instructive for modern scriptural scholarship. Each author arrived at a very different conclusion. In *Histoire et esprit*, de Lubac insisted that he was not seeking to defend Origen, though it is quite clear that he composed his book in a sympathetic spirit.[14] Most of his work was devoted to rehabilitating Origen's much-maligned legacy by challenging, among other things, the accusation that he was merely a reckless allegorist who was uncritically inspired by the Hellenistic exegetical world.[15] De Lubac argued that Origen's allegory (or "spiritual exegesis") was deeply continuous with the traditions of exegesis within the New Testament (Paul especially), and also remarkably continuous with the Greek and Latin Catholic exegetical traditions that followed him.[16] It was a "Catholic instinct" that animated Origen's "profoundly traditional" exegetical practice.[17] De Lubac was convinced, moreover, that an assessment of Origen's exegesis could not be disentangled from "a whole manner of thinking, a whole world view . . . [a] whole interpretation of Christianity."[18] Here he sought to identify the abiding value in Origen's approach to Scripture. At its best, spiritual exegesis strove to see Jesus Christ and the church, or simply the New Testament, hidden within the figures, events and institutions—the history—narrated by Israel's Scriptures.

---

[14] See most clearly H. de Lubac's introduction in *History and Spirit*, particularly, 10–14. Throughout this book de Lubac registers numerous criticisms of Origen, though he invariably casts these as trivial faults that ought not to obscure his overarching strengths (for one example, see his account of Origen's meticulous concern with "minuscule particularities" in wording at 348–353).

[15] Ibid., 9–10. Note esp. de Lubac's telling comment about Origen's allegorical interpretation of history: "Yet one thing is certain: Origen's effort was inconceivable to a Hellenic mind . . . For the moment, let us merely observe that, whatever the procedural similarities we might be able to enumerate, whatever the mutual participation we might even be able to observe in the same 'allegorizing' mentality, that effort alone is enough to place an abyss between Origen, thoroughly marked by Christianity, and those Greeks to whom he is at times thoughtlessly compared" (317).

[16] His emphasis on Origen's continuity with, and influence upon, later exegetical traditions anticipated his monumental work on medieval exegesis in which Origen plays a major role, *Exégèse médiévale: Les quatre sens de l'Écriture*, 4 vols. (Paris: Aubier, 1959–1964).

[17] *History and Spirit*, 295, 194.

[18] Ibid., 11; see also 396.

"Histoire" and *"esprit"* were, in other words, deeply woven into one another.[19] De Lubac was modest about the possibility of reviving Origen, and often admitted that in many of its details Origen's exegesis was of little value anymore. Nevertheless, Origen was a towering genius in whose work "every-thing essential" could be found.[20]

Richard Patrick Crosland Hanson conceived *Allegory* and *Event* as a calcu-lated rebuttal to de Lubac's work. From its opening page, the question propelling Hanson's study was: "Has the interpretation of the Bible as it is practised today anything seriously in common with the interpretation of the Bible as Origen, and indeed as the early Church generally, practised it?"[21] The answer to this question, posed in the halcyon days of historical-critical re-search, was somewhat predictably and with only marginal concessions, "no."[22] While Hanson could acknowledge the impressiveness of Origen's scholarly achievements within the milieu of the third century, he was insistent upon the futility of Origen for modern, professional biblical scholarship. The central reason for this negative assessment was that:

> Origen's thought remained outside the Bible and never penetrated within it. Of the great interpreters [of Scripture] . . . it is always evident that their minds were soaked in biblical thought; they give the reader the impression that they are speaking to him from inside the Bible; at least, for purposes of exposition, they have successfully put themselves into the minds of the biblical author whom they are interpreting. Origen never quite conveys this impression, and on countless occasions gives the opposite impression, that he is reading into the mind of the biblical author thoughts which are really his own.[23]

Hanson repeatedly identified two culprits that ensured Origen remained alien to the scriptural message. The first was his view of history. Origen fundamen-tally missed the biblical view of the significance of history: that history is the field in which God reveals himself. "To this insight Origen is virtually blind."[24] For Origen, history was merely symbolic or parabolic of higher truths, not a place or event where God encounters people.[25] The second and related

---

[19] *History and Spirit*, 456; 498; 503–507.

[20] Ibid., 427.

[21] R. P. C. Hanson, *Allegory and Event*, 7.

[22] See particularly his concluding thoughts on 359–374.

[23] Ibid., 363.

[24] Ibid., 363–364. So also: "In history as event, in history as the field of God's self-revelation *par excellence*, Origen is not in the least interested" (276).

[25] Hanson summarizes his assessment of Origen's view of "historicity" as follows: "We must therefore conclude, from our survey of Origen's estimate of the historical value of the Bible, that though he did regard most of the narratives and accounts in it as historical . . . he only regarded this history as valuable because of the parabolic or symbolic significance which it contained, because, in short it could be allegorized, and that this view was simply a development of the Philonic attitude to history" (285–286).

culprit was the "alchemy of allegory,"[26] the exegetical procedure that, unlike "typology," made no attempt to trace a relationship of similitude between the people and events of old and those of new. The allegorist sought, rather, to move from historical events of old into modern flights of fancy.[27] In Philo's allegory, Origen "found the means of reading into the Bible whatever non-biblical ideas were congenial to his own theological system while professing (and no doubt sincerely imagining himself) to be a particularly enthusiastic and faithful interpreter of the thought of the Bible."[28] Thus, both Origen's view of history and his practice of allegory distanced him from Scripture, and this was hardly surprising since they derived mostly "from sources extraneous to traditional Christianity, from a Platonic attitude to history and a Philonic attitude to Holy Scripture."[29] The "and" in the title *Allegory and Event* meant something like "marginalizes" or "destroys."

This is not the place to adjudicate either of these studies in depth. Clearly, however, both were fundamentally concerned with one contentious moment in Origen's exegesis, allegory. Moreover, both were cast in a polemical tone, deeply invested in an assessment of this allegory from self-conscious and clearly articulated theological perspectives. My book, in contrast, has both a broader and narrower focus. Broader in that the topic here is not simply allegory, one facet of the exegetical life, but rather more comprehensively Origen's profile of the whole exegetical life. Narrower in that I am not immediately interested in whether we ought to rehabilitate this or any other facet of Origen's vision of the exegetical life. My concern is neither to defend nor to criticize. I am concerned, rather, with whether we have understood Origen's overarching vision of the interpreter of Scripture well in the first place, and whether he would recognize in the pages that follow his account of this interpreter.

In important ways Karen Jo Torjesen's well-received *Hermeneutical Procedure and Theological Method in Origen's Exegesis* (1986) continues the line of inquiry already pursued by de Lubac and Hanson. She too is concerned with Origen's allegory; however, her study departs notably from theirs, as from most of the Origenian scholarship, with her insistence that we need to attend more carefully to Origen's audience. "[T]he essential task of exegesis

---

[26] Ibid., 362.

[27] Ibid., 7. Later in this work: Alexandrian allegory's "ultimate aim is to empty the text of any particular connection with historical events" (63). Or again, in casting Origen's allegory as Philonic, Hanson remarks: "I have deliberately labeled this type of exegesis as Philonic, because it seems to me that it involves exactly the same mode of allegory as does Philo's psychological allegory or allegory into philosophical speculation. In it the correspondence between event and event is forgotten and a biblical incident is dissolved into a timeless analysis of good and evil impulses warring within the Christian's soul" (252).

[28] Ibid., 361.

[29] Ibid., 368.

in Origen has been decisively organized around the figure of the hearer/reader."[30] In *Hermeneutical Procedure* Torjesen examines what she variously calls the "theological basis" or "theological structure" that informed Origen's exegesis.[31] For Origen, there was a twofold pedagogy of the Logos. The original, historical teaching of the Logos was found in the literal sense of Scripture, whereas the contemporary pedagogy of this Logos resided in the spiritual sense and was perpetually directed toward new audiences. The task of the allegorical exegete was to reenact the ancient teaching activity of the Logos for a contemporary audience: "Therefore Origen's exegesis moves from the saving doctrines of Christ once taught to the saints (the historical pedagogy of the Logos) to the same saving doctrines which transform his hearers today (the contemporary pedagogy)."[32] By arranging these contemporary teachings so that they corresponded well to the differing needs and levels of hearers, Origen's aim as an exegete was to facilitate "a progression of stages in the Christian's progress toward perfection."[33] In short, biblical interpretation was principally "the mediation of Christ's redemptive teaching activity to the hearer."[34]

Torjesen's study and mine can be seen as largely complementary. While she is right to insist on the hearer's progress toward perfection, such a focus on the audience does not exhaust the theological vision that informs Origen's biblical scholarship. It was not simply his audience that was moved toward Christian perfection; it was also the *interpreter* who moved toward this perfection in engaging the biblical text. Torjesen and I, then, approach the same phenomenon from opposite ends of the spectrum. Whereas she attends primarily to the object of Origen's biblical scholarship—his audience—my focus is on the subject of this biblical scholarship—the interpreter. Whether thinking of the ideal interpreter of the biblical text, or some member in his audience to whom the message of this text was addressed, for Origen both figures found themselves in their respective encounters with Scripture on a path of salvation culminating in the vision of God. At the same time, and as will become clear as this study unfolds, there are important differences in detail between the respective paths traveled by those who only heard (or read) interpreters, and those who actually interpreted Scripture.

---

[30] Torjesen, *Hermeneutical Procedure*, 12. Note that this focus on the pedagogical aims of Origen's allegory was already anticipated in important ways by W. Gruber, *Die Pneumatische Exegese bei den Alexandrinern* (n. 7 above, and *Hermeneutical Procedure*, 9); J. Daniélou, *A History of Early Christian Doctrine before the Council of Nicaea*, vol. 2: *Gospel Message and Hellenistic Culture*, transl. J. A. Baker (Philadelphia: Westminster, 1973), 274, 278; H. Crouzel, *Origen*, transl. A. S. Worrall (Edinburgh: T. & T. Clark, 1989), 75–79.

[31] Torjesen, *Hermeneutical Procedure*, vii, 1–14.

[32] Ibid., 13.   [33] Ibid., 12.   [34] Ibid., 14.

Bernhard Neuschäfer's masterful *Origenes als Philologe* (1987) rounds out this brief review. As with the preceding studies, his book stands within the general trajectory that attends to the exegetical procedures that surface in Origen's biblical scholarship. However, unlike the literature surveyed above, Neuschäfer largely eschews a discussion of allegory and Origen's theological interests that might have shaped this pattern of inquiry. Instead, he embarks upon a detailed description of Origen's other exegetical techniques. Moreover, he usefully undergirds his account with a meticulous comparative analysis of the corresponding techniques in contemporary Greco-Roman philological scholarship. As I will make clear in the first part of my book, philological scholarship unquestionably mattered to Origen, and on this topic Neuschäfer remains an invaluable guide. However, it is important to observe that such a depiction of his exegetical enterprise, or of how he thought about this enterprise, is also acutely fragmentary. For Origen, the contours of the exegetical life included, yet went far beyond, the mastery of Greco-Roman philology. It was a scholarly life that refracted these skills through the loyalties, procedural guidelines, moral dispositions, and theological perspectives of the Christian faith that, when seen as a whole, made this life both expressive of, and in continual search for, salvation. A focus, thus, on technical credentials catches only one facet of the interpreter's project. I intend to elaborate on Neuschäfer's work by specifying the ways in which Origen located the scholarly analysis of Scripture within the larger Christian drama of salvation. In so doing, I also seek to challenge a potential misreading of Neuschäfer's book. In itself, this narrow focus is not problematic, so long as it does not invite a misguided assessment that collapses Origen's extraordinarily rich vision of the exegetical life into a *mere* procedural affair. Yet this risk is especially acute in our modern setting, where there is a powerful inclination to think about biblical (or any other variety of humanistic and scientific) scholarship as simply an assortment of techniques. Where such an assumption is embraced, studies on ancient philological methods can easily, though misleadingly, be thought to be comprehensive statements on the ancient exegetical life. I resist this easy misreading by accentuating how the Christian philologist for Origen participated in the quest for salvation while studying Scripture.

OUTLINE

This book falls into two parts. In the first ("The Philologist"), the argument opens with two chapters that detail how Origen understood the scholarly credentials of Scripture's ideal interpreters. Chapter 2 outlines his educational mandate: that would-be interpreters of Scripture pursue a broad education and achieve specialized facility in literary analysis or philology. Chapter 3 elucidates what he and his contemporaries would have understood by philology. Much of the modern discussion of Origen's biblical scholarship has settled unevenly upon one particular issue: Origen the allegorist. We can trace a continuous trajectory through the contemporary literature that aims to decipher the logic of the allegorical moment in his exegetical enterprise, beginning with Charles Delarue, the eighteenth-century editor of Origen's writings.[35] Twenty years ago, B. Neuschäfer successfully challenged this picture in his aforementioned landmark study, *Origenes als Philologe*. He contended for a more contextualized portrayal of Origen's biblical scholarship. Neuschäfer persuasively demonstrated how an array of Hellenistic philological procedures, and not simply an attraction to allegory, repeatedly surfaced in Origen's own exegetical work. Today, the best portrayals of his biblical scholarship inherit, and attempt to reconcile, these two trajectories in the literature: Origen the philologist and Origen the allegorist. I will discuss three leading Greco-Roman literary procedures (text criticism, historical inquiry and literary analysis) and propose a link between them and the two main philological referents, the literal and the allegorical.

In the second part of this study ("The Philologist and Christianity"), I argue that those who studied Scripture were far more than literary technicians. At its heart, proper inquiry into Scripture for Origen played a privileged role in the interpreter's journey toward salvation. I begin my argument with the interpreter's acceptance of the educational mandate detailed in the previous part of this study. How did Origen chart onto the Christian faith those who embraced the challenge of a scholarly examination of Scripture? I answer this question in two phases. Chapter 4 contends that he located Greco-Roman scholarship, philology included, as contingent upon God's creative and providential action in the universe. Origen turned the tables on those who allotted Greco-Roman education to a foreign cultural heritage. The best of this learning was, rather, native to Christianity: it was ultimately a gift from the one true God, the ultimate source from which all true knowledge and wisdom flowed. The Christian scriptural interpreter was not acquiring a foreign education, so much as receiving divine instruction.

Chapter 5 continues this line of argument by demonstrating how, for Origen, the interpreter's decision to use Greco-Roman scholarship for the study of Scripture signaled a simultaneous devotion to God. Those who embarked upon the life of biblical scholarship were not pursuing one profession among others, but rather embracing a distinguishing feature of advanced Christianity. This was so because the would-be interpreter's conversion to a life of scriptural study plotted favorably onto Origen's sweeping discussions of the mind's competing moral commitments and its location along the

---

[35] See the literature in n. 7 above, as well as B. Neuschäfer's important overview of the modern preoccupation with Origen's allegory (*Origenes als Philologe*, 11–30).

faith–reason continuum. By devoting themselves to the study of divine Scripture interpreters signaled their commitment to God.

Chapters 4 and 5 establish how Origen contextualized two facets of the interpreter's exegetical life within the larger fabric of the Christian faith: the interpreter's expertise, Greco-Roman learning and approaches to knowledge, as well as the conversion to the life of scriptural scholarship. However, these were not the only dimensions of the interpreter's activity that Origen located within the larger Christian narrative. He knew that Greco-Roman philology could be applied to the Scriptures in any number of ways, since interpreters always embraced guidelines, loyalties, and precedents that tangibly shaped how they examined these writings. I thus advance my thesis in the next two chapters by explicating his account of his two main exegetical adversaries, the Gnostics and Jews respectively. By tracing out the boundaries he drew between their approaches to Scripture and his, we will see how problematic Gnostic and Jewish exegesis served as foils for his portrait of the ideal scriptural interpreter.

In particular, I will contend in Chapters 6 and 7 that Origen's critique of these adversaries was *not* fundamentally about procedural deficiencies (e.g. they were "literalists"). Chapter 6 demonstrates how the boundaries he drew between his exegesis and that which flourished among the "Gnostics" were confined to a handful of theologically problematic readings. These readings co-existed, as he saw it, with an uncritical encounter with Greco-Roman knowledge and a rejection of the church's rule of faith, neither of which ideal ecclesiastical interpreters were to emulate. Chapter 7 shows that when Origen criticized Jewish literalism, he was almost always leveling a charge against a handful of readings of the law and prophets that both promoted central liturgical and doctrinal tenets of Judaism and, at the same time, advanced a critique of central Christian convictions. By unfolding Origen's critique of Jewish exegesis, it will become clear how Origen exhorted ideal interpreters to embrace the exegetical tutelage of Jesus and Paul when wrestling with the enigmatic passages in the law and prophets.

Chapter 8 turns to yet another major theme: how the moral character and conduct of the Christian philologist shaped scriptural interpretation. I begin with Origen's account of how the worthy moral life helped form expectations about the Scriptures conducive to discovering their message. When challenged, moreover, by especially difficult passages, Origen repeatedly underscored the need for ideal interpreters to study Scripture with a range of exegetical virtues, and, should discouragement over an unyielding passage follow, to exercise an abiding trust that an underlying sense resided in Scripture. The worthy life, exegetical virtues, and the exercise of faith all facilitated independent scriptural study. But they also rendered the interpreter worthy of divine aid when Scripture proved impenetrable. To an interpreter who cultivated such a moral profile, especially one who prayed for this divine aid, God, the Word, and the Holy Spirit were willing to offer exegetical aid. Exegetical activity, in other words, was not simply an opportunity to express various Christian convictions; it was also a moment to welcome resources that strengthened the faith.

Chapter 9 elaborates on this issue by turning to Origen's doctrine of Scripture. It focuses on his central belief in its fecundity: it was a collection of documents given by God for new life, the salvation of the human race, including the salvation of the interpreter. I trace out this argument, beginning with his conception of Scripture's authorship, and in particular, authorial intent. I then turn to his various summaries of what he believed was the one underlying scriptural message. The chapter draws to a close by explaining how Origen envisioned Scripture's efficacy in promoting the salvation of its interpreters.

Chapter 10, the final chapter, completes the argument of my study. In the preceding chapters I demonstrate the ways in which Origen contextualized interpreters of Scripture within the middle of the Christian drama of salvation. However, this drama of salvation stretched both behind and ahead of inter-preters laboring over Scripture in this life—it had not simply a middle, but also a beginning and an end. In this final chapter I show how Origen located interpreters in the beginning and end of the cosmic story of salvation. When we cast our vision to the protological and eschatological horizons of his theology, we will see how Origen bookended the quest for salvation through scriptural exegesis in this life—the middle of the drama—with similar quests at the beginning and end of the drama. Scriptural interpretation both reprised what had fleetingly transpired at the very beginning of the mind's existence, as well as anticipated and prepared them for what would be practiced more and more perfectly in the ages to come.

In the Epilogue I gather together my argument and briefly explore the implications of my thesis for our understanding of Origen, the history of biblical interpretation, and biblical scholarship as it is practiced and under-stood today.

ORIGEN'S LIFE

A short summary of Origen's life will serve as a useful backdrop for this study, especially since his account of the scriptural interpreter was often a thinly veiled autobiography. There are many strands in Origen's story that merit close attention, though of particular interest here is his evolving, lifelong engagement with Scripture. It is also thankfully the case that, in the hands of his ancient biographers, Origen's life was repeatedly organized around the theme of biblical scholarship: how he learned it, put it into practice, published its results and, as well, taught it to his students. The following brief account of his exegetical interests draws upon these biographical reports.[36]

[36] Scattered reflections on Origen's life can be found in the writings of Rufinus, Jerome, Socrates, Epiphanius, Palladius, and Photius (for a discussion of these sources, see P. Nautin, *Origène*, 183–224). However, the two main ancient sources for reconstructing Origen's life are the *Address of Thanksgiving to Origen* (sometimes referred to as the *Panegyric*) and book six of Eusebius' *Ecclesiastical History*.

The *Address* was composed sometime between 238 and 245 (for the earlier date, see H. Crouzel, SC 148, 22; for the later, P. Nautin, *Origène*, 382). Scholars have traditionally identified the author of the *Address* as the bishop of Neocaesarea in Pontus, Gregory Thaumaturgus (the "Wonderworker"). This attribution is based both upon the manuscript tradition that assigns the work to him, as well as upon Eusebius, who suggests this attribution when he describes the bishop Gregory traveling to Caesarea in order to pursue a "love of philosophy" and "study of Divinity" under Origen's tutelage (HE 6.30/GCS 9.2, 584.15–19). This short biographical sketch dovetails with much of what we learn about the author of the *Address* from this work, in which he offers a first-hand account of Origen's school and curriculum in Caesarea. P. Nautin has, however, questioned the identification of Gregory as the author of the *Address* (*Origène*, 81–86; 183–197). For a defense of the traditional attribution to Gregory of Neocaesarea, see H. Crouzel, "Faut-il voir trois personnages en Grégoire le Thaumaturge? A propos du Remerciement à Origène et de la Lettre à Grégoire," *Gregorianum* 60 (1979): 287–320. For a mediating proposal, see M. Simonetti, "Una nuova ipotesi su Gregorio il Taumaturgo," *Rivista di storia e letteratura religiosa* 24 (1988): 17–41. For an overview of the major arguments, see R. Klein, *Oratio prosphonetica ac panegyrica in Origenem: Dankrede an Origenes*, transl. P. Guyot, FC, vol. 24 (Freiburg: Herder, 1996), 47–63.

Most of what we know of Origen's life comes from the *vita Origenis* in book six of Eusebius' *Ecclesiastical History*, first composed around the turn of the fourth century (for the various proposals on the date of this treatise, see A. Louth, "The Date of Eusebius' *Historia ecclesiastica*," *JTS* 41 [1990]: 111–123). While Eusebius' account should not be accepted uncritically, there is a good deal that speaks for its reliability. Eusebius was a pupil of Pamphilus, Origen's disciple, and along with him helped restore Origen's library in Caesarea. He also co-authored with Pamphilus the *Apology for Origen* (HE 6.33.4; see P. Nautin's reconstruction of the work in his *Origène*, 99–153, as well as R. Amacker and É. Junod's study in, *Apologie pour Origène*, vol. 2 [SC 465]). Furthermore, Eusebius tells us that he assembled one hundred of Origen's letters and that excerpts of these were anthologized in the eighth book of the *Apology* (HE 6.36.3–4), which is unfortunately no longer extant. Eusebius was deeply familiar with Origen's life and thought.

At HE 6.2.1 the historian says his account of Origen's life was drawn from two sources: "from some letters" (ἔκ τινων ἐπιστολῶν) of Origen as well as from "reports" (ἱστορίας) of those still alive who were Origen's associates (GCS 9.2, 518.15–16). Thanks largely to the work of P. Nautin, the latter of these two sources has become the subject of careful scrutiny. Prior to his study, modern biographies of Origen were largely uncritical in their acceptance of Eusebius' narrative. Nautin, however, attentively distinguishes between the bishop's alternating use of these two sources; in particular, he subjects Eusebius' oral tradition to critical analysis due to the presence of what he suspects to be hagiographical motifs (*Origène*, 20–21). At the same time, Nautin has usefully drawn our attention to the extent to which Eusebius did, in fact, rely upon solid written evidence. In particular, he identifies several passages in Eusebius' narrative that must have had an autobiographical source since no one other than Origen would have known the precise details relayed. He also reminds us that several of Eusebius' formulations (e.g. "as he himself says," at HE 6.2.14; 6.4.3; 6.14.10) explicitly convey his reliance upon Origen. (Nautin proposes that the source for this autobiographical material was a letter that Eusebius cites at length at HE 6.19.12–14.) For a recent assessment of P. Nautin's study, see the collection of essays edited by A. M. Castagno, *La biografia di Origene fra storia e agiografia: Atti del VI Convegno di Studi del Gruppo italiano di ricerca su Origene e la tradizione alessandrina* (Villa Verucchio: Pazzini, 2004).

Much of Eusebius' account—particularly of Origen's education, which is of concern to us here—uses his correspondence as a main source and is, thus, largely authentic (P. Nautin,

Origen's principal biographer, Eusebius, portrayed his subject as a scriptural prodigy. He tells us that while still very young, Origen "had stored up no small resources in the words of the faith, having been trained in the Divine Scriptures from childhood."[37] It was his father, the biographer continues, who "drilled him in sacred studies, requiring him to learn and recite every day."[38] Yet the young Origen did more than memorize Scripture. Perhaps embellishing his narrative with an editorial conceit, Eusebius foreshadows the later allegorical career of this budding scholar. Origen "was not satisfied with learning what was simple and obvious in the sacred words, but sought for something more, and even at that age busied himself with deeper speculations. So that he puzzled his father with inquiries for the true meaning of the inspired Scriptures."[39] Eusebius reports how Origen's father was later martyred in Septimius Severus' persecution in 202 and how, as a result, the family's wealth was confiscated.[40] Not quite seventeen years old, Origen found himself in want along with his mother and six younger brothers. He thus sought refuge with a wealthy Christian woman whose generous patronage made possible the continuation of his education.[41] Origen decided to specialize. "[H]e devoted himself entirely to training in literature so that he had sufficient preparation in philology [ἐπὶ τὰ γραμματικά]."[42] Shortly thereafter

---

Origène, 21–24; also see P. Nautin, *Lettres*, 132–134). There are, however, varying opinions on the reliability of Eusebius. Least critical of the bishop is H. Crouzel, who recognizes "some interesting insights" in Nautin's study, but regards his criticisms of Eusebius as "contrived" (*Origen*, 1–2). Those who take a middle path, inclining to support Eusebius' historical veracity, yet still expressing occasional reserve, include: P. Nautin, *Origène*, 31–98; R. Grant, *Eusebius as Church Historian* (Oxford: Clarendon Press, 1980), 77–83; J. W. Trigg, *Origen: The Bible and Philosophy in the Third-Century Church* (Atlanta: John Knox Press, 1983), 9; and B. Neuschäfer, *Origenes als Philologe*, 32–35. Finally, to be numbered among the more skeptical are: M. Hornschuh, "Das Leben des Origenes und die Entstehung der alexandrinischen Schule," *ZKG* 71 (1960): 13; and B. Gustafsson, "Eusebius' Principle in Handling His Sources, As Found in His 'Church History,' Books I–VII," *SP* 4 (1961): 429–441.

[37] Eusebius, HE 6.2.7/GCS 9.2, 520.22–23.

[38] Eusebius, HE 6.2.8/GCS 9.2, 520.27–28.

[39] Eusebius, HE 6.2.9/GCS 9.2, 522.1–522.5. Recall that Eusebius attributes not only Origen's education in Scripture to his father, but also his training in the other academic disciplines (HE 6.2.7, 8, 15/GCS 9.2, 520.24–25; 26–27; 524.1–2). For doubts as to whether Origen received an education from his father, see P. Nautin, *Origène*, 34–35 and B. Neuschäfer, *Origenes als Philologe*, 32.

[40] Eusebius, HE 6.2.12–13.

[41] Eusebius, HE 6.2.13–14.

[42] HE 6.2.15/GCS 9.2, 524.3–4—transl. mine. Also note Porphyry's statement on Origen cited later at HE 6.19.7: "But Origen, educated as a Greek in Greek literature [Ὠριγένης δὲ Ἕλλην ἐν Ἕλλησιν παιδευθεὶς λόγοις]" (GCS 9.2, 560.6–7), 174; R. H. Robins, s.v. "linguistics, ancient" in *OCD*, 3rd edn, ed. S. Hornblower and A. Spawforth (Oxford: Oxford University Press, 1996). Also note Origen's brief description of the "grammarian's" duties at Hom 3.6 Ps 36, where this person instructs students in a wide range of literature, from poetry, to comedy, tragedy, fiction, and history. A γραμματικός, then, is better rendered in English as a literary scholar or philologist; his discipline, as philology. For support of such a definition, s.v. γραμματικός, *LSJ*, II.2; C. Schäublin, *Untersuchungen zu Methode und Herkunft der Antiochenischen Exegese* (Cologne:

he began to earn his living in Alexandria as a teacher of the Greek language and its literature.[43]

However, within a year or so Origen began to supplement his work as a philologist. "[A]s he himself tells us," Eusebius writes, "there was no one at Alexandria to give instruction in the faith, as all were driven away by the threat of persecution, some of the heathen came to him to hear the word of God."[44] Given his profession, Origen proved useful, as well as attractive, as an instructor in the sacred writings of his church. Yet when a growing number of students came to him for catechetical instruction in Alexandria, and since he alone was providing instruction, "he considered the teaching of literature inconsistent with the study of divine subjects; not hesitating he broke these things off as useless, even his school of literature as a hindrance to sacred learning."[45] He sold his manuscripts of literature for a small fee (4 oboli per day, sufficient for only a simple existence) in order not to be in need of payment from his students.[46] Moreover, as Eusebius notes, "for the greater part of the night he gave himself to the study of the Divine Scriptures."[47] This seems to have been part of an ascetic turn in his life.[48]

Peter Hanstein, 1974), 35, n. 41; E. Dickey, *Ancient Greek Scholarship: A Guide to Finding, Reading, and Understanding Scholia, Commentaries, Lexica, and Grammatical Treatises, from Their Beginnings to the Byzantine Period* (Oxford: Oxford University Press, 2007), 230, including bibliographical references.

[43] Eusebius, HE 6.2.15.

[44] Eusebius, HE 6.3.1/GCS 9.2, 524.6–10. See P. Nautin, *Origène*, 35–37, for an analysis of the lost letter that serves as Eusebius' source here. The literature on this Alexandrian "catechetical school" is large. For orientation, see C. Scholten, "Die alexandrinische Katechetenschule," *JAC* 38 (1995): 16–37; A. van den Hoek, "The 'Catechetical' School of Early Christian Alexandria and Its Philonic Heritage," *HTR* 90 (1997): 59–87; A. Le Boulluec, "Aux origines, encore, de l''école' d'Alexandrie," *Adamantius: The International Journal of Origen and the Alexandrian Tradition* 5 (1999): 8–36.

[45] HE 6.3.8/GCS 9.2, 526.15–19—transl. mine. See P. Nautin, *Origène*, 40. This passage has caused some confusion. Origen was *not* setting aside literary scholarship, which is what Marrou suggests when he writes: "We know from Eusebius that Origen considered the role of grammarian, which he had at one time adopted, incompatible with the work of catechist which the Bishop of Alexandria had laid upon him" (*Education in Antiquity*, 321). Rather, and Eusebius stresses this as well, Origen was only setting aside his "teaching" (διδασκαλί) of literature and his "school" (διατριβή) (HE 6.3.8/GCS 9.2, 526.16–19). When Origen sold his ancient manuscripts, he created the economic means by which he could devote himself solely to the study of Scripture. He studied this collection of writings the only way he knew how: as a γραμματικός. Eusebius underscores Origen's continued practice of the philological analysis of Scripture after this conversion at HE 6.3.9–13, 6.8.6, 6.16, 18–19, and 6.23.

What is perhaps more remarkable about this passage in the *Ecclesiastical History* is that Origen would sell his library, or at least a significant part of it, only to help found, in turn, one of the more significant libraries of Christian antiquity in Caesarea Maritima. For hypotheses about how Origen developed his library in Caesarea, see J. A. McGuckin, "Caesarea Maritima as Origen Knew It," in *Orig V*: 3–25, and A. J. Carriker, *The Library of Eusebius of Caesarea* (Leiden: Brill, 2003), 2–12.

[46] HE 6.3.9.

[47] HE 6.3.9/GCS 9.2, 526.26–27.

[48] HE 6.3.9. Origen as practitioner of the ascetic or philosophic life is described at 6.3.7–13; 6.8.6. More on this theme in Chapter 5 below.

We are told that while still in Alexandria people continued to seek him out to learn Scripture. "Many others also, drawn by the fame of Origen's learning, which resounded everywhere, came to him to make trial of his skill in sacred literature."[49] Origen taught advanced students (including distinguished philosophers) "divine things," but also instructed the less learned in a number of the "common school branches, saying that these would be no small help to them in the study and understanding of the Divine Scriptures."[50] The young philologist also converted a certain Ambrose away from Valentinus' teachings.[51] This Ambrose would, in turn, become Origen's long-standing patron, providing him with numerous stenographers, copyists, as well as young women skilled in penmanship.[52] With these considerable means at his disposal, sometime in the late teens or early twenties of the third century, Origen began his prolific authorship, centered on the scholarly interpretation of Scripture.[53]

Through a complex series of events that need not detain us here, in 231/232 Origen transplanted his literary and educational activities to Caesarea (Maritima) where his ordination to the priesthood added the preaching of Scripture to his duties as well.[54] The bulk of his exegetical corpus comes down to us from this period. He would author extensive exegetical writings—scholia, homilies, and commentaries on the Bible—as well as various treatises that teemed with biblical interpretations, to say nothing of his monumental edition of the Greek versions of the Old Testament, the *Hexapla*.[55] He also founded a school in Caesarea.[56] *The Address of Thanksgiving*, traditionally attributed to Gregory Thaumaturgus who had studied under Origen during his Caesarean period, recounts in detail the curriculum of this school. Gregory speaks eloquently of his teacher, and how he persuaded him to scale the heights of the Greco-Roman educational system with a view ultimately to the study

---

[49] HE 6.18.2/GCS 9.2, 556.12–15.

[50] HE 6.18.4/GCS 9.2, 556.23–25. The reference to what Origen "says" in the above citation is important for establishing the credibility of Eusebius' biography here. P. Nautin contends that Eusebius drew upon the LA, LG, and the *Address* for this statement (*Origène*, 50–53). Also see HE 6.8.6/GCS 9.2, 536.20–21.

[51] HE 6.18.1.

[52] HE 6.23.1–2.

[53] HE 6.16; 6.23.1–2; 6.24.

[54] HE 6.8.4; 6.23.4; 6.27.

[55] This threefold characterization of Origen's exegetical genres (scholia, homilies, and commentaries) stems from Jerome's preface to his translation of Origen's *Homilies on Ezekiel*. There he provides us two of the three Greek designations alongside the Latin: σχόλια (excerpta), [ὁμιλίαι—need to supply] (homileticum genus), and τόμοι (libri and volumina) (GCS 33, 318.13–19). For an orientation to these genres and their differences, see E. Klostermann's important article, "Formen der exegetischen Arbeiten des Origenes," *Theologische Literaturzeitung* 72 (1947): 203–208, and É. Junod, "En quoi les homélies d'Origène se distinguent-elles de ses commentaires?" in *Le défi homilétique*, ed. H. Mottu and P.-A. Bettex (Geneva: Labor et Fides, 1994), 137–170.

[56] HE 6.32; 6.36.

of Scripture.[57] Gregory tells us the greatest gift Origen received from God was "that he should be an interpreter [ἑρμηνεὺς] of the words of God to humans . . ."[58] At the apex of Origen's Caesarean school, according to Gregory, his master was fulfilling the highest duty of a Christian philosopher: he was interpreting the Christian Scriptures and teaching others to pursue this task.

SOURCES

In tracing out the detailed features in Origen's vision of the interpreter, I draw on two kinds of sources. Principally, I will scour his hermeneutical thought, that is, his reflections upon the enterprise of biblical scholarship.[59] The main lines characterizing his portrait of the scriptural interpreter are found amidst these reflections. Popular perception notwithstanding, these are not restricted to the fourth book of *On First Principles*, but are in fact scattered throughout his voluminous writings. Thus an inclusionary principle guides my research: I advance my argument with passages drawn from a careful sifting of his entire corpus.[60] The second set of sources discloses information about Origen's own exegetical life. As already noted, an autobiographical element often resides deep within his vision of the scriptural exegete. Whenever relevant, then, I will turn to passages that give insight into Origen's own interpretive activity, including what his commentaries and homilies reveal of this activity, his

[57] See n. 36 above on the authorship of this work. On the character of this school, see A. Knauber, "Das Anliegen der Schule des Origenes zu Cäsarea," *MTZ* 19 (1968): 182–203; H. Crouzel, "L'École d'Origène à Césarée: Postscriptum à une édition de Grégoire le Thauma-turge," *Bulletin de littérature ecclésiastique* 71 (1970): 15–27.

[58] *Address* 15/SC 148, 170.39–40.

[59] Origen's colossal exegetical legacy has, in fact, always been twofold: he practiced biblical scholarship *and* he reflected upon it. Thus, the two panegyrical remarks quoted at the start of this chapter, while gesturing accurately to Origen's passion for scriptural exegesis, also do so incompletely. Origen was more than a practitioner of scriptural interpretation; he was also an enthusiastic hermeneut.

[60] This principle goes back at least to H. de Lubac, who wrote in *History and Spirit*: "To have any chance of reaching the authentic Origen, it is necessary to increase the quotations. Parallel passages then control, determine, and comment upon each other, especially when we have, for instance, a phrase from the Latin of Rufinus to compare with another from the Latin of Jerome and, finally, a third preserved in the original" (46). This approach does not, I also think, erroneously homogenize Origen's thought on the topic of the interpreter. On the whole, I am not convinced that there were substantial shifts or developments in his views on this theme. I do not find evidence for such flux, for which there are also good reasons: first, and more generally, much of Origen's surviving corpus stems from a period of relative intellectual maturity (for example, one of the earliest surviving works, *On First Principles*, was probably written when Origen was already 44 or 45 years old—cf. P. Nautin, *Origène*, 410); second, and more specifically, the topic of the interpreter was not simply a topic for Origen, but his vocation upon which he had embarked already in his late teens. Most of his views on this topic were probably worked out long before he even commenced his authorship.

occasional autobiographical reports of this activity, and the narratives of his main ancient biographers, Gregory Thaumaturgus and Eusebius of Caesarea.

As is well known, the condition of Origen's corpus is lamentably far from ideal. There are three basic problems. First, a sizeable portion is no longer extant, with some works partially, and others completely, lost. This disjointed state is due partly to the antiquity of his writings, though primary responsibility falls on Justinian's posthumous condemnation of Origen in the Byzantine East,[61] and the Latin West's authorization of only those works that Jerome had approved.[62] Both these decisions resulted in targeted destructions of his corpus or, tantamount to the same, refusals to copy and transmit it any further. As a consequence, today we inherit decidedly fragmentary ruins. The second (and far more delicate) problem is that even the extant literature must be cautiously assessed. The contentiousness that often surrounded Origen's theology had repercussions even for his surviving writings, as they became susceptible to that distinctive form of scribal animosity: interpolation.[63] Finally, were these difficulties not daunting enough, historians face a third challenge. Origen's extant corpus requires careful scrutiny since much of it has been transmitted indirectly in Latin translations that were only made in the fourth and fifth centuries. Since there are rarely corresponding Greek texts, the reliability of these translations has been much debated. Questions center not only on the style of these translations (when are they scrupulous and when

---

[61] This condemnation transpired amidst the so-called "Origenist controversy" (which was actually the culmination of numerous crises surrounding Origen's legacy). In 543 the emperor Justinian wrote a letter to the patriarch in Constantinople, Menas, in which he formulated nine anathemas against Origen (*Ad Menam*, text in GK, 822–825). Origen was eventually condemned as a heretic in the eleventh canon of the Second Council of Constantinople that met in 553 (GK, 825–831). For orientation to this complex topic, see F. Diekamp, *Die origenistischen Streitigkeiten im sechsten Jahrhundert und das fünfte allgemeine Concil* (Munster: Aschendorff, 1899); A. Guillaumont, "Évagre et les anathématismes antiorigénistes de 553," *SP* 3: 219–226; idem., *Les Képhalaia Gnostica d'Éuagre le Pontique et l'histoire de l'origénisme chez les Grecs et les Syriens* (Paris: Éditions du Seuil, 1962), 143–159; E. A. Clark, *The Origenist Controversy: The Cultural Construction of an Early Christian Debate* (Princeton: Princeton University Press, 1992); B. E. Daley, "What did Origenism Mean in the Sixth Century?" in *Orig VI*: 627–638; H. Crouzel, "Les condemnations subies par Origène et sa doctrine," in *Orig VII*: 311–315; D. Hombergen, *The Second Origenist Controversy: A New Perspective on Cyril of Scythopolis' Monastic Biographies as Historical Sources for Sixth-Century Origenism* (Rome: Pontificio Ateneo S. Anselmo, 2001).

[62] See the sixth-century *Decretum Gelasianum* at 4.5 (*Das Decretum Gelasianum de libris recipiendis et non recipiendis*, ed. E. von Dobschütz [Leipzig: J. C. Hinrichs, 1912], 45.239–241).

[63] Indeed, already Origen felt the need to alert readers to purposeful interpolations of his writings by his opponents. See esp. LF/Rufinus, as well as several of Rufinus' works where similar claims are made, including his translation of book one of Pamphilus' *Apology for Origen*, his own essay, *On the Corruption of Origen's Books*, and his translator's preface to Origen's *On First Principles*. On the theme of pseudepigraphy, including interpolations, in the ancient world, see G. Bardy, "Faux et fraudes littéraires dans l'Antiquité chrétienne," *RHE* 32 (1936): 5–23; 275–302; W. Speyer, *Die literarische Fälschung im heidnischen und christlichen Altertum: ein Versuch ihrer Deutung* (Munich: Beck, 1971); and N. Brox, *Falsche Verfasserangaben: zur Erklärung der frühchristlichen Pseudepigraphie* (Stuttgart: KBW, 1975).

paraphrastic?), but also upon the doctrinal commitments of the translators (to what extent are their renderings of Origen transformations that bring him up to date with later theological convictions?).[64] I will not ignore the Latin translations in this study, though I will point out where they ought to be consulted judiciously as they are often an incalculable resource. On the whole, it is my contention that, when carefully vetted, Origen's writings satisfactorily yield the details required for a reconstruction of his portrait of the scriptural interpreter.

---

[64] On the Latin translations, see G. Bardy, *Recherches sur l'histoire du texte et des versions latines du De Principiis d'Origène* (Paris: É. Champion, 1923); B. Studer, "À propos des traductions d'Origène par Jérome et Rufin," *VetChr* 5 (1968): 137–154; F. Winkelmann, "Einige Bemerkungen zu den Aussagen des Rufinus von Aquileia und des Hieronymus über ihre Übersetzungstheorie und -methode," *Kyriakon, Festschrift J. Quasten*, ed. P. Granfield and J. A. Jungmann, vol. 2 (Munster: Aschendorff, 1970), 534–538; B. Studer, "Zur Frage der dogmatischen Terminologie in der lateinischen Übersetzung von Origenes' De Principiis," in J. Fontaine and C. Kannengieser, eds., *Epektasis: Mélanges patristiques offerts au Cardinal J. Daniélou* (Paris: Beauchesne, 1972), 403–414; H. Marti, *Übersetzer der Augustin-Zeit: Interpretation von Selbstzeugnissen* (Munich: Fink, 1974); G. Lomiento, "Note sulla traduzione Geronimiana delle omelie su Geremia di Origene", in *Orig I*: 139–162. There is also a bibliography in GK, 36–43 and in H. Marti, *Übersetzer der Augustin-Zeit*, 318–332.

Part 1

The Philologist

The first part of this study outlines Origen's scholarly expectations for ideal interpreters of Christian Scripture. In his view, they ought to become competent philologists (students of the Greek language and its literature) and conversant in an array of Greco-Roman disciplines pertinent to the well-informed interpretation of Scripture. Vivid detail of the exegetical scholarship Origen was promoting can be found in his own exegetical writings, occasional autobiographical notes, and in the reports from his ancient biographers. These sources will substantiate that Origen sought to exemplify the very scholarly standards he set for other would-be scriptural interpreters. His vision of the ideal scriptural interpreter was also a deeply held personal vision.

2

Mandate: The Interpreter's Education

Origen interpreted the Christian Scriptures in an indelibly scholarly manner. He was attentive to the discrepancies in the manuscripts that transmitted these writings, examined scriptural texts with an array of Greco-Roman philological techniques, and brought to bear a wealth of knowledge that helped him elucidate passages in question. Without such a scholarly approach, he was convinced that the interpretive enterprise was doomed to uninformed, superficial and, at times, erroneous readings of these Scriptures. Thus it is not surprising that Origen issued an educational mandate: a commitment to scholarship ought to be an intrinsic feature in the profile of aspiring scriptural interpreters. In this chapter I examine his scholarly expectations of this figure; in the next, I describe in detail the interpreter's area of specialization, philology.

THE AUDIENCE

There are a handful of passages dispersed throughout Origen's corpus where he articulated an ambitious academic mandate for the would-be scriptural interpreter. These passages will allow us to sketch the first outlines of his profile of this figure. Yet before turning to the scope of this mandate, it is important to ascertain the audience to whom he customarily directed it. The setting in which Origen issued his educational mandate comes into stark focus when we consider the rarity of private access to the Christian Scriptures in antiquity. In the ancient world scribes painstakingly copied these writings by hand. This was a laborious, and thus also expensive, proposition that ensured few copies fell into the hands of individual scholars with their own private collections.[1] Most Scriptures in Origen's day were stored in ecclesiastical

---

[1] Interestingly, it appears that Origen's father was one of these rare scholars who could count at least some of the Scriptures to his private collection of books. Recall Eusebius' description of Origen's childhood tutelage in Scripture under his father's supervision (HE 6.2.7–11). On the issue of private ownership of Scriptures more generally, see C. Markschies, *Kaiserzeitliche*

libraries, alongside the other texts supporting these churches' liturgical, cate-chetical, and archival needs.[2] Thus, most people became familiar with the figures, events, and themes of the Christian Scriptures not through the direct investigation of these writings, but only when they were read and expounded upon within the setting of the liturgy.[3] It was a far smaller number who owned and read these texts privately. While there are a handful of occasions when Origen acknowledged the private reading of Scripture in his Caesarean con-gregation, it is difficult to imagine that a significant number of people in his circles owned or enjoyed private access to their Scriptures.[4]

It is no easier to imagine many possessing advanced literacy. A cursory survey of the limits of education in late antiquity indicates that Origen's scholarly mandate for interpreters would not have been received as a pedantic or even predictable directive. He expressed his mandate within an educational setting that, at least by most modern standards, was far from comprehensive.[5] While there were some in the ancient world—a very slender minority—who benefited from an extensive education, most people in Origen's day could not actually read demanding literary texts.[6] Relatively few youth had access to

---

christliche Theologie und ihre Institutionen: Prolegomena zu einer Geschichte der antiken chris-tlichen Theologie (Tübingen: Mohr Siebeck, 2007), 311–314.

[2] C. Markschies, *Kaiserzeitliche christliche Theologie*, 306–314; H. Y. Gamble, *Books and Readers in the Early Church: A History of Early Christian Texts* (New Haven: Yale University Press, 1995), 82–202.

[3] Gamble, *Books and Readers*, 205–231.

[4] For references to the private reading of Scripture in Origen's congregations, see, for instance, Hom Gen 2.5 and 12.5. For a more complete dossier of evidence, see A. Harnack, *Bible Reading in the Early Church*, transl. J. R. Wilkinson (Eugene, OR: Wipf and Stock, 2005), 68–76. It is a distinct possibility that, when compared to other pre-Nicenes, Origen's relatively frequent references to the private reading of Scripture in his homilies and commentaries reflects the presence of his pupils in his audience (more below on Origen's school in Caesarea). On the private reading of Scripture in early Christianity in general, in addition to Harnack, *Bible Reading*, see more recently, Gamble, *Books and Readers*, 231–237.

[5] Important studies on education in antiquity include: M. Lechner, *Erziehung und Bildung in der Griechisch-Römischen Antike* (Munich: Max Hueber, 1933); H. I. Marrou, *A History of Education in Antiquity*, transl. G. Lamb (New York: Sheed and Ward, 1956); F. Kühnert, *Allgemeinbildung und Fachbildung in der Antike* (Berlin: Akademie-Verlag, 1963); I. Hadot, *Arts Libéraux et Philosophie dans la Pensée Antique* (Paris: Études Augustiniennes, 1984); R. A. Kaster, *Guardians of Language: The Grammarian and Society in Late Antiquity* (Berkeley: University of California Press, 1988); R. Cribiore, *Writing, Teachers, and Students in Graeco-Roman Egypt* (Atlanta: Scholars Press, 1996); T. Morgan, *Literate Education in the Hellenistic and Roman Worlds* (Cambridge: Cambridge University Press, 1998); R. Cribiore, *Gymnastics of the Mind: Greek Education in Hellenistic and Roman Egypt* (Princeton: Princeton University Press, 2001).

[6] It is notoriously difficult to estimate literacy rates in antiquity (for Christians included); however, the numbers in the literature suggest a range from as low as 5 to as high as 20 percent. For a brief orientation to this complex issue, see Gamble, *Books and Readers*, 1–10. The most extensive recent discussion of literacy in the ancient world is by W. V. Harris, *Ancient Literacy* (Cambridge, MA: Harvard University Press, 1989). See also the respondents to Harris in J. H. Humphrey, ed. *Literacy in the Roman World* (Ann Arbor, MI: Journal of Roman Archeology, 1991).

formalized education, and among those who did, an even smaller number pursued the broad course of study over a protracted period of time that, as we will see below, Origen counseled.

He often referred to Christians with this limited educational experience or commitment as the *simpliciores*, that is, the "simpler ones."[7] While there are those in the church who have "the desire or the capacity to examine the questions with intelligence,"[8] he writes, there are also those with a "serious lack of education,"[9] the "simpler and totally innocent who are not able to examine both the depths of God and his Scriptures."[10] Origen sought to recruit scriptural scholars from these ranks, though if the following passage is indicative, it appears that he was seldom successful. He laments in his *Homilies on Ezekiel*: "frequently we exhort young people to do this [i.e. apply themselves to the divine literature], but as far as I can see, the only result is that we have wasted our time; for we have not succeeded in inducing any of them to study the Bible."[11] This lack of intellectual ability or desire for scriptural study was not unique to Origen's own day. Celsus, the second-century critic of Christianity, frequently drew attention to the low intellectual abilities among Christians, particularly when it came to studying their Scriptures. Defending himself against Celsus' scorn, Origen tellingly concedes that most members of the church have not examined the Scriptures in any depth: "Only very few have taken the trouble to understand them. They are those who have devoted their entire life, as Jesus commanded, to searching the Scriptures [cf. Jn 5:39], and have labored to study the meaning of the sacred Scriptures more than Greek philosophers have done to acquire some supposed knowledge."[12] The implication in this response is that the *simpliciores* made up the majority of Christians and that Celsus had correctly surmised that they did not possess the education, energy, or skill for informed scriptural study. Elsewhere Origen is more explicit. In his response to Celsus' charge that among Christians expressions such as "Do not examine; just believe" and "Your faith will save you" are heard, he again does not contest Celsus' accusation.

---

[7] "Simpliciores," the Latin translation of οἱ ἁπλούστεροι, was the term he often used to identify these believers (CC 3.78; Comm Jn 13.39; Lk Frg 125; PE 23.1; Comm Eph 19; etc.). The positive form (ἁπλοῖ) is found in Comm Matt 10.1 and the superlative (ἁπλούστατος) in CC 7.16, though these are relatively rare. Other designations of this group include: οἱ ἀκεραιότεροι (PA 4.2.1; Comm Jn 13.39; Lk Frg 125; Hom Jer 18.8.1), τὸ πλῆθος τῶν πιστευόντων (CC 1.9; Comm Jn 13.287; Comm Matt 13.17), ἀνεπιστήμων (PA 4.1.7), as well as οἱ πολλοί (CC 1.9; 3.21; Comm Jn 1.271), ὄχλοι (CC 2.66), νήπιοι (Hom Jer 18.6), and sometimes ἰδιῶται (CC 6.62). On Origen's account of this group, see esp. G. af Hällström, *Fides Simpliciorum according to Origen of Alexandria* (Helsinki: Societas Scientiarum Fennica, 1984).

[8] CC 4.49/SC 136, 310.6–9.

[9] CC 7.49/SC 150, 130.9–10.

[10] Comm Matt 16.4/GCS 10, 472.14–18.

[11] Hom Ez 13.3.2/GCS 8, 448.18–21.

[12] CC 6.37/SC 147, 268.22–27.

He acknowledges that it would be best if all Christians could devote themselves to the study of Scripture. However, this is not possible, "since, partly owing to the necessities of life and partly owing to human weakness," very few Christians were committed to explaining "the obscure utterances of the prophets, and the parables in the gospels, and innumerable other events or laws which have a symbolical meaning."[13] In the church it was only a minority who examined its Scriptures rigorously: those who had the education, motivation, leisure, and the financial resources to procure copies of these writings.[14]

Thus when we canvass the educational and ecclesiological contexts in Origen's day, it was only a privileged subset that was in any position to examine the Christian Scriptures first-hand and with scholarly competence. When he advocated his scholarly directive for Scripture's interpreters, then, Origen was usually not addressing himself to this group, but rather to the *simpliciores*. They would have included people who had gathered to hear him preach, and probably also some of his younger pupils or aspiring students in Alexandria and, later, Caesarea Maritima. Whether through lack of time, ability, interest, or opportunity, they did not devote sufficient energy and skill to the careful examination of Scripture. To these Origen issued his remarkable educational mandate, a mandate that would hardly have come across as perfunctory, but rather as an arduous and perhaps even daunting task.

THE DIRECTIVE

There are three passages where Origen clearly announces his educational mandate. The first of these, the golden *Letter to Gregory*, is one of his most memorable reflections on the scriptural interpreter and merits the closest attention.[15] In this short letter Origen advocates one of the interpreter's

---

[13] CC 1.9/SC 132, 100.18–23. This discussion spills over into 1.10. Note also how Origen often laments the mishandling of the scriptural text by the *simpliciores*. At times, they are literal readers when they ought not to be (a charge Origen frequently leveled against them: PA 2.11.2; 4.2.2; 4.3.2; Hom Gen 13.3; Hom Lev 10.1.1; Hom Num 22.1.3; Hom Josh 7.5; Hom Is 6.4; Hom Ez 7.10; Comm Matt Ser 15; Comm Rom 8.8; CC 1.29; 5.16). At other times, when they do strive for a nonliteral meaning, they usually go astray (PA 2.7.2; 4.2.2; Phil 27.1).

[14] For a discussion of Origen's account of the intellectual deficiency of the *simpliciores*, also see G. af Hällström, *Fides simpliciorum*, 23ff, 43–46. Other texts where Origen mentions the basic ability or competence to interpret Scripture include: Hom Gen 7.5; Hom 5.1 Ps 36; Lam Frg 8; Comm Matt 10.14; 16.20; LA 23/SC 302, 572.4–5; PA 1.6.1; 4.2.3; 4.2.8–9; 4.3.5; CC 1.18; 3.39; 4.21; 5.62; 6.37; 7.60; DH 13; Phil 12.2.

[15] Most scholars have identified this Gregory with Gregory Thaumaturgus (the "Wonderworker"), the bishop of Neocaesarea in Pontus (see, for instance, J. Dräseke, "Der Brief des Origenes an Gregorios von Neocäsarea," *Jahrbücher für protestantische Theologie* 7 [1881]: 102–126; H. Crouzel, "Faut-il voir trois personnages en Grégoire le Thaumaturge? A propos du Remerciement à Origène et de la Lettre à Grégoire," *Gregorianum* 60 [1979]: 300–318). This

defining characteristics: a commitment to scholarship. After the opening salutation to his addressee, Gregory, the *Letter* begins as follows:

> As you know, an aptitude for understanding, when supplemented by training, can achieve to the extent that this is possible (if I might call it this) its end [τέλος]—the very thing for which someone desires to train. Now your aptitude can turn you into a consummate [τέλειον] Roman lawyer and a Greek philosopher of one of the well-regarded schools. However, I have wished that you make use of all your intellectual power in a purposeful manner [τελικῶς] for Christianity. For this reason, I pray that you productively draw from Greek philosophy those things that are able to become, as it were, general teachings or preparatory studies for Christianity, as well as those from geometry and astronomy which will be useful for the interpretation of the holy Scriptures, in order that what the philosophers say about geometry and music and philology and rhetoric and astronomy—that these are philosophy's helpmates—that this too we might say concerning philosophy itself as it relates to Christianity.[16]

Origen opens his *Letter* with a splendid pun on the τέλος word group that is difficult to reproduce in English. He plays with two distinct senses of this family of terms: purpose and accomplishment.[17] Those who discipline their minds attain a desired end or purpose (τέλος). Origen's addressee has the facility for embodying the educational ideals of the Greek and Roman cultures—to become, respectively, an accomplished (τέλειον) philosopher or lawyer. Yet Origen wishes Gregory to use his prowess for what he implicitly suggests in the opening lines is another culture alongside the Greek and Roman cultures, Christianity. He is to use his abilities not for law or philosophy, but rather in a purposeful manner (τελικῶς) toward a different end, the interpretation of the Christian Scriptures.

Origen draws a bold analogy in this first section of the letter. Just as the philosophers consider the general teachings or preparatory studies (ἐγκύκλια μαθήματα ἤ προπαιδεύματα) a helpmate for their discipline, so too can Christians committed to the interpretation of the holy Scriptures consider philosophy and its subordinate disciplines their helpmate. Origen specifically mentions the fields of geometry, music, philology, rhetoric and astronomy, though he likely has a full range of academic disciplines in mind. A well-rounded education, he avers, does not inexorably lead to a distinguished public career

---

identification rests, in part, upon Eusebius describing the bishop Gregory and his brother, Athenodorus, as "deeply interested in Greek and Roman learning." While studying under Origen in Caesarea they were led "to exchange their old zeal for the study of divinity" (HE 6.30/GCS 9.2, 584.15–19). This description echoes the content of the opening section of the *Letter to Gregory*, however Eusebius does not explicitly identify this Gregory as the recipient of the *Letter*. For challenges to this identification, see P. Nautin, *Origène*, 155–157, 161. See Chapter 1, n. 36 above, on the issue of Gregory Thaumaturgus' authorship of the *Address of Thanksgiving*.

[16] LG 1/SC 148, 186.3–188.18—transl. mine.
[17] S.v. τέλος, *LSJ*, esp. senses II and III.

as a lawyer or philosopher. In another playful pun on two adverbs, he advises a productive retrieval (ποιητικῶς) of Greek philosophy and its ancillary disciplines, exhorting Gregory to pursue these studies with a different and loftier aim in mind, to use his intellectual talents in a purposeful manner (τελικῶς) for Christianity—by which Origen means the career of a biblical scholar. In these succinct and sparkling lines he proposes a remarkable reordering of the educational system for Gregory. The culmination of the *paideia* is not Roman law or Greek philosophy. This educational system has been reconceived as a propaedeutic, a course of introductory study, for a new *telos*, the examination of the church's Scriptures.

As the *Letter* continues, Origen buttresses his proposal by contending that Scripture itself "hints" at such an educational program.[18] He offers a memorable allegorical reading of the plundering of the Egyptians in which this ancient event alludes to Origen's scholarly approach to Scripture. He begins by re-telling the story of the Exodus, noting how the children of Israel, while still dwelling in the land of Egypt, were to ask their Egyptian neighbors for their vessels of silver and gold, as well as their clothing (Exodus 11:2, 12:35). He is particularly concerned with the liturgical rationale behind this request. The Hebrews did not do this for personal profit, but rather, he notes, "in order that by spoiling the Egyptians they might find material for the preparation of the things employed for the worship of God."[19] Origen lists the items in the tabernacle's holy of holies that the Israelites would later construct in the wilderness for the worship of God. He draws his summary to a close with the following question: "And why is it necessary for me, in this untimely digression, to establish how useful for the children of Israel were the things taken from Egypt, which the Egyptians did not properly use, but which the Hebrews used with the help of the Wisdom of God for the worship of God?"[20]

Origen offers a clue that helps decipher how this episode symbolically refers to the biblical scholar's use of the academic disciplines: Egypt's wealth stands for these learned disciplines.[21] With this clue in hand, much of the allegory unfolds. The Hebrew plundering of Egyptian wealth points to the biblical scholar's mastery of Greco-Roman learning. Yet it is not an unprincipled quest for learning. Origen emphasizes that the Hebrews did not plunder indiscriminately, but rather took only the finest of Egyptian wealth. This corresponds to how the exegete of Scripture should retrieve only what is most useful for the

---

[18] LG 2/SC 148, 188.19.

[19] LG 2/SC 148, 188.22–24. Other references to plundering for the sake of worship at LG 2/SC 148, 188.36–39; LG 3/SC 148, 190.65–192.68.

[20] LG 3/SC 148, 190.45–49. On the theme of usefulness in the context of Greco-Roman learning, see C. Gnilka, *ΧΡΗΣΙΣ: Die Methode der Kirchenväter im Umgang mit der Antiken Kultur*, vol. 1, *Der Begriff des "rechten Gebrauchs"* (Basel: Schwabe, 1984), 54–63.

[21] LG 3/SC 148, 190.51–53.

interpretation of Scripture.[22] Finally, the Hebrews used Egyptian splendor for the worship of God by preparing a tabernacle in which God could dwell. This points to the interpreter's use of the best of Greco-Roman learning for the worship of God as well: instead of building a tabernacle, the interpreter prepares salutary interpretations of Scripture, the place where God now dwells.[23]

Origen's educational mandate for the would-be interpreter of Scripture finds expression elsewhere in his writings. There is an important passage in *Against Celsus* where he again endorses the value of the contemporary educational system for Christian intellectuals. He is responding to Celsus' critique that Christians are in the habit of recruiting young followers when their authority figures, their fathers and teachers, are not present. Moreover, as soon as they get hold of these children, Christians try to turn them against their teachers, saying "that these talk nonsense and have no understanding, and that in reality they neither know nor are able to do anything good, but are taken up with mere empty chatter."[24] Origen unequivocally denies the charge that Christians teach the young to disregard their teachers, and in so doing, his response echoes several of the sentiments expressed above in the *Letter to Gregory*:

> But if you were to show me teachers who give preparatory teaching in philosophy and train people in philosophical study [διδασκάλους πρὸς φιλοσοφίαν προπαιδεύοντας καὶ ἐν φιλοσοφίᾳ γυμνάζοντας], I would not dissuade young men from listening to these; but after they had first been trained in a general education and in philosophical thought [προγυμνασαμένους αὐτοὺς ὡς ἐν ἐγκυκλίοις μαθήμασι καὶ τοῖς φιλοσοφουμένοις] I would try to lead them on to the exalted height, unknown to the multitude, of the profoundest doctrines of the Christians, who discourse about the greatest and most advanced truths, proving and showing that this philosophy was taught by the prophets of God and the apostles of Jesus.[25]

Origen welcomes instruction "in a general education and in philosophical thought," but then transfers his students to the even loftier teachings in the Scriptures. In the *Letter to Gregory*, Origen signaled the subordination of the general education and philosophy to Christian scriptural scholarship with the image of a helpmate—this curriculum assists the nobler task of biblical interpretation.[26] Here in *Against Celsus* the imagery shifts, though the point is still the same. Before one scales the "exalted height" of the "prophets of God

---

[22] A point Origen will revisit in the next section of this *Letter* where he warns Gregory against relying on deficient Greco-Roman learning. For more on this theme, see Chapter 6 below (the section entitled, "Exegetical Lessons: Discernment").

[23] Note that Origen elsewhere explicitly associates biblical interpretation with worship (see Comm Matt 12.32–38 and Comm Jn 13.110 and 13.146, passages discussed in more detail in "Scripture's Effects" in Chapter 9 below). For Scripture as a divine dwelling, see Hom Lev 1.1.

[24] CC 3.55/SC 136, 130.11–13.

[25] CC 3.58/SC 136, 136.26–35. Also see CC 6.13/SC 147, 210.10–12.

[26] The term is συνέριθος at LG 1/SC 148, 188.17.

and the apostles of Jesus," that is, the Christian Scriptures, one needs to begin below with a general education and philosophy.[27]

One additional passage is of interest. The fourteenth chapter of the *Philocalia* anthologizes a passage from book three of Origen's *Commentary on Genesis* in which he advocated that would-be interpreters achieve specialization in philology. Origen is commenting on Genesis 1:16–18, which he cites as follows:

> And God made the two great lights, the great light for the rulers of the day and the small light for the rulers of the night, and [God created] the stars. And God placed these in the firmament of heaven to shine on the earth and to rule the day and the night.[28]

In verse 16 it says that God created the heavenly bodies "for the rulers" (εἰς ἀρχάς) of the day and the night, but in verse 18, that they were created "to rule" (ἄρχειν) the day and the night.[29] Origen wonders if the expressions "rulers" (ἀρχαί) of the day and night are synonymous with the phrase "to rule" (ἄρχειν) the day and night.

He answers his question by taking counsel with the philologists. "Now those who concern themselves with the investigation into the meanings [of words] [τῆς τῶν σημαινομένων ἐξετάσεως] say..."[30] The grammatical rule Origen consults need not concern us here, or how, with the help of this rule, he draws a deeper sense from these verses in Genesis. What is of interest to us (and presumably also to the editors of the *Philocalia* who anthologized this passage immediately after the *Letter to Gregory*) is that Origen gradually moves into a hermeneutical discussion, reflecting on the significance of having pulled into his interpretation of Gen 1:16–18 a grammatical principle from the linguists. He writes:

> The one who finds it difficult to accept these [grammatical considerations] ought to consider if it is possible to treat a problem in ethics, or natural sciences, or theology properly without an accurate understanding of the meanings of words and of the things clarified by the topic of linguistics [κατὰ τὸν λογικὸν τόπον]. For why is it out of place [ἄτοπον] to understand the proper use of words in different languages and to carefully examine the meanings of words? There are places where we really stumble

---

[27] For two other passages where Origen helpfully discusses the value of the educational system for Christianity, see Hom Gen 11.2 and CC 6.13–14.

[28] Phil 14.1/SC 302, 406.1–6—transl. mine.

[29] Even in Aquila's translation of this passage, Origen notes, the same noun–verb relationship is maintained, though Aquila translated εἰς ἀρχάς with εἰς ἐξουσίαν and ἄρχειν with ἐξουσιάζειν (Phil 14.1/SC 302, 406.9–11). For an orientation to Aquila's translation, see N. F. Marcos, *The Septuagint in Context: Introduction to the Greek Versions of the Bible*, transl. W. G. E. Watson (Leiden: Brill, 2001), 109–122. I will discuss the ancient Greek translations of Hebrew Scripture in more detail in the next chapter.

[30] Phil 14.1/SC 302, 408.12.

because of our ignorance of words, since we have not resolved the homonyms and ambiguities and figurative and literal uses of language and punctuation.[31]

Again Origen advances his claim in this passage with a pun. The noun τόπος has the sense both of place and of topic: why is it "out of place" (ἄτοπος) to study the "topic of linguistics" (ὁ λογικὸς τόπος)?[32] It is clear from Origen's description of this discipline that he has a range of philological activities in mind: he refers to the importance of defining words, resolving homonyms and ambiguous expressions, distinguishing between literal and figurative uses of language, and solving problems with punctuation.[33] He insists that these philological branches are invaluable for deciphering topics in ethics, theology, and natural sciences. The passage draws to a close with Origen's commendation of language study for would-be biblical scholars. For those who wish not to stray concerning the truth in understanding the divine Scriptures, "it is most necessary to know the principles of language [τὰ λογικά] ..."[34] This text finely illustrates not only Origen's openness to, but also his ambitious endorsement of, the value of philological scholarship for the study of Christian Scripture.

THE DIRECTIVE AND ORIGEN'S SCHOLARLY CAREER

In each of the foregoing passages, Origen expresses a baseline conviction about ideal interpreters of Scripture: that they ought to be trained as philologists and capable in a variety of additional academic disciplines relevant to informed biblical scholarship. In giving this unmistakably ambitious counsel, however, was Origen setting a standard for others that he himself had failed to take seriously? This is our first opportunity to explore the proposal forwarded in the introduction, that Origen's vision of the ideal scriptural interpreter often

---

[31] Phil 14.2/SC 302, 408.1–410.9—transl. mine. Later in this excerpt Origen again mentions problems related to "ambiguity and punctuation" (Phil 14.2/SC 302, 410.32–33).

[32] S.v. τόπος, *LSJ*, senses I and II. It is misleading to translate ὁ λογικὸς τόπος as "logic." The discipline to which Origen here refers encompassed not only inquiry into the patterns of argument expressed through language, but also a philological assessment of language itself (as Origen's description of this discipline in the passage above also makes evident). "Linguistics" is a better rendering of this Greek expression. Note also M. Harl's translation of this expression: "la science du langage" (SC 302, 409).

[33] For a discussion of the branches of philology mentioned in this passage, see M. Harl, SC 302, 425–426; a more detailed discussion can be found in B. Neuschäfer, *Origenes als Philologe*, 35, 140–155, 202–240.

[34] Phil 14.2/SC 302, 412.37–38—transl. mine. For a similar discussion of the role of linguistics, and in particular, philology, in dealing with philosophical topics, see Comm Song of Songs prol./GCS 8, 75.6–13. This passage is discussed in more detail in Chapter 5 below.

mirrored his own interpretive life. It would be a tedious exercise to confirm this proposal by turning to Origen's own writings, and demonstrating on the basis of them how widely read he was in the scholarship of his day.[35] More interesting is the testimony of four of his ancient biographers, all of whom shared the conviction that Origen was unusually steeped in the intellectual cultures of his day. Each of these writers—both detractors and supporters alike—contended that their subject had already embraced his own educational mandate and even helped others in their quest to fulfill it. Where they differed was in their assessment of this learning.

We can begin with the church historian Eusebius, whose biography we partially examined in the previous chapter. Eusebius emphasizes that the young Origen received a double formation at the hands of his father. He was trained to read Scripture,[36] but was also instructed "in the general education" (τῇ τῶν ἐγκυκλίων παιδείᾳ) or "in the Greek disciplines" (ἐν τοῖς Ἑλλήνων μαθήμασιν).[37] Later, after his father's martyrdom, he specialized in one of these fields, philology (τὰ γραμματικά), through which he earned his living.[38] Eusebius notes, moreover, that Origen not only enjoyed a broad education, he also made it available through his own instruction. While he served as a catechetical teacher in Alexandria, he taught his more gifted pupils,

> not only in divine things, but also in foreign philosophy. For when he perceived that any persons had superior intelligence he instructed them also in the philosophic disciplines [ἐπὶ τὰ φιλόσοφα μαθήματα]—in geometry, arithmetic, and other prepara-tory studies—and then advanced to the systems of the philosophers and explained their writings. And he made observations and comments upon each of them, so that he became celebrated as a great philosopher even among the Greeks themselves. And he instructed many of the less learned in the common school branches [ἐπὶ τὰ ἐγκύκλια γράμματα]...On this account he considered it especially necessary for himself to be skilled in the cosmological and philosophical disciplines.[39]

---

[35] For quick confirmation of this point, see M. Borret's indices to the ancient authors Origen mentioned, cited, or alluded to in *Against Celsus* (SC 227, 273–299). In the next chapter I will highlight some of the ways in which Origen's wide learning surfaced in his biblical scholarship.

[36] Eusebius, HE 6.2.7–9.

[37] The former expression at Eusebius, HE 6.2.7/GCS 9.2, 520.24–25; the latter at HE 6.2.15/GCS 9.2, 524.1–2. Also see HE 6.2.8/GCS 9.2, 520.26–27.

[38] Eusebius, HE 6.2.15/GCS 9.2, 524.4.

[39] Eusebius, HE 6.18.2–4/GCS 9.2, 556.16–27—transl. amended. This biographical snippet probably relies, at least in part, on one of Origen's letters (recall Eusebius' remark at HE 6.36.3–4 that he had assembled one hundred of Origen's letters). Eusebius cites a letter of Origen a few paragraphs later in the *Ecclesiastical History* to demonstrate his "diligence in Greek learning" (HE 6.19.11/GCS 9.2, 562.5). Origen defends his continuing interest in "the Greek disciplines" and philosophy:

> When I devoted myself to the word, and the fame of my proficiency went abroad, and when heretics, and at other times those trained in the Greek disciplines and particularly in philoso-phy came to me [οἱ ἀπὸ τῶν Ἑλληνικῶν μαθημάτων καὶ μάλιστα τῶν ἐν φιλοσοφίᾳ], it seemed necessary that I should examine the doctrines of the sectarians, and what the philosophers say concerning the truth (Eusebius, HE 6.19.12/GCS 9.2, 562.8–12—transl.

This same pattern of instruction continued after he moved to Caesarea in 231/232. There Origen founded a school whose curriculum ran through several major academic disciplines. Gregory's *Address of Thanksgiving* recounts in some detail how Origen persuaded him to take up philosophy, and how he relied upon his teacher, "philosophy's guide, this divine man,"[40] for instruction:

> So to us nothing was beyond words, nor was anything hidden and inaccessible. We were permitted to learn every doctrine, both barbarian and Greek, both the most mystical and the most pragmatic, both divine and human; we pursued the ins and outs of all these more than sufficiently and examined them closely, taking our fill of everything and enjoying the good things of the soul.[41]

Gregory presents Origen as the quintessential philosopher in his *Address* and outlines the program by which Origen initiated his students into the discipline of philosophy. Origen is portrayed as a teacher of dialectics, natural sciences (including geometry and astronomy), and ethics, before teaching about divinity through a reading of philosophic and poetic discourses about God.[42] Having scaled the heights of the Greco-Roman educational system, Gregory tells his readers that Origen finally taught Scripture as the highest discourse about God. The greatest gift Origen received from God was "that he should be

mine. This letter is cited at HE 6.19.12–14. For a brief discussion, see P. Nautin in *Lettres et Écrivains Chrétien*, 126–129 and *Origène*, 53–54).

Note also two other passages in Origen's corpus where he similarly acknowledges his wider intellectual interests. In *Against Celsus*, he writes: "But although by giving all our strength to study we have examined not only the doctrines in Christianity and the different views held within it, but also to the best of our ability have honestly looked well into the teachings of the philosophers..." (CC 5.62/SC 147, 168.16–20). Again in his eleventh *Homily on Genesis* he admits an acquaintance with a host of Hellenistic disciplines. After referring to literature, grammar, geometry, mathematics, and dialectic, he says, "we bring over to our purposes all these things which have been sought from without." While this "take-over" might appear suspicious to some, Origen continues, "by disputing, by discussing, by refuting those who contradict, we shall be able to convert some to the faith, and if, overcoming them with their own reasonings and skills, we shall persuade them to receive the true philosophy of Christ and the true piety of God" (Hom Gen 11.2/GCS 6, 103.19–20; 22–25).

[40] *Address* 6/SC 148, 128.76. There are several references in this section of the *Address* to Origen as a teacher of philosophy. Recall Eusebius' account of Origen's encounter with Gregory, bishop of Neocaesarea, and how he inspired him with a "love of philosophy" (φιλοσοφίας ... ἔρωτα) (HE 6.30/GCS 9.2, 584.16–17).

[41] *Address* 15/SC 148, 170.41–47.

[42] Dialectics: διαλεκτική (*Address* 8/SC 148, 140.1); natural sciences: ... μαθήμασιν ἑτέροις, τοῖς φυσικοῖς ... (*Address* 8/SC 148, 142.6–7); ethics: τὰς θείας ἀρετὰς τὰς περὶ ἦθος (*Address* 9/SC 148, 142.5); divinity: τοὺς περὶ τοῦ θείου πάντας ... λόγους (*Address* 13/SC 148, 158.4–5). This sequence resembles Stoic divisions of philosophy—see H. von Arnim, ed., *Stoicorum Veterum Fragmenta*, vol. 2 (Leipzig: B. J. Teubner, 1923), fragments 35ff; P. Hadot, "Les division(s) des parties de la philosophie dans l'Antiquité," *MH* 36 (1979): 218–231; H. Crouzel, *Origène et la philosophie*, 22–25. Also see Origen's own discussions of the branches of philosophy at Hom Gen 6.2–3; 14.3; Hom Ex 3.3; prologue, Comm Song of Songs/GCS 8, 75.6–13; Comm Matt 17.7; Phil 14.2 (discussed above).

an interpreter of the words of God to humans…"[43] The *Address* praises Origen for his wide learning and his deployment of it in service of scriptural interpretation. This account of his pedagogical activity in Caesarea dovetails remarkably well with Eusebius' biography that focuses more on Origen's Alexandrian period.

It is notable, however, that these two loyal supporters were not the only ones who attested to Origen's proficiency in Greco-Roman scholarship. Two of his fiercest opponents, Porphyry and Epiphanius, corroborated this picture. While Eusebius and Gregory would refer to his mastery of Greco-Roman knowledge in glowing terms, however, his foes would speak scathingly of his appropriation of this very same learning. Eusebius passes along Porphyry's report from the third book of his *Against the Christians*.[44] Porphyry, the biographer of Plotinus, offers a recollection and critique of Origen. The passage merits extensive citation:

> As an example of this absurdity [the Christian allegorization of the Jewish Scriptures] take a man whom I met when I was young, and who was then greatly celebrated and still is, on account of the writings which he has left. I refer to Origen, who is highly honored by the teachers of these doctrines.[45]

---

[43] *Address* 15/SC 148, 170.39–40. Gregory's portrayal of Origen as the ideal philosopher whose philosophical activity culminated in the exercise of biblical scholarship is hardly surprising when we attend to the institutional location of philosophy in late antiquity. P. Hadot has argued that the collapse of Athens' philosophical institutions in 86 BCE, as well as the development of several diasporic philosophical schools throughout the Mediterranean world, helped inaugurate an "exegetical phase" in philosophy. This phase lasted until the third century CE (P. Hadot, s.v. "Philosophie, I.E.: Hellenismus," *HWP*, vol. 7, ed. J. Ritter and K. Gründer [Basel: Schwabe, 1989], 596). The institutional collapse of these philosophical schools resulted in a redefinition of the teaching and practice of philosophy. The schools could no longer rely on an institution or on an oral tradition. Thus these schools, dispersed throughout the Hellenic and Roman world, turned to the authoritative texts of their founders for the mediation of their discipline. The basic scholarly exercise that emerged was the explication of an authoritative text in the form of a commentary (P. Hadot, "Théologie, exégèse, révélation, écriture dans la philosophie grecque," in *Les règles de l'interprétation*, ed. M. Tardieu [Paris: Cerf, 1987], 14). Origen himself intimately associates philosophical activity with exegetical activity: see esp. CC 1.9; 2.16; 3.58; 5.58; 6.49.

[44] For a translation of the extant fragments, see *Porphyry against the Christians*, transl. R. M. Berchman (Leiden: Brill, 2005); for orientation to the complex issues surrounding this treatise, see R. Goulet, "Hypothèses récentes sur le traité de Porphyre 'Contre les chrétiens,'" in *Hellénisme et christianisme*, ed. M. Narcy and É. Rebillard (Villeneuve d'Ascq: Presses Universitaires du Septentrion, 2004), 61–109.

[45] There are questions about whether the Origen identified by Porphyry is our Origen. Eusebius accepts this identification, but contests Porphyry's claim that Origen had been raised a heathen and only later converted to Christianity (HE 6.19.9–10). Nautin (*Origène*, 199–202) is quite convinced that Porphyry is speaking about our Origen: this Origen is a Christian, benefited from Greek philosophy and wrote numerous allegorical commentaries on Scripture. Moreover, this Origen met Porphyry when the latter was a young boy (Porphyry was born *c.*232–3 in Tyre or Batanee, a village near Caesarea, and so could have met Origen before his death *c.*254). However, there has been debate about the identification of Porphyry's Origen. For a brief introduction to this question, see Crouzel, *Origen*, 10–12. For more detailed studies, consult

For this man, having been a hearer of Ammonius,[46] who had attained the greatest proficiency in philosophy of any in our day, derived much benefit from this teaching in the knowledge of the sciences; but as to the correct choice of life, he pursued a course opposite to his. For Ammonius, being a Christian, and brought up by Christian parents, when he gave himself to study and to philosophy straightway conformed to the life required by the laws.

But Origen, having been educated as a Greek in Greek literature, went over to the barbarian recklessness. And carrying over the learning which he had obtained, he hawked it about, in his life conducting himself as a Christian and contrary to the laws, but in his opinions of material things and of the Deity being like a Greek, and mingling Grecian teachings with foreign [i.e. Jewish] fables. For he was continually studying Plato, and he busied himself with the writings of Numenius and Cronius, Apollophanes, Longinus, Moderatus, and Nicomachus, and those famous among the Pythagoreans. And he used the books of Chaeremon the Stoic, and of Cornutus. Becoming acquainted through them with the figurative interpretation of the Grecian mysteries, he applied it to the Jewish Scriptures.[47]

Porphyry raises no objection to Origen being "educated as a Greek in Greek literature," or having learned the sciences and philosophy from the celebrated Ammonius. Rather, what draws Porphyry's ire is how Origen had "mingled" or contaminated this *paideia* when he later converted to Christianity. Porphyry lauds Ammonius because even though he was raised a Christian, he had the integrity to convert to a "life required by the laws" so that his life would be "conformed" to his newly acquired knowledge. Origen, by contrast, achieved scholarly proficiency while not yet a Christian.[48] But rather than keeping his life in compliance with his knowledge, he converted to the "barbarian recklessness," Christianity, and lived "contrary to the laws." In so doing, Origen "carried over" his old knowledge into a new way of life, "mingling" the two with one another. So while in his life Origen conducted himself as a Christian, he simultaneously entertained Greek doctrines about the universe and God and used Greek exegetical skills to study the "foreign fables," that is, the Jewish Scriptures. Porphyry's

---

H. Dörrie, "Ammonios der Lehrer Plotins," *Hermes* 83 (1955): 439–477; F. H. Kettler, "War Origenes Schüler des Ammonios Sakkas?" in *Epektasis: Mélanges patristiques offerts au Cardinal Jean Daniélou*, ed. J. Fontaine and C. Kannengiesser (Paris: Beauchesne, 1972), 327–335; H. Ziebritzki, *Heiliger Geist und Weltseele: Das Problem der dritten Hypostase bei Origenes, Plotin, und ihren Vorläufern* (Tübingen: Mohr Siebeck, 1994), 30–43; T. Böhm, "Origenes— Theologe und (Neu-) Platoniker? Oder: Wem soll man missvertrauen—Eusebius oder Porphyrius?" *Adamantius: The International Journal of Origen and the Alexandrian Tradition* 8 (2002): 7–23.

[46] The Ammonius in question here is the one who taught Plotinus (205–c.269), Origen's later contemporary. Ammonius is often credited with founding "Neoplatonism" (see P. Nautin, *Origène*, 200–202).

[47] Eusebius, citing Porphyry at HE 6.19.5–8/GCS 9.2, 558.23–560.17. See P. F. Beatrice, "Porphyry's Judgment on Origen," in *Orig V*: 351–367, and A. J. Carriker, *The Library of Eusebius of Caesarea*, 126–128 on the plausibility of Origen's acquaintance with these authors.

[48] Note that Eusebius contests Porphyry's claim that Origen was an adult convert to Christianity (HE 6.19.9–10).

root accusation was that Origen lived a cacophonous existence: he embraced two incompatible realities, Christianity and Greco-Roman learning.

Fascinatingly, it was the fourth-century bishop of Salamis, Epiphanius, who leveled a similar accusation against Origen. In his *Panarion* he pointedly concluded his cantankerous treatment of Origen as follows:

> And you too, Origen, blinded in your mind by the aforementioned Greek education [Ἑλληνικῆς παιδείας], have vomited venom for your followers, and have become poisonous food for them, harming the multitude with the poison by which you yourself have been harmed.[49]

Epiphanius, like Porphyry, fashioned an antagonistic relationship between Christianity and Greek education. But, of course, the bishop disagreed with Porphyry in identifying which of these two realities played the role of villain. In the latter's hands, Christianity was offensive to the *paideia*; for Epiphanius this schema was inverted, and it was the *paideia* that was deemed toxic for Christianity. Yet the point neither Epiphanius nor Porphyry contested was that Origen had indeed gained remarkable proficiency in Greek intellectual culture. On this account, these detractors said little different from Eusebius and Gregory.

These biographers confirm that the standard Origen set for others—his ambitious scholarly mandate—he had already set for himself. From his youth Origen had benefited from a broad education, and as a mature scholar continued to immerse himself in a variety of schools of thought and disciplines, usually with a particular end in view: a more informed assessment of the Christian Scriptures. What is remarkable, however, is that he did not simply challenge his audiences to aspire to the education he had received. In Alexandria and later in Caesarea, he helped his pupils realize this ambitious project for themselves. Origen, in other words, issued a scholarly mandate that he had already appropriated, and was eager to promote in his own circles.

But this first sketch of Origen's portrait of the ideal scriptural interpreter (as well as of his own scholarly commitments) does not overlap well with the picture that emerges in F. Young's seminal work, *Biblical Exegesis and the Formation of Christian Culture*. In her chapter, "Cultures and Literatures," Young writes of a "conflict" or "confrontation of cultures" that was ostensibly indicative of pre-Nicene theology:

> Prior to Nicaea Christians exploited the moral and theological shortcomings of pagan literature, adopting the well-tried methods of the schools and the well-worn arguments of the philosophers to serve their exposure of traditional religion and philosophy, and *to condemn the whole integrated literary and symbolic culture that surrounded them* (italics mine).[50]

---

[49] *Panarion* 64.72/GCS 31, 523.14–18—transl. mine.
[50] F. M. Young, *Biblical Exegesis and the Formation of Christian Culture* (Cambridge: Cambridge University Press, 1997), 70.

The passage continues: "The Bible was to provide a substitute literature, a rival *paideia*, an alternative education."[51] For Origen, Young continues in the next chapter, the "underlying assumption was that the Scriptures replaced the classics as the literature on which *paideia* was based."[52] It was only in the post-Constantinian period that this view of conflict and replacement was modified, since "cultured bishops found they could not relinquish the classics for proper linguistic training."[53]

These broad brush-strokes do not do justice to Origen, arguably the leading pre-Nicene Christian intellectual. Some of Young's claims certainly apply to Origen. He did, in fact, criticize the moral and theological shortcomings of pagan literature (as is especially clear in his *Against Celsus*).[54] It is equally indisputable that the Scriptures counted as *the* sacred writings for Origen and not, say, the works of Homer or Plato—on this issue of authority, the Scriptures had indeed usurped the classics of pagan literature. Yet both these points can be conceded without accepting Young's pre-Nicene model of "conflict and replacement" which over-interprets the situation. Origen *did* criticize non-biblical literature and did *not* view it on par with the Scriptures, but such a demotion did not imply *complete condemnation*. Indeed, as numerous passages already examined in this chapter confirm, Origen enthusiastically interacted with this literature throughout his life, both as pupil and as teacher of would-be scriptural scholars.[55] Sifted of its impurities, the *paideia* was not a "rival," as Young has it, but a "helpmate" (*Letter to Gregory*) instrumental in interpreting Christian Scripture to which it was subordinate. Thus, expressions like "battle of the literatures" strike too confrontational a note.[56]

---

[51] Ibid.

[52] Ibid., 95. Young is not the first to have made such an assertion about Origen's relation to the *paideia*. E. Molland curiously asserted that Origen "condemns philosophy *en bloc*, together with idolatry and divination" (*The Conception of the Gospel in the Alexandrian Theology* [Oslo: I Kommisjon Hos Jacob Dybwad, 1938], 87).

[53] F. M. Young, *Biblical Exegesis*, 96.

[54] See the section in Chapter 6 below entitled "Exegetical Lessons: Discernment," where I discuss Origen's argument for the judicious use of Hellenistic philosophy. Since Greek intellectual culture was not an unalloyed good, it merited (where necessary) criticism.

[55] For more on why Origen did not dismiss pagan learning outright, consult Chapter 4 below, particularly the section, "All Wisdom Comes from God," where I discuss his account of the divine provenance of all truthful knowledge, including the insights of Greek intellectual culture. Origen often acknowledges that Christians shared convictions with non-Christians, the latter having also benefited from divine revelation.

[56] F. M. Young, *Biblical Exegesis*, 56. It is important to stress here again that the young Origen's decision to sell his manuscripts of Greek literature to devote himself more fully to biblical study did *not* indicate his rejection or condemnation of this literature. Origen experienced a rivalry between his continued *teaching* of this literature and his desire to become a full-fledged student of Christian Scripture. According to Eusebius, the young Origen "considered the teaching of literature inconsistent with the study of divine subjects; not hesitating, he broke these things off as useless, even his school of literature as a hindrance to sacred learning" (HE 6.3.8/ GCS 9.2, 526.15–19—transl. emended). As the passage continues, Eusebius notes that Origen

They are not indicative of Origen's conciliatory and liberal educational mandate.[57]

Origen's ancient biographers knew what his modern readers readily discern: to a remarkable extent, his educational mandate for would-be interpreters of Scripture was a clear expression of an ideal that had animated his own scholarly career. This ideal was neither combative nor dismissive of the *paideia*, but rather appreciative, and insistent upon its usefulness for the Christian exegetical enterprise. This ideal was also an undeniably challenging prescription for would-be interpreters of Scripture, in particular the *simpliciores* in the church whom Origen often admonished to take scholarship more seriously. In a world with limited access to education, it was their task to digest carefully a wide array of Greco-Roman intellectual disciplines, and to draw upon these to facilitate the interpretation of Christian Scripture. In the next chapter I will examine more closely one particular facet of this *paideia* that we have briefly encountered above, the interpreter's area of specialization, philology.

---

gave himself more fully to the study of Scripture after he quit his school (also see Chapter 1 above, n. 45).

[57] Indeed, it is important to stress that if there was anything Origen saw rivaling an interest in Scripture, it was *not* Greco-Roman literature, but rather the mind's inordinate attraction to matters of lesser, more worldly and bodily interest. Much more on this theme below in the section, "The Ordered (and Disordered) Mind," in Chapter 5.

3

Specialization: The Elements of Philology

The scholarly examination of literature, or philology, was a well-established field of inquiry in Origen's day.[1] It was his own area of specialization and the discipline he advocated to would-be interpreters of Scripture.[2] In this chapter I will offer a sketch of ancient philology as Origen understood it, relying upon his fragmentary descriptions of this discipline, as well as his own exegetical practice. At various points I will also draw upon B. Neuschäfer's *Origenes als Philologe*, as this study already maps much of the terrain. Dionysius Thrax's (*c.*170–190 BCE) *Art of Philology*, an Alexandrian textbook that remained a standard work well into the Christian era, provides the scaffolding for Neuschäfer's monograph.[3] According to the scholia on this short treatise,

---

[1] For overviews of philology in antiquity, see J. E. Sandys, *A History of Classical Scholarship*, vol. 1, *From the Sixth Century BC to the End of the Middle Ages*, 3rd edn (New York: Hafner, 1967); R. Pfeiffer, *A History of Classical Scholarship*, vol. 1, *From the Beginnings to the End of the Hellenistic Age* (Oxford: Clarendon Press, 1968); W. Ameling and H.-G. Nesselrath, eds., *Einleitung in die griechische Philologie* (Stuttgart: Teubner, 1997). Among the numerous specialized studies on this topic, see esp. G. M. A. Grube, *The Greek and Roman Critics* (Toronto: University of Toronto Press, 1965); M. Fuhrmann, *Einführung in die antike Dichtungstheorie* (Darmstadt: Wissenschaftliche Buchgesellschaft, 1973); D. A. Russell, *Criticism in Antiquity* (Berkeley: University of California Press, 1981); R. Lamberton, *Homer the Theologian: Neoplatonist Allegorical Reading and the Growth of the Epic Tradition* (Berkeley: University of California Press, 1986); R. A. Kaster, *Guardians of Language: The Grammarian and Society in Late Antiquity* (Berkeley: University of California Press, 1988); G. A. Kennedy, ed., *Cambridge History of Literary Criticism*, vol. 1: *Classical Criticism* (Cambridge: Cambridge University Press, 1989); T. Morgan, *Literate Education in the Roman and Hellenistic Worlds* (Cambridge: Cambridge University Press, 1998).

[2] On Origen's training in this field, see the discussion above in Chapter 1 at nn. 42–43. On Origen's philological mandate for would-be interpreters of Scripture, see LG 1 and Phil 14.2, both discussed at length in the previous chapter.

[3] For editions of this text and the rich scholia on it, see Dionysius Thrax, *Dionysii Thracis: Ars Grammatica*, ed. G. Uhlig, Grammatici Graeci, 1.1 (Leipzig: B. G. Teubner, 1883; reprint, Hildesheim: Georg Olms, 1965); *Scholia in Dionysii Thracis Artem Grammaticam*, ed. A. Hilgard, Grammatici Graeci, 1.3 (Leipzig: B. G. Teubner, 1901; reprint, Hildesheim: Georg Olms, 1965). For an English translation of Dionysius' *Art of Philology*, consult A. Kemp, "The *Tekhnē Grammatikē* of Dionysius Thrax: English translation with introduction and notes," in *The History of Linguistics in the Classical Period*, ed. Daniel J. Taylor (Amsterdam: J. Benjamins, 1987), 169–189.

there were four main philological exercises in the Hellenistic classroom: text-critical analysis (διορθωτικόν), reading a passage aloud (ἀναγνωστικόν), literary and historical analysis (ἐξηγητικόν), and finally, aesthetic and moral evaluation (κρίσις ποιημάτων). The branch of ἐξηγητικόν supported four further inquiries: clarification of a word's meaning (γλωσσηματικόν); grammatical and rhetorical analysis (τεχνικόν); metrical evaluation and style criticism (μετρικόν); and finally, analysis of the historical realities mentioned in a text (ἱστορικόν). In what follows I will focus on the handful of procedures that surface most prominently in Origen's exegetical oeuvre: text criticism, historical analysis and literary analysis. For Origen, these were the staples of the interpreter's scholarly assessment of Scripture. I will, moreover, integrate into this account of ancient literary analysis the two referents that philologists sought to identify, the literal and allegorical senses of a passage. As I will stress, for Origen literal *and* allegorical interpretation were both moments within the larger philological enterprise.

PROCEDURES

Text criticism

Text criticism (διορθωτικόν) was a foundational exercise in late antique philology and proved central to Origen's own exegetical endeavors.[4] In a fragment from one of his few surviving letters, he refers to the painstaking activity of correcting discrepant copies of scriptural manuscripts. Under his patron Ambrose, he writes:

> it is neither possible to eat without conversation, nor, after having eaten, to take a walk and allow the body to rest awhile, but even during these times we are compelled to study and to correct the copies [φιλολογεῖν καὶ ἀκριβοῦν τὰ ἀντίγραφα]; nor indeed are we allowed to go to bed for the whole night in order to care for the body, since study extends deep into the night.[5]

---

[4] For orientations to Origen's text criticism, see R. M. Grant, *Letter and Spirit*, 143–144; J. Daniélou, *Origen*, 133–138; R. P. C. Hanson, *Allegory and Event*, 162–178; S. Brock, "Origen's aims as a textual critic of the Old Testament," *SP* 10 (Berlin: Akademie-Verlag, 1970): 215–218; P. Nautin, *Origène*, 344–353; M. Harl, SC 302, 126–127. The most extensive discussion occurs in B. Neuschäfer, *Origenes als Philologe*, 85–138. For additional literature, see n. 19 below on Origen's *Hexapla*.

[5] P. Nautin, *Lettres et Écrivains Chrétiens*, 250.7–251.12—transl. mine. In the preceding lines of this letter, Origen refers to Ambrose's "love for sacred studies [τῷ πρὸς τὰ ἅγια μαθήματα ἔρωτι]" which strongly suggests that the manuscripts in question here are, in fact, copies of the sacred Scriptures. Moreover, the term ἀντίγραφον often signifies a copy of these Scriptures in Origen's writings (s.v. ἀντίγραφον, Lampe, I; LA 3/SC 302, 524.20; LA 4/SC 302, 524.3, 526.24; LA 6/SC 302, 528.7–8; LA 8/SC 302, 532.2; Comm Matt 15.14/GCS 10, 387.19, 28).

Here Origen alludes to the scribe's common plight: prior to the invention of the printing press, literary works were assiduously copied by hand, line by line, word by word, letter by letter. Not surprisingly, this laborious process led to the introduction of discrepancies into manuscript copies, which required subsequent correction.[6] In a passage from his *Commentary on Matthew*, Origen points to some of the underlying causes of these discrepancies: "the differences among the copies [of the Gospels] have become great either through the negligence of some copyists, or through the perverse audacity of others, or through those who are careless in the correction of the exemplars."[7] Some errors were undoubtedly unintentional, the result of carelessness, fatigue, or simple incompetence, while others were purposeful, corruptions interpolated by mischievous scribes.

The nature of scribal transmission in antiquity presented, then, an inherent challenge to the establishment of a correct text. We find Origen engaging in text-critical activities for all the writings he considered scriptural, including those within the collection of the New Testament.[8] However, there were additional circumstances surrounding the law and prophets that considerably complicated the philologist's task. Most of these writings had originally been composed in Hebrew, yet very few Christians in Origen's day could study them in their original language.[9] Thus, they read them in translation. The most prominent

---

[6] The technical terms for these "discrepancies" are διαφορά (LA 6/SC 302, 530.27; LA 9/SC 302, 534.3, 6; Comm Matt 15.4/GCS 10, 387.29) and διαφωνία (Comm Matt 15.14/GCS 10, 387.17; 388.9, 14). Origen repeatedly highlights three sorts of textual corruption: additions, omissions (see Comm Matt 15.4/GCS 10, 388.5–7; LA 5/SC 302, 526.1–3) and transpositions (see LA 7/SC 302, 530.2). Also see Origen's *Letter to Friends in Alexandria* where he says his own writings were subjected to these three forms of corruption (LF/Rufinus).

[7] Comm Matt 15.14/GCS 10, 387.28–388.4—transl. mine. In Comm Matt 15.14, 16.19; and Hom Jer 16.5.2, Origen again suggests scribal ignorance as a cause of divergences in the manuscript copies. Interestingly, in the latter passage he is willing to entertain the notion that the error goes back to the translators of the Septuagint itself. As for the charge of intentional scribal corruption, this accusation was widespread in late antiquity. Origen raises the charge with respect to his own writings (see Chapter 1 above, at n. 63). For a discussion of this theme, see A. Bludau, *Die Schriftsfälschungen der Häretiker: ein Beitrag zur Textkritik der Bibel* (Munster: Aschendorf, 1925), and more recently, B. Ehrman, *The Orthodox Corruption of Scripture: The Effect of Early Christological Controversies on the Text of the New Testament* (New York, NY: Oxford University Press, 1993).

[8] J. Daniélou's contention that "Origen never undertook any critical work on the New Testament" is erroneous (*Origen*, 137). For examples of Origen's text-critical work on the New Testament, see Comm Matt 15.14, 16.19, Comm Jn 2.132, 6.204ff, 20.144ff. Also recall his comments about the Marcionite corruption of the NT text (Comm Rom 10.43.2; LF/Rufinus; CC 2.27). For literature on Origen's NT textual criticism, see J.-P. P. Martin, *Origène et la critique textuelle du Nouveau Testament* (Paris: V. Palmé, 1885); R. P. C. Hanson, *Allegory and Event*, 176–177; B. M. Metzger, "Explicit references in the works of Origen to variant readings in New Testament manuscripts," in *Biblical and Patristic Studies in Memory of Robert Pierce Casey*, ed. J. N. Birdsall and R. W. Thomson (Freiburg: Herder, 1963), 78–95.

[9] Eusebius makes brief mention of Origen's knowledge of Hebrew—simply that "he learned the Hebrew language" (HE 6.16.1/GCS 9.2, 552.27). It is not clear from this statement what level of proficiency he attained, and H. Crouzel is certainly correct to observe that there "can be all

translation into Greek was the Septuagint (*LXX*),[10] but several other Greek translations existed as well. By the early third century, the major versions of Aquila, Symmachus, and Theodotion also circulated throughout Christian networks—Origen often referred to these collectively as "the remaining versions" (οἱ λοιπαὶ ἐκδόσεις).[11] For would-be text critics of the law and prophets there emerged, then, a series of Old Testaments, each with its own complex manuscript tradition. In principle—should scholars have access to a rich cache of manuscripts—they could pursue two types of comparative textual analysis. They could examine the discrepancies that surfaced *within* each of these Old Testament manuscript traditions: the differences among the multiple Hebrew copies in circulation, as well as the differences among the multiple copies *within* each of the distinct families of Greek translations.[12] But of course, they could also examine the disagreements *between* each of these Old Testaments. As we will see below, it was the discrepancies within the septuagintal family that would prove especially decisive for Origen's own text-critical work, though he also consulted the other Greek translations and Hebrew copies to sort out these difficulties. The Septuagint was the Greek-speaking church's official version of the law and prophets in his day, and when Origen attempted to emend an Old Testament text, he invariably aimed at securing its correct septuagintal version.[13]

Reconstructing Origen's text-critical procedures is a notoriously difficult task. This is so, in part, because he had very little to say about them, even when his exegetical work clearly reflected text-critical decisions.[14] Another obstacle is that the *Hexapla* (τὰ Ἑξαπλᾶ[15]), the multi-columned edition of the Old

---

manner of levels in one's knowledge of a language" (*Origen*, 12). Most scholars regard Origen's knowledge of Hebrew as slender. Note esp. Hom Num 14.1.3 where he distances himself from a knowledge of this language.

[10] The title "Septuagint" is from the Latin for "seventy" (septuaginta), the ostensible number of translators who participated in this translation project. Origen can designate this work as "the translation of the seventy" (ἡ ἑρμηνεία τῶν ἑβδομήκοντα in LA 9/SC 302, 534.7) or simply "the seventy" (ἑβδομήκοντα in Comm Matt 15.14/GCS 10, 388.7–24). For orientations to this Greek translation, see H. B. Swete, *An Introduction to the Old Testament in Greek*, rev. R. R. Ottley (Cambridge: Cambridge University Press, 1914); S. Jellicoe, *The Septuagint and Modern Study* (Oxford: Clarendon Press, 1968); G. Dorival, M. Harl, and O. Munnich, *La Bible grecque des Septante: Du judaïsme hellénistique au christianisme ancien* (Paris: Éditions du Cerf, 1988); N. F. Marcos, *The Septuagint in Context: Introduction to the Greek Versions of the Bible*, transl. W. G. E. Watson (Leiden: Brill, 2001); most recently, T. Rajak, *Translation and Survival: The Greek Bible and the Ancient Jewish Diaspora* (Oxford: Oxford University Press, 2009).

[11] On these and other Greek translations, see N. F. Marcos, *The Septuagint in Context*, 109–173.

[12] Scholars often fail to stress that Origen had access to several Hebrew copies (LA 3/SC 302, 524.20; Comm Jn 6.212/GCS 4, 150.23; also Eusebius, H.E. 6.16.1). On possessing multiple copies of the Septuagint, see Comm Matt 15.14 (discussed more fully below).

[13] For clear statements on the authority of the *LXX*, see LA 8 and Hom Jer 15.5.2.

[14] Particularly curious are those passages where he announced a textual difficulty, noted variant readings, adopted one, yet remained entirely silent about his decision-making process (see, for instance, Hom Jd 1.1 and Jer Frg 14).

[15] As it is called by Eusebius at HE 6.16.4/GCS 9, 554.15. At least in the writings that have come down to us, Origen does not provide a name for this reference work.

Testament that facilitated text-critical activity, only survives in fragments.[16] There are, moreover, only a few passages in which Origen actually gestures toward this work;[17] beyond these passages we find scattered descriptions from fourth century authors, some of whom probably handled it personally.[18] There are still any number of disputes in the scholarship about the physical form of the *Hexapla*, its layout, how it was composed, its contents, and even the ends that it served.[19] In what follows I offer a cautious description of this enormous project, "absolutely unique in its genre in antique Christian literature."[20]

Origen probably began his compilation of the *Hexapla* while he was still in Alexandria.[21] This multi-volume work presented the Old Testament in a grid of columns and rows. The first column on the left margin of the page contained the Hebrew text in Hebrew characters. It was followed to the right by a column with the Hebrew text transliterated into Greek characters; thereafter came the four Greek translations of Aquila, Symmachus, the Septuagint, and Theodotion. For some books Origen also affixed to the right of Theodotion's text a fifth, sixth, and even seventh translation (referred to as the Quinta, Sexta, and Septima).[22] There were, then, as many as nine columns of

---

[16] The last edition of the *Hexapla* was published by F. Field, ed., *Origenis Hexaplorum*, 2 vols. (Oxford: Clarendon Press, 1875). P. Nautin, *Origène*, 303–309 and A. Grafton and M. Williams, *Christianity and the Transformation of the Book*, 96–102 discuss the fragments that have been discovered since this publication. For a list of the editions for the hexaplaric material recovered after Field's edition, see D. Barthélemy, *Critique textuelle de l'Ancien Testament*, vol. 3 (Fribourg: Éditions Universitaires, 1992), clx–clxi.

[17] Origen alludes to this work in his *Letter to Africanus* and at Comm Matt 15.14.

[18] Eusebius, H.E. 6.16.1–4 (as well as Rufinus' Latin translation that diverges at points); Jerome, Comm Tit 3.9 and *On Illustrious Men* 54; Epiphanius, *Panarion* 64, 3.5–7 and *On Weights and Measures* 17. For a quick overview of these passages, see M. Williams and A. Grafton, *Christianity and the Transformation of the Book*, 89–96; for a more substantial discussion, consult P. Nautin, *Origène*, 311–332 and B. Neuschäfer, *Origenes als Philologe*, 86–87, esp. nn. 14–16.

[19] For an overview of the *Hexapla*, see A. Grafton and M. Williams, *Christianity and the Transformation of the Book*, 86–132. For more detailed discussions, consult: H. B. Swete, *Introduction to the Old Testament in Greek*, 59–86; R. Devreesse, *Introduction à l'étude des manuscrits grecs* (Paris: Librairie C. Klincksieck, 1954), 101–117; P. E. Kahle, *The Cairo Geniza*, 2nd edn (Oxford: Basil Blackwell, 1959), 157–164, 239–247; S. Jellicoe, *The Septuagint and Modern Study*, 100–146; D. Barthélemy, "Origène et le texte de l'Ancien Testament," in *Epektasis: Mélanges patristiques offerts au Cardinal Jean Daniélou*, ed. J. Fontaine and C. Kannengiesser (Paris: Beauchesne, 1972), 247–261; G. Dorival, "L'apport des chaînes exégétiques à une réédition des Hexaples d'Origène," *RHT* 4 (1974): 45–74; A. Schenker, *Hexaplarische Psalmenbruchstücke: die hexaplarischen Psalmenfragmente der Handschriften Vaticanus graecus 752 und Canonicianus graecus 62* (Freiburg: Universitätsverlag, 1975), 3–7; P. Nautin, *Origène*, 303–361; J. N. Guinot, "La fortune des Hexaples d'Origèneau IVè et Vè siècles en milieu antiochien," *Orig VI*: 215–225; A. Salvesen, ed., *Origen's Hexapla and Fragments: Papers Presented at the Rich Seminar on the Hexapla* (Tübingen: Mohr Siebeck, 1998); N. Fernández Marcos, *The Septuagint in Context*, 204–238 with a bibliography.

[20] P. Nautin, *Origène*, 303.

[21] Ibid., 369.

[22] Note, for instance, Origen's reference to a fifth Greek translation of Zechariah in Comm Matt 16.16. The evidence for this physical description of the *Hexapla*, especially the order of the columns, comes from Jerome, Comm Tit 3.9 and Rufinus, HE 6.16.4. Additional evidence for

biblical text on some of the pages of the *Hexapla*. Scholars would have read a biblical passage in this work from the top of the page to the bottom: after identifying a column of interest, their eyes would scan down the page, encountering with each new (i.e. lower) row, the next word or phrase in the biblical text. If these scholars wished to compare the text in their column with that in any another column, they could pause at a word or phrase, and then read to the left or right within that row, ultimately moving across all the columns on the hexaplaric page. This procedure quickly allowed readers to determine whether there were any discrepancies among the Greek translations of a particular Hebrew passage. Since each row of the *Hexapla* was devoted to such a small amount of text (a single word or phrase), this work quickly became colossal in size: best estimates suggest between forty and fifty codices.[23]

Why did Origen construct this monumental reference work? The answer to this question is hardly straightforward. In his *Letter to Africanus* he contended that this exegetical tool promoted an informed Jewish–Christian dialogue.[24] It is hard to believe, however, that this was the sole, or perhaps even primary, purpose behind devising this work. The desire to know the Hebrew text for his discussions with the Jews was perhaps *a* reason for constructing the *Hexapla* (or a happy result of the construction) but it was not the only one, and probably not the most important one. Origen also had an interest in correcting the copies of the Septuagint that lay before him, the church's official version of the Old Testament.

The *Letter to Africanus* offers tantalizing, though incomplete, evidence for this latter activity. Origen notes that there were discrepancies between the Greek and Hebrew copies of Genesis and observes that the words "God saw that it was good" (Gen 1:8) were not in the Hebrew manuscripts, though they could be found in the Septuagint (*LXX*). In this context he mentions two text-critical sigla, the obelus (ὀβελός) and asterisk (ἀστερίσκος), which annotated at least one of his septuagintal texts.[25] "And it is also possible to find other

---

this sequence of columns derives from the fragment from the Cairo Genizah, which displays five Greek columns on Psalm 22: the Greek transliteration of the Hebrew, followed by the versions of Aquila, Symmachus, the Septuagint and Theodotion. See C. Taylor, *Hebrew-Greek Cairo Genizah Palimpsests from the Taylor-Schechter Collection: Including a Fragment of the Twenty-Second Psalm According to Origen's Hexapla* (Cambridge: Cambridge University Press, 1900), 13–15.

[23] F. Field estimated that it consisted of fifty volumes (*Origenis Hexaplorum*, xcviii). Williams suggests close to forty codices, each with 400 leaves (800 pages) (*Christianity and the Transformation of the Book*, 104–105).

[24] The letter is dated to 248–50 by de Lange, SC 302, 501 and P. Nautin, *Origène*, 182. For interpretations of Origen's discussion of text criticism in this letter, see D. Barthélemy, "Origène," 248–251; S. Brock, "Origen's aims as a textual critic of the Old Testament," 215–218; N. R. M. de Lange, "The letter to Africanus: Origen's recantation," in *SP* 16: 242–247; P. Nautin, *Origène*, 176–182, 344–347; B. Neuschäfer, *Origenes als Philologe*, 93.

[25] It is not clear whether the septuagintal text in the fifth column of the *Hexapla* contained these sigla, or whether some other edition of the *LXX* did (or both). For an overview, see M. Williams and A. Grafton, *Christianity and the Transformation of the Book*, 88, 108, 116–117.

passages in Genesis by which we have placed [signs] which the Greeks call obeli in order that such a situation be noticeable to us," that is, the situation where there was more text in the *LXX* than in the Hebrew. "On the other hand," Origen continues, "we put asterisks by those passages which exist in the Hebrew but are not found among us."[26] The signs to which Origen here refers had a long tradition in Hellenistic philology. In his hands the obelus signified a passage in the *LXX* that was lengthier than its corresponding text in the Hebrew, whereas the asterisk notified the reader that the septuagintal reading was shorter than the Hebrew.[27] Origen offers little more in this *Letter* to help explain how he corrected discrepant manuscripts.

A slightly more informative description of these sigla and the aims of the *Hexapla* occurs in Origen's *Commentary on Matthew*. There he writes:

> We have been able, with God helping us, to repair the difference between the copies of the Old Testament, by using the remaining versions [of the OT] as a criterion. Based upon these remaining versions, we made a judgment about the uncertainties in the Septuagint due to the difference in its copies. We kept what is in agreement with these [versions]. We marked some passages with an obelus that are not in the Hebrew (we did not dare to completely strike these out); but we added others with asterisks in order to make it clear that what we supplied was not in the Septuagint but from the remaining translations harmonious with the Hebrew.[28]

In this notoriously dense passage Origen explicitly announces his concern for the correction ("repair"—ἰάομαι) of the multiple and sometimes discrepant copies of the Septuagint before him. To help decipher this passage, it is important to keep in mind that Origen was envisioning a very particular

---

[26] Καὶ ἄλλα δέ ἐστιν εὑρεῖν ἐν τῇ Γενέσει, οἷς ἡμεῖς [σημεῖα] παρεθήκαμεν τοὺς καλουμένους παρ᾿ Ἕλλησιν ὀβελούς, ἵν᾿ ἡμῖν γνώριμον ᾖ τὸ τοιοῦτον· ὡς πάλιν ἀστερίσκους τοῖς κειμένοις μὲν ἐν τῷ Ἑβραϊκῷ, παρ᾿ ἡμῖν δὲ μὴ εὑρισκομένοις (LA 7/SC 302, 530.6–532.10—transl. mine). Note the mistranslation of this last clause in the ANF, vol. 4, p. 387, col. 1, section 4 (and preserved in A. Grafton and M. Williams, *Christianity and the Transformation of the Book*, 120–121), which wrongly reads: "and on the other hand, I marked with an asterisk those passages in our copies which are not found in the Hebrew." This translation attributes the function of the obelus to the asterisk.

[27] On the history of these sigla that trace back to Zenodotus, the scholar at the Alexandrian Museum, see R. Pfeiffer, *History of Classical Scholarship*, 115. For the various forms of these sigla, see F. Field, *Origenis Hexaplorum*, lii–lx; H. B. Swete, *Introduction to the Old Testament in Greek*, 69–73. In addition to the passages discussed below, also see references to the obelus at PE 14.4 (the Jewish use of it in copies of Daniel); Comm Jn 28.137/GCS 4, 410.15–16; Comm Rom 6.2/J. Scherer, *Le Commentaire d'Origène sur Rom. III.5–V.7 d'après les extraits du Papyrus n. 88748 du Musée du Caire et les fragments de la Philocalie et du Vaticanus gr. 762* (Cairo: L'Institut Français d'Archéologie Orientale, 1957), 192.20.

[28] τὴν μὲν οὖν ἐν τοῖς ἀντιγράφοις τῆς παλαιᾶς διαθήκης διαφωνίαν θεοῦ διδόντος εὕρομεν ἰάσασθαι, κριτηρίῳ χρησάμενοι ταῖς λοιπαῖς ἐκδόσεσιν· τῶν γὰρ ἀμφιβαλλομένων παρὰ τοῖς Ἑβδομήκοντα διὰ τὴν τῶν ἀντιγράφων διαφωνίαν τὴν κρίσιν ποιησάμενοι ἀπὸ τῶν λοιπῶν ἐκδόσεων τὸ συνᾷδον ἐκείναις ἐφυλάξαμεν, καὶ τινὰ μὲν ὠβελίσαμεν <ὡς> ἐν τῷ Ἑβραϊκῷ μὴ κείμενα (οὐ τολμήσαντες αὐτὰ πάντη περιελεῖν), τινὰ δὲ μετ᾿ ἀστερίσκων προσεθήκαμεν, ἵνα δῆλον ᾖ ὅτι μὴ κείμενα παρὰ τοῖς Ἑβδομήκοντα ἐκ τῶν λοιπῶν ἐκδόσεων συμφώνως τῷ Ἑβραϊκῷ προσεθήκαμεν (Comm Matt 15.14/GCS 10, 388.7–24)—transl. mine.

textual problem.[29] There were multiple *LXX* manuscripts on his desk, and a consensus reading for a particular verse emerged between most of these, as well as between these and the Hebrew and other Greek versions (by Aquila, Symmachus, and Theodotion). However, in the scenario Origen here describes, at least one of the *LXX* manuscripts before him deviated from this consensus. In such a circumstance, the "remaining versions," οἱ λοιπαὶ ἐκδόσεις, would serve as a "criterion" for adjudicating the diverse witnesses among the *LXX* copies. The reading in the *LXX* manuscripts that formed a consensus with the other versions was "kept." However, the deviating *LXX* manuscripts were marked with text-critical sigla. The obelus, as we have already seen above, marked these manuscripts if they had more text than the emergent consensus (though, Origen quickly notes, this additional text was not actually erased). If, however, the *LXX* manuscripts deviated by having too little text, they were marked with an asterisk and the missing passage was added "from those remaining translations harmonious with the Hebrew." Either way, the divergent manuscript was "repaired." Here, then, in the *Commentary on Matthew*, Origen outlines one (and only one) highly specific text-critical scenario. There were, of course, other scenarios he encountered, though how he dealt with them remains largely opaque to us.[30]

---

[29] This difficult passage has elicited much commentary. My translation and interpretation draw heavily upon the literary context in the *Commentary* where Origen sees a parallel between his work on OT manuscripts and the problem he was encountering with the text of Mt 19:19. This verse was found in some manuscripts of Matthew, but was missing from others; it was, furthermore, missing from the synoptic parallels of Mark and Luke. This situation paralleled what Origen often encountered with the multiple *LXX* manuscripts before him (as with the multiple manuscripts of Matthew on his desk)—that is, cases when one *LXX* copy was in agreement with every other Greek translation and the Hebrew, but another *LXX* copy was out of step with all these other texts. For other examples where Origen wrestles, as he does here, with a discrepant text, while a consensus emerges among all the other versions, Hebrew included, see Hom Jer 14.3.1, 16.10.1; Comm Jn 6.40, 6.212, 28.137. For literature on this passage, see I. Soisalon-Soininen, *Der Charakter der asterisierten Zusätze in der Septuaginta* (Helsinki: Suomalainen Tiedeakatemia, 1959), 12; P. Nautin, *Origène*, 347–350; and most exhaustively, B. Neuschäfer, *Origenes als Philologe*, 87–100.

[30] For instance, what happened when the issue with the deviating manuscript was not too much or too little text, but a transposed text (see LA 7/SC 302, 530.2)? Or, what happened when a consensus failed to emerge between the other Greek translations so that they did not uniformly support a septuagintal reading? It is evident from a wider examination of Origen's corpus that no version of the Old Testament, the Hebrew text included, consistently served as an infallible criterion. There are examples when Origen sides with the Hebrew against all the Greek translations (see esp. CC 5.48). But there are also other examples where he sides with the *LXX* when it is at odds with the Hebrew (Gen Frg/PG 12.97; Hom Lev 12.5; Comm Rom 8.6.2, 8.8.4). These passages are particularly important since they challenge S. Brock's claim that Origen labored to develop "a text that would be acceptable in the authoritative eyes of contemporary Jewish scholars" ("Origen's aims as a textual critic of the Old Testament," 216). This is simply wrong. In fact, Origen can express alarm at those who wish uncritically to adopt the Jewish Bible on the grounds that, since discrepancies emerge between it and the Septuagint, the latter is necessarily corrupt (see esp. LA 4 where Origen contends that Jewish Bibles are not free from forgery). And finally we can complicate the picture even more by noting that Origen could reach conclusions about readings based *not* upon the comparison of various textual variants, but rather upon the content or sense of the variant in question (see Hom Lev 12.5; Hom Jer 16.5.2, 16.10.1, 20.5.1; Comm Matt Ser 121; Comm Jn 6.204–216).

The correction of septuagintal manuscripts, as well as those of New Testament writings, was a pressing concern for Origen. Yet even here it is important to sound a note of caution. While Origen was certainly alert to variant readings in the manuscript traditions before him, it is striking that we sometimes observe him *not* making a decision about which variant to adopt, but rather simply alerting his audience to multiple readings.[31] Indeed, there are also times when Origen has a clear preference for a particular reading, yet still offers an interpretation of the unfavorable reading.[32] These sorts of practices suggest that the goal of correcting a text was not always paramount, or at least pressing. Nevertheless, as we have seen, Origen *did* engage in διορθωτικόν. However obscure his text-critical activity still remains to us, for him the ideal interpreter of Scripture was implicated in the activity of correcting manuscripts, and of drawing upon an awareness of discrepant manuscript traditions to inform the interpretation of Christian Scripture.

In the Hellenistic classroom, the establishment of a text served as a basis for further philological inquiry. According to Dionysius Thrax's *Art of Philology*, once a scholar had settled upon a variant reading, the passage in question was read aloud (ἀναγνωστικόν).[33] This was an especially important aid for comprehension in the ancient world since books were not adorned with spaces between words, punctuation marks or capital letters—aids for reading that we take for granted today.[34] Once this step was taken, the scholar embarked upon historical and literary analysis (ἐξηγητικόν) of the text in question, often the most demanding moments in the philological enterprise. In the next two sections I will highlight Origen's historical analysis (ἱστορικόν) followed by the two leading features of his literary inquiry, clarification of a word's meaning (γλωσσηματικόν) and discussion of the grammatical and rhetorical features of the text in question (τεχνικόν).

Historical analysis

At a basic level, historical analysis (ἱστορικόν) began with the issue of facticity: did passages narrate what actually transpired? Ancient literary scholars assessed this sort of probability by applying the methods of refutation

---

[31] In addition to the examples provided by P. Nautin, *Origène*, 351–352, see Hom Gen 3.5; Comm Jn 20.187; Comm Rom 2.13.8, 2.13.25; LA 7 where Origen uses the *Hexapla* simply to determine what the Hebrew reading was, and not to correct the *LXX*.

[32] See esp. Hom Jer 14.3 and 15.5.

[33] Though silent reading was not as rare as scholars have customarily thought. See B. M. W. Knox, "Silent reading in antiquity," *Greek, Roman and Byzantine Studies* 9 (1968): 421–435; A. K. Gavrilov, "Reading techniques in classical antiquity," *Classical Quarterly* 47 (1997): 56–73; and M. Burnyeat, "Postscript on silent reading," *Classical Quarterly* 47 (1997): 74–76.

[34] See Phil 14.2 where Origen twice mentions difficulties with punctuation (discussed above in Chapter 2).

(ἀνασκευή) and confirmation (κατασκευή). Origen discusses this issue at length in *On First Principles*:

> Nevertheless, the exact reader will hesitate in regard to some passages, finding himself unable to decide without considerable investigation whether a particular incident, believed to be history, actually happened or not [πότερον ἥδε ἡ νομιζομένη ἱστορία γέγονε κατὰ τὴν λέξιν ἢ οὔ], and whether the literal meaning of a particular law is to be observed or not [καὶ τῆσδε τῆς νομοθεσίας τὸ ῥητὸν τηρητέον ἢ οὔ].[35]

He catalogues a series of events from both the Old and New Testaments whose historicity he doubts. He calls into question, for instance, whether God actually planted a tree in Eden whose literal fruit granted eternal life, or whether anyone could literally believe that there was a mountaintop from which the devil could show Jesus all the kingdoms of the world (Matt 4:8). The careful reader, Origen contends, will see "that events which did not take place [ἕτερα μὴ συμβεβηκότα] are woven into the narratives of what literally transpired."[36] As for the facticity of sayings, Origen enumerates a number of passages that were either irrational (ἄλογος) or impossible (ἀδύνατος). It is irrational, for instance, for Moses to have uttered a prohibition to eat vultures (Lev 11:13; Deut 14:12), since nobody in the worst of famines ever ate such a creature. Nor is it rational when Jesus commands: "Salute no man by the way" (Lk 10:4).[37] Origen admonishes readers not to accept gullibly everything at the level of the letter, "for occasionally the records taken in a literal sense are not true, but actually absurd and impossible."[38] While he was convinced passages that were historically *true* outnumbered those that were not,[39] there are several instances in his surviving exegetical corpus where we see him wrestling with the plausibility of biblical narratives. Sometimes he confirms them, other times he refutes (i.e. rejects) them.[40]

If philologists were convinced in the historicity of an event or reasonability of a saying, they drew upon a full spectrum of knowledge to help illuminate the passage in question. This is the moment in the exegetical enterprise where the multi-disciplinary expertise Origen counseled in his *Letter to Gregory* became relevant. In his writings we find any number of instances where he called upon a variety of fields within the ἐγκύκλιος παιδεία to facilitate his

---

[35] PA 4.3.5/GK 744, 330.14–746, 331.3.
[36] PA 4.3.1/GK 734, 325.3–4—transl. mine. Also in the same section: that events such as these are "recorded as if they have happened, but in fact these have not happened according to the letter" (PA 4.3.1/GK 732, 324.8–9—transl. mine).
[37] PA 4.3.2 and 4.3.3.
[38] PA 4.3.4/GK 740, 328.13–15.
[39] PA 4.3.4.
[40] See R. M. Grant, *The Earliest Lives of Jesus*, 38–49 for a brief discussion of this concern in Greco-Roman rhetorical handbooks, and 62–79 for Origen's interest in this same issue. For other instances where Origen engages in this sort of inquiry, see Hom Sam 5.2–4; Comm Jn 10.119–122, 10.129–130; CC 1.42; P.A. 4.2.8–4.3.5.

biblical scholarship. Brief illustrations now follow of how Hellenistic scholarship surfaced in his scriptural interpretation.

Origen drew upon his knowledge of *topography* to correct New Testament manuscripts. For instance, while a majority of manuscripts (including probably the earliest) read, "These things were done in Bethany beyond the Jordan where John was baptizing" (Jn 1:28), Origen still suspects a corrupt text. This reading ought to be overturned based upon his personal knowledge of the region, "since we have been in the places, so far as the historical account is concerned, of the footprints of Jesus and his disciples and the prophets."[41] The Bethany Origen was familiar with was far removed from the Jordan river; moreover, no town in the vicinity of the Jordan river was called Bethany, though there was a Bethabara on the banks of this river.[42]

A knowledge of *customs* expedited biblical scholarship. Commenting on Mary's greeting to Elizabeth in Lk 1:41, Origen notes that the verb ἀσπάζεσθαι ("to greet") did not signify a greeting kiss, but rather a word of peace, which was a "custom among the Hebrews."[43]

The work of *historians* played a significant role in his exegesis. Origen reminds Celsus that it was not only the gospels that testified to John the Baptist, but also Josephus in the eighteenth book of his *Antiquities*.[44] On several occasions he draws upon Josephus' narrative to relay details surrounding the Roman conquest of Jerusalem.[45] Origen also refers several times to Phlegon's *Chronicle* to confirm several gospel affirmations about Jesus.[46]

Origen had an active interest in *cosmology*. In *On First Principles* he asks whether the sun, moon, and stars are to be ranked among the "principalities" mentioned in Col 1:16–18. His ensuing discussion, about whether stars are exempt from change and ought to count as living and rational beings, reflects an awareness of current opinion on these topics.[47] In *Against Celsus* he comments on the star at Jesus' birth (Matt 2:1–12) and remarks that he has

---

[41] Comm Jn 6.204/GCS 4, 149.15–17.

[42] Comm Jn 6.204–205. For other topographical comments, see the discussion of Gerasa/ Gadara/Gergesa (Comm Jn 6.208–216); Jerusalem (Lk Frg 30); Sea of Galilee or Lake of Gennesaret (Comm Matt 11.18); wells of Ascalon (CC 4.44); the city of Elat on the Red Sea (Jer Frg 24); the location and description of Babylon (Jer Frgs 41 and 44, probably relying upon Herodotus' descriptions in his *Histories*).

[43] Lk Frg 30/GCS 9, 238.7–11. For another instance of knowledge of customs, see Comm Matt Ser 124.

[44] CC 1.47.

[45] CC 1.47, 2.13; Comm Matt 10.17. Also see Jer Frg 14, as well as possible anonymous references to him at Comm Matt 10.21, 17.25; and Comm Jn 13.251.

[46] That Jesus was a prophet with foreknowledge (CC 2.14), including foreknowledge of Jerusalem's destruction (Comm Matt Ser 40), and that there was an eclipse and earthquake that accompanied his death (CC 2.33, 2.59; Comm Matt Ser 134). For additional texts and discussion of the chronological information Origen drew upon, particularly for Jesus' birth, death and the destruction of Jerusalem, see B. Neuschäfer, *Origenes als Philologe*, 176–185.

[47] See esp. PA 1.7.2–3. On this topic, see A. B. Scott, *Origen and the Life of the Stars: A History of an Idea* (Oxford: Oxford University Press, 1991).

read "the book on comets by Chaeremon the Stoic" that secures the point that comets have sometimes appeared when good events are about to happen.[48] There are also occasional *meteorological* comments in his corpus. Interpreting Jeremiah 10:13 ("And he has raised up the clouds from the last of the earth, and he made lightning for the rain"), Origen defers to experts: "Certain people say concerning these things that the producing of lightning from the clouds arises from clouds which are rubbed against one another."[49]

In his second *Homily on Genesis* Origen draws upon *geometry* to explain the cubits with which Noah's ark was constructed. His opponent, Apelles, thinks the dimensions of the ark are too small to accommodate the animals claimed to have entered it, but Origen remarks that "Moses ... reckoned the number of cubits in this passage according to the art of geometry in which the Egyptians especially are skilful. For with geometricians, according to that computation which they call the second power, one cubit ... is considered as six ... or as three."[50]

We find scattered references to *mineralogy* and *zoology* in his biblical scholarship. In the *Commentary on Matthew* he reaches Matthew 13:45 where the kingdom of heaven is likened to someone in search of pearls. Origen offers a lengthy excursus on the nature of pearls and openly draws upon the opinion of anonymous experts: "We find then among those who discuss stones, concerning the nature of the pearl ... "[51] There are also occasional references to the characteristics and symbolic values of animals mentioned in Scripture: the deer is invulnerable to the poison of snakes,[52] the partridge is malicious and unscrupulous,[53] foxes are crafty,[54] leopards and lions are lethal,[55] etc.

When Celsus denigrated Christianity for its division into multiple sects, Origen responded that any teaching beneficial to life had proliferated into multiple sects, and this included medicine and its various schools.[56] This comment implies an awareness of the state of *medicine* in his day. Origen's knowledge of this discipline surfaces frequently in his writings. In his *Homilies on Leviticus* he addresses the medicinal benefits of hyssop (Lev 14:4)—"This kind of herb, doctors say, has a nature to wash and purify, if any uncleannesses

---

[48] CC 1.58–59. Note also the cosmological discussion surrounding the various senses of the term κόσμος at PA 2.3.6. Of particular interest is Origen's assessment of astrology in book three of his *Commentary on Genesis* where he offers a lengthy and technical critique of determinism (excerpted in Phil 23).

[49] Hom Jer 8.4.2/SC 232, 366.23–25.

[50] Hom Gen 2.2/GCS 6, 29.3–6. Also see CC 4.41.

[51] Comm Matt 10.7/GCS 10, 7.6–7. For an assessment of his reflections on the topaz in Psalm 118, see B. Neuschäfer, *Origenes als Philologe*, 191–192.

[52] Hom Jer 18.9.1; Comm Matt 11.18; CC 2.48.

[53] Hom Jer 17.1.

[54] Hom Ez 2.4.

[55] Jer Frg 3. Other references to animals and their symbolic values: Hom Lev 9.8.4; Comm Jn 10.142.

[56] CC 3.12.

of the human breast should become entrenched from the corruption of a noxious humor."[57] Or again, he offers an excursus on the principles of genera- tion when he discusses the "seed of Abraham" mentioned in John 8:37.[58]

There are, finally, a range of reflections drawn from the philosophers on *anthropology, language, moral theory,* and *theism* that inform topics that repeatedly surface in his biblical scholarship. Origen comments, for instance, on the soul–body relationship,[59] the soul as a self-determining principle of movement,[60] offers a well-developed account of the mind,[61] and a series of basic distinctions in cognitive activity such as between knowledge and truth, opinion, and error, the intelligible and visible, and reason as conceived or expressed.[62] He draws upon the much-discussed question of the origin of language in connection with his etymological analysis of proper nouns in Scripture.[63] Origen relies upon Stoic moral discourse (in particular, the dis- tinction between actions good, bad, and indifferent) to help soften the dis- creditable features of the story of Lot's intercourse with his daughters.[64] He draws upon the Stoic notion of universal ideas ($\kappa o\iota\nu\alpha\grave{\iota}\,\breve{\epsilon}\nu\nu o\iota\alpha\iota$) when discuss- ing Romans 2:15 and the just judgment of Gentiles who have not been given the law.[65] And on the topic of theism he picks up discussions that echoed throughout philosophical circles in antiquity—"We candidly admit," he writes to Celsus, "that some Greek philosophers did know God, since God made it plain to them."[66] In his writings we find him reflecting upon a range of motifs discussed in his day: for instance, whether God can be named or known,[67] whether God is a body or not,[68] how God communicates with or inspires mortals,[69] the sort of abode God has created for the blessed,[70] or how God transcends mind and being.[71]

In sum, after determining the historical or logical plausibility of a passage in Scripture, the philologist's historical analysis consisted primarily in

[57] Hom Lev 8.10.11/GCS 6, 410.6–8.

[58] Comm Jn 20.3; again at 20.34–36 and Comm Matt 15.3. Other medicinal reflections at Hom Lev 9.8.4; Hom Num 17.1.3; Comm Matt 13.6; PA 2.10.4.

[59] For instance, PA pref.5, 1.1.3, 1.7.3; CC 1.33, 4.30.

[60] PA 3.1.2; PE 6.1.

[61] PA 1.1.6.

[62] CC 6.65, 7.45–46.

[63] CC 1.24. Several other references to theories of signification can be found at Hom Ex 5.2; Jn 6.216; CC 1.24–25, 5.45, 6.39; Phil 14 and 17; LA 18. Recall Phil 14, discussed in the previous chapter, where Origen explicitly draws upon philologists to solve a grammatical problem.

[64] CC 4.45.

[65] CC 1.4.

[66] CC 4.30.

[67] CC 6.65, 7.42.

[68] PA 1.1–3; CC 6.62–64, 6.70–72.

[69] CC 7.3, 7.7.

[70] CC 7.28–30.

[71] PA 1.1–9; CC 6.64, 7.38.

drawing upon a wealth of background knowledge to illuminate the passage in question.

Literary analysis

One of Origen's baseline convictions was that the authors of Scripture composed their writings with literary precision.[72] This presupposition about the literary care with which Scripture was crafted conditioned, in turn, the exegetical enterprise: would-be interpreters needed to attend to its precise literary features. Two of the ways interpreters did this were through γλωσσηματικόν, the explanation of individual words, and τεχνικόν, grammatical and rhetorical analysis. Brief accounts of both of these procedures now follow.

For Origen, part of γλωσσηματικόν involved defining unknown or difficult terms in the biblical text. He puzzles, for instance, over the adjective ἐπιούσιος in the Lord's Prayer ("give us this day our ἐπιούσιον bread"—Matt 6:11 and Lk 11:3). "Now I must consider what ἐπιούσιον means. The first point to know is that the expression ἐπιούσιον is not employed by any of the Greeks or of the wise, nor is it in colloquial use among the common people. Rather, it seems to have been invented by the evangelists."[73] After comparing the adjective to another similar term, he suggests that its sense ought to be derived from its constituent parts: the bread Jesus' followers ask for is ἐπι-ούσιον since it is, quite literally, "for our being."[74] There are numerous similar instances of Origen at work defining difficult or important terms in Scripture.[75]

The etymological analysis of proper nouns (individual and place names) played a prominent role in late antique philology as well.[76] As a rule, Origen did not develop etymologies himself, but rather relied upon existing reference

---

[72] The technical rhetorical term for this exactness is ἀκρίβεια (Comm Matt 14.13/GCS 10, 311.22–24; Hom Lk 32.1/GCS 9, 181.11–14; Comm Jn 13.360/GCS 4, 283.1; Jn Frg 29/GCS 4, 505.1–2; Phil 2.4/SC 302, 244.3–246.4; Phil 2.5/SC 302, 248.8–11).

[73] PE 27.7/GCS 2, 366.33–367.2.

[74] PE 27.7–9/GCS 2, 369.25–26.

[75] See, for example, his definitions of sanctus (ἅγιος) in Hom Lev 11.1.2–3; θάνατος in DH 25.4–24; εὐχή in PE 3.1–4; κόσμος in Comm Matt 13.20; ἀρχή in Comm Jn 1.90–124; δόξα in Comm Jn 32.330–338; νομός in Phil 9; εὐχαριστία in Comm Eph 23; πάσχα in Pascha 1. Note also how he can parse Hebraisms, as, for example, at CC 6.17. Additional examples of definitions occur at Hom Lev 5.8.1–2; Hom Jer 18.6.3–7, 19.13.1–5; Comm Jn 5.4–5, 13.285–297; Comm Cor 19. For further discussion of definitions, see B. Neuschäfer, *Origenes als Philologe*, 140–155.

[76] In Dionysius Thrax's *Art of Philology* the discovery of a word's etymology was the fourth part of philology: Μέρη δὲ αὐτῆς [i.e. γραμματικῆς] ἐστιν ἕξ...τέταρτον ἐτυμολογίας εὕρεσις (Dionysius Thrax, *Ars Grammatica*, ed. G. Uhlig: 1.1/5.4–6.2). For discussions of etymology, see the scholia to this work (A. Hilgard, ed., *Scholia in Dionysii Thracis Artem Grammaticam*, 14.23ff, 169.19–22, 302.6, 303.8, 303.18, etc.).

works.[77] Nevertheless, etymological analyses were important for him. "Indeed," he wrote, "we ought not despise the proper names, since things are signified by them which are useful for the interpretation of passages [in Scripture]."[78] According to the literal sense, for example, the Word came to the prophet Hosea son of Beeri, but according to the mystical sense the Word is sent to the one who is saved—"since 'Hosea' is translated as 'saved.'"[79] Or again, after the wedding in Cana, Jesus went to "Capharnaum" which translates as "field of exhortation"—a fitting meaning, Origen says, since after the good cheer of the wedding Jesus would have exhorted his disciples in the mission to which he had entrusted them.[80] Etymologies abound in his exegetical corpus.[81]

There are also instances, though they are less frequent, when Origen explores the symbolic value of numbers. He offers a lengthy commentary on the dimensions of the ark in his second *Homily on Genesis*. The ark is three hundred cubits long, fifty wide, and thirty high. To begin with, three hundred is three one hundreds, and "the number one hundred is shown to be full and perfect in everything and to contain the mystery of the whole rational creation." The number fifty, in turn, symbolizes "forgiveness and remission. For according to the law there was a remission in the fiftieth year... Therefore Christ, the spiritual Noah, in his ark in which he frees the human race from destruction, that is, in his Church, has established in its breadth the number fifty, the number of forgiveness." And as for thirty, it is like three hundred. "For what a hundred multiplied by three makes there, ten multiplied by three makes here"—here Origen alludes to the symbolic value of ten, a figure that repeatedly signifies perfection in his writings. Origen continues his commentary on the

---

[77] He acknowledges, for instance, his dependence upon the work ἑρμηνεία τῶν ἑβραϊκῶν ὀνομάτων: "In *interpretatione Hebraicorum nominum*...invenimus..." (Hom Num 20.3/GCS 7, 191.9–10). There is a similar acknowledgment in a passage in the *Commentary on John*: εὕρομεν τοίνυν ἐν τῇ ἑρμηνείᾳ τῶν ὀνομάτων (Comm Jn 2.197/GCS 4, 90.17–18; 22). Also see Hom Num 27.12 and Hom Ex 5.2. On the sources for Origen's etymologies, see R. P. C. Hanson, "Interpretations of Hebrew names in Origen," in *VChr* 10 (1956): 103–123; W. Gruber, *Pneumatische Exegese*, 61–62 on his dependence upon Philo; N. R. M. de Lange, *Origen and the Jews*, 121.

[78] Comm Jn 6.216/GCS 4, 151.6–7—transl. mine. For similar sentiments about the importance of the meaning of names, see Hom Num 27.5 and 27.12; Hom Josh 23.4; Comm Jn 2.196; LA 12; PE 24.2.

[79] Comm Jn 2.4/GCS 4, 52.20–21.

[80] Comm Jn 10.37–38.

[81] For additional examples, see Hom Jer 9.2.1 ("Jerusalem"), 10.4.2 ("Anathoth"), 19.14.2 ("Babylon"); Comm Jn 2.197 ("Elizabeth"), 6.120 and 13.389 ("Pharisees"), 6.206 ("Bethabara" and "Bethania"); 6.217–220 ("Jordan"), 10.63 ("Gergesa"), 10.286 ("Tyrians"), 13.81 ("Jeroboam"), CC 5.30 ("Shinar"), 6.44 ("Satan"), Hom Ez 1.3 ("Jerusalem," "Babylon," and "Ezra"); see esp. Hom Num 27 *passim*. For lists of Origen's etymologies, see R. Heine, *Origen: Homilies on Genesis and Exodus* (Washington: Catholic University of America Press, 1982), 389–396, and F. Wutz, *Onomastica Sacra: Untersuchungen zum Liber Interpretationis Nominum Hebraicorum des hl. Hieronymus*, TU 11.1–2 (Leipzig: J. C. Hinrichs, 1914–15), where a partial list of the names mentioned by Origen is provided, along with their interpretations and references to where they are found in Origen's works (739–748).

ark's dimensions by reminding his congregation of the numerous cases where these three numbers—three hundred, fifty, and thirty—are used in Scripture in association with momentous dates and events. Finally, he turns to the number one: one ark was constructed, because "'there is one God and Father from whom are all things, and one Lord' [1 Cor 8:6] and 'one faith of the Church, one baptism, one body and the one spirit' [Eph 4:5, 4] and all things hasten to the one goal of the perfection of God."[82] There are several other instances where Origen offers symbolic assessments of numbers in the Scriptures.[83]

In addition to γλωσσηματικόν (defining terms), grammatical and rhetorical explanation (τεχνικόν) constituted another important facet of late antique exegesis. In his *Commentary on John*, Origen contends that since the evangelist knew "Greek precision" (ἑλληνικὴ ἀκριβολογία), he was intentional about where he inserted definite articles and where he omitted them.[84] This leads Origen into a reflection upon the use of the definite article in John 1:1 ([1a] Ἐν ἀρχῇ ἦν ὁ λόγος, [1b] καὶ ὁ λόγος ἦν πρὸς τὸν θεόν, [1c] καὶ θεὸς ἦν ὁ λόγος). Why, he wonders, is the article present before θεός in 1b, but not before the same noun in 1c? The significance, he suggests, behind this alternative use of the article is that when present before θεός in 1b it signifies God, the uncreated cause of the universe, but when it is not present before this noun in 1c, it refers to the λόγος as God.[85] The difference, Origen continues, between "God" with the article and "God" without the article is as follows: ὁ θεός is the true God, the creator of the cosmos; anything else termed θεός is formed as an image of this God, the prototype. The way in which the Word is θεός is, however, unique: it is the archetypal image, the first to be with God, in an everlasting relationship of contemplation with the Father and, through his ministry, the source of anything else becoming θεός.[86]

Any number of other grammatical inquiries characterize the work of a literary scholar. Origen is attentive to the plural (πληθυντικός) and singular (ἑνικός) forms of verbs,[87] to the significance of tenses,[88] and reflects on grammatical errors or solecisms (σολοικισμός)—some only ostensible,[89] and

---

[82] Hom Gen 2.5/GCS 6, 34.12–35.7.

[83] Hom Gen 16.6 (5 and 10); Hom Ex 7.5 (6), 9.3 (7, 10 and 28); Hom Lev 13.4.1 (10), 13.5.1 (6); Hom Num 5.2.2–3 (5, 25, 50, 500), 22.1.3 (5); Hom Josh 10.3 (6 and 7); Hom Jud 4.2 (6), etc. On this theme, see J. Kalvesmaki, "Formation of Early Christian Theology of Arithmetic: Number Symbolism in the Late Second and Early Third Century," Dissertation, Catholic University of America, 18 April 2006.

[84] Comm Jn 2.13/GCS 4, 54.12–14.

[85] Comm Jn 2.14.

[86] Comm Jn 2.17–18. Other reflections on the use of the article: Comm Matt 11.5; Comm Jn 6.46 (see B. Neuschäfer, *Origenes als Philologe*, 202–207). Also see Comm Eph 1 where Origen comments on Paul's curious use of prepositions.

[87] Phil 8.1/SC 302, 336.9–11.

[88] On the future form, ζήσομαι, see Ps Frg/SC 189, 214.1–4.

[89] As in the shift from the plural verb to the singular in Hosea 12:4 (Phil 8.1–3).

others not. In his *Commentary on Ephesians* he remarks on the muddled syntactical structure of 1:15–18a and offers a correction:

> The phrase, "in recognition of him the eyes of your heart having been enlightened," [Eph 1:18a] will appear to be expressed incorrectly [δόξει σόλοικον εἶναι] unless we interpret it as expressed in inverted order [ὑπερβατὸν]. Wherefore I think the grammatical sequence of the context is as follows...[90]

Origen is attentive to ambiguous grammatical forms. For instance, he notices how the verbs in Psalm 4:5 (ὀργίζεσθε καὶ μὴ ἁμαρτάνετε) can be either imperative (προστακτικός) or indicative (ὁριστικός).[91] He wonders what sort of sentence Jesus uttered in association with his footwashing when he said: Γινώσκετε τί πεποίηκα ὑμῖν (Jn 13:12). According to Origen, this sentence can be read either as a question ("Do you know what I have done for you?"), in order to demonstrate how great Jesus' deed was, or as a command ("Know what I have done for you!"), that he might arrest the disciples' attention with the footwashing.[92]

The exegete who has mastered τεχνικόν is also able to distinguish a range of tropes (τρόποι) and figures (σχήματα).[93] Origen comments on the following in his writings: onomatopoeia (ὀνοματοποιία), the novel formation of a word, sometimes from a sound associated with what is named;[94] catachresis (κατάχρησις), the incorrect use of a word, frequently distinguished from using a word properly (κυρίως);[95] metaphor (μεταφορά);[96] paradox (παράδοξος);[97] synecdoche (συνεκδοχή), where the part stands for the whole;[98] significance or emphasis (ἔμφασις);[99] periphrasis (περίφρασις), indirect and circumlocutory writing;[100] tautology (ταυτολογία), saying the same thing twice in different words;[101] epitasis (ἐπίτασις), exaggeration or amplification;[102] hyperbaton (ὑπερβατόν), an inversion of the normal order of words;[103] ἀπὸ κοινοῦ (from the common attribution), namely, the modifier of one word in a pair of words

---

[90] Comm Eph 9/*JTS* 3 (1902), 398.2–10. On another solecism in Ephesians, see Comm Eph 13/*JTS* 3 (1902), 408.11–15.

[91] Ps Frg/*PG* 12.1141–1144.

[92] Comm Jn 32.112–123.

[93] For a longer discussion of many of these that now follow, see B. Neuschäfer, *Origenes als Philologe*, 202–240.

[94] On the *LXX* reading ἐφρύαξαν at *PG* 12.1101c–d; on εὐδοκία at Comm Eph 3/*JTS* 3 (1902): 237.29–30.

[95] Hom 1.1 Ps 36; Comm Song of Songs prol./*GCS* 8, 71.1–4, 75.13–15; Comm Matt 15.10; Phil 14.2.

[96] Comm Jn 10.221; Comm Rom 6.1.8.

[97] Comm Jn 2.112–114.

[98] Comm Matt 12.38.

[99] Lam Frg 18; Lk Frg 53; CC 6.57.

[100] Ps Frg/*PG* 12.1137c–d.

[101] Comm Jn 2.64.

[102] Lk Frg 59.

[103] Lk Frg 20; Comm Rom 1.13.1, 6.7.6; Comm Eph 9.

also modifies the other;[104] παρασιώπησις (passing over in silence), usually where two items are presupposed in a sentence, but only one is expressed;[105] allegory (ἀλληγορία), where one thing is signified, but another actually meant;[106] hyperbole (ὑπερβολή);[107] ellipsis (ἔλλειψις), the omission of superfluous words;[108] and the homonym (ὁμώνυμος), the same word but with different meanings.[109]

Three additional exegetical techniques prominently characterized Origen's philology: attending to the voice of the speaker, observing the sequence or arrangement of a passage, and clarifying obscure texts in light of clearer texts. A brief explanation of these procedures follows.

Exegetes were repeatedly deciphering the voice of the person actually speaking (πρόσωπον λέγον) in a particular passage.[110] While in Alexandria, Origen composed his short *Commentary on the Song of Songs* in which he reflected upon the difficulties that alternating speakers presented the interpreters of Scripture:

> Any one who does not understand the peculiar character of the persons in Scripture [τὸ ἰδίωμα τῶν προσώπων τῆς γραφῆς], both as regards the speakers and the persons addressed, must be much perplexed by what he reads; he will ask who is speaking, who is spoken to, and when does the speaker cease to speak. For it often happens that the same person is addressed, though a third person speaks to him; or the person addressed is no longer the same, and a different person takes up what is said, while the same person speaks. And sometimes both the speaker and the person addressed are changed; or, further, though both are unchanged, it is not clear that they are... It is also the way of Scripture to jump suddenly from one discourse to another. The prophets, above all, do this, obscuring their sense and more or less confusing the reader.[111]

A fine illustration of this concern for identifying the speaker can be found in Origen's *Homilies on Samuel*, where he reaches the vexing passage of the necromancer who ostensibly raised Samuel's soul from Hades at the behest of

---

[104] Hom Lk 32.4 on Is 61:1 where it says "preach release to captives and sight to blind." Origen understands the "preaching" to be "ἀπὸ κοινοῦ" since it applies both to the captives as well as to the blind. Other examples: Lk Frg 209; PE 26.2.

[105] Gen Frg/PG 12.137a.

[106] While Origen never offered a definition of ἀλληγορία, there are several clear accounts of allegorical expressions and allegorical interpretations: see Hom Ez 1.3.6; Comm Matt 12.3; PA 4.2.2; CC 2.68–69. Also see the discussion below in "Referents: Literal and allegorical."

[107] Origen defines it at Comm 1 Cor 49; see also Lam Frg 59; Comm Matt Ser 134; PE 27.16.

[108] Comm Rom 1.13.1.

[109] See the lengthy discussion of homonyms in Phil 9.1–3; also Hom 1.4 Ps 36; Hom Jer 20.1.2; CC 7.31; 7.34; Phil 14.2; DH 11.

[110] On this important exegetical technique in Origen, see M.-J. Rondeau, *Les Commentaires patristiques du Psautier (IIIe–Ve siècles)*, vol. 2 (Rome: Pontificium Institutum Studiorum Orientalium, 1985), 21–135; B. Neuschäfer, *Origenes als Philologe*, 263–276; M. Harl, SC 302, 330–333.

[111] Phil 7.1/SC 302, 326.1–17. See the ensuing illustration of this sort of confusion at Phil 7.2.

Saul (1 Sam 28:3–25). Origen challenges a regnant interpretation that says the necromancer misleads when she claims she has seen Samuel. Origen calls attention to the fact that the woman's claim to have seen Samuel was relayed by the person of the narrator (τὸ διηγηματικὸν πρόσωπον). Referring to the verse: "And the woman said, 'Whom shall I summon for you?'" [1 Sam 28:11], Origen asks:

> What person speaks [Τίνος πρόσωπόν ἐστιν τὸ λέγον], "And the woman said"? Is it, in fact, the person of the Holy Spirit, by whom Scripture is believed to be written, or is it some other person? For the narrator, as they know who study any kind of discourse, is certainly the author, but the author of these discourses is not believed to be a man, but the Holy Spirit is the author who has moved people.[112]

This exegetical technique helps Origen insist that the woman did, in fact, see Samuel, and thus compels him to explain why such an event ever transpired.[113]

Another widespread literary technique was attentiveness to the τάξις ("order"), ἀκολουθία ("sequence"), or εἱρμός ("series," "sequence") of a passage.[114] Origen thought pericopes within Scripture were characterized by a variety of orders, sequences, or series (e.g. series of speakers, audiences addressed, of events and actions depicted, of arguments, etc.). Well-schooled readers were alert to the sequence of a passage, avoided disturbing it, and were particularly attentive when its authors had intentionally disrupted it. In his extensive hermeneutical tractate in book four of *On First Principles*, Origen comments upon the sequentially arranged spiritual message of Scripture, and how it corresponds to the arrangement of the historical events that symbolized this message:

> that because the principal aim was to announce the sequence [εἱρμὸν] that exists among spiritual things...whenever the Word found that historical events could be harmonized with these mystical events he used [them], hiding from the multitude their deeper meaning.[115]

But the sequences in Scripture were not exclusively reserved for spiritual meanings. The "bodily part" of Scripture was also recorded "with a sequence [εἱρμῷ] and with a power which is truly appropriate to the Wisdom of

---

[112] Hom Sam 5.4/SC 328, 180.9–16—Trigg modified.

[113] For other instances of this technique, see Hom 5.5 Ps 36; Hom 2.5 Ps 37; Frg Ps/PG 12.1100d; Hom Jer 14.11–12; Comm Song of Songs prol.; Comm Jn 1.284–287, 2.116, 6.50–53; Comm Rom 9.1.15.

[114] Origen could use these terms interchangeably: see esp. CC 1.41/SC 132, 184.4–5. For literature on this exegetical procedure, see B. Neuschäfer, *Origenes als Philologe*, 239–240 and D. Dawson, "Allegorical reading and the embodiment of the soul in Origen," in *Christian Origins: Theology, Rhetoric and Community*, ed. L. Ayres and G. Jones (London: Routledge, 1998), 30–38.

[115] PA 4.2.9/GK 726, 321.11–15—transl. mine.

God."[116] In his twenty-seventh *Homily on Numbers*, Origen attends famously
to the series of stations in the wilderness that the Hebrews traversed. It is clear
that at the level of the letter the geographic stations were linked to one another
in a series of events—they constituted stages in the Israelites' journey. If the
stages at the level of the letter were linked together as part of a journey, then
the stages in the soul's spiritual journey must also be linked together, and so
Origen insists: one must examine "the entire order [ordinem] of stages."[117]

However, the sequences of scriptural pericopes were often broken, and
Origen found this so conspicuous that he proposed a reason for it: authors
were putting readers on alert to search for another, hidden sense in the
passage. "If the usefulness of the law and the sequence and ease of the
narrative" were evident to interpreters, how would they know that there was
any message waiting for them beyond the obvious meaning in Scripture? The
cue to the reader, Origen answers, is that the author has disturbed the
usefulness of the law and the sequence of a narrative:

> Consequently, the Word of God has arranged for certain stumbling blocks, as it were,
> and hindrances and impossibilities to be inserted in the midst of the law and the
> history, in order that we may not be completely drawn away by the sheer attractiveness
> of the language...[118]

The sorts of "stumbling blocks" Origen has in mind are the insertions of
useless and impossible laws, or in the case of histories, the insertion of fictive
elements. An example of something unhistorical inserted into a narrative can
be found in John's gospel where the evangelist, Origen says, has not preserved
the ἀκολουθία, for how can he say that Jesus arose from supper to wash his
disciples' feet when guests customarily wash their feet not after, but *before*,
supper? This disturbance of the sequence has been done "to raise our understanding to the spiritual sense of the details in this passage."[119] What registers
as a sequential disruption of Scripture at the level of the letter is usually
designed to alert readers to an allegorical meaning.[120]

---

[116] PA 4.2.8/GK 724, 320.14–15—transl. mine. On this passage, see M. Harl, SC 302, 87–89, as
well as CC 1.62 where the rhetoric of Jesus' followers is said to lack δύναμις and τάξις (a synonym
for εἱρμός).

[117] Hom Num 27.6/GCS 7, 263.20. "Ordo" here likely translates τάξις. For a similar approach
to the wilderness pericope, see Hom Ex 5 and Hom Ex 7.3. For other examples where Origen
searches for the sequence of a passage, see Hom Josh 25.1; Hom 4.2 Ps 36; Hom 2.6 Ps 38; Frg Ps/
PG 12.1074d; Frg Ps 118/SC 189, 458.49; Comm Matt 12.34, 13.17, 16.16, 17.26; Comm Jn
2.1–12, 6.11, 6.34, 6.147, 10.159–161; Comm Rom 3.1.3; Phil 25.2; CC 2.24, 4.40. Passages where
Origen breaks the sequence of Scripture include Comm Jn 6.11, 6.34; Comm Rom/JTS 13 (1912),
214.

[118] PA 4.2.9/GK 726, 321.6–9.

[119] Comm Jn 32.11/GCS 4, 426.30–427.1—transl. mine.

[120] For other examples of intentionally disrupted sequences, see Comm Jn 10.18–20, 13.364–
370; Phil 9.3. However, there is a significant exception to this theory. On occasion, Origen claims
that a passage in Scripture was simply written in a poor style, a style without τάξις and ἀκολουθία

Origen's third common literary technique used clearer passages to illuminate related, yet obscure, passages.[121] Indeed, the principle that one ought to
explain Scripture with Scripture is probably the most frequently mentioned
exegetical procedure in Origen's writings and probably also the most frequently practiced. He often expresses this principle in the language of 1 Corinthians
2:13: "comparing spiritual things with spiritual."[122] In his *Commentary on
First Corinthians* he explains this enigmatic Pauline phrase as follows: "by
searching out and examining such and such a text along with such and such
another text and bringing together what they have in common, the mind (as it
were) of Scripture will be unveiled."[123] In *Against Celsus* Origen responds to
his opponent's claim that the prophets' writings are incoherent and totally
obscure:

> It is only a person who is wise and truly in Christ who could give as a connected whole
> the interpretation of the obscure passages in the prophets by "comparing spiritual
> things with spiritual" [1 Cor 2:13] and by explaining each phrase found in the text
> from the common usage of that phrase elsewhere in scripture.[124]

Arguably the most famous discussion of this procedure occurs in Origen's
prologue to the *Commentary on the Psalms*. There are passages in the Scriptures, he admits, that are "closed and sealed." How, then, does the reader open
such passages? According to that "most pleasing tradition handed down by a
Hebrew to us," Origen recounts,

> the whole inspired Scripture resembles, on account of its obscurity, many rooms that
> are locked shut in one house. A key lies next to each room, but it does not correspond
> to it, and so the keys for the rooms are scattered, each not corresponding to those
> [rooms] which they lie beside. And it is a great labor both to discover the keys and to

---

(see esp. CC 1.62, 6.1). In such cases, the broken sequence of Scripture was *not* a clue to the
reader to search for a deeper message, but rather merely an indication of the low literary skill of
its author (see esp. Comm Jn 13.364–367 and Comm Rom 3.1). B. Neuschäfer remarks that in
cases such as these, we find Origen practicing another dimension of philology: aesthetic evaluation (κρίσις ποιημάτων) (*Origenes als Philologe*, 241–243, 255–257).

[121] For literature on this exegetical procedure, see esp. M. Harl, SC 302, 141–145;
B. Neuschäfer, *Origenes als Philologe*, 276–285; F. Young, *Biblical Exegesis*, 133–137. In the
subsequent history of literary criticism this procedure has often been called interpreting "Homer
with Homer." On the history of the expression Ὅμηρον ἐξ Ὁμήρου σαφηνίζειν and the principle
behind it, see *Origenes als Philologe*, 276–280 and C. Schäublin, "Homerum ex Homero," *MH* 34
(1977): 221–227.

[122] See Hom Num 16.9.4; Hom 1.1 Ps 36; Comm Matt 14.14; Comm Matt Ser 52; Comm Jn
13.361; Phil 2.3; CC 4.71, 7.11, etc. Note at PA 4.3.5 where a different verse expresses this
principle: Jn 5:39 ("Search the Scriptures"). At Comm Matt 10.15 and Hom Jer 1.7.3 Origen
alludes to 2 Cor 13:1/Deut 19:15 ("Every matter must be established by the testimony of two or
three witnesses"). However, Origen utilizes 1 Cor 2:13 far more often to express this exegetical
principle.

[123] Comm Cor 11/*JTS* 9 [1908] 240.20–22—transl. mine. Also see Comm Matt 10.15, 17.17;
Comm Jn 6.127 and CC 7.11 where Origen describes this exegetical principle similarly.

[124] CC 7.11/SC 150, 40.15–19.

match them to the rooms which they are able to open. Therefore we understand these obscure Scriptures when we take starting points for understanding not from any other place than from other passages which have the interpretation dispersed throughout them. At any rate, I think that even the apostle suggests a similar way for understanding the divine words when he says: "And we speak these things not in words taught by human wisdom but in those taught by the Spirit, comparing spiritual things with spiritual things" [1 Cor 2:13].[125]

For our purposes, one illustration of this straightforward procedure should suffice. In his eleventh *Homily on Leviticus* Origen expounds on the verse, "Be holy as I am also holy, says the Lord" (Lev 20:7). Like any well-trained philologist interested in γλωσσηματικόν, he asks what the term "holy" means. He quickly compiles an inventory of passages where the noun is used, noting how not only people, but also animals, vessels, garments, and places can be called holy in various parts of the Scriptures.[126] Origen then extrapolates from these references to holiness scattered throughout Scripture, suggesting what the command in Leviticus 20:7 means: someone is holy who is "separated and set apart from the rest of men who live carnally and are bound with mundane affairs, and does not seek things which are upon the earth but which are in heaven."[127] This exegetical principle is at work on seemingly every page of Origen's exegetical corpus.[128]

Finally, in all these text-critical, historical, and literary labors over the biblical text, it is important to round out our discussion by calling attention to Origen's reliance upon, or at least awareness of, previous philological work. According to Eusebius, he procured biblical commentaries of Symmachus (one of the translators of the Hebrew Scriptures into Greek).[129] He knew of Aristobulus' and Philo's exegetical works,[130] had Heracleon's *Exegetical Notes* on John's Gospel before him,[131] and refers to his Hebrew teacher on several occasions.[132] Origen credits an elder for help in refuting Valentinians with particular scriptural passages.[133] He also produces statements scattered

---

[125] Phil 2.3/SC 302, 244.4–17—transl. mine. Other occasions where this procedure is said to help in interpreting difficult passages: Hom Num 12.1; Comm Jn 20.74; PA 4.3.5; CC 4.71–73.

[126] Hom Lev 11.1.2.

[127] Hom Lev 11.1.4/GCS 6, 447.12–17.

[128] For other examples of this philological procedure at work, see Hom Lev 5.8.1–2; Hom Jer 12.1.2, 19.13.2, 27.1; Hom 1.1 Ps 36; Hom 3.2 Ps 36; Hom 1.9 Ps 38; Comm Matt 16.4; Comm Matt Ser 52; Comm Jn 13.285; DH 25.4; Comm Cor 19; Phil 8.1; CC 7.11, etc.

[129] Eusebius, HE 6.17.

[130] On the former, see the reference at CC 4.51; on Philo, see esp. Comm Matt 15.3, 17.18; CC 4.51, 6.21. For Origen's use of Philo, see D. T. Runia, *Philo in Early Christian Literature: A Survey* (Minneapolis: Fortress Press, 1993), 157–183.

[131] On Heracleon and his commentary, see E. Pagels, *The Johannine Gospel in Gnostic Exegesis: Heracleon's* Commentary on John (Nashville: Abingdon Press, 1973).

[132] See PA 1.3.4, 4.3.14. Also see Hom Jer 20.2.2 for an interpretation from a Jew who has become a Christian. Origen also explicitly mentions taking up Jewish interpretations of Scripture: Hom Gen 2.2, 12.4; Hom Ex 5.2; Hom Num 14.1.3; Hom Josh 15.6; Hom Ez 4.5, 4.8; CC 4.34.

[133] Hom 2.6 Ps 36.

throughout his writings that point to anonymous exegetical precedent: "We maintain that the law has a twofold interpretation, one literal and the other spiritual, as was also taught by some of our predecessors."[134]

REFERENTS: LITERAL AND ALLEGORICAL

If these are the main features of philology as Origen understood it, how do they relate to allegory? In the concluding lines of *Origenes als Philologe*, Bernhard Neuschäfer challenged his readers to wrestle with two regnant portraits of Origen: the older portrait that presented him as an allegorist, and the newer that depicted him as a philologist. Were these two conflicting tendencies within the exegete or could they be harmoniously integrated into a single picture?[135] He left the question unanswered. For Origen, I propose, the answer was clear: allegorical interpretation was a legitimate dimension of philological inquiry. Indeed, we have already traced several of the philological principles—etymological analysis, number symbolism, and interpreting Scripture with Scripture—that were indispensable techniques for helping him discover the allegorical sense of passages. For Origen there were in principle two referents of any given scriptural text: the literal and the "nonliteral" (i.e., allegorical, figurative, symbolic, spiritual, mystical or deeper).[136] Ideal philologists pursued a broad education and cultivated a series of exegetical techniques with the intent of deciphering *both* the literal *and* the allegorical referents of a passage. Philology, in other words, could be practiced in a literal or an allegorical mode—but it was always philology.[137]

---

[134] CC 7.20/SC 150, 60.6–7. Additional references to earlier exegetical work can be found at Hom Gen 5.5; Hom Jd 8.4; Hom 4.1 Ps 36; Hom Jer 11.3; Comm Matt 13.18, 17.28; Comm Matt Ser 31, 126; Comm Rom 2.13; PA 2.3.6, 2.8.5; CC 3.23, 4.17, 4.38, 4.48, 5.38, 5.57–58, 6.49, 8.66–67. Also recall Porphyry's comments examined in the previous chapter about Origen's numerous sources and how they helped him read the Jewish Scriptures (Eusebius, HE 6.19.7–9). For a plausible reconstruction of Origen's library, see A. Carriker, *The Library of Eusebius of Caesarea*, 5–11.

[135] *Origenes als Philologe*, 292.

[136] I say "in principle", since not every scriptural text for Origen had both an allegorical and a literal referent (see PA 4.2.5 and 4.3.1–3 where Origen insists some passages have no literal sense). For more on this theme, see the section "One Message" in Chapter 9 below.

[137] See especially Origen's defense of the allegorical interpretation of the Hebrew Scriptures in *Against Celsus*, beginning at 4.37. At 4.51 he justifies the allegorical interpretation of the law by referring to Aristobulus, Philo, and especially Numenius the Pythagorean. "[W]e approve of him [Numenius]," Origen writes, "because he had a greater desire than Celsus and other Greeks to examine even our writings in a scholarly way [φιλομαθῶς], and was led to regard them as books which are to be interpreted allegorically [περὶ τροπολογουμένων] and which are not foolish" (SC 136, 316.25–28). This is one of Origen's clearest statements about allegorical interpretation as a serious, scholarly activity.

While Origen never offered a straightforward definition of allegory in his extant writings (i.e., "by allegory I mean...."), we can surmise a suitable working definition of the pair ἀλληγορία and ἀλληγορέω since he employed numerous words that were interchangeable with them.[138] One of these terms is σύμβολον and it surfaces in one of Origen's more concise and illuminating discussions of allegorical exegesis.[139] In this passage Celsus raises the charge that if Jesus was so great, he should have exhibited his divinity by disappearing from the cross, rather than enduring it.[140] In his response Origen wishes to show that it was advantageous for Jesus *not* to have suddenly disappeared from the cross. There he writes:

> The events recorded to have happened to Jesus do not possess the full view of the truth in the mere letter and history [ἐν ψιλῇ τῇ λέξει καὶ τῇ ἱστορίᾳ]; for each recorded event is shown to be also a symbol of something else [σύμβολόν τινος εἶναι] by those who read Scripture more intelligently.[141]

Here we have the basic account of an allegorical exegesis: the intelligent reader is not content with only the letter and history of a passage, but can also show how such a passage is a "symbol of something else." In the case of this excerpt from *Against Celsus*, Origen recognizes that Jesus' crucifixion was an event that had transpired and had significance for its time and place, that this event had a "literal significance [τὰ δὲ τῆς λέξεως]."[142] But this event also symbolized, Origen insists, the truth indicated in the verse: "I am crucified with Christ" (Gal 2:20), and he

---

[138] For example, ἀλληγορία and ἀλληγορέω are used interchangeably with τροπολογία (CC 4.38/SC 136, 278.6–7; 4.44/SC 136, 298.24; 4.48/SC 136, 306.1–308.17 with 308, 35–36; 4.49/SC 136, 310.4–12) and τροπολογέω (see CC 1.17/SC 132, 120.4; 1.18/SC 132, 122.9–10; 4.49/SC 136, 310.9–15), with ἀναγωγή (Comm Jn 4.22/GCS 4, 111.7; 13.101/GCS 4, 240.31–32) and ἀνάγω (Comm Jn 1.180/GCS 4, 33.23–24; 10.174/GCS 4, 201.26–27; 13.270–271/GCS 4, 267.1, 4, 6; 13.454/GCS 4, 297.11–13; 20.166/GCS 4, 352.14–15), with πνευματικός (two very similar dossiers of Pauline texts supporting nonliteral interpretation are cited at CC 4.49/SC 136, 310.18 and PA 4.2.6/GK 714, 315.15, and in the latter they are considered instances of a πνευματικὴ διήγησις whereas in the former, instances of ἀλληγορία) and πνευματικῶς (CC 2.3/SC 132, 286.15–18; Comm Jn 20.67/GCS 4, 337.31–32), and also with ὑπόνοια (CC 4.38/SC 136, 292.64–66). In fact, the general principle appears to be that while Origen draws upon a rich vocabulary to describe his exegetical practice, most of these terms fall into two categories: those that describe nonliteral (ascending, figurative, tropological, allegorical, spiritual, symbolic, etc.) exegesis on the one hand, and those that describe literal exegesis (exegesis according to the letter, according to history) on the other.

[139] A "symbol" in Scripture is an "allegory," and as such is receptive of an "allegorical" interpretation. For example, the things that happened to Abraham, Origen says, "happened allegorically [Gal 4:24]" (Comm Jn 20.74) and thus "we must [interpret] the whole story of Abraham allegorically" [δεῖ πᾶσαν τὴν κατὰ τὸν Ἀβραὰμ ἀλληγοροῦντα ἱστορίαν] (Comm Jn 20.67/GCS 4, 337.31). A few lines later, referring to one episode in this story (Gen 12:4 where it says: "And Lot went with him [Abram]" as the two departed Haran) Origen tellingly writes: "it was a symbol" [σύμβολον ἦν] (Comm Jn 20.69/GCS 4, 338.20).

[140] CC 2.68.

[141] CC 2.69/SC 132, 446.3–7—transl. mine.

[142] CC 2.69/SC 132, 450.49.

provides several other Pauline texts where the crucifixion and death of Christ are referred symbolically, that is, allegorically, to something other than the actual event, namely to the "crucifixion" and "death" of Christians.

Several other passages confirm this understanding of, and distinction between, allegorical and literal exegesis. In his opening *Homily on Ezekiel*, Origen speaks of the captivity of Israel as a "sign" (*signum*): "Therefore, when you hear about the captivity of the people, to be sure you should believe that the captivity really happened in accordance with the reliable testimony of history. Yet it came first as a sign of something else [*in signum rei alterius*], and it pointed to a subsequent mystery."[143] The captivity transpired, Origen insists, and so it had an historical or literal sense. But it was also a "sign of something else," and so admitted a mystical interpretation as well. Again in *On First Principles* Origen comments on how the simpler Christians interpret the tabernacle in Exodus allegorically. He contends that, "so far as believing that the tabernacle is a figure of something [τύπος τινός] they do not err; but so far as properly applying the passage of Scripture to some particular thing of which the tabernacle is a figure, here they sometimes fall into error."[144] The tabernacle, in other words, is not just an historical object; it is also a "figure of some [other] thing" that some allegorical readers properly discern and others (the *simpliciores*) do not. And as a final illustration of Origen's distinction between literal and "nonliteral" interpretation, we can turn to the twelfth book of his *Commentary on Matthew* where Origen reflects upon signs in Scripture. In Matthew 16:4 Jesus says: "An evil and adulterous generation seeks after a sign [σημεῖον], and there shall be no sign given to it, but the sign of Jonah the prophet." Origen notes that while the Savior was admonishing his interlocutors, nevertheless from his great mercy he offered them a sign: the sign of Jonah. The sign of Jonah,

> became indicative of this, so that the elucidation of that sign, which was obscure on the face of it, might be found in the fact that the Savior suffered, and passed three days and three nights in the heart of the earth. At the same time, also, we learn the general principle that, if the sign signifies something [εἴπερ τὸ σημεῖον σημαίνει τι], each of the signs which are recorded, whether as in actual history, or by way of precept, is indicative of something afterwards fulfilled [δηλωτικόν τινός ἐστιν ὕστερον πληρουμένου]; as for example, the sign of Jonah going out after three days from the whale's belly was indicative of the resurrection of our Savior, rising after three days and three nights from the dead...[145]

Unlike the passage from *Against Celsus* discussed above, where Jesus' crucifixion was an historical event that admitted an allegorical referent, here Origen sees Jesus' crucifixion (and resurrection) as the allegorical referent of an earlier event, Jonah's encounter with the whale. That earlier event had a significance—it was

---

[143] Hom Ez 1.3.6/GCS 8, 325.13–16.
[144] PA 4.2.2/GK 702, 309.10–13—transl. mine.
[145] Comm Matt 12.3/GCS 10, 73.7–17.

"actual history"—but it was also a sign of something else. As Origen continues, he counsels his readers: "Seek you also every sign in the Old Scriptures as a figure of some thing in the New Scripture, and that which is named a sign in the New Testament as indicative of something either in the future age, or even in the subsequent generations after the sign has taken place."[146]

In each of these passages we see how at least some of the Scriptures for Origen were *composed* as a twofold communication: words had their basic referent, but they were also symbolic of some other referent. This twofold compositional character corresponded to literal and allegorical *interpretation*, both of which were responsible for these respective communications. The task of literal exegesis was to identify the basic ("immediate," "at hand," "obvious") referent, whereas allegorical exegesis identified this other ("lofty," "deeper") referent.[147] Philologists, the students of words, sought after the referents of words, be they literal or allegorical.[148]

This chapter completes the first part of this study. In this section ("The Philologist") I have elucidated Origen's educational expectations for ideal interpreters of Christian Scripture. They ought to become able philologists, students of the Greek language and its literature, as well as become conversant in an array of Greco-Roman disciplines that promoted an enlightened interpretation of Scripture. These scholarly credentials were unquestionably integral to Origen's vision of the ideal interpreter of Scripture. Yet they were just as clearly insufficient. Close inspection of his writings reveals that those who studied Scripture well were far more than cultured literary technicians. Greco-Roman scholarship contextualized scriptural exegesis, but so too did the Christian faith. I develop this argument in the next part of this study.

---

[146] Comm Matt 12.3/GCS 10, 73.17–20—transl. mine.

[147] Adjectives such as πρόχειρος (Phil 27.12/SC 226, 308.6) and ἐπιπόλαιος (PA 4.3.11/GK 762, 340.4; Hom Jer 18.4.1/SC 238, 186.4), both of which mean "within reach" or "obvious," can describe literal exegesis. On the other hand, terms such as βαθύτερον ("deeper") (CC 3.7/SC 136, 26.1; Comm Matt 13.2/GCS 10, 183.28) and the "ascent" family (ἀναγωγή, etc.—see n. 138 above) are affiliated with allegorical exegesis.

[148] For other instances of this understanding of literal and allegorical exegesis, see Hom 3.6 Ps 36/Prinzivalli, 126–134; Comm Song of Songs prol./GCS 8, 76.20–22; PA 4.2.2/GK 702, 309.10–11; and esp. 4.2.6/GK 714, 315.15–716, 316.1. Also see my essay, "Revisiting the allegory/typology distinction: The case of Origen," *JECS* 16 (2008): 283–317, for a fuller discussion of Origen's exegetical terminology and his distinction between literal and nonliteral exegesis.

Part 2

The Philologist and Christianity

The first part of this study demonstrated how Origen located the interpreter of Scripture within the Greco-Roman educational system. His baseline expectation was that ideal interpreters would become well-rounded scholars with particular fluency in philology. The second part of this study fills out this portrait by arguing that Origen's horizons for describing the interpreter extended far beyond the bounds set by the educational system. He explicitly positioned the exegete within the all-encompassing Christian drama of salvation. As each of the chapters that now follow will demonstrate, in a variety of ways this drama formed the overarching context for his understanding of the interpreter. In Origen's hands, exegetes did not simply offer scholarly assessments of the message of salvation inscribed on Scripture's pages; the exercise of biblical interpretation was also a means of participating in this living drama of salvation, a way of life culminating in the vision of God.

4

Scholarship: Divine Provenance

Origen's profile of the scriptural interpreter remains monochromatic, and certainly incomplete, if we fail to grasp how he contextualized this figure within the Christian faith. Scholarship mattered, but so too did a commitment to Christianity from which this interpreter gained a spectrum of loyalties, guidelines, dispositions, relationships, and doctrines that tangibly informed biblical scholarship. Origen offered a vivid account of the scriptural interpreter, and it is the main task of this part of the study to do justice to this colorful portrait. A convenient place to begin is with the interpreter's acceptance of the educational mandate detailed in Part I of this study. How did Origen chart those who embraced the challenge of a scholarly examination of Scripture onto the Christian faith? I will answer this question in two stages. In this chapter I will examine how he delineated Greco-Roman scholarship, philology included, as contingent upon God's creative and providential action in the universe. In the next chapter I will demonstrate how, for Origen, the interpreter's decision to apply this scholarship to the study of Scripture signaled a simultaneous devotion to God.

Before we can address how Origen assessed the life given over to scriptural scholarship, it is important to clarify his perspective on scholarship itself. On the surface, his insistence that Greco-Roman philology was integral to the biblical scholar's profile renders our thesis untenable. After all, as his critics both within and without the church saw it, the literary scholarship endorsed by Origen enjoyed a *Greco-Roman*, and not Christian, provenance. As we will see below, Celsus asserted that any insightful teachings espoused by Christianity were ultimately foreign to it. These had been originally devised and pristinely embodied in other ancient cultures, especially the Greco-Roman. Thus, as his argument ran, when these teachings surfaced in Christian circles it was only because they had been borrowed, or perhaps even stolen. Origen countered this argument with a very different genealogy of the mind and the intellectual culture that sprang from it. Following a long tradition of Christian apologists, he famously contended that the best of Greco-Roman (or any other) learning was, in fact, native to Christianity. This knowledge ultimately enjoyed divine provenance and only surfaced because God and God's Son, the very Wisdom and Reason of God, had gifted it. This thesis was applicable to the debate about the interpreter's particular field of expertise, philology, including its contentious allegorical configuration. It too was ultimately a gift from God. Thus, by mastering the Greco-Roman scholarship relevant to scriptural exegesis, Christian interpreters were not acquiring a foreign training, so much as receiving and sharing in divine instruction.

CELSUS' POLEMIC

By the beginning of the third century, Origen stood within a well-developed tradition of Christian apologetic discourse. Over the course of the previous hundred years or so, leading Christian intellectuals had risen to the challenge of defending their fledgling movement against a range of objections from Greco-Roman intellectuals. One of the recurring issues concerned origins. Christianity, it was claimed, was dubious since it was a relatively young religion with a parasitic existence. At its best, it merely parroted the insights of the established conventions and wisdom embodied by the Greco-Roman tradition. At its worst, it misunderstood, corrupted, or was entirely ignorant of these insights. Whatever wisdom Christianity had, it was not original to it, since it had been expressed earlier and more completely in ancient Greco-Roman culture.[1]

Christians were certainly not alone when it came to this question of provenance. The ancient world was replete with debates about the antiquity (and hence superiority) of varieties of cultures, religions, and philosophical schools.[2] The Jewish apologetic tradition, for instance, had already crafted a defense of itself against similar charges, contending for the antiquity of the patriarchs and Moses, including their responsibility for helping shape other civilizations (and not the other way around).[3] The Christian apologetic tradition continued, and developed, this response. Prior to Origen, a series of authors, such as Aristides, Justin, Tatian, Theophilus, and Clement of Alexandria, turned

---

[1] For orientation to this large topic, see P. Labriolle, *La réaction païenne: Etude sur la polémique antichrétienne du Ie au VIe siècle* (Paris: L'Artisan du Livre, 1948; Paris: Cerf, 2005); R. Wilken, *The Christians as the Romans Saw Them* (New Haven: Yale University Press, 1984); X. Levieils, *Contra Christianos: Le critique sociale et religieuse du christianisme des origines au concile de Nicée (45–325)* (Berlin: W. de Gruyter, 2007).

[2] For a quick overview of this debate in antiquity, and particularly how non-Hellenistic civilizations turned the argument about antiquity to their advantage in their polemic with the Greeks, see A. J. Droge, *Homer or Moses? Early Christian Interpretations of the History of Culture* (Tübingen: Mohr Siebeck, 1989), 1–11.

[3] See A. J. Droge, *Homer or Moses?*, 12–48 and G. R. Boys-Stones, *Post-Hellenistic Philosophy: A Study of its Development from the Stoics to Origen* (Oxford: Oxford University Press, 2001), 76–95.

their opponents' polemic on its head, advancing some variant of the general thesis that the Judaeo-Christian heritage was, in fact, more ancient than the Hellenistic or other venerable Eastern cultures, and that the latter were dependent on the former, not the other way around.[4]

Origen thrust himself into this old debate when he devised his response to Celsus' *True Discourse*.[5] At several places in this work Celsus challenged Christianity, including the Judaism from which it emerged, for its lack of antiquity. "There is an ancient doctrine," Celsus writes, "which has existed from the beginning, which has always been maintained by the wisest nations and cities and wise men."[6] He then lists the Egyptians, Assyrians, Indians, Persians, Odrysians, Samothracians, Eleusinians, and Hyperboreans who shared this ancient doctrine. Yet Origen notes one ancient people missing from this list: "for some unknown reason he [Celsus] misrepresents the Jews alone, and does not include their race in the list with the others."[7] Indeed, "it is only the Hebrews that he rejects, as far as he can, in respect of both antiquity and wisdom."[8] According to Celsus, long before the Jews (to say nothing of Christians) stepped onto the stage of world history, there were venerable civilizations that had discovered and cultivated a rich body of doctrines and practices. Foremost among these civilizations were the Greeks.[9] Celsus reminds his readers that the Jews emerged recently, alluding to the Exodus when he asserts that they were actually Egyptians who fomented a rebellion against other members of their community.[10] And as for Christians, they were simply Jews who, like their forefathers at the Exodus, had recently incited a rebellion

---

[4] In addition to the two studies in n. 3, also see D. Ridings, *The Attic Moses: The Dependency Theme in Some Early Christian Writers* (Gothenburg: Acta Universitatis Gothoburgensis, 1995).

[5] Celsus was a second-century philosopher and opponent of Christianity. His treatise, *True Discourse*, is the earliest literary critique of Christianity (176–180). It survives only in the excerpts cited and paraphrased by Origen in his *Against Celsus*. Critical edition of Celsus' text: R. Bader, *Der Ἀληθὴς Λόγος des Kelsos* (Stuttgart: Kohlhammer, 1940), 39–216. See the German translation and commentary, *Die Wahre Lehre des Kelsos*, transl. and ed. H. E. Lona (Freiburg: Herder, 2005).

For literature on Celsus' critique and Origen's response, see esp. L. Rougier, *Celse ou le conflit de la civilisation antique et du monde chrétien* (Paris: Éditions du Siècle, 1926); A. Miura-Stange, *Celsus und Origenes: Das Gemeinsame ihrer Weltanschauung* (Giessen: Töpelmann, 1926); C. Andresen, *Logos und Nomos: Die Polemik des Kelsos Wider das Christentum* (Berlin: W. de Gruyter, 1955); K. Pichler, *Streit um das Christentum: Der Angriff des Kelsos und die Antwort des Origenes* (Frankfurt: Lang, 1980); R. L. Wilken, *The Christians as the Romans Saw Them*, 94–125.

[6] CC 1.14/SC 132, 114.27–29. Also see CC 4.14 where Celsus presents himself as an exponent of these "ancient doctrines."

[7] CC 1.14/SC 132, 112.44–114.5.

[8] CC 1.16/SC 132, 118.20–21. Note also in this section how Celsus fails to mention Moses in his list of "ancient and wise men who were of service to their contemporaries and to posterity by their writings."

[9] See esp. CC 1.2 where Celsus admits that the Greeks came after the "barbarians" who had discovered doctrines. However, Celsus continues by claiming that the Greeks were better able to judge the worth of these teachings, defend them, and put them into practice.

[10] CC 3.5; also see 4.31.

against their own people.[11] "I will ask them [Christians] where they have come from, or who is the author of their traditional laws. Nobody, they will say. In fact, they themselves originated from Judaism, and they cannot name any other source for their teacher and chorus-leader."[12]

According to Celsus' argument, neither Christians nor Jews could claim any sort of antiquity that rivaled the great Mediterranean or eastern civilizations. Thus, when a trace of teaching surfaced in the Judaeo-Christian tradition that bore some resemblance to what had already been developed elsewhere and earlier, Celsus was quick to propose dependence. At their best, the Jews were derivative, as was the case with elements in the Mosaic cosmogony that had been borrowed from earlier writers.[13] At their worst, they had "misunderstood" what was said by earlier writers,[14] "corrupted" pre-existing narratives,[15] or simply out of ignorance made their own futile attempts at what had already been expressed well by earlier, inspired writers.[16] When he turned to Christianity, Celsus proposed a very similar narrative. Jesus' followers, like Moses and the prophets, had misunderstood or corrupted their ancestral heritage.[17] And even if there were cases where Christians had hit upon something worthwhile, Celsus contended that they were only saying something (whether they knew it or not) that some Greek had already said long before and better.[18] Indeed, more often than not, much of the wisdom that resided in ancient cultures simply went unclaimed by Jews and Christians.

In sum, a leading edge in Celsus' polemic against Christianity (and the Judaism from which it gradually emerged) was his assertion that a venerable body of doctrines and practices resided natively within a host of cultures far older than either Judaism or Christianity. When traces of these traditions surfaced within Christianity, it was only because this new religion had borrowed (usually quite carelessly) from this vast and foreign cultural heritage. Thus, the argument concluded, Christianity's youth and reliance upon others rendered it suspect.

ALL WISDOM COMES FROM GOD

Origen accepted little of this argument. Most important for our purposes was his counter-assertion that the interpreter's expertise—Greco-Roman scholarship

---

[11] CC 3.5; also 2.1, 2.4, 3.14, and 5.33.
[12] CC 5.33/SC 147, 96.4–7.
[13] CC 1.19–21.
[14] See CC 6.7, 6.15.
[15] CC 4.21; also 4.41–42.
[16] CC 4.36.
[17] CC 3.16, 4.11, 5.65, 6.19, 6.43, 7.58.
[18] See CC 5.65 and 7.58–61. For more on Celsus' criticism of Christianity as derivative, see C. Andresen, *Logos und Nomos*, 146–166.

and philology in particular—took its origins ultimately from the Christian God. However, to appreciate this conspicuous claim, it is first necessary to examine Origen's alternative account of the mind and learning. For him, every human mind was profoundly dependent upon God. Not only was the mind created by God, but its very activity in pursuit of knowledge, and indeed, even the knowledge it gathered, were contingent upon God's providential involvement in the cosmos. Put concisely, minds and the intellectual culture that sprung from them enjoyed divine provenance.

This thesis comes into immediate focus in the opening chapter of *On First Principles*. "God," Origen writes, is an incorporeal, incomprehensible "Mind," a single and simple intellectual existence.[19] Among all existing things, this Mind alone is uncreated.[20] As Creator, then, God stands as the source behind all things that come to be. But in the case of intelligent creatures like humans, God fashions a particularly intimate bond with them since they, like God, are rational. God is "the Mind and Fount from which originates all intellectual existence or mind."[21] This is the most fundamental way in which Origen traced intellectual culture back to God. The very capacity for rational thought in creatures was sourced in the creative activity of the supreme Mind.

But God did not simply create the capacity for thought. God also continuously sustained the activity of thought. Origen closes his first survey of God, Christ, and the Holy Spirit in *On First Principles* with a wide-ranging discussion of the activities these divine agents perform in the world.[22] One of these activities is to sustain or nourish human rational thought. While some divine actions, Origen insists, are intended only for those who are advancing in their hold on Christianity, there are others that are directed "indiscriminately" toward "saints" and "sinners" alike:

> That the activity of the Father and the Son is to be found both in saints and in sinners is clear from the fact that all rational beings are partakers of the Word of God, that is, of Reason, and so have implanted within them some seeds, as it were, of Wisdom and Righteousness, "which is Christ" [Gal 3:16].[23]

In this section of *On First Principles*, Origen repeatedly stresses that where creatures come to exercise their minds, this fact alone already points to God and God's Son—the Wisdom of God—engaging in an "activity" or "work" on

---

[19] PA 1.1.6/GK 110, 21.10–14. On God as Mind, also see PA 1.2.3 and Comm Jn 1.277–278.

[20] See, for instance, PA pref.4, 1.3.5–8; Comm Jn 2.14, etc.

[21] PA 1.1.6/GK 110, 21.13–4—Butterworth modified. For other statements on the affinity between our minds and God the supreme Mind, see PA 1.1.7, 4.4.9–10, as well as the more general discussions about humans made according to the image of God at PA 1.2.6; Comm Jn 1.104–5, 2.20; CC 4.30, 6.63, 7.66. See as well "The ordered (and disordered) mind" in Chapter 5 below.

[22] PA 1.3.5–8.

[23] PA 1.3.6/GK 170, 56.19–57.1—Butterworth modified.

their behalf.[24] Origen describes this activity variously as a "grace," "gift," and "blessing," and even an "implanting," "bestowal," and "revealing." As intellectual creatures begin to exercise their rational capacities they are said, as a result, to "participate in," "partake of," or be in "communion with" God and the Son.[25] To the extent, then, that people use their minds, they draw upon God, the Mind, and God's Son, the Wisdom and Word of God. There is a bond or communion that exists between God and rational creatures simply in virtue of the latter pursuing the life of the mind.[26]

God created the capacity for thought, sustained the activity of thought, but also conveyed the content of thought. Origen did not hesitate to identify specific intellectual traditions that depended upon God's revelatory action. Here again, these insights were distributed widely, both to those within and those without the Judaeo-Christian tradition. For those within, the consummate expression of divine illumination was the Christian Scriptures, writings that enjoyed a dual authorship, as humans assisted by divine authors composed a collection of writings instrumental to the advancement of the divine plan of salvation.[27] But God also revealed insights to those outside this

---

[24] For Origen's discussions of these loftier intellectual aspects of the Son, see esp. PA 1.2.2–3, 1.3.5–8; Comm Jn 1.90–124 (Wisdom); 1.266–288, 2.46–63 (Word). On the Son as the very Image of God, see PA 1.2.6; Comm Jn 1.104–5, 2.20; CC 6.63. On the topic of the Son as revealer, see M. Harl, *Origène et la fonction révélatrice du Verbe incarné* (Paris: Éditions du Seuil, 1958).

[25] PA 1.3.6–8/GK 170, 56.19–184, 63.7. Other particularly clear passages include: "Christ is 'in the heart' [Rom 10:8] of all men, in virtue of his being the Word or Reason, by sharing in which men are rational" (PA 1.3.6/GK 172, 57.10–11—Butterworth modified). A few paragraphs later, Origen refers to the mere presence of rational activity among humans as Christ conferring "the natural gift of reason" on creatures (PA 1.3.7/GK 178, 60.8–9). Rational activity broadly construed, thus, already places humans in a relationship with God and God's Son, since "a participation in Christ, in virtue of his being the Word or Reason, makes them rational" (PA 1.3.8/GK 178, 60.24–180, 61.1. For additional texts on the ubiquitous work of God's Wisdom and Word in sustaining rational activity in all people, see Comm Jn 1.246, 1.269–276, 2.19–33.

[26] It is interesting to note one passage in *Against Celsus* where Origen supplements the argument I am outlining here: he proposes that an intentional *lack of assistance* on God's part also stimulated minds to begin work at the dawn of civilization. Celsus charged Christians with erroneously thinking that "God made all things for the sake of man" (CC 4.74), a position difficult to maintain since humans, unlike animals, need to struggle in order to survive. In his response to this critique, Origen argued that a broad spectrum of skills for survival first emerged because human reason was placed in a providentially arranged set of circumstances that allowed for the cultivation of these arts. "He [Celsus] does not see that from a desire that human understanding should be exercised everywhere, in order that it might not remain idle and ignorant of the arts [τῶν τεχνῶν], God made man a needy being, so that by his very need he has been compelled to discover arts, some for food and others for protection" (CC 4.76/SC 136, 374.5–10). Origen proceeds to list an array of skills and trades such as agriculture, viticulture, gardening, weaving, architecture, carpentry, navigation, and sailing that all emerged because a God-given capacity for rational thought was exercised when a providentially arranged set of circumstances placed humans in a situation of need. For a longer discussion of this passage, contextualizing both Celsus' and Origen's arguments in their respective philosophical settings, see A. J. Droge, *Homer or Moses?*, 153–157.

[27] Much more on Scripture's dual authorship and its role in the plan of salvation in Chapter 9 below.

tradition.[28] In *Against Celsus*, for example, Origen transmits his challenger's claim that Plato spoke truly about the highest good when he said that this good could not be expressed in words. Origen in no way denies this claim. Instead, he replies: "When we hear this, we also agree that this is well said; for God revealed to them these things and all other truths which they stated rightly."[29] At other junctures in *Against Celsus* Origen states quite openly (thus again agreeing with his challenger) that there were affinities between the teachings in the Christian Scriptures and those in circulation in Greco-Roman intellectual traditions. "Do not suppose," he writes, "that it is not consistent with Christian doctrine when in my reply to Celsus I accepted the opinions of those philosophers who have affirmed the immortality or the survival of the soul. We have some ideas in common with them."[30] Or again, in the midst of a long discussion of Celsus' assertion that God has made all things not simply for humans, but also for irrational creatures, Origen remarks: "If he had been a philosopher with any sense of obligation to his fellow-men, he ought to have avoided destroying with Christianity the helpful beliefs which are commonly held among men, and should have given his support, if he could, to the fine doctrines which Christianity has in common with the rest of mankind."[31] For Origen there was nothing surprising about the emergence of similar teachings in otherwise heterogeneous communities since these teachings were, ultimately, explained by their common source. When Celsus criticizes "our ethical teaching on the grounds that it is commonplace and in comparison with the other philosophers contains no teaching that is impressive or new," Origen responds: "There is therefore nothing amazing about it if the same God has implanted in the souls of all men the truths which He taught through the prophets and the Savior; He did this that every man might be without excuse at the divine judgment, having the requirement of the law written in his heart [cf. Rom 2:15]."[32] There was, of course, not a perfect or complete overlap in teachings, but there *was* overlap.[33]

---

[28] In light of the passages that now follow, F. Young's assertion is particularly jarring that Origen and other pre-Nicenes condemned and sought to replace the literary classics of the Greco-Roman *paideia* (see the discussion at the end of Chapter 2).

[29] CC 6.3/SC 147, 184.7–8.

[30] CC 3.81/SC 136, 182.1–4.

[31] CC 4.83/SC 136, 390.27–31. Other texts where the philosophers (or others) have teachings similar, if not identical, to those expressed by Christians: CC 1.4–5, 3.40, 3.80–81, 4.30, 6.7, 6.13–14, 7.45–47, 7.71, 8.52; PA 1.3.1; Comm Jn 2.19–33. These decisively refute the claim made by E. Molland, that Origen "condemns philosophy *en bloc*" (*The Conception of the Gospel*, 87).

[32] CC 1.4/SC 132, 84.6–86.11. For similar sentiments about God's revelation even to those outside the Judaeo-Christian heritage, see CC 1.5 and 4.30.

[33] It is important to stress that even when the Greeks (or anyone else) erred, this too plotted on Christian coordinates for Origen: they borrowed badly from Israel's Scriptures (CC 4.12, 4.21), or were under demonic influence (Hom Num 16.7, 18.3.5–6; Hom Jer 5.3; PA 3.3.1–3; CC 7.3, 8.4), or participated deficiently in God's Wisdom (Hom Num 18.3; Comm Jn 2.30). See particularly

Contrary, then, to Celsus' claims about the cultural provenance of venerable doctrines, Origen insisted that those outside the Judaeo-Christian heritage (as well as those within it) were cast in a dependent posture, all parties deriving their insights ultimately from God's self-disclosure. Naturally, this alternative account of the mind's contingency upon God had ramifications for the debate about borrowing. If there was borrowing, Origen insisted, it was not in the direction Celsus claimed, but rather the other way around. On several occasions in *Against Celsus* he set the record straight on the issue of antiquity. He reminded his readers that Moses was older than Plato, Hesiod, and Homer, and even the Greek alphabet.[34] Given the antiquity of Moses and the prophets, then, it was not the Jews who were borrowing from the Greeks, but the latter from the former:

> The highest good, towards which all rational nature is progressing, and which is also called the end of all things, is defined by very many even among philosophers in the following way, namely, that the highest good is to become as far as possible like God [cf. Plato, *Theaetetus*, 176 B]. But this definition is not so much, I think, a discovery of their own, as something taken by them out of the divine books. For Moses, before all others, points to it when in recording the first creation of man he says, "And God said, Let us make man in our own image and likeness" [Gen 1:26].[35]

We find several other passages like this one in *Against Celsus*, where Origen claims that at least some of the similarities between Greek teachings and those found within the Christian Scriptures were to be attributed to the former drawing upon the latter.[36] The Greeks who stood outside the Judaeo-Christian heritage were, thus, always dependent upon God for their insight: they either derived it directly from God's revelation to them, or indirectly, by borrowing from God's revelations to the Jews.

Thus we see in this section how Origen proposed an alternative genealogy of intellectual culture. He directly challenged Celsus' contention that an ancient body of doctrine resided natively among a host of ancient civilizations, only to be borrowed (usually sloppily) by Jews and Christians at a later date. It is important to stress that Origen did *not* deny similarities between teachings in the Scriptures and those in circulation in Greek literary and philosophical

---

Chapter 6 below where Origen criticizes Gnostic exegetes for their uncritical reliance on the deficient elements in Greco-Roman learning.

[34] CC 4.11, 4.21, 4.36, 6.7, 6.43, 7.28. On the antiquity of Judaeo-Christian teaching, also see CC 1.15–16, 6.4–5, 6.15, 7.39, 7.51, 7.59. Also of interest are those passages where Origen reminded his readers that while antiquity of intellectual traditions was important, it alone did not establish the truthfulness of these traditions (see CC 1.21, 4.20, 7.46, 7.58–59).

[35] PA 3.6.1/GK 642, 280.2–8.

[36] See CC 4.11–12, 4.21, 4.39, 5.15, 6.4, 6.19, 6.43, 7.30. G. R. Boys-Stones curiously contends: "For Origen did not accuse the pagans of theft (at least, such accusations did not form part of his general strategy against them)" (*Post-Hellenistic Philosophy*, 195). While the language of "theft" was not prominent, Origen certainly envisioned dependence.

circles. What he *did* deny was the proposal that these common convictions were best explained by Jews and Christians borrowing from foreign circles. Origen's counter-argument, anchored in the conviction of a God who was rational, creative, and magnanimous, dramatically reoriented Celsus' contention about the cultural origins of ancient doctrines and practices. This God, the supreme Mind, along with God's Son, the very Wisdom and Reason of God, created human minds with the capacity to think, sustained their thought, and nourished them with insight. These insights, moreover, were revealed generously to those within, as well as without, the Judaeo-Christian heritage. Thus, whatever was valuable in the Greco-Roman civilization (or any other civilization for that matter) was not original or native to it, but rather ultimately traced back to the Christian God. As a result, whenever similarities surfaced between Hellenistic and Christian teachings, these were best explained not by Celsus' proposal, but by the dependence of the former on Christianity's Scripture and, ultimately, its God.

THE ORIGINS OF PHILOLOGY

Without an appreciation for our author's overarching thesis about the divine provenance of intellectual culture, his account of the origins of the scriptural interpreter's area of specialization, philology, makes little sense. This discipline, he stressed, was not foreign to Christianity. In this section I will examine a handful of the more important passages where Origen contends that philology, allegory included, was ultimately a divine gift. In making such an assertion about the status of this discipline, Origen echoes the argument outlined above, that all of the mind's genuine intellectual achievements were contingent upon God.

In his eighteenth *Homily on Numbers*, Origen is inquiring into Balaam's fourth prophecy when he reaches the verse that claims this seer "knows the knowledge of the Most High" (Num 24:16). He is perplexed about how something so lofty could be attributed to this prophet, since no one in Scripture, not even the apostle Paul, ever dared to make such a claim for himself.[37] Origen hopes to clarify this conundrum with another, clearer verse in Scripture: "All wisdom is from God" (Sirach 1:1). After explaining that this verse could not possibly refer to the false wisdom of the world that is destined for destruction (alluding to Paul in 1 Cor 2:6), he proposes that only knowledge considered indispensable for the practice of arts useful to humans, or which assists them in gaining knowledge of anything, is properly considered

---

[37] Hom Num 18.3.1.

wisdom that comes from God. "[W]e may designate as wisdom given by the Lord either every skill that is considered necessary for human use in a craft, or the knowledge of any matter."[38] Origen substantiates this claim by referring to several passages in Scripture where it is explicitly stated that the skills of the weaver, craftsman, geometer, musician, and medical doctor are dependent on wisdom bestowed from God.[39] Returning to the scriptural claim that Balaam possessed "the knowledge of the Most High," Origen concludes that this must have signified the divine origins of this seer's knowledge about the natures of animals, movements of birds, and differences of sounds.[40] Significant for our purposes is that in this context Origen recalls an episode in Scripture where the discipline of philology was also attributed to God. He briefly recounts the details surrounding the story of Daniel and his companions who were in exile in Babylon. Nebuchadnezzar, the Babylonian king, provided three years of education in the literature and language of the Chaldeans for Daniel and his friends, so that they could serve in the royal court (cf. Dan 1:3–6). However, Origen points out, the biblical narrative ultimately attributed Daniel's philological skill to God's beneficence: "The Lord gave to them [Daniel and his friends] knowledge and understanding and prudence in every philological art [*in omni arte grammatica*] [Dan 1:17]."[41] Amidst a commentary, then, on the verse that "All wisdom is from God," Origen mentions a number of skills and disciplines that enjoy divine provenance, and philology is one of these.

A more extended discussion of the divine origins of philology occurs in the prologue to Origen's *Commentary on the Song of Songs*, a *locus classicus* for his reflections on the interpreter of Scripture. Here he proposes that God inspired Solomon with philology, and that Solomon, in turn, taught it to others through his writings. We pick up Origen's argument with his discussion of the significance of the order of the Solomonic books.[42] He asks why the three Solomonic books accepted as scriptural in the churches are arranged in the order they are: Proverbs first, Ecclesiastes second, and the Song of Songs third. He begins his response by reminding his readers of a common threefold division of philosophy in antiquity:

---

[38] Hom Num 18.3.2/GCS 7, 170.19–21.

[39] Hom Num 18.3.3.

[40] Origen also notes that Balaam used his knowledge wickedly by taking knowledge of good things and putting it into service of evil. Here he is drawing upon the negative Balaam tradition in Scripture where he is said to have practiced divination (cf. Josh 13:22) (Hom Num 18.3.4).

[41] Hom Num 18.3.6/GCS 7, 172.4–5. The Latin "*in omni arte grammatica*" is most likely Rufinus' translation of: ἐν πάσῃ γραμματικῇ τέχνῃ. On defining the adjective γραμματικός as "philological," see Chapter 1, n. 42.

[42] This is a typically philological inquiry into the order (τάξις) of what was being read (see B. Neuschäfer, *Origenes als Philologe*, 79–84).

The basic disciplines through which one attains to the knowledge of things are the three which the Greeks called ethics, physics and the esoteric discipline [*ethicam, physicam, epopticen*]; these we may call the moral, natural, and contemplative [*moralem, naturalem, inspectivam*]. There are admittedly some among the Greeks who also count linguistics [*logicen*] as a fourth, which we can call rational [*rationalem*]. Others have said that the latter is not extrinsic, but is rather interwoven through these three disciplines which we mentioned above and is incorporated into the whole group.[43]

We can pass over Origen's descriptions of ethics, physics, and the esoteric discipline.[44] Important for our purposes is his reference to the fourth philosophical discipline which I have translated as "linguistics" (the Latin term is *logice*, most likely Rufinus' transliteration of Origen's ἡ λογική). The English translator of this *Commentary* renders the Latin expression unhelpfully, I think, as "logic." It is important to remember that ἡ λογικὴ τέχνη, the linguistic discipline, often encompassed in antiquity far more than what is customarily meant by logic today. "Linguistics" is probably a more helpful translation since it catches better the wide spectrum of this ancient scholarly discipline: it certainly included inquiry into the patterns of argument expressed through language (resembling our logic), but it also comprised an assessment of language itself, that is, the sorts of issues philologists addressed. Indeed, here as elsewhere in his writings, Origen appears to have been most interested in this latter, philological component of ἡ λογική.[45] We gather this from his ensuing description of the discipline in the *Commentary*: this discipline "seems to consist of the literal and figurative definitions of words and expressions, of genres and their kinds, and to teach the tropes of each sort of expression."[46] This concise description strikingly resembles the branch of philology concerned with literary analysis (ἐξηγητικόν) as we sketched it

---

[43] GCS 8, 75.6–13—transl. mine. Note the correction of Baehrens' text, replacing "enopticen" with "epopticen." There are several variants here, though epopticen is now widely preferred in the scholarship because of precedents in the philosophical and theological literature, as well as other parallel passages in Origen's writings (e.g., see Lk Frg 218/GCS 9, 321). For a discussion of this issue, see J. Kirchmeyer, "Origène, commentaire sur le cantique prol.," *SP* 10: 230–235; P. Hadot, s.v. "Epopteia," *HWP*, vol. 2, ed. J. Ritter (Basel: Schwabe, 1972), 599; SC 376, 755, n. 4.

[44] For his other divisions of philosophy, see Hom Gen 6.2–3, 14.3; Hom Ex 3.3; Lam Frg 14; Phil 14.2. See H. Koch, *Pronoia und Paideusis: Studien über Origenes und sein Verhältnis zum Platonismus* (Berlin: W. de Gruyter, 1932), 247–248; H. Crouzel, *Connaissance mystique*, 50–52, 62–63, 65, 249–251; P. Hadot, "La logique, partie ou instrument de la philosophie?" in *Simplicius, Commentaire sur les Catégories*, fasc. 1, transl. and commented by I. Hadot (Leiden: Brill, 1989), 183–188; and more generally, P. Hadot, s.v. "Philosophie, I.F.: Die Einteilung der Philosophie in der Antike," *HWP*, vol. 7, ed. J. Ritter and K. Gründer (Basel: Schwabe, 1989), 603–605.

[45] As in Phil 14.2 discussed above in Chapter 2. H. Koch claims, puzzlingly, that Origen did not explain what he meant by this discipline (*Pronoia und Paideusis*, 249). As the *Commentary* continues, however, Origen offers numerous descriptions of this mode of inquiry. See the next two footnotes.

[46] Est enim logice haec vel, ut nos dicimus, rationalis, quae verborum dictorumque videtur continere rationes proprietatesque et improprietates, generaque et species, et figuras singulorum quorumque edocere dictorum (GCS 8, 75.13–16)—transl. mine.

above in Chapter 3. This branch was concerned with the clarification of a word's meaning (γλωσσηματικόν) as well as with rhetorical analysis (τεχνικόν). Origen points to both of these facets of ἐξηγητικόν when he remarks, above, that the linguistic discipline is interested in the definitions of "words and expressions" as well as the distinctions between "tropes" and "genres."[47]

Having rehearsed for his readers the threefold division of philosophy in antiquity, Origen returns to his initial question: why did Solomon write and arrange three books as he did? He revisits the debate about borrowing or dependence in antiquity that we have analyzed in the previous sections of this chapter. The Greek wise men did not invent these branches of philosophy, even though they tried to pass them off as their inventions. Rather, they possessed them second-hand. They borrowed from Solomon, who was first taught wisdom by the Spirit of God, long before the Greek philosophers.[48] Solomon, Origen continues, was the first to teach people philosophy, and for the purposes of ordering the wisdom he received from God, he wrote three books and arranged them in a meaningful sequence. The three branches of philosophy cultivated by the Greeks at a much later date were dependent upon the three Solomonic writings, the philosophic curriculum par excellence. And philology too, Origen insists, was taught by Solomon—not in some fourth book, but rather in the book of Proverbs, "through which the contents of words and significance of expressions are taught and the proper use of each discourse is clearly and rationally distinguished."[49] The scriptural interpreter's

---

[47] Origen offers several additional descriptions of ἡ λογική in the prologue to this *Commentary* that confirm he has the philological side of linguistics in mind. Origen will argue that Solomon teaches this discipline through Proverbs. To begin with, the very title of this book (Παροιμίαι) indicates the two basic philological referents, the literal and the allegorical, for the title "denotes that one thing is openly said, and another is inwardly meant [quod utique nomen significat aliud quidem palam dici, aliud vero intrinsecus indicari]" (GCS 8, 76.20–22). This assessment of the title follows from the etymology of the noun παροιμία, from παρά and οἴμη, i.e. "alongside the song" (see a very similar reference to the title "Proverbs" in CC 4.87). Moreover, Origen continues, in this book Solomon expresses an interest in γλωσσηματικόν when he distinguishes between the shades of meaning of related words such as scientia, sapientia, disciplina, and intellectum verborum (GCS 8, 76.27–33). And finally, he remarks, Solomon admonishes interpreters of Proverbs to understand various tropes (τεχνικόν), since he knew: "that in the divine words . . . there are diverse figures of expression and various forms of speaking and knowing that among these there is a figure that is called a 'parable,' and another which is called 'obscure speech,' and others that are named 'enigmas' [Prov 1:6]" (GCS 8, 77.8–12)— transl. mine. Origen affiliated Solomon's book of Proverbs with philological counsel elsewhere. Recall the preamble to his famous discussion of the threefold manner of interpretation in PA 4.2.4 where he cites a passage from Prov 22:20–21 to justify this way of interpretation.

[48] GCS 8, 75.23–26. In addition to Solomon's chronological priority over the Greek philosophers, Origen cites 1 Kings 4:29–30 to support his claim that the king drew his wisdom from God ("And God gave understanding to Solomon and exceedingly great wisdom . . .").

[49] GCS 8, 77.1–3—transl. mine.

area of specialization, then, ultimately enjoyed divine provenance. It was taught by God to Solomon and found expression in his writing.[50]

In these two passages from the *Homilies on Numbers* and *Commentary on the Song of Songs*, Origen asserts the divine provenance of philology (and several other disciplines as well). Interestingly, he made the same claim for that particularly contentious moment in his philological enterprise: allegorical exegesis. The critique to which he was responding when he advanced that claim was part of the same general polemic sketched at the start of this chapter: that Christianity occupied a derivative place in Greco-Roman society. Yet part of this critique also included the more hostile assertion that most of the wisdom within these ancient cultures simply went unclaimed by Christians. This included allegory. According to Celsus, as well as people in Origen's Caesarean congregation, allegorical composition and interpretation not only flourished on soil foreign to the Christian Scriptures, but also, the very authors of these Scriptures had *failed* to borrow either rhetorical or exegetical allegory. Thus, as the argument ran, Christians were in no position to interpret their sacred writings allegorically. This critique and Origen's response merit closer attention.

Already in Origen's day, his allegorical interpretation of Scripture proved controversial. Here again he found himself in a debate with Celsus. "If Celsus had read the Bible impartially, he would not have said that our writings 'are incapable of being interpreted allegorically.'"[51] Celsus' denial of the allegorical interpretation of Christian Scripture was rooted in a more fundamental denial: that the Bible had not been *composed* allegorically in the first place. "But Celsus thinks the books of Jews and Christians are utterly crude and illiterate, and supposes that those who allegorize them force the meaning of the authors in so doing."[52] At several points in *Against Celsus* Origen wonders if his challenger's difficulties with a particular biblical passage were based on the assumption that the passage in question was not composed allegorically. Celsus ridicules, for instance, the text where God brought a trance upon Adam and from one of his ribs made a woman (Gen 2:21–22). Origen responded: "But he does not quote the passage one has only to hear to understand that it is to be interpreted allegorically. In fact, he wanted to pretend that such stories are not allegories."[53] There is another passage in *Against Celsus* where Origen relays his challenger's critique that the laws given by Moses and Jesus contradicted one another. Origen responds: "He [Celsus] thinks that in the law and prophets there is no deeper doctrine beyond that of

---

[50] Recall the discussion in Chapter 2 (at n. 43) about exegetical analysis as a privileged mode of philosophical inquiry in antiquity. It is not an accident that Origen speaks of philology as a philosophical discipline here in the prologue to the *Commentary on the Song of Songs*.

[51] CC 4.49/SC 136, 308.37–39. See also CC 1.17.

[52] CC 4.87/SC 136, 402.32–35.

[53] CC 4.38/SC 136, 278.6–7.

the literal meaning of the words."[54] For Celsus, the Old Testament was composed in a thoroughly literal manner.

What especially unsettled Origen was his suspicion that his critic was denying a level of literary and religious sophistication to the Jews while, on the other hand, happily discovering the deepest allegorical truths in non-Jewish literature.[55] This was yet another venerable practice to which many ancient civilizations had been apprenticed, with the notable exception of the Jews.[56] "And if the Egyptians relate this mythology, they are believed [by Celsus] to be concealing philosophy in obscurities and mysteries; but if Moses wrote for a whole nation and left them histories and laws, his words are considered to be 'empty myths not even capable of being interpreted allegorically.'"[57] Origen makes this point more forcefully later in book four of *Against Celsus* when he wonders why Celsus gladly allegorizes the Hesiodic myth about a woman given to men as punishment for having stolen fire, but when he comes to the story of God making a woman from the rib of a man (Gen 2:21–22), this story has no deeper sense: "But it is not treating the matter fairly to refuse to laugh at the former as being a legend, and to admire the philosophical truths contained in it, and yet to sneer at the biblical stories and think that they are worthless, your judgment being based upon the literal meaning alone."[58] Celsus' objection, then, to the allegorical interpretation of the Scriptures—the books of the law in particular—was grounded in a basic denial that they had ever been composed allegorically. While other, ostensibly more ancient, cultures were well-versed in allegorical composition, this rhetorical procedure was absent from the sacred literature of the Hebrews. Once again, the Jews were strangers to an esteemed, ancient literary practice.

A related version of this argument surfaced in Origen's own day within his congregation in Caesarea. We catch a glimpse of this critique in his *Homilies on Genesis*. There Origen proposes a playful allegorical interpretation of Isaac and his servants digging wells (Gen 26): he allegorizes this event to refer to his own (!) allegorizing of Scripture. Isaac and his servants digging wells point symbolically to himself whenever he begins "to discuss the words of the ancients and to seek in them a spiritual meaning" so as to "renew his hearers."[59] However, Origen continues more soberly, just like the Philistines

---

[54] CC 7.18/SC 150, 54.20–23. See related passages at CC 1.17, 4.17, 4.48, 4.51, 4.55. Given the absence of the allegorical composition of Scripture, Celsus proposed that the underlying motivation for their allegorical interpretation was shame over their embarrassing contents: see CC 4.38, 4.48, 4.51.

[55] See esp. CC 3.43 and 6.42.

[56] See CC 1.14–16 on the Jews being strangers to the "ancient doctrine" in circulation among other civilizations.

[57] CC 1.20/SC 132, 126.19–128.2.

[58] CC 4.38/SC 136, 278.18–21. On Celsus' purported double standard, also see CC 4.17 and the remainder of the discussion at 4.38–41.

[59] Hom Gen 13.3/GCS 6, 116.17–18.

quarreled with Isaac and his servants over their wells, contending that "The water is ours" (Gen 26:20), so too does he have to deal with adversaries who "lie in ambush for me."[60] These "friends of the letter," like Isaac's Philistines, are territorial. Origen voices their objection:

> But also if one of those who knows secular literature should now hear me preaching, he is perhaps saying: "These things are ours of which you speak and it is the learning of our discipline. This very eloquence with which you discuss and teach is ours." And, like some Philistine, he stirs up quarrels with me saying: "You dug a well in my soil." And he will seem right to himself to lay claim to those things which are of his own land.[61]

Whereas Celsus contended that allegorical *composition* was foreign to, and absent from, the Jewish Scriptures, the criticism from Origen's congregation in Caesarea focused on the foreign provenance of allegorical *exegesis*. This interpretive practice sprouted on soil alien to the Christian Scriptures, and just as the ancient wells mentioned in Genesis had sole proprietary rights, so too did allegorical exegesis. It did not exist (so the criticism) in two places at once. Thus, its foreign origins simultaneously implied its absence from the Christian Scriptures and, in turn, yielded to the conclusion that its interpreters could not lay legitimate claim to it. In short, both of Origen's critics agreed with one another: the absence of either allegorical composition or exegesis from the Christian Scriptures necessitated the conclusion that these writings ought not to be interpreted allegorically.[62]

Origen's subversion of this argument against the allegorical interpretation of the Christian Scriptures repeatedly came back to the same point: these writings were legitimately allegorized because—contrary to the aforementioned criticisms—their allegorical exegesis was already present *within* them. Origen concedes that if it was only the Jews and Christians "of our own time"

---

[60] Hom Gen 13.3/GCS 6, 116.20–21. Other passages in his homilies where Origen responds to the perceived scandal of allegory in his congregants include Hom Lev 1.1.2 and 7.4.1–2.

[61] Hom Gen 13.3/GCS 6, 116.28–117.4—Heine modified.

[62] The charge that allegorical interpretation was foreign and, thus, off-limits to Christians did not abate in Origen's own lifetime. In the fourth century, additional versions of this critique were directed posthumously against Origen. For instance, in a fragment from his third book *Against Christians*, Porphyry echoed Celsus' sentiments, insinuating that the Jewish Scriptures were not written allegorically, and claiming that Hellenistic allegorical exegesis was inappropriately applied to these "foreign fables" (Eusebius, HE 6.19.4–8, and discussed above in Chapter 2). This critique also found a home within Christian circles. Theodore of Mopsuestia raised similar issues in his *Commentary on the Psalms*, insisting that Origen's allegory was additionally tainted by its deep indebtedness to Philo. See L. van Rompay, transl., *Théodore de Mopsueste: Fragments syriaques du Commentaire des Psaumes* (Louvain: Peeters, 1982), 14–15; F. G. McLeod, *Theodore of Mopsuestia* (London: Routledge, 2009), 75–79. Much of the modern discussion of early Christian allegory echoes these late antique debates, seeking to locate allegory in foreign religious, philosophical, educational, and cultural contexts, and thereby also usually to marginalize it. See P. W. Martens, "Revisiting the allegory/typology distinction: The case of Origen," *JECS* 16 (2008): 283–296.

who read Scripture allegorically, his critics might have scored an important point.[63] However, it was not simply Origen's contemporaries who studied the Scriptures allegorically. Those who composed Scripture had already interpreted other parts of Scripture allegorically. Repeatedly Origen sought precedent for the allegorical interpretation of Scripture in Paul's letters:

> We will quote a few examples out of a great number in order to show that Celsus falsely accuses the Bible to no purpose when he says that it cannot be interpreted allegorically. Paul, the apostle of Jesus, says: "It is written in the law, Thou shalt not muzzle the ox that treadeth out the corn. Does God care for oxen? Or does He say this altogether on our account? For on our account it was written, because he that ploughs ought to plough in hope, and he that threshes ought to thresh in hope of partaking" [1 Cor 9:9–10, citing Deut 25:4]. And in another place the same man says: "For it is written that for this cause a man shall leave his father and his mother and shall cleave unto his wife, and the two shall become one flesh. This is a great mystery; but I speak concerning Christ and his church" [Eph 5:31–32, citing Gen 2:24]. And again in another passage: "And we know that all our fathers were under the cloud, and all passed through the sea, and were all baptized unto Moses in the cloud and in the sea" [2 Cor 10:1–2]. Then he interprets the story of the manna and of the water which is recorded to have come miraculously out of the rock, saying as follows: "And they all ate the same spiritual meat, and they all drank the same spiritual drink; for they drank of the spiritual rock which followed them; and the rock was Christ" [1 Cor 10:3–4].[64]

We find a very similar dossier of evidence in one of Origen's earliest writings, *On First Principles*. In book four of this treatise he contends that the Scriptures need to be interpreted not simply literally but also allegorically. He justifies this latter contention by reminding his audience that the apostle Paul set a precedent for an interpretation of the law and prophets that moved beyond the literal or bodily sense to the other two loftier, allegorical senses. Origen refers to 1 Cor 9:9–10 ("is it for the oxen that God cares? Or does he say it altogether for our sake?") to illustrate the sort of allegorical interpretation that detects the "soul" of Scripture. Immediately thereafter he catalogues a long list of Pauline passages where the apostle exhorts an allegorical interpretation that detects the "spirit" of Scripture, either explicitly indicating that the law and prophets contain figures, copies, and shadows of something else (Heb 8:5; 10:1; 1 Cor 10:11; Col 2:16ff), or actually pursuing an allegorical interpretation of a particular passage (1 Cor 10:4; Gal 4:21–24; Rom 11:4–5).[65]

---

[63] CC 4.49.

[64] CC 4.49/SC 136, 310.16–312.36.

[65] PA 4.2.6. Note also Origen's brief recourse to two other scriptural passages in this section of *On First Principles*. Both of these hint, or so he thinks, at the allegorical interpretation of Scripture. He famously opens his discussion of the threefold manner of scriptural interpretation with a reference to Solomon: "The right way, therefore as it appears to us, of approaching the scriptures and gathering their meaning, is the following, which is *extracted from the writings themselves*" (PA 4.2.4/GK 708, 312.1–3). Origen proceeds to cite Prov 22:20–21 on portraying knowledge in a "threefold" manner. Later in PA 4.2.6 Origen proposes that the reference in Jn 2:6

Passages such as these sufficed to refute the critique that emerged from Origen's Caesarean congregation. So long as he could point to the presence of the allegorical interpretation of the Scriptures already within these Scriptures—that is, later scriptural authors interpreting earlier authors allegorically—he squarely met the challenge. After all, it was not just the Hellenistically trained Origen who interpreted these writings allegorically, it was the authors of these writings themselves who did so. At the same time, how effective was such a dossier of New Testament allegorizations of the law and prophets in the response to Celsus? Origen seems to have anticipated Celsus' rejoinder that even the apostle Paul—no different from later Christians like Origen—was making forced allegorical readings of the law and prophets. Thus Origen extended his argument by turning to the Old Testament writings themselves, noting how even within Israel's Scriptures there was evidence for allegorical interpretation. Origen reminds Celsus that the psalmist Asaph, for instance,

> showed that the stories in Exodus and Numbers are "problems" and "parables," as it is written in the book of Psalms. For when about to recount these narratives he prefaces his account in this way: "Give ear, O my people, to my law, incline your ears to the words of my mouth. I will open my mouth in parables, I will utter problems of old, which we have heard and read, and our fathers have told us" [Ps 77:1–3].[66]

Indeed, Origen continues in his response to Celsus, if

> the law of Moses contained within it nothing to be interpreted as containing hidden meaning, the prophet would not have said to God in his prayer "Open thou mine eyes, that I may understand thy wonders out of thy law" [Ps 118:18]. Here he knew that there is a veil of ignorance lying upon the heart of those who read and do not understand the allegorical meaning [cf. 2 Cor 3:13–16].[67]

Of course, to offer a decisive refutation of Celsus' claim that the law and prophets had not been composed with allegorical intent was very difficult.

---

to waterpots each holding "two or three *metretes*" also signifies the literal and allegorical interpretations of Scripture.

In general, however, Origen invoked Paul's and Jesus' allegorical interpretations of Scripture. When his congregants in Caesarea recoiled at what they perceived to be a foreign exegetical approach to the book of Genesis, he quickly reminded them that Jesus spoke well of the scribe who was trained in the kingdom of heaven. Jesus spoke of this scribe as an allegorist, since "he brings forth from his treasures new things and old" (Mt 13:52). If so, then why could Origen not do similarly, discovering the new spiritual message in the books of the old covenant (Hom Gen 13.3)? For additional references to Jesus' and Paul's exegetical, esp. allegorical, tutelage, see the more detailed discussion in Chapter 7 below. As will become clear in that section, Origen invoked the exegetical precedent of Jesus and Paul in two distinct ways: here in this chapter, the precedent establishes the *importance* of being willing to interpret Scripture allegorically; in Chapter 7 below, I discuss those passages where Origen turns to Jesus and Paul as precedent for doing *a particular sort* of allegorical exegesis of the law and prophets.

[66] CC 4.49/SC 136, 312.36–44.
[67] CC 4.50/SC 136, 312.1–7.

Who really could determine their purpose? But if it was difficult for Origen to ascertain it, surely it was no easier for Celsus to secure his claim about authorial intent. However, as Origen saw it, the weight of evidence was on his side. After all, he reasoned, "since the very authors of the doctrines themselves and the writers interpreted these narratives allegorically, what else can we suppose except that they were written with the primary intention that they should be allegorized?"[68]

Unlike his opponents, then, Origen was convinced that the allegorical interpretation of the Christian Scriptures was a legitimate practice. There was clear precedent for this practice within them, and thus by implication, the strong suggestion that what had been interpreted allegorically had also been composed allegorically. Of course, in defending allegorical exegesis in this way, Origen was not reversing his opponents' claim, contending now that allegorical exegesis was (somehow) unique to the Christian Scriptures. This was never an argument about the uniqueness of allegory, or even about its originality, to Christianity—Origen did not deny the widespread presence of allegorical composition and interpretation in Hellenistic literature.[69] Rather, Origen was arguing for the *presence* of allegorical exegesis and rhetoric in the Christian Scriptures, and thus, by extension, that this was yet another area of commonality between Christianity and Greco-Roman intellectual culture.

---

[68] CC 4.49/SC 136, 310.12–15.

[69] Origen was fully aware that there was a long tradition of allegorical interpretation that predated Christianity and could be found outside of the Christianity of his day. He applied the pair of Greek terms ἀλληγορία and ἀλληγορέω to all sorts of readers and texts: to the Greeks interpreting Hesiod's myths (CC 4.38), to those who, with insight into Plato's teachings, allegorized his myths (CC 7.30), to the allegorical readers of Homer (CC 8.68), and other Greek writers (CC 1.18, 4.48), but also to the heterodox interpreters of Scripture (Comm Jn 20.166), to Jews and Christians in the reading of the Old Testament (CC 4.38, 4.49, 4.87), and to Christians interpreting Scripture in accordance with Gal 4:24 ("Now this is an allegory: these women are two covenants...") (Comm Jn 20.74; PA 4.2.6; CC 4.44). Of course, Origen could speak of himself as an allegorist: "And we must first say that just as when we find written of God that he has eyes and eyelids and ears, hands and arms and feet, and indeed even wings, we change what is written into an allegory..." (Comm Jn 13.131/GCS 4, 245.24–27. Also see Comm Matt 17.35; Comm Jn 1.180, 20.67, 20.329, 13.101; PA 4.2.6).

There is little if any indication from Origen's pen that allegorical interpretation was somehow original, let alone unique, to Christians. He knew it was widely practiced. The question was whether the Christian Scriptures had been composed allegorically and whether there was also a compelling tradition of their allegorical interpretation emerging from within these Scriptures. R. P. C. Hanson deals unsatisfactorily with Origen's attribution of allegory to the apostles. Hanson makes it sound as if Origen, when he refers to apostolic precedent for allegorizing Scripture, thought allegory was somehow unique to the church. "Origen consistently claims that the allegorization of Scripture is the Church's *special way* of interpreting the Bible, handed down to her by the apostles [italics mine]" (*Origen's Doctrine of Tradition*, 101). This is a misleading claim—at most Origen would say that allegory was characteristic of how the church read Scripture, but I am not aware of any passage where he contends that Christians are somehow unique or special in practicing allegorical exegesis.

In light of the foregoing discussion in this chapter, it is also clear that Origen would never have conceded that the presence of allegory in the Christian Scriptures implied a foreign derivation. These Scriptures, after all, were divinely inspired.[70] Their allegorical rhetoric was a divine rhetoric. Origen makes this point many times, but nowhere as clearly as in the preface to *On First Principles*. There he announces the ecclesiastical rule's teaching on Scripture, and how it was divinely authored to convey both a literal and allegorical sense: "Then there is the doctrine that the Scriptures were composed through the Spirit of God and that they have not only that meaning which is obvious, but also another which is hidden from the majority of readers."[71] If these Scriptures were composed allegorically under divine influence, this clearly invited their allegorical assessment. Yet no one less than the divinely inspired Paul and Jesus, God's Word made flesh, had already interpreted the law and prophets allegorically. Who, then, could doubt that the allegorical exegesis of Scripture enjoyed divine provenance?

On the surface, Origen's insistence that the ideal interpreter harness the Greco-Roman intellectual traditions for the purposes of biblical scholarship could be seen as a powerful critique of the main thesis in this book. Was not any attempt to frame a figure with this sort of expertise within the parameters of the Christian faith misguided from the start? Indeed, as we have seen, Origen's ancient critics raised a version of this question. They contended that the learning he advocated had been developed independently of Christianity; it had resided originally and pristinely in Greco-Roman intellectual culture and was, thus, foreign to Christianity. But as I have demonstrated in this chapter, Origen countered this critique by explicitly contextualizing the interpreter's expertise—commendable Greco-Roman knowledge and approaches to knowledge—within the larger Christian narrative. Philology, and any other discipline relevant to informed scriptural inquiry, enjoyed divine provenance. God, the supreme Mind, had created minds with the capacity for thought, sustained these minds in their intellectual activity, and even conveyed to them specific teachings, practices, and skills. The interpreter's expertise was not borrowed or stolen from a foreign culture, but rather bestowed by the Christian God. The gradual participation in this expertise ushered the interpreter into a relationship with God, the ultimate source from which all knowledge and wisdom flowed.

---

[70] For a dossier of passages where Origen makes this claim, see Chapter 9 below, especially the section "Authorial intent."

[71] PA pref.8/GK 94, 14.6–8. See esp. PA 4.2.7–9.

5

Conversion: Sanctified Study

In the previous chapter I examined the status Origen assigned to the best of Greco-Roman learning. In his view, this learning ultimately enjoyed divine provenance, and thus as scholars—both Christians and non-Christians alike—gradually mastered it, they came into an increasingly profound relationship with God. Yet what about Christians who wished to use Greco-Roman scholarship for interpreting *their Scriptures*? How did Origen assess the decision to embark upon the life of scriptural scholarship? As we will discover in this chapter, biblical interpretation for Origen was not simply one profession among others. It was arguably the consummate way of life to which he exhorted his readers and congregations. Indeed, he elevated this way of life to the point that it became a hallmark of advanced Christianity. Yet why he did so might not, at first glance, be transparent. An answer to this question crystallizes when we scrutinize how the would-be interpreter's conversion to a life of scriptural study plotted favorably onto Origen's sweeping discussions of the mind's competing moral commitments and its location along the faith–reason continuum. We will discover how, for him, interpreters who devoted themselves to the study of divine Scripture signaled their simultaneous devotion to God.

THE LIFE OF SCRIPTURAL INTERPRETATION

Already in one of Origen's earliest surviving writings, he proposed that scriptural interpretation was a practice intrinsic to mature Christianity. He famously advances this thesis in the opening paragraphs of his *Commentary on John* when he turns to the Apocalypse (he considered this work and the gospel that he was expounding upon to be authored by the same John). Origen notices two cryptic references in the Apocalypse to the 144,000 servants of God (Rev 7:4, 14:3). He wishes to ascertain the precise identity of these mysterious figures, and in so doing offers a remarkably imaginative interpretation of the ancient Levites. This select group within the larger Israelite society symbolized another select group within the new children of Israel, Christians. The Levites signified those advanced Christians who attested to their dedication by immersing themselves in scriptural scholarship. This passage from the *Commentary* merits closer examination.

Origen detects a handful of references in the Apocalypse to the 144,000 servants of God, a select group of people who have the names of the Lamb and God his Father inscribed on their foreheads (Rev 7:3–4, 14:1–5). But these servants are also curiously described as a subset taken from "every tribe of the children of Israel" (Rev 7:4), a designation that gives Origen pause.[1] Who precisely are these 144,000 who have the name of *Jesus*, the Lamb, written on their foreheads, yet are *also* designated "children of Israel"? Origen surmises that despite the obvious sense of this latter designation, John could only have had Gentile believers in Christ in mind, whose "physical race does not appear to go back to the seed of the patriarchs."[2] After all, he observes, "a believer from Israel according to the flesh is rare."[3] John, in other words, was not using the designation "children of Israel" literally to refer to believers in Jesus of Jewish extraction; rather this was an allegorical label, referring to Gentiles who had come to believe in Christ.[4]

If, then, these 144,000 servants of God are a select number of believers in Jesus, taken from the larger Gentile Christian community, what demarcates them from their fellow believers? Origen makes two moves to help him answer this question. The first identifies a correspondence between this select group of Christians and an analogously select group within ancient Israelite society. He seeks this particular correspondence since, as noted above, John curiously designated Christians as "children of Israel," a nomenclature that suggests profound similarities between the Christian and Israelite communities. Since John's 144,000 servants of God are a chosen subset within the modern "children of Israel," that is, the larger Gentile Christian population, Origen proposes that there should be a parallel group, distinguished as well in its service to God, within the original children of Israel. The Levites were precisely this group, he continues, since they alone rendered sacerdotal service unto God within the larger Israelite society. The basic twofold structure among the "people of old, who were called the people of God," is also to be found among the new "people of Christ," who possess the characteristics of ancient Jewish society, although, Origen is quick to add, they possess these in a "more mystical manner [μυστικώτερον]."[5]

---

[1] Comm Jn 1.2–3.

[2] Comm Jn 1.4/GCS 4, 4.14–15.

[3] Comm Jn 1.7/GCS 4, 4.30–31.

[4] For more on Origen's view of these Jewish Christians, see "Literalism and Ebionite exegesis" in Chapter 7 below.

[5] Comm Jn 1.1/GCS 4, 3.1–6. For the view that Origen is reflecting here on the structure of the Christian community in Alexandria, see A. Jakab, *Ecclesia Alexandrina* (Bern: Peter Lang, 2001), 194–196.

Origen's next move is to determine the identity of these "levitical" Christians. He does so by drawing upon a vivid epithet applied to the 144,000 in John's Apocalypse: these are "firstfruits for God and for the Lamb" (Rev 14:4). In ancient Israelite society, Origen notes, the Levites had a different relationship to the firstfruits than the rest of the twelve tribes. While the latter offered firstfruits to God, they did not consider all their possessions firstfruits since only some of their belongings were offered to God. The Levites, however, considered *all* their possessions firstfruits and, in turn, offered all of these to God.[6] But the reference to "firstfruits," Origen contends, "admits in addition an elevated sense [ἐπιδέχεται ἀναγωγήν]."[7]

He proposes that among Christians, the new Israelites, "those who devote themselves to the divine Word and truly exist by the service of God alone will properly be said to be Levites and priests in accordance with the excellence of their activities in this work."[8] There is a delightful pun in this passage on two senses of the noun λόγος. The reference to select Christians, who "devote themselves to the divine Word [τῷ θείῳ λόγῳ]," can refer to the Son of God, whom the *new* children of Israel worship, but it can also refer to the written word of God, Scripture, which they ceaselessly study. As the opening lines of the *Commentary on John* unfurl, this latter reading becomes explicit: the all-engrossing activity that demarcates mature Christians from the simpler is their unreserved commitment to scriptural scholarship. Origen explains to his patron Ambrose how the activity of biblical scholarship, to which he has been commissioned, constitutes these figurative firstfruits:

> Since we are eager for those things which are better, all our activity and our entire life being dedicated to God and we wish to have all our activity as the firstfruits of many firstfruits—unless, indeed, we are mistaken when we think this—what more excellent activity ought there be…than the careful examination of the gospel [τὴν περὶ εὐαγγελίου ἐξέτασιν]?[9]

For Origen, then, the select 144,000 in the Apocalypse cryptically symbolized those few in the Christian ambit like himself who dedicated all their lives to a particular activity, the interpretation of the gospel. Indeed, as Origen will quickly argue in the subsequent paragraphs of his *Commentary*, these advanced Christians actually devoted their lives to the interpretation of *all* of Scripture.[10] These opening paragraphs of the *Commentary on John* offer us one of Origen's earliest statements about the privileged place biblical scholarship occupied in Christianity. In his view, an absorbing commitment to

---

[6] Comm Jn 1.9.
[7] Comm Jn 1.8/GCS 4, 5.6—transl. mine.
[8] Comm Jn 1.10/GCS 4, 5.20–22.
[9] Comm Jn 1.12/GCS 4, 5.34–6.6.
[10] See Comm Jn 1.13–26, which includes further reflections on the theme of firstfruits.

scriptural interpretation was a measure of one's heightened commitment to this faith.[11]

As I have already argued, Origen's vision of the scriptural interpreter was often reflexive. In the opening paragraphs of his *Commentary on John*, he makes the bold assertion that the project of scriptural study was a hallmark of a more robust form of Christianity. But this claim is also unmistakably autobiographical. Origen was an unflagging interpreter of Scripture, and he aspired through a more zealous investigation of Scripture to signal his deepening commitment to Christianity ("all our activity and our entire life being dedicated to God"). Origen viewed *his own* devotion to scriptural scholarship as a barometer of his growing devotion to Christianity. Along these lines, it is certainly interesting to note how Eusebius shared Origen's autobiographical assessment of his own commitment to scriptural interpretation. In his biography of Origen, the historian tellingly portrays how his subject's diligent scriptural study only transpired after he converted to a more dedicated variety of Christianity. Moreover, Origen's newfound passion for the study of Scripture was pursued alongside other undeniably earnest forms of Christian expression. The passage from the *Ecclesiastical History* deserves generous citation. Describing this conversion, Eusebius reports that Origen

> disposed of whatever valuable books of ancient literature he possessed, being satisfied with receiving from the purchaser four oboli a day. For many years he lived philosophically in this manner, putting away all the incentives of youthful desires. Through the entire day he endured no small amount of discipline; *and for the greater part of the night he gave himself to the study of the Divine Scriptures.* He restrained himself as much as possible by a most philosophic life; sometimes by the discipline of fasting, again by limited time for sleep. And in his zeal he never lay upon a bed, but upon the ground. Most of all, he thought that the words of the Saviour in the Gospel should be observed, in which he exhorts not to have two coats nor to use shoes, nor to occupy oneself with cares for the future. With a zeal beyond his age he continued in cold and nakedness; and, going to the very extreme of poverty, he greatly astonished those about him... He is said to have walked for a number of years never wearing a shoe, and, for a great many years, to have abstained from the use of wine, and of all other things beyond his necessary food; so that he was in danger of breaking down and destroying his constitution. (italics mine)[12]

In this passage, Eusebius unmistakably locates Origen's decision to embark upon a life of scriptural scholarship as a part of a larger ascetic turn (living

---

[11]   And by implication, since these mystical Levites were distinguished by their all-engrossing commitment to biblical interpretation, it was the Christian *hoi polloi*—the *simpliciores*—who gave only fleeting attention to the biblical text. Origen claims this as well in his interpretation of the 144,000: most Christians, in fact, have "much time for the activities of life" and only "offer a few acts to God" (Comm Jn 1.10/GCS 4, 5.17–18). For more on the *simpliciores*, see the section, "The audience," in Chapter 2 above.

[12]   Eusebius, HE 6.3.9–12/GCS 9.2, 526.20–528.14. See P. Nautin, *Origène*, 39–41 for an analysis of Eusebius' possible sources here.

"philosophically," as many fourth century authors termed it). Origen's fervent pursuit of Christianity did not simply entail a series of ascetical practices such as renouncing worldly possessions, "youthful desires," food, clothing and sleep. Also intrinsic to this more austere form of Christianity was the dedicated study of Scripture. The portrait of Origen that emerges in the *Ecclesiastical History* is that his scriptural study was emblematic of his desire to be uncompromisingly Christian.[13]

At some level, Origen's lofty valorization of scriptural exegesis followed his own pursuit of this scholarly vocation. He was an indefatigable interpreter and, as we have already seen, the *vitae* of his principal ancient biographers presented their ecclesiastical luminary as the scriptural scholar par excellence: Origen embodied this way of life and also helped his students in Alexandria and Caesarea realize this way of life for themselves. But there was certainly more to his elevation of scriptural study into a hallmark (and perhaps *the* hallmark) of serious Christian commitment. Origen often aligned his advocacy of this life with Jesus' command to "Search the Scriptures" (Jn 5:39). The *simpliciores*, he laments in *Against Celsus*, were not "willing to spend time searching Scripture [σχολάσαι τῇ ἐρεύνῃ τῆς γραφῆς], though Jesus says 'search the scriptures' [Jn 5:39]."[14] On several occasions Origen exhorts obedience to this dominical command, thus framing the life devoted to scriptural interpretation as one of the characteristics of Christian discipleship.[15] Yet even this does not fully explain why scriptural scholarship was a mark of the advanced (or advancing) Christian.

In order to better understand how Origen thought about this matter, it is important to recognize that he situated a life infused with scriptural learning within two larger and overlapping moral visions. The first of these visions (discussed in the following section) focused on the mind and the two worlds—incorporeal and corporeal—that competed for its attention. For Origen,

---

[13] There seems little reason for calling into question the reliability of at least the general contours of Eusebius' account of Origen's conversion, since it coincides strongly with Origen's own account. Indeed, recall how in the opening paragraphs of his *Commentary on John*, it is not only Origen's zealous commitment to scriptural study that demonstrates his engrossing dedication to God, but also his sexual renunciation: "what more excellent activity ought there be, after our physical separation from one another, than the careful examination of the gospel?" (1.12/ GCS 4, 5.34–6.6). The expression "physical separation from one another" is a reference to virginity—see Origen's previous citation of Rev 14:1–5 where John speaks of the 144,000 as virgins (Comm Jn 1.3, 5, 7–8). There is a striking resemblance, then, between how Eusebius and Origen narrate his conversion to a more serious variety of Christianity: both claim scriptural study and ascetic renunciation were intrinsic to this conversion. It is true that Eusebius does not explicitly mention sexual renunciation here at HE 6.3.9–12. However, a few paragraphs later when he resumes his history of the young Origen's career in Alexandria, he revisits his newfound asceticism by referring (notoriously) to his self-castration (HE 6.8.1–5).

[14] CC 5.16/SC 147, 54.10–11—transl. mine.

[15] For additional passages where Origen discusses the acceptance of Jesus' mandate in Jn 5:39, see Comm Jn 6.303; PA 4.3.5; CC 3.33.

scriptural exegesis aimed for one, and only one, of these worlds: scholars who embarked upon a course of scriptural study signaled their commitment to pursue the incorporeal God at the expense of an inordinate attraction for their bodies and the larger corporeal universe. In what follows, I draw mainly upon the treatise *On First Principles* to elucidate the key details in Origen's sweeping drama of human minds and their position between these two worlds. Thereafter, I will discuss several passages in which he claims that minds journeyed toward the incorporeal God along the path of scriptural study.

THE ORDERED (AND DISORDERED) MIND

The theme of the opening chapter of *On First Principles* is God the Father and what sort of existence God enjoys. Here, as elsewhere in his writings, Origen stresses that God is *not* corporeal, a position he regards as faulty, though some within the Christian sphere entertain it.[16] Even though much of the language and imagery in the Christian Scriptures suggests that God is, or has, a body, Origen insists that a proper reading of these disputed texts confirms that God is actually incorporeal.[17] How, then, does God exist? "God therefore must not be thought to be any kind of body, nor to exist in a body, but to be a simple intellectual existence,"[18] or, as he says a few lines later, "Mind."[19]

This fundamental assertion about God's identity leads to another of Origen's oft-repeated theses about how God is (and is not) known by humans. There are two basic ways in which humans perceive: either through their five bodily senses or through the "sense of mind" [*sensus mentis*].[20] Each of these six senses is yoked, as it were, to its own particular object. In the former set, sight is associated with color, shape, and size; hearing is tied to sound; smelling to vapors; taste to flavors; and touch to hot and cold, rough and soft. Yet when it comes to the "sense of mind," this is far superior to the former senses in that it has for its object intellectual substances. "To see and to be seen"—and as he

---

[16] The theme of God's incorporeality is a recurring motif in Origen's theology: see PA pref.8; Hom Gen 3.1–2; Comm Jn 13.123–150; CC 2.71, 3.40, 4.37, 6.69–6.70, 7.27, 8.49; PE 23.3. Origen criticizes the anthropomorphic account of God that he finds in Melito of Sardis (Gen Frg/*PG* 12.93A), in Gnostic writings (PA 2.4.3), among the *simpliciores* (PE 23.1), in Celsus (CC 6.62–64), and even among some Jews of his day (Hom Gen 3.1).

[17] See PA 1.1.1–4 where Origen contests the interpretations of numerous passages in the Old and New Testaments that suggest God is corporeal. A similar discussion of biblical passages occurs at Comm Jn 13.123–150 and CC 6.70.

[18] PA 1.1.6/GK 110, 21.10–11. Also see CC 6.69.

[19] PA 1.1.6/GK 110, 21.13–14. Also see CC 4.54 and 4.75 for similar assertions about God, as well as the passages in Scripture that clearly support this contention, briefly listed and discussed at PA 1.1.8.

[20] PA 1.1.7/GK 114, 24.3–116, 24.21.

elsewhere adds, to hear and be heard, to smell and be smelt, to taste and be tasted, to touch and be touched—"is a property of bodies; to know and to be known is an attribute of intellectual existence."[21]

Since God is not a body, it follows that God is also not perceived through the five bodily senses. God, the supreme Mind, is known, rather, through our minds. This is because "there is a certain affinity between the mind and God, of whom the mind is an intellectual image, and that by reason of this fact the mind, especially if it is purified and separated from bodily matter, is able to have some perception of the divine nature."[22] Origen is even more evocative in the concluding paragraphs of *On First Principles* where he argues that traces of the divine image in humans are not to be found in their bodies, but rather in their minds, on the basis of which they enjoy "a kind of blood-relationship with God [*consanguinitatem quandam . . . ad deum*]."[23] To stress his conviction that the mind is the superior faculty, that it is immortal and intellectual, not mortal and corruptible, and that it has God the divine Mind as its highest object, Origen can call this intellectual sense the "divine sense [*sensum divinum*]."[24]

While he is quick to qualify that our minds are inadequate to God—God "is far and away better than our thoughts about him"[25]—he does not think we are completely incognizant of God. Our minds are able to have some perception of God, however dim, if only because, as we saw above, they are derived from, and thus bear some similitude to, this divine mind. Yet one of the obstacles that hinders the mind's perception of God can be traced back to this mind's prelapsarian state. At several junctures in *On First Principles* Origen revisits the question of how rational minds in their original disembodied state of divine contemplation fell away from this splendid activity. His hypothesis about the primordial fall consistently returns to the themes of the mind's loss of interest in God, its negligence, or even laziness. "But sloth and weariness of taking trouble to preserve the good, coupled with disregard and neglect of better things, began the process of withdrawal from the good."[26] Earlier in this work he likens this act of negligence to someone who studies geometry or

---

[21] PA 1.1.8/GK 118, 26.2–4.

[22] PA 1.1.7/GK 116, 24.18–21.

[23] PA 4.4.10/GK 818, 363.29–30. For other clear passages on the mind's (and not body's) perception of God, see PA 2.4.3, 4.4.9; On Martyr. 47; CC 7.33.

[24] PA 1.1.9/GK 120, 27.6–14 and borrowing from Prov 2:5 ("You shall find a divine sense"). Also see Hom Lev 3.7.2; PA 1.1.7, 2.4.3, 4.4.10. This "divine sense(s)" is the same as the "spiritual sense(s)." Origen often argues against the literalist reading of those biblical passages that suggest God is literally "seen," "heard," "tasted," etc. These are, rather, references to spiritual sight, hearing, and taste, i.e., to the mind's perception of God. See esp. CC 1.48, 7.34; Comm Song of Songs 1/GCS 8, 104.22–05.32, 107.1–11.

[25] PA 1.1.5/GK 106, 20.8–9. On God's incomprehensibility also see PA 1.1.5/GK 108, 20.19–23 and CC 6.17–18.

[26] PA 2.9.2/GK 404, 165.27–28.

medicine. If such a person has been thoroughly trained in these disciplines so as to master them, it surely will not happen that he falls asleep with this mastery, only to wake up without it. "If, however, he loses interest in these exercises and neglects to work, then through this negligence his knowledge is gradually lost, a few details at first, then more, and so on until after a long time the whole vanishes into oblivion and is utterly erased from his memory."[27] So it is with minds in their prelapsarian states: with the exception of Jesus' soul that clung in "loving affection" to God,[28] they have all fallen away in varying degrees from this activity of contemplation.[29] Prelapsarian apathy toward God continues to color these minds after their fall. Indeed, this state of distracted focus on God is exacerbated by the fact that, after the fall, minds have become embodied and reside in a vast corporeal universe.[30] This universe is certainly good, since it derives from the good Creator.[31] However, it too easily becomes a source of distraction from God as minds become inordinately attracted to it, i.e. attracted to it for its own sake, instead of ascending through and beyond it to its Creator.[32]

With this corporeal obstacle to the contemplation of God, Origen signals one of his cornerstone spiritual doctrines. He repeatedly dichotomizes human conduct into two antagonistic impulses.[33] On the one hand, there is the negligent mind, inattentive to God and enamored by the "world," "bodies," or "flesh and blood"; on the other hand, there is the attentive mind "purified" and no longer "associated" with this corporeal realm, directing its energies to spiritual, intellectual, or divine matters.[34] This dichotomy pervades Origen's thought. So, for instance, in *On First Principles* he tellingly divides all human occupations into these two categories. Most people have as their sole interest "bodily experiences" and "the pleasures and lusts of the body";[35] a far smaller number, however, pursue loftier interests beyond the body, namely, the study of wisdom, knowledge, and truth. So, Origen exhorts, "if there be a man who can discern something better than these activities, which appear to be connected with the body, and can give diligent attention to wisdom and

---

[27] PA 1.4.1/GK 184, 63.22–186, 63.26.

[28] PA 2.6.3.

[29] Other texts on this loss or falling away: PA 1.3.8, 1.4.1, 1.6.2, 1.8.1, 1.8.2, 1.8.4, 2.6.3, 2.8.4, 2.9.2, 3.3.5, 3.5.5. Much more on Origen's protological thought in the section "In the beginning" in Chapter 10 below.

[30] PA 1.6.2, 1.7.1, 1.8.4, 2.1.1, 2.9.3, 2.9.6.

[31] PA pref.1, 1.1.6, 4.1.7.

[32] See esp. PA 1.1.6.

[33] For more on this dichotomous portrayal of the Christian life, see esp. E. Schockenhoff, *Zum Fest der Freiheit: Theologie des christlichen Handelns bei Origenes* (Mainz: Matthias-Grünewald, 1990), 239–251.

[34] PA 1.1.7/GK 116, 24.20. The language of purity abounds: PA 1.1.5; CC 6.17, 6.69, 7.33, 7.45; on association with bodies: PA 1.1.5; CC 6.17, 7.45; On Martyr. 47.

[35] PA 2.11.1/GK 438, 183.18–20.

knowledge, he will undoubtedly direct all his efforts towards studies of this sort, with the object of learning, through inquiry into truth, what are the causes and reason of things."[36]

As he does in this passage, Origen usually casts the mind's two interests as mutually exclusive: to the extent that the mind is oriented to the world, it is not directed to higher things; conversely, to the extent that the mind is committed to an examination of spiritual affairs, it has left behind material preoccupations.[37] Thus, for instance, in *Against Celsus* he clarifies for his interlocutor what the church's teachers strive to impart:

> See here how he [i.e. Celsus] ridicules our teachers of the gospel who try to elevate the soul in every way to the Creator of the universe and who show how men ought to despise all that is sensible and temporary and visible, and who urge them to do all they can to attain to fellowship with God and contemplation of intelligible and invisible things, and to reach the blessed life with God and the friends of God.[38]

Or again, in the midst of his discussion of the divine or spiritual senses in his *Commentary on the Song of Songs*, Origen juxtaposes the two competing realms that can occupy the mind's attention, and privileges one of these:

> But to those who follow the leading of their subtle spiritual sense and perceive that there is greater truth in the things that are not seen, than there is in those that are seen, and that the things invisible and spiritual are closer to God than are the bodily and visible...they recognize that this is the way of understanding truth that leads to God.[39]

In passages such as these, Origen spells out the mind's basic moral dilemma between succumbing to the world or directing its attention to God. It only follows, then, that it is a mark of progress or advance in Christianity when this mind transforms its interests away from the distractions of the world to loftier intellectual and spiritual matters. So, for example, in his *Homilies on Numbers*, Origen exhorts his congregation in Caesarea to embark upon their journey to God, leaving behind the "vanities of the world" and "earthly things" in the quest for virtue. Moses composed an allegory when he wrote of the stations that the Hebrews traversed in the wilderness, signifying by these stations the figurative markers along the Christian journey. He did this,

---

[36] PA 2.11.1/GK 440, 183.23–26. Also see PA 1.4.1 where learning and study are presented as the proper response to the temptation to neglect contemplating God.

[37] Origen often cites Pauline texts such as the following when he dichotomizes these two trajectories of human interest: "a law in our members fighting against the law of our mind and leading us captive in the law of sin" (Rom 7:23); "You are not in the flesh but in the spirit if the Spirit of God dwells in you" (Rom 8:9); or "the flesh lusts against the spirit and the spirit against the flesh and these are contrary to one another" (Gal 5:17) (see, for example, Hom Gen 7.2).

[38] CC 3.56/SC 136, 130.1–7. Also see CC 3.59–62 and 7.39; PA 1.1.7, 2.11.1, 2.11.7, 4.4.10.

[39] Comm Song of Songs 1/GCS 8, 106.19–25. For other similar passages, see Hom Lev 11.1.4–7; PA 1.4.1.

so that we may prepare ourselves for this way [that leads to the kingdom of God] and, by considering the journey that lies ahead of us, we may not allow the time of our life to be ruined by laziness and negligence. Otherwise, while we linger in the vanities of this world and take delight in each of the sensations that come to our sight or hearing or even to touch, smell and taste, the days may slip by, the time may pass, and we shall not find any opportunity for completing the journey that lies ahead ... Thus, we are making a journey, and the reason we have come into this world is so that we may pass "from virtue to virtue" [cf. Ps 83:8], not to remain on the earth for earthly things ... [40]

Elsewhere Origen discusses progress in Christianity in a similar way. In his fourth *Homily on Psalm 36* he comments on the verse: "The steps of a man are guided by the Lord" (Ps 36:23). Origen explains to his congregation that the steps in question are the "stages of progress" people make as they move toward virtue and, ultimately, the knowledge of God.[41] As people embark on this journey their first steps take them past the "place of wickedness" so that they can ultimately "see a great sight." "For no one who is still in the midst of wickedness and who has not stepped around or bypassed it will be able to gaze fully at the great sight of the hidden things of God, which is to say Knowledge and Wisdom. It is a great sight, when God is seen by a pure heart [cf. Matt 5:8]."[42] Progress in Christianity is marked by the mind's movement away from vice and corporeality, toward virtue and the contemplation of the living God.

I have outlined in some detail the contours of this larger drama of embodied minds and their competing objects of affection, since this is the setting in which Origen locates the life of scriptural study. Those who commenced the examination of Scripture signaled that they were leaving behind distracting affairs of the world and turning their attention to the God who had disclosed himself in Scripture.[43] There are a number of passages where Origen explicitly positions the interpretation of Scripture within this loftier way of life. In his eleventh *Homily on Leviticus*, for instance, he comments on the verse: "Be holy as I am also holy" (Lev 20:7). Those who are unholy mire themselves in "secular affairs," live "carnally," and are occupied with "mundane affairs"; they are involved in "earthly deeds" and the "desire of the flesh." On the other

---

[40] Hom Num 27.7/GCS 7, 265.10–20.

[41] Hom 4.1 Ps 36/Prinzivalli 166.27–32. For other passages where progress in Christianity is described as a traversal of stages, see Hom Gen 1.7; Hom Lev 1.4.3; Comm Song of Songs prol.; Comm Matt 12.37–38; PA 1.3.1–8, 2.7.3, 3.3.3, 4.2.4; CC 2.4, 4.16, 6.10, 6.68; Pascha 18. On this theme more generally, see esp. G. Gruber, *ZΩH—Wesen, Stufen und Mitteilung des wahren Lebens bei Origenes* (Munich: M. Hueber, 1962).

[42] Hom 4.1 Ps 36/Prinzivalli 168.43–47. For similar passages about the mind's interest in God serving as a marker for growth in Christianity as it leaves behind a fixation with earthly affairs, see PA 2.11.7, 4.4.10.

[43] Much more on encountering God through the study of Scripture in Chapter 8 below (esp. the sections "Divine aid" and "Prayer"), as well as on the larger issue of Scripture as the instrument or vehicle through which God communicates with humans in Chapter 9.

hand, those who are holy are set apart, avoiding such dishonorable activities as they devote themselves fully to God.[44] One way they do this, Origen insists, is through scriptural study: in the church "that one is set apart and separated 'who meditates on the Law of God day and night' [Ps 1:2] and who 'exceedingly desires his precepts' [Ps 111:1]."[45]

There are other passages written to similar effect. In his third *Homily on Exodus* Origen comments on Moses' commission to tell Pharaoh to let the Hebrews travel three days' journey into the wilderness to worship God (Ex 3:18). Moses, the allegorical Origen insists, did not simply lead God's people out of Egypt ages ago; he does so even now when, through his writings, he directs God's people out of their world, the new Egypt, to a new Sinai. This new exodus transpires when the words of Moses "stir a soul to the service of God, invite it to depart from the world, to renounce all things which it possesses, to give attention to the divine Law and to follow the word of God."[46] Here Origen's familiar contrast of human conduct into two competing impulses clearly surfaces. Those who wish to serve God on the new Sinai abandon Egypt: they depart from the world, renounce all their possessions, and direct their attention to worthy matters, which includes the study of the divine law.

Origen revisits this theme later in his twelfth *Homily on Exodus* where he explains with particular clarity how the diligent study of Scripture replaces a disordered attention to the corporeal world. Here he is commenting at length upon Paul's dictum in 2 Corinthians that those who "turn to the Lord" have the veil over their minds removed when they read the law (2 Cor 3:14–16). Before explaining what a mind "turned to the Lord" means, Origen explores what "turning away" could signify. In what follows he enumerates the ways in which the mind turned away, the worldly mind, fails to embark upon the diligent study of Scripture:

> Everyone who is occupied with common stories when the words of the Law are read is turned away. Everyone who is concerned about affairs of the world, about money, about profits "when Moses is read" [2 Cor 3:15] is turned away. Everyone who is tied up with concerns for possessions and distracted by the desire for riches, who is zealous for the glory of the age and honors of the world is turned away. But he also is turned away who appears to be a stranger to the attitudes we have just mentioned; who stands and hears the words of the Law intent both in countenance and eyes, but wanders in his heart and thoughts.[47]

So what does it mean, Origen continues, to be turned *to* the Lord? He answers: "If we turn our backs on all these things and give attention to the word of God with zeal, actions, mind, and care; if 'we meditate on his Law day and night'

---

[44] Hom Lev 11.1.4–5.   [45] Hom Lev 11.1.5/GCS 6, 448.9–10.
[46] Hom Ex 3.3/GCS 6, 168.14–17.   [47] Hom Ex 12.2/GCS 6, 263.11–18.

[Ps 1:2]; if, all things having been disregarded, we devote ourselves to God, if we are exercised in his testimonies, this is to 'turn to' [2 Cor 3:16] the Lord."[48] In this homily Origen identifies the mind converted to the life of careful scriptural study as the mind simultaneously converted away from the distractions of the corporeal world. The exegetical life is a life that has made progress in Christianity.[49]

Before turning to the next section of this chapter, it is important to observe once again how Eusebius' biography of Origen distinctly echoes what his subject says here about biblical scholarship and the mind's competing interests. There are, in fact, *two ways* in which Eusebius presents the young Origen's commitment to scriptural study as the abandonment of the distractions of the corporeal world. Eusebius writes that when Origen received increasing numbers of students in Alexandria looking for "instruction in the faith" and "divine subjects," he found it progressively difficult to continue his work as a professional teacher of Greek literature.[50] As his biographer presents it, Origen faced a dilemma: to continue dividing his attention between his professional and ecclesiastical duties, or to opt solely for the latter. Origen ultimately decided to devote himself more fully to Christianity, since he "considered the teaching of literature inconsistent with the study of divine subjects; not hesitating, he broke these things off as useless, even his school of literature as a hindrance to sacred learning."[51] It is significant that on the heels of this decision to give up his professional school of literature, Eusebius says that Origen "gave himself to the study of the Divine Scriptures" (presumably the core of his curriculum in Alexandria).[52] By sequencing these events in his narrative in such a manner, Eusebius strongly intimates that Origen's renunciation of teaching secular literature was a precondition for commencing a life of serious scriptural study. In other words, already in Origen's own life, he experienced a version of the dilemma that we have discussed above. Would he opt, on the one hand, for a prolonged engagement with "worldly" literature that inevitably took time and energy away from the study of Scripture, or, on the other hand, would he choose to devote himself extensively to scriptural scholarship at the expense of his former career?[53]

Yet as we have also seen above, Eusebius presents Origen's newfound commitment to scriptural study as itself accompanied by a series of additional

---

[48] Hom Ex 12.2/GCS 6, 263.18–22.

[49] For other passages where this sort of claim about biblical scholarship is made, see Hom Gen 16.4; Hom Lev 11.1.4–7; Hom Ez 3.7.1; Comm Rom 7.17.4; PA 1.4.1.

[50] Eusebius, HE 6.3.1, 6.3.8.

[51] Eusebius, HE 6.3.8/GCS 9.2, 526.15–19—transl. emended.

[52] Eusebius, HE 6.3.9/GCS 9.2, 526.26–27.

[53] Perhaps Origen himself briefly hints at this dilemma in his preface to *On First Principles*, where he says he gave up the search for truth among "Greeks and barbarians" and sought it, instead, from Jesus Christ and his teaching in Scripture (PA pref.2).

renunciatory practices (repudiating worldly possessions, food, clothing, sleep, and sex).[54] It is highly unlikely that Origen saw these practices as unrelated to his renunciation of his professional school. Just as his abandonment of the distractions of this school served as a *prior* condition for serious scriptural study, so did his relinquishment of the distractions of food and sleep in particular serve as an *ongoing* condition for his careful nightly examination of Scripture. Scriptural study was always in competition with some other activity or distraction. Eusebius' narrative strongly intimates, then, that when Origen spoke of scriptural study occurring within the drama of the mind's competing interests, he was also voicing an episode from his own biography.

ADVANCING FROM FAITH TO REASON

The conversion to a life of scriptural study was, then, a distinguishing feature of the advanced, or advancing, Christian. Within Origen's vision of the mind and its competing interests, such an activity signaled a departure from less promising pursuits to a burgeoning devotion to God, as the mind slowly made its way back to the divine contemplation it had once enjoyed. However, this account of the mind and its battling interests was not Origen's only barometer for gauging commitment to Christianity. As important as an interest in loftier matters was, what also mattered was *how* the mind pursued this interest. Were people content with simply accepting from their priests and teachers a straightforward account of Christian doctrine, or did they progress to a first-hand and penetrating examination of this doctrine? Origen often spoke of this sort of spiritual growth as a movement from "faith" to "reason." Scriptural scholarship was relevant to this movement since it was one of the privileged ways Christians could pursue rational activity: those who left behind an unquestioning acceptance of others' interpretations of Scripture and decided to examine it carefully for themselves gestured their commitment to a life of reason within the church, one of the hallmarks of advanced Origenian Christianity.

It is important to note at the start that the distinctions Origen drew between faith ($\pi i \sigma \tau \iota s$) and reason ($\lambda \acute{o} \gamma o s$, and cognate terms such as $\gamma \nu \tilde{\omega} \sigma \iota s \, \acute{\epsilon} \pi \iota \sigma \tau \acute{\eta} \mu \eta$, $\sigma o \phi \acute{\iota} a$) were vexingly fluid. This is due in large measure to two different understandings of faith that he entertained.[55] In some contexts, "faith"

[54] HE 6.3.9–12.

[55] For brief yet instructive overviews of faith according to Origen, see D. Lührmann, s.v. "Glaube," in *RAC* 11 (1981): 91–94 and L. Perrone, s.v. "Fede/Ragione," in *Origene: Dizionario. La cultura-il pensiero-le opere*, ed. A. M. Castagno (Rome: Città Nuova, 2000), though note that the definition of faith at *PG* 12.1576C is incorrectly cited in this latter article—faith is an "assent" ($\sigma \nu \gamma \kappa a \tau \acute{a} \theta \epsilon \sigma \iota s$) and not a "condescension" ($\sigma \nu \gamma \kappa a \tau \acute{a} \beta a \sigma \iota s$). Other literature on faith (and its relationship to reason): W. Völker, *Das Vollkommenheitsideal des Origenes: Eine Untersuchung*

referred to an intellectual disposition: it was the unstudied, uncritical or second-hand assent to the truthfulness of a teaching, be it Christian or any other. In his response to Celsus, for example, Origen insists that for Christians "it is far better to accept doctrines with reason and wisdom than with mere faith [μετὰ λόγου καὶ σοφίας ... ἤπερ μετὰ ψιλῆς τῆς πίστεως]."[56] This sort of faith was also practiced outside of Christian circles. Particularly illuminating is Origen's response to Celsus' critique that Christians merely accept, without any further investigation, the truthfulness of their teachings and Scriptures. Origen replies that this sort of faith is just as much a characteristic of philosophers as it is of Christians. When people join a particular philosophical school, it is not because they have first listened to all the arguments made for and against the philosophers who represent each of the schools. Rather, a pupil joins a school because "he believes [τῷ πιστεύειν]" one school or teacher is better than the rest: it is "by an unreasoning impulse [ἀλλ᾽ ἀλόγῳ τινί ... φορᾷ]" that people become Stoics, and not, say, Platonists.[57] Origen described such faith as "irrational and unlearned."[58]

Not surprisingly, when he spoke of faith in this way, his tone was usually critical. He relegates this act of faith in Christian circles to the simpler: "we accept it as useful for the multitude."[59] Knowledge, on the other hand, is found among the advanced, who have left faith behind: they "know how to advance beyond mere faith" to possess knowledge, wisdom and reason.[60] In Origen's writings, where "faith" signifies unexamined assent to the truth of Christianity's teachings, the goal for the Christian is to replace or overcome it with a studied, rational assent to these teachings.

There are, however, passages where Origen's account of faith is unmistakably different. "Faith" is an assent to the truthfulness of Christian teaching *without implying* anything about whether this assent is rational or not. This understanding is expressed in a famous definition that surfaces in the *Commentary on John*: "For faith is, properly speaking, the acceptance with the

---

zur Geschichte der Frömmigkeit und zu den Anfängen christlicher Mystik (Tübingen: J. C. B. Mohr, 1931), 77–85; H. Crouzel, Origène et la "connaissance mystique," 444–450; U. Wickert, "Glauben und Denken bei Tertullian und Origenes," Zeitschrift für Theologie und Kirche 62 (1965): 153–177; M. Harl, SC 302, 64–65, 147–148; T. Heither, "Glaube in der Theologie des Origenes," Erbe und Auftrag 67 (1991): 255–265; C. Reemts, Vernunftsgemässer Glaube: Die Begründung des Christentums in der Schrift des Origenes gegen Celsus (Bonn: Borengässer, 1998).

[56]   CC 1.13/SC 132, 110.23–25.

[57]   CC 1.10/SC 132, 102.14–15. Also see CC 3.24 on the function of belief in the Asclepius cult.

[58]   Comm Jn 5.8/GCS 4, 105.16–17. Also see CC 1.10. Along similar lines, the noun πίστις is often qualified derogatorily by the adjective ψιλή ("mere"): see CC 1.9/SC 132, 100.32; 1.13/SC 132, 110.25; 3.33/SC 136, 78.14; 4.54/SC 136, 324.43. Moreover, δόξα ("opinion") is a synonym for faith, as at CC 6.40/SC 147, 274.10–14 where Origen takes over Celsus' language approvingly.

[59]   CC 1.10/SC 132, 102.2–3.

[60]   CC 3.33/SC 136, 78.12–14. Also see PA pref.3, CC 7.46, and Comm Jn 13.352–362 where Origen tends to see faith and reason as mutually exclusive, the former belonging to the simpler, the latter to the more advanced. On this topic, see esp. G. af Hällström, Fides simpliciorum, 11–42.

whole soul of that which was believed at baptism."⁶¹ "Faith" so understood is not something that demarcates simpler Christians from the more advanced, but rather something that binds them to one another, since both accept the truthfulness of Christian teaching. Yet at the same time, the simpler and advanced hold this faith differently. Later in his *Commentary on John*, Origen distinguishes between those with partial and full faith in the church's rule, the latter practicing it more rationally since it is faith they have "without doubt" (ἀδιστάκτως) and "with certainty" (βεβαίως).⁶² Even more clearly in *Against Celsus*, Origen admits the simple believe (ἀλόγως), but there are also advanced Christians, that is, "those of us who attempt to believe μετὰ λόγου."⁶³ Indeed, for Origen, advancement in Christianity can even be described as a faith increasingly fortified with reason.⁶⁴

When Origen understands faith this second way, the goal for a Christian is not *to replace* it with reason (as with the first definition, when it is *per definitionem* irrational), but rather *to bolster* it by supplementing it with first-hand inquiry into what is already believed or held as true. Thus comments like, "Let us attempt to strengthen our faith with reason,"⁶⁵ are not that uncommon. Along the same lines, Origen agrees with Celsus' claim, "that it is necessary not simply to believe but also to supply a reason for the things one believes."⁶⁶ Or again: "Now there is a great difference between knowing that takes place alongside believing, and only believing."⁶⁷ According to this definition of faith, it is something assigned to both the simpler and advanced Christians, the latter distinguishing themselves from the former because they have supplied their assent to Christian teaching, their belief, with reasons for accepting it as true.

While there are ambiguities, then, surrounding Origen's use of "faith," these terminological vicissitudes should not obscure how, for him, the movement from simpler to more advanced Christianity was consistently a movement toward a more personal and profound encounter with Christian teaching. The simpler assented in an unexamined manner to this teaching, usually on the strength of someone else's authority; the advanced, however, approached this teaching more "rationally." Rational inquiry for Origen covered a range of activities. It confirmed the truthfulness of what was believed on the basis of

---

⁶¹ κυρίως γὰρ πίστις ἐστὶν κατὰ τὸ βάπτισμα τοῦ ὅλῃ ψυχῇ παραδεχομένου τὸ πιστευόμενον (Comm Jn 10.298/GCS 4, 221.15–16). Also see PA pref.3.

⁶² Comm Jn 32.183/GCS 4, 450.35 and 451.1.

⁶³ CC 3.16/SC 136, 44.21–22.

⁶⁴ Comm Matt 12.6; Comm Jn 10.298–306, 32.169–182; perhaps also Ps Frg/PG 12.1576C where Origen says that faith is the ψυχῆς αὐτεξουσίου λογικὴ συγκατάθεσις, i.e., "the rational assent of the soul endowed with the power of choice."

⁶⁵ PA 4.1.1/GK 668, 292.12–670, 293.1. Also see CC 5.20/SC 147, 62.8–9.

⁶⁶ CC 6.10/SC 147, 200.5–6.

⁶⁷ Comm Jn 19.20/GCS 4, 302.6–7—transl. mine.

careful, personal investigation. This investigation, moreover, often opened additional, expansive vistas of Christian teaching, since it uncovered the deeper rationale—the "hows" and "whys"—of this teaching that easily eluded simpler Christians. Thus, while the terminology that marked this sort of progress in Christianity was unsettled (a reason that had replaced faith, or a faith that was practiced reasonably), for Origen advanced Christians were always exercising their minds in a more vigorous, inquisitive, and studied manner toward Christian teaching.

For our purposes, what is significant is that the interpretation of Scripture was often the epitome of rational activity for Origen, as it afforded the opportunity to investigate Christian teaching in greater depth and on a first-hand basis. One of his most important discussions of faith, reason, and scriptural interpretation occurs early in *Against Celsus* (1.9–13). In this section Celsus accuses Christian leaders of only encouraging uncritical belief in, and not the examination of, Christian teaching. In response to this charge, Origen does not deny that Christian teachers encourage some of their followers who do not have the time or ability to study Scripture, "to believe even without thought [πιστεύειν καὶ ἀλόγως]."[68] It is simply the case that for various reasons not all people can examine the sorts of teachings to which they wish to adhere. But Origen will also insist in his response that not all Christians accept their teachings as true without any further thought. Those Christians who *study Scripture* provide the evidence for the sort of rational inquiry Celsus implores: "For in Christianity, if I make no vulgar boasting, there will be found no less profound study [ἐξέτασις] of beliefs and examination [διήγησις] of the enigmas in the prophets and of the parables in the gospels and of the other myriad events and laws that have a symbolic meaning."[69] The distinction Origen draws here is between simple Christians who assent to Christian teaching in Scripture in an unexamined manner "without thought" through the mediation of a teacher, and advanced Christians who accept it because they have exercised their minds by studying Scripture carefully for themselves.[70]

Later in *Against Celsus*, Origen makes a similar association between the study of Scripture and the life of reason in the church. Responding to Celsus' denial of Jesus' divinity, Origen remarks that this critic was ignoring the evidences for Jesus' divinity found among his followers. These proofs included not simply the "Churches of people who have been helped, the prophecies spoken about him, the cures which are done in his name, the knowledge and

---

[68] CC 1.10/SC 132, 102.3.

[69] CC 1.9/SC 132, 98.16–100.21.

[70] It is also instructive to note in this section of *Against Celsus* (1.9–13) how Origen puns on the noun λόγος. While there are Christians who believe ἀλόγως (CC 1.10/SC 132, 102.3), there are others who are committed to λόγος—a term Origen here employs to designate both rational inquiry, and that which is examined, Scripture (see both uses of the noun in the sentence at CC 1.13/SC 132, 110.23–25).

wisdom in Christ," but also, Origen adds, the "reason [λόγος] which is to be found in those who know how to advance beyond mere faith [ἀπὸ τῆς ψιλῆς πίστεως], and how to search out the meaning of the divine Scriptures. Jesus commanded this when he said 'search the scriptures' [Jn 5:39]."[71] Here Origen makes the claim that advanced Christians actually examine Scripture for themselves, and interestingly, buttresses this assertion by juxtaposing two rationale for scriptural study: this study exemplifies a reason transcending mere faith, and it also fulfills Jesus' command, mentioned earlier in this chapter, to "search the Scriptures."

We can highlight one final passage where Origen associates the examination of Scripture with the movement toward a more intelligent Christianity. In the preface to *On First Principles,* he acknowledges debate among professing followers of Jesus about how to interpret Scripture well. To adjudicate these sometimes-competing interpretations, a reliable guide for interpretation is needed. Origen proposes that such a guide can be found within the "tradition of the church and the apostles" which offers a "definite line and unmistakable rule."[72] This rule, he continues, can be traced back to the apostolic preaching in Scripture. The apostles delivered indispensable doctrines in a straightforward manner "to all believers, even to such as appeared to be somewhat dull in the investigation of divine knowledge."[73] These are the articles of the church's rule that are scattered throughout the apostolic writings, and they are "to be believed [*credenda est*]."[74] But advanced Christians, Origen insists, do more than simply accept these as true; they examine the apostolic writings first-hand, pursuing the "hows" and "whys" behind the statements that the apostles deliberately did not disclose. "The grounds of their statements they [i.e. the apostles] left to be investigated by such as should merit the higher gifts of the Spirit and in particular by such as should afterwards receive through the Holy Spirit himself the graces of language, wisdom and knowledge."[75] While the simpler Christians, then, hold a few central apostolic teachings as true, there are also people in the church who have received the "higher gifts of the Spirit" and who studiously inquire into the apostolic writings themselves, uncovering layers of teaching that escape most Christians. In passages such as these from *On First Principles* and *Against Celsus,* we see that one of the privileged ways Origen thought people could practice a "reasonable" Christianity was by devoting themselves to studious inquiry into Scripture. Those who embarked on such inquiry made progress along their Christian journey.

This depiction of scriptural inquiry as a rational activity advances the larger argument of this chapter. I have contended that an all-embracing commitment to scriptural interpretation for Origen helped distinguish simpler from

---

[71] CC 3.33/SC 136, 78.10–16. [72] PA pref.2/GK 84, 8.19, 8.28.
[73] PA pref.3/GK 86, 9.2–4. [74] PA pref.2/GK 84, 8.27.
[75] PA pref.3/GK 86, 9.4–7.

advanced or advancing Christians. This commitment to Scripture mapped in several ways onto the coordinates of the Christian faith. It certainly manifested obedience to Jesus' command to "search the Scriptures," but it also demonstrated the mind's abandonment of the world as it pursued the words of God, and signaled the exercise of reason through a more personal and profound acquaintance with Christian teachings. As several autobiographical and biographical remarks confirm, for Origen, the conversion to a life of scriptural study was not simply a professional decision; it was a religious one, and one he had already made.

In Chapters 4 and 5 I have demonstrated how Origen contextualized two facets of the interpreter's exegetical life within the larger fabric of the Christian faith: the interpreter's expertise, Greco-Roman learning, and approaches to knowledge, as well as the conversion to the life of scriptural scholarship. However, these were not the only facets of the interpreter that Origen located within the larger Christian narrative. He knew that the Greco-Roman philological apparatus could be deployed in any number of ways, since interpreters always embraced guidelines, loyalties, and precedents that tangibly shaped how they examined the scriptural text. Some of these were salutary and others less so. In the next two chapters I will turn to Origen's accounts of his two main exegetical adversaries, the Gnostics and Jews, and demonstrate how his assessment of interpreters in these communities sheds additional light on his portrait of the ideal scriptural interpreter.

6

Boundaries (Part I): Interpretation among the Heterodox

The interpretation of commonly held Scriptures was the principle arena in which Origen contested with his chief religious adversaries, heterodox Christians and the Jews. Since suspect pieties and religious teachings could almost always be implicated in suspect biblical exegesis, we often find Origen constructing an elaborate polemic against the exegetical practices of his two main rivals. This polemic is vital to our topic. By closely scrutinizing what rendered these interpreters less than ideal for Origen, we will at the same time grasp more clearly the contours of his portrait of Scripture's ideal interpreter.

Yet Origen's assessment of interpreters he deemed suspect requires careful examination. He often accused his opponents of reading "according to the letter," and occasionally profiled them simply as "friends of the letter."[1] In one particularly famous passage in *On First Principles*, he argued that his exegetical adversaries continued to produce contentious readings of Scripture, because "Scripture is not discerned according to its spiritual sense, but is understood according to the mere letter."[2] But as I will argue, the suggestion that literalism was the cardinal exegetical deficiency of his rivals is unhelpful, if not misleading. We should not overlook that Origen leveled numerous other criticisms against his opponents' exegesis, not simply that they were occasionally literalists. Moreover, the charge of literalism to modern ears often suggests merely a procedural error on the part of his opponents, whereas, in fact, Origen's most trenchant critique of his two main exegetical rivals was profoundly doctrinal. This will be my central contention in this and the following chapter, devoted respectively to his assessments of heretical Christian and Jewish exegesis. This chapter argues that the boundaries Origen drew between his exegesis and that which flourished among those commonly called "Gnostics" today were

---

[1] See Hom Gen 6.3/GCS 6, 69.5 (*amici et defensores litterae*); 13.3/GCS 6, 116.20–21 (*amici litterae*); PA 2.11.2/GK 440, 184.7 (*litterae solius discipuli*), etc. More pejoratively, "slaves of the letter" (οἱ τῆς λέξεως δοῦλοι) at Comm Jn 10.103/GCS 4, 188.16; 10.276/GCS 4, 217.27–28.

[2] PA 4.2.2/GK 700, 308.9–11—transl. mine.

confined to a handful of theologically problematic readings. In his mind, these readings were accompanied by an uncritical encounter with Greco-Roman knowledge and a recalcitrance toward the church's rule of faith, neither of which ideal ecclesiastical interpreters were to emulate.

A PRELIMINARY NOTE ON TERMS

There were numerous figures and groups in the Christian ambit that Origen counted among his rivals in providing a sound interpretation of the Christian faith. In one of the few surviving fragments from his *Commentary on Titus*, he offers a long list of contentious figures: the trio of Marcion, Valentinus, Basilides (and all their followers), the Sethiani, Apelles, the Ebionites, the Patripassianists, and Cataphrygae.[3] However, it is usually the case that when Origen referred to the "heretics,"[4] those who "profess to believe in Christ,"[5] his "opponents,"[6] or the "heterodox,"[7] he singled out three specific figures: Valentinus, Basilides, and Marcion. Occasionally Origen referred to one or another of these figures (or their movements) individually. But it is more often

---

[3] This fragment from the *Commentary* (where Origen interprets Titus 3:10–11) survives in Rufinus' translation of Pamphilus and Eusebius' *Apology for Origen* 33/SC 464, 80.9–10, 82.23, 84.50; 35/SC 464, 90.2. Other personalities or groups mentioned in Origen's writings include: Heracleon, Elkesites (Eusebius, HE 6.38), the Ophites (Comm Matt Ser 33; Comm Cor 47; CC 6.24–35 and 3.13 where they are mentioned together with the Cainites), Dositheus the Samaritan (PA 4.3.2; CC 6.11), and Apelles (Hom Gen 2.2; CC 5.54; LF/Rufinus). The case of Heracleon is interesting. Origen suspected that he was a Valentinian (Comm Jn 2.100), though he seldom numbered him along with Valentinus, Basilides, and Marcion (a rare instance of this occurs at Comm Jn 6.116). This restraint could very well be due to the fact that he knew one of Heracleon's writings well (he usually did not have such first-hand knowledge of his other opponents' texts) and was not convinced that Heracleon always fit the Valentinian mold. On these figures, see A. von Harnack, *Kirchengeschichtliche Ertrag*, vol. 1, 30–38; vol. 2, 54–81; A. Le Boulluec, *La notion d'hérésie dans la littérature grecque IIe–IIIe siècles*, vol. 2 (Paris: Études Augustiniennes, 1985), 524–545; and for a more general orientation, A. Marjanen and P. Luomanen, eds., *A Companion to Second-Century Christian "Heretics"* (Leiden: Brill, 2005).

[4] οἵ τε ἀπὸ τῶν αἱρέσεων (PA 4.2.1/GK 698, 307.4). For this phrase, also see Hom Jer 5.14.1, 12.5.1; Comm Cor 15, 19, 44; Phil 1.30, etc. Origen uses αἵρεσις in two distinct ways: with little pejorative coloration, to designate various groups or schools of Christians, as in the following passage from *Against Celsus* where he speaks of "sects among the Christians" (περὶ τῶν ἐν Χριστιανοῖς αἱρέσεων) (CC 3.13/SC 136, 36.2). He also uses the term more polemically, to label a group or school that embraced false teaching, i.e., "heresy." On this important term, and how this second use gradually emerged in early Christianity, see esp. A. Le Boulluec, *La notion d'hérésie*, 41ff.

[5] *qui Christo se credere profitentur* (PA, pref.2/GK 84, 8.14). Also see Hom Jd 8.1 where they welcome the "name of Christ."

[6] ὁ ἐξ ἐναντίας (PA 3.1.16/GK 518, 223.14) and οἱ γὰρ ἐπιλαμβανόμενοί (PA 3.1.18/GK 530, 229.9).

[7] οἱ ἑτερόδοξοι (Comm Jn 1.82/GCS 4, 18.24; CC 5.63/SC 147, 170.23–24; PA 3.1.16/GK 520, 224.10–11, etc.).

the case that he envisioned them collectively, since he considered their theologies—or at least their departures from what he considered orthodox teaching—as closely related.[8] As such, he frequently grouped them together, either creating a list on which each was named, or by categorizing them sweepingly (and anonymously) as "heretics" or "heterodox."[9]

On occasion I will speak of this trio and their followers collectively as "Gnostics." I do so advisedly, however, since in the modern scholarship on Gnosticism several significant (and slippery) issues have prompted historians to question how helpful, and perhaps even valid, this category remains.[10] One of the issues concerns the label itself: "Gnostic/Gnosticism." It appears that this label only became a technical term in the eighteenth century to designate a variety of figures and movements from the second and third centuries in the Roman Empire, many with a Christian coloration yet also strong dualistic tendencies.[11] There is a dearth of evidence suggesting that *gnosis* and *gnostikos* (or any other terms for that matter) functioned for the ancients as they do for scholars today, as distinctive labels identifying a particular (and controversial) subset of Christians. No extant writing from someone we would today customarily call "Gnostic" uses the Greek terms *gnosis* or *gnostikos* (or their Coptic equivalents) as self-designating markers.[12] And for our purposes it is important to note also that Origen never labeled his principal adversaries *gnostikoi*.[13]

---

[8] Indeed on only rare occasions did Origen distinguish from one another the theological profiles of the individual heretical figures and movements (e.g. Comm Matt Ser 38 and 46). On this issue, see esp. A. Le Boulluec's discussion "Distinctions entre les erreurs," in *La notion d'hérésie*, 519–542.

[9] For references to each figure in this trio, see Hom Num 12.2; Hom Josh 7.7, 12.3; Hom Jer 10.5.1, 17.2.1; Hom 3.11 Ps 36; Hom 2.8 Ps 37; Hom Ez 2.5, 7.4, 8.2; Comm Matt 12.12; Comm Matt Ser 38; Hom Lk 29.4, 31.3; PA 2.9.5, etc. There are numerous occasions where Origen refers by name to only one or two of these. Marcion is mentioned in Comm Rom 2.10.2, LF/Rufinus and Hom Jd 1.1 (where he is associated simply with the "heretics"); Marcion and Valentinus in Hom Ex 3.2; Hom Ez 2.5; Comm Rom 4.12.1; PA 2.7.1; Marcion and Basilides in Hom Num 9.1.3; Valentinus and Basilides in Comm Rom 8.11.2; Basilides alone in Comm Rom 5.1.27. Sometimes the list of names is longer (Comm Matt Ser 33, 46, 47; see Comm Titus above at n. 3).

[10] See B. Layton, "Prolegomena to the study of ancient Gnosticism," in *The Social World of the First Christians: Essays in Honor of Wayne A. Meeks*, ed. L. M. White and O. L. Yarbrough (Minneapolis: Fortress Press, 1995), 334–350; M. A. Williams, *Rethinking "Gnosticism": An Argument for Dismantling a Dubious Category* (Princeton: Princeton University Press, 1996); and more recently, K. L. King, *What is Gnosticism?* (Cambridge, MA: Harvard University Press, 2003).

[11] *Lampe*, s.v. γνωστικός, II.B.

[12] They deployed other terms, such as "Christians," "pneumatics," and "elect," but not *gnostikoi*. Helpful in this regard: F. Sieger, "Selbstbezeichnungen der Gnostiker in den Nag-Hammadi-Texten," *ZNW* 71 (1980): 129–132; M. Smith, "The history of the term Gnostikos," in *The Rediscovery of Gnosticism: Proceedings of the International Conference on Gnosticism at Yale, New Haven, Connecticut, March 28–31, 1978*, ed. B. Layton, vol. 2 (Leiden: Brill, 1981), 796–807; C. Markschies, *Gnosis: An Introduction*, transl. J. Bowden (London: T. & T. Clark, 2003), 10–11.

[13] There is one passage in *Against Celsus* where the term γνωστικοί appears to mark a particular subset of Christians. Celsus attacks the plurality within Christianity by noting,

At the same time, even if the terms *gnosis* and *gnostikos* were not used in the ancient world as labels to designate a distinctive subset of Christians, they were certainly used descriptively of these Christians.[14] In the case of Origen, he occasionally ascribed the words γνῶσις and γνωστικός to those he deemed to be of dubious Christian lineage, using these terms to denote a particular quality or feature of their Christianity: they practiced an ostensibly "learned" or "knowledgeable" Christianity.[15] However, it is just as important to note that Origen did not use these terms exclusively of groups he considered heretical. While critical of an array of heterodox figures and movements concerned with gnosis, he *also* held out the ideal of true gnosis for his own form of Christianity.[16] For Origen, the terms *gnosis* and *gnostikos* had broad application to a wide spectrum of Christians. They certainly were not reserved as exclusive markers for a distinct subset of problematic Christians.

Nevertheless, on occasion I will use the term "Gnostic," largely as a matter of convenience. In keeping with modern scholarly convention, it will serve as a collective label that designates early Christian figures like Valentinus and Basilides who are thought to have held certain teachings in common. While Origen did not use the term in this way, he too was interested in lumping together many of these same figures (Marcion included) for precisely the same reason: the familial resemblance of several of their teachings.[17] In what follows

"there are some too who profess to be Gnostics." Who precisely Celsus has in mind is not clear (thus it is also not clear if these overlap with those customarily deemed "Gnostics" today). Origen takes his opponent's nomenclature to be referring very broadly to those "who introduce strange new ideas which do not harmonize with the traditional doctrines received from Jesus" (CC 5.61/SC 147, 166.22). This account of the "Gnostics" is curiously vague. It is such a featureless description of these figures that it suggests Origen was not familiar with Celsus' use of the term γνωστικοί. This suspicion is further confirmed, I think, by the fact that while Origen does not correct his opponent's nomenclature, elsewhere he never uses this term as Celsus does, for some distinct group of Christians.

[14] Indeed, there is strong circumstantial evidence from the writings of early Christian heresiologists that their opponents used these terms as self-descriptors. See the review of evidence by M. A. Williams, *Rethinking "Gnosticism,"* 33–43.

[15] See esp. Comm Jn 5.8/GCS 4, 105.4 and 13.98/GCS 4, 240.9. Origen could also apply 1 Tim 6:20 ("the knowledge [γνῶσις] falsely so-called") to them at Hom Jd 1.1/GCS 7, 466.24–25; Comm Matt 12.12/GCS 10, 91.31–92.3; Comm Jn 5.8/GCS 4, 105.12–13, etc.

[16] On γνῶσις as an Origenian ideal for Christians: Comm Cor 2; PA pref.1; CC 3.33. Of course, also recall the previous chapter in which I demonstrated at some length how the life of scriptural interpretation signaled for Origen the reasonable, intelligent pursuit of God.

[17] Whereas contemporary scholarship distinguishes Marcion/ites from Gnostics, such a demarcation usually does not occur with Origen (see n. 9 above). He customarily numbers Marcion and his followers among Valentinus and Basilides since he sees all these parties committing the chief heresy of distinguishing the just God from the good God (Comm Jn 32.190), the Creator of the OT from the saving God of the NT, and as a result, devaluing the OT (Hom Josh 12.3; PA 2.7.1; Comm Rom 2.13.27, etc.). From his perspective all these figures also deny the freedom of rational creatures (Comm Rom 4.12.1; PA 2.9.5, etc.). These are the two issues, for Origen, that bind Marcion to Valentinus and Basilides. Intriguingly, the second of these issues provides the basis for the only expression I have found in his writings that classifies these figures descriptively on the basis of a common teaching: "those who introduce the natures"

I will not take into consideration the writings of Valentinus, Basilides or Marcion. My real concern is with Origen's account of these figures as scriptural interpreters and the light this sheds on his vision of the ideal scholar of Scripture.

ORIGEN AMONG THE GNOSTIC HETERODOX

The triumvirate of Valentinus, Basilides, and Marcion proved to be one of the decisive forces that shaped Origen's ecclesiastical career.[18] While the evidence does not point to overwhelming first-hand contact with their writings or their followers, these nevertheless made a profound impact on him.[19] His autobiographical reflections already confirm this. Lamenting before his congregation in Caesarea how these "heretics" teach that the Creator God of the Old Testament is savage, Origen confesses a rival loyalty: "But I hope to be a man of the Church. I hope to be addressed not by the name of some heresiarch

(Comm Jn 20.54, 20.135, 28.179; PA 1.8.2, 3.1.23; CC 5.61). Compare this with M. A. Williams' suggestion that these groups ought to be labeled "biblical demiurgical," taking his cues from the first theme Origen thought linked this trio of Gnostic theologians, their dualistic account of God (*Rethinking "Gnosticism,"* 51–53).

[18] Though to what extent is a notoriously complex issue. While he seldom expresses a sympathetic view towards them, he certainly shared many positions with them that he would not have deemed controversial (this is acknowledged in varying degrees at Hom Num 9.1.1–7 and CC 3.12–13, 5.61). To what extent Origen's thought was continuous with, and even indebted to, the theology of his Christian opponents has been a matter of debate for over a century. The most recent attempt to sort out the influence of Valentinianism on Origen can be found in H. Strutwolf, *Gnosis als System: Zur Rezeption der valentinianischen Gnosis bei Origenes* (Göttingen: Vandenhoeck & Ruprecht, 1993), 23–24 and esp. part 2: "Die Rezeption der valentinianischen Gnosis bei Origenes," 210–356.

[19] Origen probably encountered followers of Valentinus in Alexandria. His Alexandrian patron Ambrose, for instance, was apparently a follower of Valentinus (Comm Jn 5.8; Eusebius, HE 6.18.1); one of Origen's letters preserved by Eusebius shows him referring to "heretics" as his pupils in Alexandria (HE 6.19.12); Eusebius also refers at HE 6.2.13–14 to the heretic Paul whom Origen met as a young man in Alexandria. Jerome reports that there also existed a Greek dialogue between Origen and a Valentinian by the name of Candidus on whether Christ was an emanation (προβολή) (*Apology against Rufinus*, 2.19). In terms of writings, Origen possessed a copy of Heracleon's *Exegetical Notes on the Gospel of John* (and knew of his followers—see Comm Jn 20.170), tells us he had procured an Ophite cosmological diagram (CC 6.24), and knew the contents of Marcion's New Testament (Comm Rom 10.43.2).

While towards the end of his career he could write that he had "examined not only the doctrines in Christianity" but also "the different views held within it" (CC 5.62), it is nevertheless difficult to assert that Origen had significant immediate contact with these groups and their writings. I say this for two reasons. First, it is noteworthy that with the exception of Heracleon's *Exegetical Notes*, Origen rarely, if ever, cites the texts of those he deemed heterodox. This would be a puzzling oversight if he actually had access to their writings. And second, he tends to offer highly schematic accounts of his opponents' positions with little effort toward articulating distinctive profiles (see nn. 8, 9, and 17 above). These two factors strongly suggest limited first-hand acquaintance with his opponents' writings.

[*ab haeresiarchae aliquo*], but by the name of Christ. I hope to have his name, which is blessed upon the earth. I desire, both in deed and in thought both to be and to be called a Christian."[20] On a number of occasions, Origen envisioned himself not simply as an ecclesiastic who was loyal to his church, but also as this church's ambassador in its dispute with the heterodox.[21]

Invariably, Origen conducted this dispute through the vehicle of biblical scholarship. To appreciate why this was so, it is important to stress how profoundly he saw the plurality within the Christianity of his day as exegetically rooted. Different approaches to the Scriptures explained the emergence of different factions within Christianity. In *Against Celsus*, for instance, he accounted for the diversity of schools within Christianity not primarily in terms of their differing doctrinal commitments, but in terms of what explained these differing commitments: their divergent approaches to Scripture. When Celsus criticized Christianity because it had fractured into multiple sects, Origen coolly responded that any teaching beneficial to life, such as medicine or philosophy, split into factions. As for Christianity, he contended that from its beginning numerous scholars directed their attention to its Scriptures. "The result of this," he continued, "was that they interpreted differently the scriptures universally believed to be divine, and sects [αἱρέσεις] arose named after those who, although they admired the origin of the word, were impelled by certain reasons which convinced them to disagree with one another."[22] We find a similar sentiment in book four of *On First Principles*, this time applied more widely to include both the *simpliciores* within the church, and the Jews without. After spelling out a series of doctrinal deficiencies among Jews, the Gnostic heterodox and the simpler believers in the church, Origen proposes an explanation that accounts for their disparate teachings:

> Now the reason why all those we have mentioned hold false opinions and make impious or ignorant assertions about God appears to be nothing else but this, that Scripture is not understood in its spiritual sense, but is interpreted according to the bare letter. On this account we must explain...what are the ways of interpretation that appear right to us, who keep to the rule of the heavenly Church of Jesus Christ through the succession from the apostles.[23]

---

[20] Hom Lk 16.6/GCS 9, 97.28–98.3.

[21] For other autobiographical statements in which he presents himself as "man of the church [vir ecclesiasticus]" or holder of the church's rule, see Hom Lev 1.1.4–6; Hom Josh 7.6, 9.8; Hom Is 7.3; Hom Jer 5.14.1; Hom Ez 2.2; Hom Lk 16.6; Comm Jn 6.66, 32.183–193; Comm Rom 3.1.18; DH 10.14. Also recall Eusebius' account of the young Origen's stay with a wealthy woman who had entertained a heretic by the name of Paul: "for he [Origen] held, while still a boy, the rule of the Church [φυλάττων ἐξ ἔτι παιδὸς κανόνα ἐκκλησίας], and abominated, as he somewhere expresses it, heretical teachings" (HE 6.2.14/GCS 9.2, 522.29–30). On Eusebius' source for this anecdote, see P. Nautin, *Origène*, 21–24, 34–35.

[22] CC 3.12/SC 136.36.29–33 (see n. 4 above on this use of the term αἵρεσις). Also see PA pref.1–2 and Hom Num 9.1.2.

[23] PA 4.2.2/GK 700, 308.8–16—Butterworth slightly modified.

Passages such as these help explain how, for Origen, biblical exegesis became the main arena in which he contested with his religious adversaries, the Gnostics included.

Several explicit autobiographical comments confirm his loyalty to the church in its dispute with the heterodox, and how this dispute played itself out in the sphere of scriptural scholarship. Two passages from early in his career are of particular interest. In the preface to *On First Principles*, Origen identifies his adherence to the church's rule of faith as an antidote to toxic Gnostic readings of Scripture. He opens his preface acknowledging strongly conflicting interpretations of Scripture within the Christian community, and many on issues of great import. What guideline can the interpreter embrace to avoid erroneous interpretations? Origen proposes that his readers embrace the "definite line and unmistakable rule [*certam lineam manifestamque regulam*]" of the church, "handed down in unbroken succession from the apostles." "We maintain," he underscores, "that that only is to be believed as the truth which in no way conflicts with the tradition of the church and the apostles."[24] Those who adhere to the church's rule of faith, like Origen, have a guideline for scriptural interpretation that steers them clear of the Gnostic exegetical fallacies. We find a similar sentiment in the opening lines of book five of the *Commentary on John*. There Origen speaks with rare candor about how his overarching exegetical project was an expression of his debate with the heterodox who denied common teachings between the Old and New Testaments. He writes:

> But even now the heterodox [τῶν ἑτεροδόξων], with a pretense of knowledge [προφάσει γνώσεως], are rising up against the holy Church of Christ and are bringing compositions in many books, announcing an interpretation of the texts both of the Gospels and of the apostles. If we are silent and do not set the true and sound teachings down in opposition to them, they will prevail over inquisitive souls which, in the lack of saving nourishment, hasten to foods that are forbidden and are truly unclean and abominable. For this reason it seems necessary to me that one who is able intercede in a genuine manner on behalf of the teaching of the Church and reprove those who pursue the knowledge falsely [γνῶσιν] so-called [cf. 1 Tim 6:20]. He must take a stand against the heretical fabrications [κατὰ τῶν αἱρετικῶν ἀναπλασμάτων] by adducing in opposition the sublimity of the gospel message, which has been fulfilled in the agreements of the common doctrines in what is called the Old Testament with that which is named the New.[25]

Origen's vocation of biblical scholarship was at some level a refutation of the scriptural scholarship advanced by the Gnostic heterodox who saw a conflict between the messages in the Old and New Testaments. It should not surprise, then, that the Gnostic heterodox would vividly color his account of the interpreter of Scripture. Their less than ideal engagement with the biblical

---

[24] PA pref.2/GK 84, 8.18–28.   [25] Comm Jn 5.8/GCS 4, 105.4–16.

text often became a foil for Origen's account of the ideal scriptural interpreter. We need to inquire more closely, as a result, into Origen's assessment of the deficiencies in Gnostic exegesis.

GNOSTIC EXEGESIS AND DOCTRINE

Throughout his career, Origen leveled numerous criticisms against the teachings, procedures and piety of the Gnostics, including their scriptural exegesis. As he saw it, they usually did not read Scripture well.[26] A quick survey of his writings shows him directing a variety of criticisms against their approach to scriptural interpretation. He faults, for instance, their literal readings: because they "discern nothing spiritual in these writings, nothing worthy of God, I would say that they now possess only the 'letter that kills'" (2 Cor 3:6).[27] Yet he also criticized them for inadequate *allegorical* interpretations: "If however they interpret spiritually, even with this very spiritual understanding they do not hold to the rule of apostolic truth."[28] He identified, moreover, a range of procedural deficiencies: their text criticism was at times suspect,[29] as was their literary inquiry into an established text.[30] He also charged them with an

---

[26] Origen's interaction with Heracleon serves as the notable exception. Even though Origen suspected that he was a Valentinian (Comm Jn 2.100), he did not object to all of Heracleon's interpretations. In fact, he accepted a good number (Comm Jn 6.115, 6.126, 6.197, 13.59–61, 13.95), agreed to some provided they did not imply a problematic Valentinian position (Comm Jn 13.57–61, 13.63–64), and sometimes offered another plausible interpretation of John's gospel alongside Heracleon's, yet with no announcement of censure (Comm Jn 10.261–262, 13.226). For studies of Heracleon's exegesis, see Y. Janssens, "Héracléon: Commentaire sur l'Évangile selon Jean," *Le Muséon* 72 (1959): 101–151, 277–299; M. Simonetti, "Eracleone e Origene," *VetChr* 3 (1966): 111–141; 4 (1967): 23–64; E. H. Pagels, *The Johannine Gospel in Gnostic Exegesis: Heracleon's Commentary on John* (Nashville: Abingdon, 1973); C. Blanc, "Le Commentaire de Héracléon sur Jean 4 et 8," *Aug* 15 (1975): 81–124; J.-M. Poffet, *La Méthode exégétique d'Héracléon et d'Origène: commentateurs de Jn 4: Jésus, la Samaritaine et les Samaritains* (Fribourg: Éditions Universitaires, 1985); A. Castellano, *La Exegesis de Origenes y de Heracleon a Los Testimonios del Bautista* (Santiago: Pontificia Universidad Católica de Chile, 1998); A. Wucherpfennig, *Heracleon Philologus: Gnostische Johannesexegese im zweiten Jahrhundert* (Tübingen: Mohr Siebeck, 2002) with extensive bibliography.

[27] Comm Rom 2.14.11/Bammel 182, 120–122. Other texts where he criticizes the literal reading of heretics: Hom 5.5 Ps 36; Comm Matt 15.3; Comm Matt Ser 27; Lk Frg 180; Comm Rom 2.13.27; PA 2.4.4, 2.5.1–2, 3.1.15, 4.2.2; Phil 26.4, 27.12.

[28] Si vero spiritaliter intellegant [haeretici], in ipso autem spiritali intellectu apostolicae non teneant regulam veritatis (Hom 4.1 Ps 36/Prinzivalli, 172, 109–111—transl. mine). Also see Hom Lk 16.6; Lk Frg 165; the criticisms of Heracleon's allegories at Comm Jn 6.201, 10.48, 13.115.

[29] On a handful of occasions Origen censures the Marcionites, Valentinians, and perhaps followers of Lucan for altering the text of the gospels (CC 2.27). He accuses Marcion of deleting portions of the later chapters of Romans (Comm Rom 10.43.2; perhaps also Comm Jn 5.7 and Phil 8.1). Note also the reference to Marcion and Apelles altering the gospels and Paul (LF/Rufinus).

[30] For instance, Origen charges Heracleon with disregarding the sequence of biblical passages at Comm Jn 10.223 and 13.102.

assortment of reading vices: they did not read carefully, consistently or attentively, thereby distorting the texts they were examining.[31] There were, moreover, many other occasions when Origen simply registered his disagreement with a particular Gnostic interpretation of Scripture, without attempting to identify a cause, such as those mentioned above, that accounted for how the resulting interpretation had become defective.[32]

It is helpful to keep this panoply of criticisms in mind from the start. It discourages a simplistic reading of Origen's assessment of his opponents' scriptural exegesis: "literalism," for instance, hardly begins to encapsulate the issue, even if there is an occasional passage where he suggests it does.[33] Moreover, the recognition that Origen directed such a profusion of critique against his opponents might lead us to wonder if, perhaps, something simpler and more fundamental lay behind it. It will be my contention that when we parse his kaleidoscopic series of criticisms more closely, examining the larger literary contexts in which these surfaced, a striking pattern emerges. As a rule, Origen was targeting a more basic and deficient *doctrinal current* that ran through Gnostic scriptural interpretation: its philology was deficient when (and only when) it promulgated a teaching at odds with the sort of Christianity Origen represented.

It turns out to be the case that there were two interpretations of Scripture among the Gnostic heterodox that repeatedly preoccupied Origen: a dualistic account of God and a deterministic theory of rational nature. As already noted above, one of the reasons he frequently listed Marcion, Valentinus, and Basilides together as a trio, or grouped them under the umbrella label "heretics," was that he thought they all shared these two positions. For Origen, these two views quintessentially identified where these heterodox differed from his own understanding of Christianity. Concerning the former view, at least as Origen understood it, his opponents entertained a belief in two Gods: the God of the law and prophets on the one hand, and the God of Jesus on the other. The former was the Creator, a draconian figure given to violence and evil, with followers equally prone to these deficiencies. The God of Jesus, on the other hand, was good and perfect.[34] In *On First Principles* Origen offers a quick summary of the sorts of passages his opponents rallied around when they wished to argue for this dualistic view of God:

---

[31] I examine these criticisms in Chapter 8 below (the section "Exegetical virtues") since they are not particular to the Gnostic heterodox—he can direct them against the *simpliciores* and Celsus as well.

[32] As in the statement: "Our opponents, therefore, have not rightly explained the meaning of the passage" (PA 3.1.19), or in Hom Ez 1.11 where they simply "do not understand" the passage in question. Also see similar discussions of Gnostic exegesis at PA 3.1.7–15, 1.8.2; Comm Rom 1.3.1–3, 5.1.27.

[33] See especially PA 4.2.2/GK 700, 308.8–11 (cited above at n. 23).

[34] For a clear discussion of the Gnostic pantheon as Origen understood it, see PA 2.4–5. Other illuminating passages include Hom Lev 13.4.2; Hom Jd 1.1; Hom 5.5 Ps 36; Comm Rom 2.14.11; PA 3.1.16; Phil 1.30.

And those of the heretical groups [Οἵ τε ἀπὸ τῶν αἱρέσεων], reading the passage, "A fire has been kindled from my wrath" [cf. Jer 15:14], and "I am a jealous God, visiting the sins of the fathers to children until the third and fourth generation" [Ex 20:5] and "I repented of having anointed Saul to be king" [1 Sam 15:11] and "I, God, make peace and create evil" [cf. Is 45:7], and in other passages, "There is no evil in a city, which the Lord did not do" [cf. Amos 3:6], and still further, "Evils descended from the Lord upon the gates of Jerusalem" [cf. Micah 1:12] and "An evil spirit from the Lord troubled Saul" [cf. 1 Sam 18:10], and myriads of similar passages like these, have admittedly not dared to disbelieve that these writings are from God, yet believe them to be from the Creator, whom the Jews worship.[35]

It is on the basis of passages like these, he continues, that they introduce notions of an inferior Creator alongside a perfect God: "Consequently they think that since the Creator is imperfect and not good, the Savior came here to proclaim a more perfect God who they say is not the Creator, and about whom they entertain diverse opinions."[36] In his writings Origen repeatedly offers alternative interpretations of passages like those listed above that were read as promoting this pantheon.[37] A significant part of his critique of Gnostic exegesis targeted its doctrine of God ostensibly drawn from the Old and New Testaments.

The second central issue in his polemic with Gnostic exegesis was self-determination (τὸ αὐτεξούσιον).[38] As he presented it, his opponents denied that humans had free will, that is, the capacity to make independent decisions for which God could hold them accountable. Instead, humans possessed pre-determined rational natures, some lost, incapable of receiving salvation, and others saved, incapable of being lost.[39] On this topic as well, Origen knew that there were passages in both the Old and New Testaments that inclined to his opponents' position, "namely, that it is not in our power whether we keep the commandments and are saved or transgress them and are lost."[40] The *locus*

---

[35] PA 4.2.1/GK 698, 307.4–12—Butterworth slightly emended. For another catalogue of difficult scriptural passages, see PA 2.5.1.

[36] PA 4.2.1/GK 698, 307.12–15.

[37] See, for instance, his interpretations of Ex 15:16 (where God is said to "acquire" the Hebrews as his people) at Hom Ex 6.9; Deut 32:39 ("I shall kill and I shall make alive") at Hom Jer 1.16.2–3 and Hom Lk 16.5; Ps 2:5 ("Then shall he speak unto them in his wrath") at PA 2.4.4; Jer 20:7 ("You have deceived me, Lord") at Hom Jer 20.1–4; Jer 13:14 ("I will not regret and I will not spare and I will not pity their destruction") at Hom Jer 12.5.1.

[38] PA 3.1.1/GK 462, 195.8.

[39] For Origen, this teaching was espoused so distinctively by Marcion, Valentinus and Basilides, that he occasionally grouped them together as "those who introduce the natures [οἱ τὰς φύσεις εἰσάγοντες]" (Comm Jn 20.54, 20.135, 28.179; PA 1.8.2, 3.2.23; CC 5.61). Origen's lost treatise, *On Natures*, appears to have been concerned with Valentinian determinism (see R. E. Heine, *Origen: Scholarship in Service of the Church* [Oxford: Oxford University Press, 2010], 127–128).

[40] PA 3.1.7/GK 480, 204.7–9. The theodicy that helped shape his opponents' view of human nature is detailed helpfully by Origen at PA 2.9.5; the biblical verses that suggested their view are listed at PA 3.1.7–8. Origen's own positive account of human freedom is explicated clearly at PA 3.1.1–6.

classicus for his refutation of the Gnostic claim that the denial of a free will had an exegetical basis is found in book three of *On First Principles*. Here Origen explicitly refutes, at some length, half a dozen of the more contentious passages in Scripture that could be read as supporting this position, beginning with the vexing assertion attributed to God in Exodus: "I will harden Pharaoh's heart" (Ex 4:21; 7:3).[41] In this section of *On First Principles* Origen tackles difficult passages from the law, prophets, gospels and apostolic writings, to discredit such an interpretation as best he can.[42] There are several other places where Origen challenged the Gnostic attempt to derive the deterministic theory of natures from Scripture.[43]

A careful examination of the larger settings in which Origen's criticisms of Gnostic exegesis surface demonstrates that he did not criticize their philology in abstraction from the interpretations it produced. Rather, he criticized it when it was marshaled to produce offending interpretations, invariably the two outlined above. So, for instance, in the passage cited earlier from the *Commentary on Romans* where Origen censured a literal exegesis in Gnostic circles,[44] a wider examination of the literary context shows that he had a *specific* literal interpretation in mind: tearing asunder the unity of God, and thus, also, the law from the gospel.[45] Origen was not leveling a general critique against the practice of any and all literal exegesis (which he himself also practiced), but rather a critique against a particularly troubling interpretation that happened to result from literal exegesis. The same pattern holds for other criticisms of his opponents' scriptural interpretations. In his opprobrium of Marcion's text criticism, Origen has Romans 16:25–27 in mind, where the mystery of Christ has been disclosed through the "prophetic Scriptures" according to the command of "eternal God." Marcion illegitimately excised this passage since it challenged his view of the unity of the Scriptures and God.[46] The issue here was not text criticism per se, or even the need to excise an interpolated passage, but the ideological ends this particular text-critical decision served. In the critique of Heracleon's "spiritual level of understanding [κατὰ δὲ τὸ νοούμενον]," Origen obviously did not censure the general

---

[41] PA 3.1.8–14.

[42] See his discussion at PA 3.1.7–14 of Ezekiel 11:19–20 ("I will take away their stony hearts and will put in them hearts of flesh, that they may walk in my statutes and keep my judgments"); Mark 4:12 ("That seeing they may not see, and hearing they may hear and not understand, lest haply they should be converted and it should be forgiven them"); Phil 2:13 ("Both to will and to do are of God"); Rom 9:18 ("So then he [God] hath mercy on whom he will, and whom he will he hardeneth"); Gal 5:8 ("The persuasion is of him that calleth," i.e., and not of us); Rom 9:18–21 ("So then he hath mercy on whom he will, and whom he will he hardeneth," etc.).

[43] The issue of human freedom is a major theme in the Comm Rom: preface from Origen 1, 1.3.1–3, 2.4.7–8, 2.10.2, 4.12.1, etc. Also see Hom Jer 21.12; Comm Matt 10.11; Comm Jn 20.96–127, 135, 168–170, 287ff; 28.179ff, etc.

[44] See n. 27 above.

[45] Comm Rom 2.14.11.

[46] Comm Rom 10.43.1–2.

principle of allegorical exegesis, but rather the particular allegorical interpretation forwarded: according to Heracleon's reading of John 4:22 ("Because salvation is of the Jews") the Jews are "images of those in the Pleroma."[47] As passages such as these demonstrate, what was invariably at stake for Origen in his critique of Gnostic philology was a specifically contentious theological interpretation that could often be traced back to a distinct exegetical move, such as a literal reading, an allegorical exegesis, or a text-critical decision. Indeed, there is additional confirmation for the thesis that what truly mattered for Origen was not exegetical technique, but the theological interpretation it promoted. Very frequently he did not even mention a philological cause, such as literalism, that lay behind a Gnostic exegetical fallacy—he simply criticized the resulting interpretation.[48]

In short, Origen's critique of the exegesis of the Gnostic heterodox was not propelled by his perception of philological weakness per se, but rather by the conviction that doctrinal deficiencies could be sustained by philological decisions.[49] Whether leveling wide-ranging accusations that sought to identify a cause for erroneous interpretations (they were mere literalists, offered unacceptable allegories, edited texts poorly, etc.), or simply objecting to the interpretations themselves, Origen's critique of Gnostic philology converged on the same point: their exegesis was objectionable when it promulgated teachings at odds with the church's, in particular, its accounts of God and human accountability. Inevitably, these two doctrines resided at the heart of his critique of Gnostic scriptural interpretation.[50]

---

[47] Comm Jn 13.115/GCS 4, 243.19–22.

[48] Indeed, very frequently Origen did *not* expressly associate "literal" exegesis with Gnostic exegesis. For instance, see the following criticisms of the Gnostic view of God ostensibly derived from Scripture, where Origen makes *no* explicit mention of literal exegesis: Hom Ex 6.9; Hom Josh 12.3; Hom Jer 1.16.1–3, 12.5.1; Comm Matt Ser 117; Hom Lk 16.4; Comm Jn 13.73–74; Comm Rom 4.4.3, 8.11.4; Comm Eph 2; PA 1.8.2, 2.4.3, 2.5.4, 3.1.9, 3.1.16, 3.1.18; Phil 21.15. This same tendency is even more pronounced in Origen's criticisms of the exegesis that denies humans the power of meaningful choice. In his lengthy discussion of the problem of determinism beginning at PA 3.1.7 he explicitly refutes the Gnostic exegesis of numerous biblical passages, but refers only once to a literal interpretation of a passage that could generate this view (at PA 3.1.15).

[49] His critique of Heracleon's exegesis fits the pattern I have been tracing in this section as well—it is centrally a critique of doctrines ostensibly discovered in Scripture. For instance, when Heracleon's readings clearly agree with Gnostic positions, like the suggestion that the Creator God, or the OT in general, is inferior, Origen charges him with "impious" and "slanderous" interpretations and locates him among the heterodox (Comm Jn 6.108, 6.116, 6.199, 20.358–362). Other Gnostic positions that surface in Heracleon's exegesis include the teaching about determined natures (Comm Jn 13.120–122, 20.168–170), the pleroma (Comm Jn 10.211, 13.67–74), and the woman transformed into a man (Comm Jn 6.111). Only rarely does Origen register his disapproval of Heracleon's interpretations when they are *not* identifiably Gnostic (on John's response to the Pharisees at Jn 1:26, see Comm Jn 6.153; on the temple Jesus was referencing in Jn 2:20, see Comm Jn 10.254–261).

[50] For comparatively rare examples of criticisms not linked to these two teachings, see Origen's critique of the doctrine of metempsychosis, which he attributes to Basilides (Comm Matt 11.17, 13.1; Comm Jn 6.62–66; Comm Rom 5.1.27, 5.9.11); the Valentinians' notion of

EXEGETICAL LESSONS

Yet there were additional features in Origen's heresiological portrait of Gnostic exegesis. He was convinced that more lay behind his opponents' puzzling accounts of God and human nature than sporadic, and usually highly debatable, scriptural texts. Where these aforementioned suspect scriptural interpretations circulated, he maintained that perceptive critics would find two further problems: an uncritical acceptance of erroneous teachings in circulation outside the church, and the rejection of the church's doctrinal guideline, the rule of faith. For Origen these issues were clearly related. When professing Christians turned *against* teachings embodied in the church's rule they were, simultaneously, turning *toward* competing teachings outside the church.[51] By examining both of these deficiencies below, we illumine two important features in Origen's profile of the ideal scriptural interpreter.

Discernment

One of the leitmotifs in early Christian accounts of heresy was that suspect Christian teachings could be traced back to an uncritical dependence upon deficient elements in Greco-Roman intellectual culture.[52] Origen accepted and developed this argument. Novel heretical doctrines found their origins in teachings "foreign" or "alien" to the church.[53] There are those, he writes, who claim to be Christians but "who introduce strange new ideas [οἱ τὰ ἀλλόκοτα ἀναπλάσματα . . . ἐπεισαγαγόντες] which do not harmonize with the traditional doctrines received from Jesus."[54] The Valentinians and Marcionites "introduce heresies foreign [καὶ αἱρέσεις ξένας ἐπεισάγοντες] to the meaning of Jesus' teaching."[55] As we will see below, the point Origen makes in

---

προβολή (emanation) (Comm Jn 20.157–159; PA 1.2.6, 4.4.1); the invisibility and incorporeality of God (PA 1.1.1).

[51] On this relationship between the church's rule and foreign teaching, see the important discussion at Hom Num 20.3.2–3.

[52] For a discussion of this theme in ante-Nicene literature, see esp. A. Le Boulluec, *La notion d'hérésie*. On occasion, Origen voices the extreme view that his opponents derived their ideas from the devil or opposing powers: see Hom 4.4 Ps 36; Hom 5.5 Ps 36.

[53] Hom Ez 7.7; Hom Jer 5.14.1; CC 1.69, 4.2, 5.63, 6.32.

[54] CC 5.61/SC 147, 166.25–27.

[55] CC 2.27/SC 132, 356.13–14. Also see Hom Gen 2.4. It is important to add here that while Origen never wavered in his presentation of heresy as foreign to authentic Christianity, he was not consistent about whether it could be considered a version of Christianity in itself. He usually considered heresy non-Christian—it looked in from the outside. However, there are a handful of passages where he seems to have considered it a distinctive *part* of Christianity, albeit an illegitimate part (see especially CC 3.12 and 5.61–62; perhaps also Hom Num 9.1.2). In other words, while heresy was always foreign to true Christianity, it could either be envisioned as

passages like these is not simply that professing Christians introduced teachings from outside the church, but more specifically, that they introduced teachings that conflicted with or undermined his church's message.[56]

The usual culprits were the Greco-Roman philosophers and poets. Origen often found some way to link these to his Christian opponents, thereby conveying their dubious affinity for one another.[57] For instance, in his seventh *Homily on Joshua* he argues that Valentinus, Basilides, and Marcion went astray because of their dependence upon the "philosophers and rhetoricians," the people who are not of the church, but rather "of this world." Origen's springboard for his claim is the fall of Jericho, and in particular, Achan's violation of the divine decree not to take any objects of value from Jericho (Josh 6:18–19; 7:21). Ever the homilist, Origen inquires into the deeper sense of Achan's theft, wondering if this passage might in some way apply to his audience. He preaches:

> There is much elegance in words and much beauty in the discourses of philosophers and rhetoricians, who are all of the city of Jericho, that is, people of this world. If, therefore, you should find among the philosophers perverse doctrines of a splendid discourse with beautiful assertions, this is the tongue of gold. But beware lest the splendor of the performance beguile you, lest the beauty of the golden discourse seize you. Remember that Joshua commanded all the gold found in Jericho to be an accursed thing. If you read a poet with properly measured verses, weaving gods and goddesses in a very bright tune, lest you be seduced by the sweetness of eloquence, remember: it is a tongue of gold. If you take it up and place it in your tent, if you introduce into your heart those things which are declared by the poets and philosophers, then you will pollute the whole church of the Lord. This the unhappy Valentinus did and Basilides, this also did Marcion. Those persons stole the tongues of gold from Jericho, and they attempted to introduce into the churches sects [sectas] not fitting to us, and to pollute all the church of the Lord.[58]

This allegorical interpretation of Achan's theft finely illustrates Origen's genealogical account of heresy. His contention is that Valentinus, Basilides, and Marcion were to the church what Achan was to Israel: defectors who polluted

---

external to it, or as a subset of Christianity foreign to its true version. For a discussion of this issue, see A. Le Boulluec, *La notion d'hérésie*, 443–452, esp. 451–452. Recall the related discussion of the two senses of αἵρεσις above in n. 4.

[56] This critique that follows serves as the key qualification of Origen's endorsement of Greco-Roman learning, discussed above in Chapters 2 and 4. While he unambiguously approved of this learning when its message harmonized with the Christian faith, this endorsement did not blind him to its perceived shortcomings. See, for example, Hom 3.6 Ps 36; CC 1.2, 3.75, 3.81, 6.2ff where Origen criticizes the Greco-Roman disciplines, and especially the philosophical schools, for falling short of Christianity. For more on this theme, see M. J. Edwards, *Origen against Plato* (Aldershot: Ashgate, 2002).

[57] See Hom Gen 2.4; Hom Josh 18.3; Hom Jd 1.1, 8.1; Hom 3.11 Ps 36; Hom 4.1 Ps 36; Hom Jer 5.14.1, 16.9.1; Hom Ez 7.7; Comm Matt 15.4; CC 6.22–6.38; esp. Eusebius, HE 6.19.12, where he is quoting an otherwise lost letter from Origen.

[58] Hom Josh 7.7/GCS 7, 334.25–335.12.

their respective communities with something foreign. Whereas Achan was prohibited from despoiling Jericho of its literal gold, this trio was to be on guard against the figurative gold of the philosophers and poets, who were "all of the city of Jericho," a symbol of the "people of this world." Yet just as Achan succumbed to the temptation of foreign gold, this trio was beguiled by the rhetorical brilliance of these figures—their "golden discourse"—into accepting "perverse doctrines." Origen tellingly highlights how polytheistic temptations (the "gods and goddesses" of the poets) seduced his opponents, no doubt taking aim at the dualistic account of God in their circles. The result of their temptation was that the church was polluted by the introduction of contaminated foreign doctrines. Origen concludes by warning his congregation not to be similarly beguiled into accepting dangerous teachings that swirl outside the church. Integral to his account of heresy was a critique not simply of its foreign ancestry, but of a foreign ancestry that conflicted with prevailing Christian convictions.

Not surprisingly, the same problem lurked within Gnostic exegesis. There are two illuminating passages where Origen contends that his opponents relied uncritically upon foreign ideologies when they interpreted Scripture. In these passages he makes his point through figurative readings of the rebellions fomented by Korah and Jeroboam against divinely ordained leaders, Aaron and Solomon respectively. Origen seizes upon both of these passages (as he did with the passage about Achan) since they highlighted a situation in ancient Israel that he thought was analogous to the situation of the church in his own day: the rebellions instigated within Israel by these two figures pointed symbolically to the Gnostic rebellion in the church. Moreover, as we will see, in their narrative detail Origen was convinced that both of these passages yielded a promising allegorical interpretation: as these rebellions in ancient Israel betrayed foreign influence, so the heterodox drew upon deficient foreign themes as they mingled them into their interpretations of the church's Scriptures.[59]

In his *Homilies on Numbers*, Origen preaches on Korah's insurrection within the Israelite camp (Num 16). Korah and his allies had challenged the exclusive rights of the Aaronic priesthood. In response, Moses created a trial whereby Korah and his allies, along with Aaron, were to burn incense in their bronze censers before the entrance of the tabernacle. God would choose the lawful priest. According to the narrative in Numbers, God struck down Korah and his allies with fire since they had lit a "strange fire" (cf. Num 26:61) in the bronze censers. Origen elaborates on Korah's sacrilege with an allegorical interpretation. Korah stands for the Gnostics, and the bronze censers, holy appurtenances for worship,

---

[59] Indeed, it is especially noteworthy that Origen goes to some length to argue against the Gnostic heterodox, as he does here, *from the Old Testament* itself. By drawing upon this collection of writings, he was making another trenchant point: that the Old Testament his opponents rejected, actually anticipated, and indeed spoke out against, the very Gnostics who would later reject it.

serve as a "figure of the divine Scripture [*figuram . . . Scripturae divinae*]." What, then, does the "strange fire" that Korah placed in these censers symbolize? "On this Scripture," Origen answers, "the heretics place 'strange fire,' that is to say, by introducing a meaning and an interpretation that is foreign to God [*sensum et intelligentiam alienam a Deo*] and contrary to the truth, they offer not a sweet incense to the Lord, but a detestable kind."[60] The strange fire in the censer symbolizes an interpretation foisted upon Scripture that is strange or foreign to God. Thus, Korah and his allies, foreign to the exclusive privileges of the Aaronic priesthood, represent a heretical exegesis that similarly stands outside the church. And just as Korah introduced "strange fire" to the censers, so these heretical interpreters introduce interpretations of the Scriptures that are foreign or incompatible with them.

A similar, yet more elaborate, account of heretical scriptural exegesis surfaces in Origen's *Letter to Gregory*. Here he explicitly identifies the foreign element in heretical exegesis with the corrupted portions of the Greek intellectual disciplines. As we have already seen in Chapter 2, in this *Letter* Origen proposes a remarkable reordering of the educational system. For Christians like Gregory, the culmination of the antique *paideia* was not Roman law or Greek philosophy, but the scholarly interpretation of his Scriptures that drew upon a philosophical training, and all it presupposed. To buttress this proposal Origen offered an allegorical interpretation of the Exodus. The construction of the tabernacle in the Sinai wilderness from the spoils of Egypt symbolized the discerning retrieval of Hellenistic learning for the purposes of biblical scholarship. However, in the third section of the *Letter* Origen sounds a warning that this *paideia* can also be disruptive to the undiscerning. He emphasizes, thus, the need for a judicious appropriation of Hellenistic learning. Revealingly, Origen makes this point with another liturgical analogy drawn from the Old Testament, likening the unhappy retrieval of Greek learning not to the construction of the tabernacle, but rather to the idolatrous worship promoted later in Israelite history by Jeroboam.[61]

"Divine Scripture knows," Origen writes, "that there was a bad outcome for some who descended from the land of the children of Israel into Egypt. It hints that there will be a bad outcome for some who dwell among the

---

[60] Hom Num 9.1.2/GCS 7, 54.18–23—Scheck modified. For a related passage where Origen distinguishes between interpretations "estranged from God" and those native to the thoughts of God, see Hom Ez 2.2.4.

[61] The Exodus provides the specific link between the two passages Origen allegorizes in this *Letter*. Whereas Egyptian gold was used to construct the tabernacle (symbolizing the productive use of Hellenistic learning), some of this gold had also been used to construct a golden calf (cf. Ex 32:2–4). In the biblical text, Jeroboam alludes to this latter episode when he erects his golden calves in Bethel and Dan: "Here are your gods, O Israel, who brought you up out of Egypt" (1 Kings 12:28). For more on Origen's association of biblical scholarship with worship, see Chapter 9 below (section "Scripture's effects").

Egyptians... after having been trained by the law of God and the Israelitish worship of him."[62] Origen continues with an illustration of one such Israelite who fared badly after dwelling among the Egyptians. He summarizes episodes from the life of Jeroboam who traversed into Egypt only later to return home, erect two golden calves and assume kingship over Israel (thus rivaling the kingship in Judah).[63] So long as Jeroboam resided in Israel, Origen notes, he worshiped God. But when he descended into Egypt, having fled from the "wise Solomon" and the "Wisdom of God," he married the sister of Pharaoh's wife, had a son with her, and raised him among Pharaoh's children. Upon returning to the land of Israel, Jeroboam became an idolater, fabricating golden calves and setting up a rival worship to Jerusalem in Bethel and Dan.

Origen leaves it to his reader to unpack the deeper sense of this passage, though he provides several important clues about how he wishes a number of the details in this episode to be read. The allegory begins to unfold when we notice that the corrupted Jeroboam stands for the heterodox who "beget heretical ideas [αἱρετικὰ γεννήσαντες νοήματα]."[64] As Jeroboam fled Solomon to forge an alliance with Pharaoh's household, so there are figures who leave the church and draw uncritically upon "Egypt," a symbol, Origen notes, of the "learned disciplines of the world [μαθήματα τοῦ κόσμου]."[65] A few lines later Origen specifies that these figures draw upon the worst in these disciplines— "Greek ingenuity"—thus highlighting for his addressee Gregory that he is only

---

[62] LG 3/SC 148, 190.49–54—transl. mine.

[63] Origen mistakenly calls Jeroboam (1 Kings 11:26–12:33) Ader the Idumaean, mentioned a few lines earlier in 1 Kings 11.

[64] LG 3/SC 148, 192.69–73. And there are several other clues as well. Like Jeroboam, the heterodox (1) divide the people of God. The term Origen uses for Jeroboam's "divide" of the nation into two kingdoms is διασχίζω, punning thereby on another sense of the σχίζω word group: "schismatic" (LG 3/SC 148, 190.62). Elsewhere in his writings Origen associates Jeroboam's division or separation of the Israelites with the similar action of the heterodox in the church: see Comm Jn 13.81–82, as well as Hom Ez 3.5–6. Another clue (2) in the *Letter* is that these modern-day Jeroboams have erected their own "imaginations [ἀναπλάσματα]" in Scripture (LG 3/SC 148, 192.69–73). Here, as elsewhere, Origen often describes Gnostic doctrines as "theories," "myths," "inventions," "fictions," or "imaginations." Note the expression, "fabricating mythical theories for themselves [μυθοποιοῦντες ἑαυτοῖς ὑποθέσεις]" (PA 4.2.1/GK 700, 308.2). "The heterodox," Origen writes elsewhere, "do not know what they worship because it is something they have made up, and not truth; it is a myth and [not] a mystery [ὅτι πλάσμα ἐστὶν καὶ οὐκ ἀλήθεια καὶ μῦθος καὶ (οὐ) μυστήρια]" (Comm Jn 13.103/GCS 4, 241.8–9). The noun ἀναπλάσματα is used at PA 4.2.1; three times at Hom Jer 16.9.1 where Origen says the philosophers and Gnostics erect doctrinal idols with the help of their "imaginations"; there is also talk of an "invented God [ἀναπεπλασμένου θεοῦ]" (Phil 23.2). For bringing "inventions" to Scripture, see also Hom 5.5 Ps 36; Hom Ez 2.2.4, 7.7; PA 1.8.2, 3.4.5. Finally, (3) it is noteworthy that Origen claims these modern-day interpreters are like Jeroboam who, "after having been trained *by the law of God*", takes up a new dwelling in the land of Egypt. The reference to "law" is ambiguous, but it too suggests the Gnostic heterodox. Origen could be referring to the typical denigration of the Jewish law among his opponents (see Phil 1.30; Hom Num 27.2), or to their refusal to subscribe to the church's law, i.e. its rule of faith (more on this point below).

[65] LG 3/SC 148, 190.53.

to avoid what is deficient in Greco-Roman learning, and not, in fact, all of this learning.[66] Those who do not avoid these deficiencies become latter-day Jeroboams, the heterodox. Once again, the topos of the Greco-Roman origins of heresy surfaces.

The picture comes into sharper focus when we realize that Origen's allegorical Jeroboams are specifically heretical *interpreters of Scripture*. The literal Jeroboam, he observes, returned from Egypt and perpetrated idolatry at Bethel where he erected one of his golden calves. This is a significant detail for Origen. The etymological meaning of Bethel is "house of God," and thus this town refers allegorically to the Scriptures since this is "where the Word of God dwells."[67] It is here where the heterodox return after drawing upon extra-ecclesial traditions devoid of wisdom: they introduce their fantastical interpretations in the pages of Scripture. There is significance in seemingly every detail of this story for Origen. He notes that Jeroboam also committed idolatry in the region of Dan. Dan, he carefully continues, was "on the frontier district, close to the region of the Gentiles." This geographic locale for Jeroboam's idolatry allows Origen to stress yet again the foreign provenance of dubious heretical scriptural interpretations. While in Dan, Jeroboam was in the vicinity of Gentile territory, and this geographic proximity can be taken as a symbol for modern-day Jeroboams whose interpretations of Scripture reside on another sort of frontier: between the church and those conflicting Greco-Roman traditions that flourish beyond its boundaries.

As we gather from these allegorical interpretations of the episodes concerning Korah and Jeroboam, for Origen the Christian heterodox failed to exercise discernment in their interactions with Greco-Roman learning and, thus, introduced deficient elements into their interpretations of Scripture. Like other Christians in his day, Origen was convinced that the Greco-Roman *paideia* was of ambiguous value. Despite the real danger associated with its shortcomings, this certainly did not serve as a pretext for complete rejection. Rather, interpreters needed to approach the *paideia* critically. One of the

---

[66] LG 3/SC 148, 192.69. Earlier in this *Letter* Origen drops a few additional hints about the inadequacy of the *paideia*. For instance, in the opening section of the *Letter* Origen writes: "For this reason I have prayed that you productively draw from Greek philosophy those things that are able to become, as it were, general teachings or propaedeutics for Christianity, as well as those from geometry and astronomy which will be useful for the interpretation of the holy Scriptures" (LG 1/SC 148, 186.10–188.14—transl. mine). The insinuation is that not everything is able to become valuable or useful for scriptural interpretation. Another clue is given in the second section of the *Letter* when Origen retells the story of the Hebrew plundering of the Egyptians. He stresses that the Hebrews did not plunder indiscriminately, but rather took the very finest of Egyptian wealth: several grades of gold, silver, and clothing, again implying that not everything in Egypt was worth taking for the construction of the tabernacle. For other statements on the limits or deficiencies of Greco-Roman learning, see Hom Lev 5.7.5; Hom Num 20.3.2–3; Hom Jd 2.3; PA 3.3.2; CC 1.2, 3.75, 3.81, 6.5.

[67] LG 3/SC 148, 192.71–74.

principal reasons the Gnostics erred in their reading of Scripture was because they had failed to exercise sufficient discretion in their engagement with this checkered learning. Origen cautioned his addressee Gregory: "And I, having learned from experience, can say that few have taken anything useful from Egypt and have come out from there and prepared objects for the worship of God."[68] Origen called for precisely this sort of discernment toward foreign learning elsewhere.[69]

In his *Homilies on Leviticus*, for instance, he commented upon a stricture in the book of Deuteronomy (21:10–13) about seizing a "woman with a beautiful figure" in warfare. According to this passage, she could only become the warrior's wife if the hair of her head was shaved, her nails pared down, she was dressed in mourning clothes, and allowed to grieve for her lost family. Only after thirty days could she become his wife. Origen offers an allegorical interpretation of this legislation, explaining how interpreters of Scripture are spiritual warriors:

> But nevertheless, I also frequently "have gone out to war against my enemies and I saw there" in the plunder "a woman with a beautiful figure" [cf. Deut 21:10-11]. For whatever we find said well and reasonably among our enemies, or we read anything said among them wisely and knowingly, we must cleanse it also from the knowledge which is among them, remove and cut off all that is dead and worthless—namely all the hairs of the head and the nails of the woman taken from the spoils of the enemy— and so at last make her your wife when she has nothing of the things which are called dead through infidelity . . . For the women of our enemies have nothing pure because there is no wisdom among them with which something unclean was not mixed.[70]

Here Origen identifies himself as the allegorical referent of the deuteronomic warrior. In his regular encounter with the learning of his "enemies" he too chances upon a "beautiful figure." He renders this woman allegorically as the comely figure of what he finds to be "said well" and written "wisely and knowingly." The Septuagint rendering of "a woman with a beautiful *figure*"— γυναῖκα καλὴν τῷ εἴδει—undoubtedly invited Origen to allegorize this woman into what was expressed in an eloquent literary style. The noun εἶδος can designate not simply the figure, shape or physique of a person, but also literary form or style.[71] Origen needs to cleanse and remove what is unworthy from the blemished literature of the Greek philosophers and poets.

Interpreters of Scripture were more than spiritual warriors. They were also allegorical polygamists. The patriarchs sometimes took many wives, Origen

---

[68] LG 3/SC 148, 190.65–192.68—transl. mine.

[69] On this larger theme in early Christian literature, see C. Gnilka, *ΧΡΗΣΙΣ: Die Methode der Kirchenväter im Umgang mit der Antiken Kultur*, vol. 1, *Der Begriff des "rechten Gebrauchs"* (Basel: Schwabe, 1984).

[70] Hom Lev 7.6.7/GCS 6, 390.24–391.11.

[71] S.v. εἶδος, *LSJ*, senses I and II.

notes in his eleventh *Homily on Genesis*, yet they were not teaching men in the church to become literal polygamists. Rather, they were instructing them to multiply in spiritual marriages since "the Scripture designates the progress of the saints figuratively by marriages."[72] One form of saintly progress symbolized by the patriarchal marriages was a growing intimacy with a variety of academic disciplines. Yet just as the Scriptures present the patriarchs taking on multiple wives prudently in their old age, so is this knowledge not to be pursued recklessly or indiscriminately. Origen remarks:

> If we are also in touch with some of these instructions which appear to be on the outside in the world—for example, as the knowledge of literature or the theory of grammar, as geometry or mathematics or even the discipline of dialectic—*and we bring over to our purposes* all these things which have been sought from without and we approve them . . . then we will appear to have taken in marriage either foreign wives or even concubines [italics mine].[73]

What is important for Origen is that those who have growing acquaintance with several academic disciplines exercise discernment: "we bring over to our purposes" those things learned from without. A very similar allegorical reading of polygamy transpires in his *Homilies on Numbers* where Origen remarks that Solomon was deceived by his many wives into idolatry (1 Kings 11:1–6). "I think that the many wives represent the many dogmas and the different philosophies of the many nations." Though Solomon wanted to investigate all these teachings, he was, in the end, deceived by them. "Thus it is a grand thing and truly a work of God," Origen concludes, "to intermingle with many dogmas, as with wives, and yet not to turn aside from the rule of truth . . ."[74]

Ideal interpreters, unlike their heretical counterparts, exercised discernment when they encountered Greco-Roman learning. Not surprisingly, Origen advocated this same stance toward the scriptural interpretations of his *Christian* opponents. They too, after all, were outsiders.[75] Yet despite his frequent polemic against their exegesis, he did not advocate a complete rejection of their work. Rather, as was the case with the philosophers and poets, he consistently pleaded for a careful adjudication of their scholarship. In his *Homilies on Numbers*, for instance, Origen urges his congregation that while there are interpretations in the writings of the heretics that should be expelled from the church, it is also the case that "some things from the meanings of the divine Scripture are found inserted into the words even of heretics." In such a case, Origen continues, "let these things not be rejected equally with those things that are contrary to the truth and to the faith."[76]

---

[72] Hom Gen 11.2/GCS 6, 102.28–103.1.
[73] Hom Gen 11.2/GCS 6, 103.16–22.
[74] Hom Num 20.3.3/GCS 7, 192.19–28.
[75] See esp. n. 55 above.
[76] Hom Num 9.1.2/GCS 7, 54.25–28.

Fidelity to the church's rule[77]

Alongside the uncritical acceptance of deficient Greco-Roman learning, Origen identified the failure to hold to the church's rule of faith as a characteristic of the Gnostic exegetical enterprise.[78] As noted above, these twin failures were closely linked to Origen. The flipside of *embracing* foreign teachings incompatible with the Christian faith was *rejecting* the teachings constitutive of this faith. There are two passages in *On First Principles* where Origen portrays adherence to the church's rule of faith as a hallmark of the ideal scriptural interpreter. Conversely, suspect Gnostic interpretations of Scripture betrayed a rejection of this rule.

Origen lists the most extensive rule in his surviving corpus in the preface to book one of *On First Principles*.[79] The circumstance that elicits his discussion of this rule is his awareness of rival interpretations of Scripture within the Christian community. He opens this work with the assertion that those who

---

[77] The modern literature on the rule is large. See D. F. Kattenbusch, *Das Apostolische Symbol: Seine Entstehung, sein geschichtlicher Sinn, seine urprüngliche Stellung im Kultus und in der Theologie der Kirche*, vol. 2, *Verbreitung und Bedeutung des Taufsymbols* (Leipzig: J. C. Hinrich, 1900 [the first seven chapters of this vol. published in 1897]), 134–179; J. Kunze, *Glaubensregel, Heilige Schrift und Taufbekenntnis* (Leipzig: Dörffling & Franke, 1899), 158–167; G. Bardy, "La Règle de Foi d'Origène," *RSR* 9 (1919): 162–196; D. van den Eynde, *Les normes de l'enseignement chrétien dans la littérature patristique des trois premiers siècles* (Paris: Gabalda & Fils, 1933), 304–311; H. Oppel, "$Kανών$. Zur Bedeutungsgeschichte des Wortes und seiner lateinischen Entsprechungen (Regula-Norma)," *Philologus*, supplement vol. 30.4 (1937); E. Molland, *The Conception of the Gospel in the Alexandrian Theology*, 90ff; A. C. Outler, "Origen and the 'Regula fidei,'" *CH* 8 (1939): 212–221 [corrected version reprinted in *Second Century* 4 (1984): 133–147]; R. P. C. Hanson, "Origen's Doctrine of Tradition," *JTS* 49 (1949): 17–27; H. de Lubac, *History and Spirit*, 60–76; R. P. C. Hanson, *Origen's Doctrine of Tradition*, 91–126; R. C. Baud, "Les 'Règles' de la théologie d'Origène," *RSR* 55 (1967): 161–208; R. T. Etcheverría, "Orígenes y la regula fidei," *Orig* I: 327–338; H. Ohme, *Kanon ekklesiastikos: Die Bedeutung des altkirchlichen Kanonbegriffs* (Berlin: W. de Gruyter, 1998), 181–218; R. Williams, s.v. "Regola di Fede," in *Origene: Dizionario. La cultura-il pensiero-le opere*, ed. A. M. Castagno (Rome: Città Nuova, 2000).

[78] Key terms for this "rule" include: $κανών$ (PA 4.2.2; DH 10.14); $κανὼν ἐκκλησιαστικός$ (Hom Jer 5.14.1; Comm Cor 74; in the plural, Comm Cor 4); $κανὼν τῆς ἐκκλησίας$ (Comm Matt Ser 46; PA 4.2.2). Note that the expressions $κανὼν τῆς πίστεως$ and $κανὼν τῆς ἀληθείας$ are *not* found in Origen's Greek corpus. The Latin terms include: *regula* (PA pref.2); *regula ecclesiastica* (Comm Titus 4); *ecclesiastica et apostolica traditio* (PA pref.2); *regula apostolicae veritatis* (Hom 4.1 Ps 36); *regula pietatis* (PA 3.5.3); *regula christianae veritatis* (PA 3.3.4); *regula evangelica* (Hom Josh 7.6); *canon ecclesiarum* (Comm Matt Ser 28); *regula fidei* (Comm Rom 2.7.3), etc. See Hanson, *Tradition*, 91–98 and Ohme, *Kanon ekklesiastikos*, 193–213 for a discussion of terminology, and in particular, the care that must be taken with the Latin translations. R. C. Baud's important essay on the rule in Origen took "*regula*" as the consistently faithful Latin translation of $κανών$ ("Les 'Règles,'" 164). Several scholars, however, have convincingly argued that Origen's Latin translators, and Rufinus in particular, were more liberal with "*regula*" and similar expressions in their translations than Origen himself was (see F. Kattenbusch, *Symbol*, 137, n. 4; G. Bardy, "La Règle," 181; D. van den Eynde, *Les normes*, 230, 308–310). On the inflation of the use of "*regula*" in the Latin translations, see H. Ohme's fine discussion, *Kanon ekklesiastikos*, 185–192.

[79] The most elaborate rule that survives in the Greek can be found at Comm Jn 32.186–193. For partial rules, see Comm Matt Ser 33; Comm Rom 4.6.3; CC 1.7.

believe grace and truth have come through Jesus Christ derive the knowledge
of the "good and blessed manner of living from no other source than the very
words and teaching of Christ."[80] Yet Origen continues, insisting significantly
that the teaching of Christ is not to be taken in a narrow sense, restricted only
to what is found in the gospels. Rather, his teaching is dispersed throughout
the law and the prophets of the Old Testament, and even the apostolic writings
of the New Testament. The argument for this claim need not detain us here. It
suffices to say that by drawing explicit attention to the law and prophets as an
additional source for the words of Jesus Christ, Origen is already hinting at
those in the Christian community who would find this claim difficult—the trio
of Marcion, Valentinus, and Basilides, along with their followers. As Origen
continues, he notes that there are significant disagreements among Christians
about how their Scriptures should be interpreted. "[M]any of those who profess
to believe in Christ disagree not only in small and trivial but also in great and
important matters—of God, for example, or of the Lord Jesus Christ himself, or
of the Holy Spirit, and not only of these, but also of others who are creatures,
that is of the dominions or the holy powers."[81] The problem, as Origen presents
it in the opening paragraphs of *On First Principles*, is that there are conflicting
interpretations of the same Scriptures among those who avow allegiance to
Christ. Or, as he puts it a few lines later, some professing Christians put forward
interpretations "differing from the Christians of earlier times."[82]

He proposes a solution to this problem. "[I]t seems therefore necessary
concerning each of these matters to first lay down a sure line and clear rule
[*certam lineam manifestamque regulam*]..."[83] This rule, he continues, is
derived from the apostolic preaching itself. The apostles delivered doctrines
that they believed to be necessary in simple terms, accessible to all believers.[84]
This teaching was "handed down in unbroken succession from the apostles"
and is "still preserved and continues to exist in the churches up to the present
day."[85] This teaching, enumerated under several headings, constitutes the "sure
line and clear rule" that will serve as a guideline for interpreting Scripture well
and thus, also, as an arbitrator between competing interpretations.

As Origen proceeds to summarize this rule, it becomes increasingly clear
that he has his Gnostic opponents in view. Several of the articles in this rule
explicitly challenge the two features of the Gnostic theological vision he found
so offensive. The first article, for instance, expresses a belief in one God,

---

[80] PA pref.1/GK 82, 7.9–13—Butterworth emended.
[81] PA pref.2/GK 84, 8.14–18.
[82] PA pref.2/GK 84, 8.25.
[83] PA pref.2/GK 84, 8.14–20—transl. mine. Rufinus' *regula* probably translates κανών. It is
unlikely Rufinus interpolated Origen's Greek text here with an auxiliary "*regula*" since most of
Origen's preface is, in fact, devoted to a discussion of this rule.
[84] PA pref.3.
[85] PA pref.2/GK 84, 8.25–28.

creator and sustainer of the universe, who sent Jesus Christ to call both Israel and the Gentiles. "This just and good God, the Father of our Lord Jesus Christ, himself gave the law, the prophets and the gospels, and he is God both of the apostles and also of the Old and New Testaments."[86] Without ever mentioning his opponents by name, Origen clearly disputes the dualistic account of God and the Scriptures that he so frequently attributed to the Gnostic coalition.[87] In the article on the soul he touches upon the other issue he consistently disputed with his opponents: the capacity of rational souls to make meaningful choices.

> This also is laid down in the Church's teaching, that every rational soul is possessed of free will and choice [*rationabilem liberi arbitrii et voluntatis*]; and also, that it is engaged in a struggle against the devil and his angels and the opposing powers; for these strive to weigh the soul down with sins, whereas we, if we lead a wise and upright life, endeavour to free ourselves from such a burden. There follows from this the conviction that we are not subject to necessity [*non nos necessitati esse subiectos*], so as to be compelled by every means, even against our will, to do either good or evil. For if we have a will [*Si enim nostri arbitrii sumus*], some powers may very likely be able to urge us on to sin and others to assist us to salvation; we are not, however, compelled by necessity to act either rightly or wrongly... [88]

According to this article in the rule, the soul is not fated to its actions, but rather is capable of choice and will be judged after its departure from the world according to its deeds, either rewarded with eternal life or punished in accordance with its crimes. This soul is not subject to necessity, and even if other spiritual powers persuade it to act in one way or another, it is still capable of self-determination.[89]

In these opening paragraphs of *On First Principles* Origen provides an important insight into his portrait of Scripture's ideal and less than ideal interpreters. Ideal interpreters embrace this rule as a guideline for their exegetical work. Gnostic interpreters, he insists, reject important portions of it. Toward the end of *On First Principles* the church's rule surfaces again. Here Origen revisits the topic he raised in the preface of his treatise, offering another account of how Scripture ought to be read, given the plurality of interpretations in circulation. However, Origen's discussion is more explicitly polemical than it was in his preface. It is no longer conflicting interpretations of the same Scriptures that worry him, but rather erroneous interpretations.

---

[86] PA pref.4/GK 88, 10.2–4.

[87] This polemic surfaces in the rule's article on the Holy Spirit as well. "It is, however, certainly taught with utmost clearness in the Church, that this Spirit inspired each one of the saints, both the prophets and the apostles, and that there was not one Spirit in the men of old and another in those who were inspired at the coming of Christ" (PA pref.4/GK 90, 11.7–10).

[88] PA pref.5/GK 90, 12.8–92, 13.3—Butterworth modified.

[89] For a more complete discussion of the contents of this rule, see the discussion in Chapter 9 below (in the section "Contours of the message").

> After having spoken cursorily about the divine Scriptures being inspired by God, it is necessary to discuss the manner for reading and understanding them, since many errors have emerged because the way in which we should approach the holy writings has not been discovered by the multitude.[90]

Origen continues, enumerating not one group as he did in the opening lines of his preface, but rather three groups that compose this uninformed "multitude": the Jews, heterodox Christians, and the *simpliciores*. He catalogues how each group in its own way derives a false understanding of God (or Jesus Christ) from a mistaken interpretation of Scripture. Those of interest here, the "heterodox" interpreters, read anthropomorphic depictions of God in the Old Testament in a draconian manner, attributing them to an inferior Creator.[91] Again, Origen has the Gnostic coalition in mind.

A new way of reading Scripture must then be proposed that facilitates the discernment of the true sense of Scripture. Origen announces two religious qualifications for ideal readers: that they believe (as it were) in the "trinitarian" authorship of Scripture, and that they hold to the church's rule:

> Therefore we must show to those who believe that the sacred books are writings not from men, but that they were composed and have come down to us from the inspiration of the Holy Spirit by the will of the Father of the universe through Jesus Christ, what are the apparent ways [of interpretation] for those who hold to the rule of the heavenly church of Jesus Christ through the succession of the apostles [ἐχομένοις τοῦ κανόνος τῆς Ἰησοῦ Χριστοῦ κατὰ διαδοχὴν τῶν ἀποστόλων οὐρανίου ἐκκλησίας].[92]

There has been a fair amount of debate about the meaning of κανών in this passage; however, there are several indications that the "rule" to which Origen refers is the church's rule of faith.[93] Here in book four Origen is revisiting the topic with which he opened *On First Principles*: contested interpretations of Scripture and how to adjudicate them. There, as here, disagreements surface about how to read Scripture, and as there, so here, Origen introduces the

---

[90] PA 4.2.1/GK 694–6, 305.10–306.2—transl. mine.

[91] PA 4.2.1, cited above at nn. 35 and 36.

[92] PA 4.2.2/GK 700, 308.11–16—transl. mine. See Chapter 9 below (section "Authorial intent") for a discussion of the divine inspiration of Scripture.

[93] There are five positions in the literature: (1) G. Bardy and R. C. Baud understand the "rule" to be the content of the ecclesiastical preaching as enumerated in the preface to PA (G. Bardy, "La Règle," 177, n. 1; R. C. Baud, "'Les Règles,'" 171). The majority of scholars (2) see the κανών here as referring to the principle of allegorical exegesis (F. Kattenbusch, *Das apostolische Symbol*, 143–144, n. 15; J. Kunze, *Glaubensregel*, 166; J. Daniélou, *Origen*, 139). Lebreton (3) thinks the rule is the superior knowledge of the perfect, based on their spiritual interpretation of Scripture and opposed to the initial and elementary teaching of Christ (J. Lebreton, "Les degrés de la connaissance religieuse d'après Origène," *RSR* 12 [1922]: 289–291). E. Molland (4) has furnished another view: Origen "probably" has the "canon of Scripture" here in mind (*Gospel*, 92–93, n. 5). Finally (5) Outler, latching onto the adjective "celestial," understands the "celestial church" to relate to the earthly church in the way that the "eternal gospel" relates to the "temporal gospel." Thus, the rule of the heavenly church "refers to the rational archetype which is only partially exemplified in the existing rule of the churches" (A. Outler, "Origen and the 'Regula fidei,'" 220).

κανών/*regula* as a safeguard against the erroneous reading of Scripture. In both places, moreover, the κανών/*regula* is described in similar terms: there, it is "handed down by the apostles in the order of succession [*per successionis ordinem ab apostolis tradita*]," and here it is "transmitted through the succession of the apostles [κατὰ διαδοχὴν τῶν ἀποστόλων]."[94] In short, both of these passages from *On First Principles* emphasize the integral role of the church's rule of faith in successful scriptural interpretation. Adherence to this rule was a distinguishing feature of the ideal scriptural interpreter and, conversely, a missing feature from the profile of the Gnostic exegete.

For Origen, ideal scriptural interpreters were more than scholars: *how* they approached the Bible with their philological expertise also mattered. I have confirmed this point in this chapter by retracing the lines Origen drew between Gnostic exegesis and the ecclesial interpretation of Scripture. He registered a series of complaints about how these heterodox Christians mishandled the Greco-Roman philological apparatus and, as I demonstrated, these boundaries went far deeper than a catalogue of procedural deficiencies (such as perpetrating literal exegesis). At the heart of his critique were doctrines, dispositions, and loyalties that these interpreters had embraced, yet that were out of step with the Christian faith, as he understood it. For Origen, the Gnostic exegetical enterprise became misshapen when (and only when) it yielded doctrines about God and the soul at odds with those in circulation throughout most churches. These readings, moreover, were accompanied by an uncritical disposition toward Greco-Roman learning and a refusal to hold to the church's rule.

This Gnostic exegete was a foil for Origen's account of the ideal interpreter of Scripture. For aspiring interpreters (and this included Origen, as several autobiographical passages indicate) adherence to the church's rule of faith and a discerning engagement with the Greco-Roman disciplines yielded viable interpretations of Scripture—or at the very least, safeguarded interpreters from the sorts of doctrinal errors committed in Gnostic exegetical circles. In these tangible ways, then, the exercise of biblical interpretation afforded interpreters an opportunity to express distinct Christian convictions. In the next chapter I will examine Origen's critique of Jewish exegesis, his other significant exegetical adversary. This critique will shed additional light on how Origen envisioned ideal scriptural interpreters as participants in the Christian drama of salvation.

---

[94] There are several other references to the rule (or synonymous expressions) in Origen's writings where it explicitly functions to distinguish spurious from authentic Christian interpretations of Scripture. See Hom 4.1 Ps 36; Comm Matt 11.17, 13.1; Comm Matt Ser 33; Comm Jn 6.62–66; Comm Rom 5.1.27; perhaps Phil 6.2; Phil 11.2.

7

Boundaries (Part II): Interpretation in the New Israel

On the surface, Origen's critique of Jewish scriptural exegesis is far more straightforward than his assessment of Gnostic interpretation. Against the latter he levels a wide range of criticisms that he seldom directs against the Jews. Overzealous text-critical emendations, failures to detect the literary sequences in passages, deficiencies not simply in literal but also in allegorical interpretations, and curiously, a whole series of reading vices that are ostensibly perpetrated by his Gnostic adversaries—this panoply of exegetical deficiencies Origen finds among his Christian opponents, but curiously *not* in the scriptural interpretations of his Jewish opponents. Against the latter, rather, there is only one charge that he consistently levels: they are literalists.

But this seemingly fortuitous observation does little to mask a series of formidable problems. To begin with, why did Origen associate Jewish exegetical fallacies nearly exclusively with literalism, precisely what he did not do with Gnostic misinterpretations of Scripture? Most scholars have not detected this discrepancy in Origen's assessment of his two principal exegetical adversaries. Yet even if we can propose a satisfactory answer to this question, it still leaves a more fundamental issue unresolved: why did Origen accuse his Jewish contemporaries of literalism in the first place? This charge in particular has puzzled his modern readers. Most notably, there is the challenge of reconciling this charge with his acknowledgment elsewhere that allegory also flourished within contemporary Jewish exegetical traditions. This twofold and seemingly contradictory assessment of Jewish exegesis has baffled many of Origen's commentators. Why level the accusation of literalism when he knew full well that Jewish scholars often had recourse to allegorical exegesis? Alongside this obvious difficulty, there are additional complications that lurk behind the charge of literalism. There are, for instance, hints of hypocrisy. How do we make sense of this critique of Jewish exegesis as literalist when Origen was himself a practitioner of literal exegesis? Indeed, how does his seemingly wholesale critique of Jewish exegesis dovetail with his decision to incorporate successful Jewish interpretations into his own readings of Scripture? Finally, careful readers will wonder if Origen's censure of Jewish literalism is not greatly exaggerated. There are a handful of passages in his corpus where he will demarcate Jews from Christians simply in terms of how they approach their shared Scriptures. The old Israel examines it literally but most Christians do not, and these different exegetical decisions astonishingly account, or so it seems, for the chief boundaries between these two religious communities. In short, the charge of Jewish literalism requires careful analysis.

In order to shed light on Origen's critique of Jewish exegesis (and of a version of this exegesis circulating within the Christian community), I will adopt a strategy similar to the one pursued in the previous chapter. I will contend that we understand his critique poorly if we think it identifies a procedural flaw that runs throughout all Jewish exegesis—that is, as if the fundamental exegetical deficiency among the Jews was their singular insistence upon discovering the literal referents of Scripture. If this is how Origen understood Jewish literalism, then we will indeed face intractable difficulties in our attempts to make sense of this critique. Yet the evidence suggests something different. It turns out that Origen meant something much more specific when he spoke critically of Jewish literalism. Just as was the case with his censure of Gnostic exegesis, so too this charge against Jewish exegesis is best read not simply or even primarily as a disapproval of philological procedures, but rather as a critique of a particular set of literal interpretations supportive of troubling liturgical and doctrinal commitments. As we will see below, when Origen criticized his Jewish opponents for being literalists, he was consistently leveling a charge against a handful of readings of the law and prophets that both promoted central tenets of Judaism and, at the same time, advanced a critique of central Christian convictions. Origen also directed this critique against some in the Christian community who perpetrated a narrower version of Jewish literalism. He usually identified these figures as Ebionites. The Ebionites believed in Jesus as the Messiah, yet interpreted and followed literally several precepts of the Jewish law.

By unfolding Origen's critique against Jewish and Ebionite exegesis, additional contours in his portrait of Scripture's ideal interpreter will come to light. He repeatedly implicated these related (and troubling) exegetical approaches to the law and prophets in the rejection of Jesus' and Paul's exegetical tutelage. Ideal interpreters, by contrast, were exhorted to embrace this tutelage when wrestling with the enigmatic passages in the Scriptures that were held in common by the old and new Israel.

ORIGEN AMONG THE JEWS

A resident first of Alexandria and then later of Caesarea (Maritima), two cities with thriving Jewish populations, Origen was certainly familiar with the Judaisms of his day.[1] Some of this knowledge would have been garnered from first-hand encounters with Jews, whom he usually refers to as Ἰουδαῖοι, Ἑβραῖοι, or Ἰσραηλῖται.[2] There are a handful of references to such conversations in his writings.[3] Origen also acknowledges his awareness of the writings of Philo[4] and Josephus,[5] as well as of the rabbinic exegetical traditions that surface occasionally in his own exegetical work.[6] It is not surprising, then, that

---

[1] For literature on Origen's relationship with Judaism, see G. Bardy, "Les traditions juives dans l'oeuvre d'Origène," *RB* 34 (1925): 217–252; R. P. C. Hanson, *Origen's Doctrine of Tradition*, 146–156; R. P. C. Hanson, *Allegory and Event*, 155–157; E. Urbach, "Rabbinic exegesis and Origen's commentary on the Song of Songs and Jewish-Christian polemics," *Tarbiz* 30 (1960): 148–170; H. Crouzel, *Origène et la "Connaissance Mystique"* (Paris: Desclée de Brouwer, 1961), 312–322; A. J. Philippou, "Origen and the early Jewish-Christian debate," *GOTR* 15 (1970): 140–152; E. Urbach, "Homiletical interpretations of the sages and the expositions of Origen on the canticles, and the Jewish-Christian disputation," *Scripta Hierosolymitana* 22 (1971): 247–275; H. Bietenhard, *Caesarea, Origenes und die Juden* (Stuttgart: Kohlhammer, 1974); N. R. M. de Lange, *Origen and the Jews: Studies in Jewish-Christian Relations in Third-Century Palestine* (Cambridge: Cambridge University Press, 1976), esp. 82–84, 103–121; A. Wasserstein, "A Rabbinic midrash as a source of Origen's homily on Ezekiel," *Tel Aviv* 46 (1977): 317–318; R. Kimelman, "Rabbi Yohanan and Origen on the Song of Songs: A third-century Jewish-Christian disputation," *HTR* 73 (1980): 567–595; D. J. Halperin, "Origen, Ezekiel's Merkabah, and the Ascension of Moses," *CH* 50 (1981): 261–275; G. Sgherri, *Chiesa e Sinagoga nelle opere di Origene* (Milan: Vita e Pensiero, 1982); M. Harl, SC 302, 47–51; P. M. Blowers, "Origen, the rabbis, and the Bible: Toward a picture of Judaism and Christianity in third-century Caesarea," in *Origen of Alexandria: His World and His Legacy*, ed. by C. Kannengiesser and W. L. Petersen (Notre Dame: University of Notre Dame Press, 1988), 96–116; J. A. McGuckin, "Origen on the Jews," in *Christianity and Judaism*, ed. by D. Wood (Oxford: Blackwell, 1992), 1–13.

[2] For Ἰουδαῖοι, see CC 1.15/SC 132, 116.6, 1.18, 1.26, etc.; for Ἰουδαϊσμός, see CC 1.2/SC 132, 80.2 and esp. CC 3.14/SC 136, 40.19–20 where it is juxtaposed to Χριστιανισμός; for Ἑβραῖοι, see CC 1.21/SC 132, 128.5; PA 4.1.4, etc.; for Ἰσραηλῖται, see PA 3.1.23/GK 554, 241.6, etc. There are several other designations, such as: οἱ ἐκ περιτομῆς ("the members of the circumcision" [PA 4.3.2/GK 736, 326.8]; the rabbis can be referred to simply as σοφοι ("wise") [LA 7/SC 302, 538.2 and n. 2 on that page]). On Origen's use of terms like "Jew," "Hebrew," "Israelite," and even "Pharisee" for contemporary rabbinic Jews (Jn Frg/GCS 4, 510.2), see N. de Lange, *Origen and the Jews*, 29–33, 35–37. Note also how Origen can appropriate this terminology to speak of Christians. They are "Hebrews in the mystical sense" (Comm Matt 11.5/GCS 10, 41.3; On Martyr. 33, etc.), "invisible Jews" (Hom Lev 5.1.2/GCS 6, 333.6; PA 4.2.5; Comm Jn 1.259—based on Rom 2:29), and "Israel according to the Spirit" (PA 4.3.6/GK 748, 332.8–9; Comm Rom 7.14.1–3—based on 1 Cor 10:18 and Rom 9:6).

[3] In *Against Celsus* Origen occasionally refers to discussions with Jews: CC 1.45; perhaps 1.49, 1.55, 2.3, 2.30, 2.31. Also see LA 9–12 and perhaps also Pascha 1–2; H. Bietenhard, *Caesarea, Origenes und die Juden* (Stuttgart: Kohlhammer, 1974), 49; N. de Lange, *Origen and the Jews*, esp. ch. 8.

[4] See CC 4.51, 6.21. For more on Origen's use of Philo, see D. T. Runia, *Philo in Early Christian Literature: A Survey* (Minneapolis: Fortress Press, 1993).

[5] CC 1.16, 1.47, 2.13, 4.11; Comm Matt 10.17.

[6] Hom Gen 2.2; Hom Num 13.5, 14.1, 27.12; Hom Is 9; Hom Jer 20.2; Hom Ez 10.3; Comm Matt 11.9; PA 4.3.14; LA 7. See R. P. C. Hanson, *Tradition*, 149–156 and esp. N. de Lange, *Origen and the Jews*, chs. 5, 9–10.

his writings offer a remarkable wealth of information about the institutions, social practices and doctrines of ancient Judaism.[7] Particularly important are his extensive and often detailed comments on Judaism in *Against Celsus*. In this work he frequently criticizes Celsus' fictitious Jew through whom attacks on Christianity are made. Origen was sufficiently confident in his knowledge of Judaism to be able to castigate Celsus for putting words into the mouth of his literary Jew that were inconsistent with what Origen thought a real Jew in his day would claim.[8] Also fascinating in this work is how Origen undertakes a lengthy defense of Judaism against Celsus, who was attempting to establish the falsity of Christianity by attacking its origin in Judaism.[9] Origen was, then, not only familiar with Judaism, but could also express his sympathies with it, even though this support was predictably limited to what a Christian, who acknowledged Jesus as the anticipated Messiah, could offer.[10]

When it came to scriptural interpretation, Origen was adamant that he, along with his fellow Christians, did not (or at least ought not to) interpret Scripture like the Jews. As was the case with the Gnostic heterodox, Origen's self-understanding as an ecclesiastical interpreter of Scripture was closely tied to his simultaneous rejection of a significant element of Jewish exegesis. He opens, for instance, his first *Homily on Leviticus* by questioning those in his congregation who would be content with a literal interpretation of the liturgical precepts in the book of Leviticus, an interpretation that would have been offered by the Jews when they still had their temple. "For if I should follow the simple understanding, as certain ones among us do, without using in their terms of ridicule the 'stratagems of language' or the 'cloud of allegory,' I would draw out the voice of the Lawgiver."[11] Origen continues, spelling out for his congregation the stark implications of eschewing, as they would have it, an allegorical exegesis of Leviticus:

> I, myself a man of the Church, living under the faith of Christ and placed in the midst of the Church, am compelled by the authority of the divine precept to sacrifice

---

[7] See R. P. C. Hanson, *Tradition*, 152–153; N. de Lange, *Origen and the Jews*, 33–47.

[8] Celsus introduces this figure at CC 1.28. See Origen's refutation of Celsus' Jew at CC 1.48–49, 2.1ff, 2.28, 2.31, 2.34, 2.55, 2.57, 2.77, 2.79, 4.2, 5.6, 5.8.

[9] CC 1.22. Also see CC 1.16.

[10] R. L. Wilken draws attention to Origen's commendation of Jews: "And what is most extraordinary for a[n early] Christian writer, Origen has something to say in praise of the Jews" (in *Judaism and the Early Christian Mind: A Study of Cyril of Alexandria's Exegesis and Theology* [New Haven: Yale University Press, 1971], 43). De Lange also notices this: "His remarks about them [Jews] are on the whole surprisingly free from the ill-informed rancour which pervades much of the literature on the subject which survives from the early Church" (76). Especially helpful on Origen's account of the salvation of the Jews is H. Bietenhard, *Caesarea, Origenes und die Juden*, 61–73. Texts where Judaism receives a strikingly positive evaluation include: CC 1.26, 2.4, 4.31, 5.6–7, 5.41–50, 8.48; Comm Matt 14.20; Comm Rom 3.1.3. Note particularly the discussions of Rom 11:25–26 ("all Israel will be saved"): Hom Ex 6.9; Hom Num 6.4.2; CC 6.80; and Comm Rom 8.12.1–8.

[11] Hom Lev 1.1.2/GCS 6, 280.20–281.3—Barkley emended.

calves and lambs and to offer fine wheat flour with incense and oil. For they do this who force us to be subservient to the historical sense and to keep to the letter of the law ... [12]

A literal, historical interpretation of Leviticus would compel Christians to follow its priestly prescriptions, a confounding activity for someone like Origen who was a "man of the Church" and had put his faith in Jesus as the Christ. Origen suggests, rather, a different way of reading Leviticus that moves beyond the letter of the text and that reflects his distinctive, ecclesial location: "Therefore, let us fall, if it is necessary, into your detractions so long as the Church, which has already turned to Christ the Lord, may know the truth of the Word which is completely covered under the veil of the letter [cf. 2 Cor 3:16–17]."[13]

Elsewhere Origen elaborates on this point, that the Christian and Jewish communities of his day could be demarcated simply in terms of their respective exegetical strategies regarding their shared Scriptures. For instance, in the opening lines of the ninth book of his *Commentary on Romans*, he summarizes Paul's argument in this letter: "In the entire preceding text of the epistle [Rom 1–11] the apostle had taught how the essence of religion has been transferred from the Jews to the Gentiles, from circumcision to faith, from the letter to the spirit, from shadow to truth, from the fleshly observance to spiritual observance."[14] Noteworthy in this passage is that Origen marks the shift in God's plan of salvation with exegetical vocabulary. The Gentiles have a religion characterized by an adherence to the "spirit" and "truth" of Scripture, not as is the case among the Jews, who are marked by a "fleshly" commitment to Scripture's "letter" and "shadow." In *Against Celsus* Origen makes this same point even more clearly:

We both [Jews and Christians] confess that the books [of the law and prophets] were written by the divine Spirit, but concerning the interpretation of the contents of the books we no longer speak alike. In fact, the reason we do not live like Jews is that we think the literal interpretation of the laws does not contain the meaning of the legislation [τὴν κατὰ τὸ ῥητὸν ἐκδοχὴν τῶν νόμων εἶναι τὴν περιέχουσαν τὸ βούλημα τῆς νομοθεσίας].[15]

In passages such as these Origen succinctly insists that the differences between Jews and Christians in the first half of the third century could be explained by the differing ways in which these communities interpreted the Scriptures they held in common.[16] This account of religious diversity echoes what we saw in

---

[12] Hom Lev 1.1.2–3/GCS 6, 281.3–7.

[13] Hom Lev 1.1.4/GCS 6, 281.14–16.

[14] Comm Rom 9.1.1/Bammel 710.1–5—Scheck modified.

[15] CC 5.60/SC 147, 162.3–164.7—Chadwick modified.

[16] Also see Hom Gen 3.5, 6.1, 6.3; Hom Ex 5.1, 7.1; Hom Lev 3.3.1–6, 5.5.1, 6.3.5, 7.5.7, 10.2.1–6; esp. Hom Num 7.2.4; Hom Jer 12.13.1–2, 14.12.2; Hom Ez 14.2; Comm Matt 10.14,

the previous chapter where Origen contended that interpretive disagreements about commonly shared Scriptures accounted for the emergence of different sects *within* Christianity.

In several of the passages that we will examine in greater detail below, it will become evident that Origen's identity as a Christian interpreter of Scripture was closely tied to his repudiation of the interpretive practices cultivated in the Jewish communities of his day. He repeatedly demarcated an ecclesiastical style of interpretation that he wished to epitomize from the sort of interpretation that flourished in Jewish circles. How precisely, then, did he distinguish ecclesiastical interpreters from "disciples of the Synagogue"?[17]

A PUZZLING CHARGE

In the fourth book of *On First Principles*, Origen offers his readers guidelines by which to interpret the Scriptures. It is important to present these guidelines, he insists, "since many errors have emerged because the way in which one ought to approach the holy writings has not been discovered by the multitude."[18] He offers illustrations of how his main exegetical rivals, the Jews included, misread Scripture, and then follows this with a concise assessment of their cardinal exegetical deficiency:

> Now the reason why all those we have mentioned hold false opinions and make impious or ignorant assertions about God appears to be nothing else but this: that Scripture is not understood in its spiritual sense [κατὰ τὰ πνευματικὰ], but is interpreted according to the bare letter [πρὸς τὸ ψιλὸν γράμμα].[19]

This is his fundamental charge brought against the Jewish exegetical tradition: it is literalist. We see this charge scattered throughout his writings. The Jews are those "who maintain that nothing more than the letter is signified."[20] The scribes and Pharisees of Jesus' day "put an earthly and fleshly interpretation on the Law and close up the spiritual and mystical interpretation."[21] When Celsus' Jew criticizes Christianity for taking its origin from Judaism, yet under the pretense of a progress in knowledge distances itself from Judaism,

11.14; Comm Matt Ser 10, 23, 89; Comm Jn 28.95–97; Comm Rom 2.14.14, 6.7.18; PA 2.7.2, 4.3.2; Pascha 28–29; CC 2.76, 3.4, 6.70, 7.26; esp. CC 2.1–6 where Origen distinguishes Christianity and Judaism based on their respective readings of the law (this passage will be discussed more thoroughly below).

[17] See Hom Ex 5.1/GCS 6, 183.11–21 for the distinction between the "disciples of Jesus" and the "disciples of the Synagogue." This passage is quoted below at n. 101.

[18] PA 4.2.1/GK 696, 306—transl. mine.

[19] PA 4.2.2/GK 700, 308.8–11.

[20] PA 4.3.2/GK 736, 326.7–9—transl. mine.

[21] Hom Gen 13.2/GCS 6, 114.26–28.

Origen responds: the Christian faith is indeed based upon the law and prophets, but whereas the Jews "read them superficially and only as stories," Christians delve deeply into their "wise and mysterious doctrines."[22] It is also interesting how Origen's language makes the charge of literalism. Occasionally the adverb Ἰουδαϊκῶς ("in the Jewish manner, like Jews") signifies literal exegesis: "to understand the promises recorded in the prophets . . . like Jews," is to fail to grasp their spiritual sense.[23] And when Origen wishes to invoke apostolic precedent for this charge, he often turns to 2 Cor 3:15 ("When Moses is read a veil lies upon their hearts"). The occluding "veil" is a symbol of the literalism that blinds the hearts of those who aspire to Moses' true message.[24] There are any number of instances where this charge of literalism is directed against Jewish exegesis.[25]

However, this criticism can be complicated in several ways. First, while Origen censured Jewish exegetical traditions as literalist, he also happily borrowed their interpretations and hermeneutical principles, incorporating these into his own writings.[26] Second, while he castigated literalism among his opponents, he himself endorsed (and practiced) the literal reading of

---

[22] CC 2.4/SC 132, 290.17–19.

[23] Comm Jn 10.291/GCS 4, 219.25–26. Also see Lk Frg 171. So too for Rufinus' Latin adjective Iudaicus in PA 2.11.2 (which most likely translates Ἰουδαϊκός), where, speaking of otherwise anonymous Christians, Origen notes that "since they understand the divine scriptures in a Judaistic sense [*Iudaico autem quodam sensu scripturas divinas intellegentes*]" they learn nothing worthy of the divine promises (PA 2.11.2/GK 442, 186.1–3). Also see Hom Josh 7.5, 15.1. For a similar use of the Greek adjective Ἰουδαϊκός, see CC 7.29.

[24] References to Jews who read the Scriptures with a "veil" include Hom Ex 12.1; Hom Lev 4.7.3; Hom Num 7.2.4; Hom Ez 14.2; Comm Rom 6.7.18; CC 5.60. Other NT passages that are invoked to describe the deficiencies in Jewish exegesis include Titus 1:14 ("pay attention to no Jewish myths") (Hom Gen 13.3; Hom Ex 5.1; Hom Num 13.4.2, 26.3.5; CC 2.5, 2.6, 2.52, esp. 7.29); 1 Tim 1:4 ("myths" and "endless genealogies") (Hom Gen 13.3); 2 Tim 4:4 ("They will turn their ears away from the truth and turn aside to myths") (Hom Gen 13.3).

[25] See Hom Gen 3.1, 3.5; Hom Ex 5.1, 7.3; Hom Lev 3.3.1, 4.7.3, 5.1.2, 5.8.3, 10.1.1, 12.4.3, 16.1.3, 16.2.2; Hom Josh 8.7; Hom Jer 12.13.1; Comm Matt 11.14, 16.10; Hom Lk 5.3; Comm Jn 10.291; Comm Rom 8.8.10; Comm Eph 31; CC 2.1, 2.6, 2.10, 6.70.

[26] There are numerous places where Origen explicitly mentions taking up Jewish interpretations of Scripture: Hom Gen 2.2, 12.4; Hom Ex 5.2; Hom Num 14.1.3; Hom Josh 15.6; Hom Jer 20.2.2; Hom Ez 4.5, 4.8; CC 4.34. Some of the Jewish interpretations Origen approves come, no doubt, from Jewish converts to Christianity. (See the references to his Hebrew teacher in PA 1.3.4 and 4.3.14 who offers an interpretation of Is 6:2 with reference to "our Lord Jesus Christ." Similarly, at Hom Jer 20.2.2 there is reference to a Jew who has become a Christian and who relays a Hebrew tradition about Jer 20:7.) Origen borrows not only from Jewish exegesis, but also from its hermeneutics. In Phil 2.3, for instance, he refers to the "most pleasing tradition handed down to us by a Hebrew" where the obscure passages in Scripture are likened to many locked rooms in a house. Origen also cites with approval the Jewish tradition that only the mature should be allowed to read the Song of Songs and that it should be left to the wise to teach the young Scripture, leaving the δευτερώσεις (beginning of Genesis, the first and last chapters of Ezekiel, and the Song of Songs) for the end of this instruction (Comm Song of Songs prol.). On Origen's retrievals of Jewish exegesis, see G. Bardy, 'Les traditions juives dans l'oeuvre d'Origène,' *RB* 34 (1925): 217–252, and N. de Lange, *Origen and the Jews*, chs. 9 and 10.

Scripture.[27] There also appears to be historical dissonance in Origen's charge of literalism. Jewish allegorical reading of Scripture flourished in Alexandria prior to Origen's own exegetical activity.[28] Indeed, we find several passages where Origen himself acknowledged the presence of allegory in this exegetical tradition.[29] Not surprisingly, then, Nicholas de Lange expressed amazement over this criticism from Origen: "It may be thought remarkable that Origen, of all people, who was well acquainted with Jewish exegesis in all its aspects, should have perpetuated this myth of 'Jewish literalism,' but perpetuate it he certainly does."[30] Along the same lines, Marguerite Harl, noting Origen's awareness of rabbinical allegories, writes: "The polemic against Jewish exegesis is especially in Origen a residue of previous [Christian] polemics. It appears in his work as an archaism . . ."[31] And more recently, Guy Stroumsa has called Origen's critique of Jewish literalism, despite his awareness of its allegorical commitments, a "major paradox," and, following Harl and de Lange, suggests that this critique results from his inheritance of "the (then already) traditional *adversus iudaeos* in Patristic literature."[32] Each of these commentators has noted a basic and troubling incommensurability between the presence of Jewish allegory in antiquity and Origen's critique of Jewish literalism. On the surface, this charge of literalism certainly puzzles.

A SPECIES OF LITERALISM

Yet as I will contend below, much of the confusion dissipates when we examine the specific literary contexts in which this criticism emerges. Rarely

---

[27] For discussions of the value of the literal sense of Scripture, see PA 4.2.4, 4.2.8, 4.3.4; Comm Jn 13.38–39. On Origen's own practice of literal exegesis on the OT, see Hom Gen 2; Hom Jer 15.5.1; Hom Sam 5, etc. Much of his NT analysis is literal, esp. his commentary on Paul's letters.

[28] J. C. Joosen and J. H. Waszink, s.v. "Allegorese A. III," in *RAC*, vol. 1, ed. T. Klauser (Stuttgart: Hiersemann, 1950). Also see R. Grant, *The Letter and the Spirit* (London: SPCK, 1957), 31–40; R. P. C. Hanson, *Allegory and Event*, 11–36; N. de Lange, *Origen and the Jews*, 106–109, 112ff; D. Dawson, *Allegorical Readers and Cultural Revision in Ancient Alexandria* (Berkeley: University of California Press, 1992), 73–126.

[29] See CC 4.21 where Origen refers to the allegories of the law in Philo, Aristobulus, and Numenius; also see CC 4.48–49, 6.49, 7.20, 7.70. R. P. C. Hanson's remark that "no Jewish school of thought with which Origen was in touch was willing to allegorize" is incorrect (*Allegory and Event*, 35, n. 1).

[30] N. de Lange, *Origen and the Jews*, 83.

[31] M. Harl, SC 302, 51. She is perhaps borrowing from H. de Lubac, who was nervous with Origen's claim that only the disciples of Christ, and not the Jews, discerned the meaning of the Jewish Scriptures. On this issue, de Lubac writes, Origen was "most dated" (*History and Spirit*, 126).

[32] G. Stroumsa, "Clement, Origen, and Jewish esoteric traditions," *Orig VI*: 60. The same claim is made later in this essay: "Here Origen's polemics against Jewish literalism reflects the remnant of earlier polemics" (68).

does Origen speak of Jewish literalism in abstraction; he speaks, rather, of particularly troubling literal interpretations. An inspection of his wider corpus reveals the conspicuous pattern that the charge of literalism was invariably linked to two particular literal interpretations, both of which challenged central Christian convictions.

The first Jewish literal interpretation that drew Origen's repeated censure was the interpretation that endorsed the continued adherence to the Jewish law, in particular, its liturgical and ceremonial customs such as circumcision, keeping the Passover, Sabbath regulations, dietary customs, and the distinctions between pure and impure. Only a few passages need to be examined to illustrate this point. For instance, in his *Homilies on Joshua* he preaches on Caleb's destruction of Kiriath-sepher during the conquest of Canaan (Josh 15:15–16). Origen offers "city of letters" as the etymological meaning of Kiriath-sepher, and takes this city's destruction to refer allegorically to the destruction of the "letter" of Scripture and what this letter advocates.[33] Origen preaches:

> Now I . . . who, with the letter of the law destroyed and shattered, inquire after its spiritual sense [*Ego autem . . . qui exscisa ac discussa legis littera sensum in ea spiritalem requiro*]. Moreover, I destroy the letter when I am now not circumcised according to the flesh, and when I do not eat unleavened bread according to the flesh, and when I fail to observe the Passover along with the Jews, and when I do not keep the Sabbath according to the letter.[34]

This forceful passage conveys well several important features in Origen's larger critique of Jewish literalism. To begin with, we see how his critique centers specifically on a handful of ceremonial precepts in the law. It is not a universal dismissal of all Jewish exegesis, but rather a critique focusing on the literal interpretation of a very particular set of passages within the law. Related to this point, we also see how this criticism of Jewish exegesis entails far more than a scholarly dispute. When the relevant passages in question were interpreted literally, the law gave rise to a distinctive Jewish pattern of living not adopted by most Christians: among other things, it obliged the practice of circumcision, eating unleavened bread, observing the Passover, and keeping the Jewish Sabbath. This intimate association between literal interpretation of the law and a distinctive way of life helps explain passages such as the one already cited above from *Against Celsus* that at first glance appear to make inflated claims for the social and religious implications of literal interpretation: "In fact, the reason why we do not live like the Jews [οἵ γε οὐδὲ βιοῦμεν ὡς Ἰουδαῖοι] is that we think the literal interpretation of the laws does not contain the meaning of the legislation."[35]

---

[33] Hom Josh 20.5/GCS 7, 424.8–10.   [34] Hom Josh 20.6/GCS 7, 426.1–6.
[35] CC 5.60/SC 147, 162.5–164.7. The same point is repeatedly made elsewhere (see the references in n. 16 above).

The final point of interest in this passage from the *Homilies on Joshua* is that Origen is careful *not* to advocate that Christians discard those portions of the law that spoke of liturgical and ceremonial customs. In so doing, he was walking a careful line between two opposing positions prevalent in his day. On the one hand, there was a propensity in Christian circles, associated especially with the Ebionites, to adopt these customs literally. An example of this was already provided above, when Origen opened his *Homilies on Leviticus* by turning to his congregation and dismissing a literal interpretation of that book, lest the "voice of the Lawgiver," namely Moses, be literally followed and the command to sacrifice animals and to offer wheat flour with incense and oil be taken at face value.[36] On the other hand, there was a tendency that pulled in precisely the opposite direction. In his *Homilies on Numbers* Origen remarks how, when a passage from Leviticus or Numbers is read before his congregation,

> those who hear the rites of sacrifice, or the observation of Sabbaths, or of other similar things being read aloud in the Church are offended and say: "What need is there for this to be read in the Church? What good are Judaic precepts to us and the observances of a rejected people? These things belong to the Jews; let the Jews look after them!"[37]

Faced with these competing voices within his own congregation, Origen adroitly positioned himself between them. Neither embracing these legal stipulations literally, nor rejecting them unreservedly, he argued for a mediating position: that such precepts in the law be interpreted allegorically. Returning to the passage from his *Homilies on Joshua*, he insists that after the letter of the law is "destroyed and shattered," Christians are obliged to search for the "spiritual sense" in these very passages. In so doing, they mark out for themselves a way of living that is distinct from their Jewish contemporaries; but it is also a way of living symbolized by the Jewish law.

There is another passage in his *Commentary on Matthew* where Origen offers one of his most transparent accounts of how the ceremonial prescriptions in the law could be followed in two very different ways, physically or spiritually. He is explicating Jesus' denunciation of the scribes and Pharisees, and in particular the verse: "Therefore, do whatever they teach you and follow it; but do not do as they do" (Matt 23:3). He introduces a distinction between what the teachers of the law fittingly spoke, and what they poorly understood and correspondingly practiced. They commendably spoke of the law, but they did not understand it properly due to their commitment to its physical sense, and thus practiced it physically as well. Christians, on the other hand, fulfill the dominical command in Matthew's gospel when they listen to the law these

---

[36] Hom Lev 1.1.2.   [37] Hom Num 7.2.4/GCS 7, 40.19–23.

teachers spoke, yet understand it differently from them by following its spiritual intent.

> They [Jews] talk about circumcision, about the Passover, about unleavened bread, of meals and of feasts and of new moons and of Sabbaths and of the remaining commands of the Law, but they do not act according to the intent of the law [*voluntatem legis*]. They are not circumcised, as is the meaning of the law (for this reason, the apostle says: "We indeed are the circumcision, who serve God in the Spirit and do not trust in the flesh" [Phil 3:3]), nor do they sacrifice the Passover (because they do not know that "Christ our Passover is sacrificed for us" [1 Cor 5:7]), nor do they eat unleavened bread according to the intent of the law (which the apostle explains, when he says: "Let us celebrate the festival, not with the old yeast, nor the yeast of malice and evil, but with the unleavened bread of sincerity and truth" [1 Cor 5:8]) . . . We who are the disciples of Jesus, however, understand those, "who sit on Moses' seat, the scribes and Pharisees" [Matt 23:2], as those who practice the circumcisions and the other physical commands of the law, but who are far removed from the spiritual commands of the law [*a spiritalibus legis mandatis*]. We do and observe whatever they say to us about the law, since we understand the sense of the law . . .[38]

In this illuminating passage it is clear once again that Origen does not think literalism plagues Jewish exegesis as a whole, but only the interpretation of particular ceremonial customs in the law. He outlines the two ways these passages in the Mosaic law were kept in his day. Following the scribes and Pharisees, they were interpreted literally in Jewish circles, thus resulting in an approval of their distinctive legislated customs in their obvious and physical sense. Conversely, the Christian community read these passages differently. Following Paul's apostolic precedent in his letters, we "disciples of Jesus," Origen remarks, interpret the same laws spiritually, thus approving their customs in their spiritual configuration and simultaneously censuring them in their physical form. Christians still observe the law, but not in the Jewish manner. So convinced was Origen that this spiritual sense of the law was the only authentic interpretation of it after Jesus' ministry, that he could, as in the above passage, refer to it simply as "the meaning," "intent," or "sense of the law."[39]

Exegesis in Jewish circles was objectionable, then, when it rendered the prescriptions to follow the ceremonial customs in the law literally. Alongside this critique, Origen reproached a second variety of literalism in the Jewish communities of his day that denied Jesus was the Messiah predicted in the law and prophetic writings. There is an insightful passage in *Against Celsus* where

---

[38] Comm Matt Ser 10/GCS 11, 19.26–20.3, 20.6–11—transl. mine.

[39] Also note how Origen can identify this spiritual sense as the "sense of Christ [*sensum Christi*]" (Comm Rom 2.14.14/Bammel 183.140) or the "apostolic sense [*apostolorum sensum*]" (PA 2.11.3/GK 442, 186.4). For similar passages where Origen speaks of the two different senses of the law that were embraced in Jewish and Christian communities respectively, see the passages listed in n. 16.

Origen responds to Celsus' contention that both Christians and Jews wrangle with one another in vain about the prophesied Messiah, likening this debate to the proverbial "fight about the shadow of an ass."[40] Origen counters that the debate is, in fact, carried out with perfect seriousness, but that Jews and Christians differ in who they think fulfills the Messianic prophecies:

> We [Jews and Christians] seek to have clear evidence about the person proclaimed beforehand, and to find out what kind of person was prophesied, what he is to do, and, if possible, when also he will come. We said earlier that Jesus was the prophesied Christ and quoted a few out of several prophecies on this point [cf. *Against Celsus* 1.49–57]. Accordingly, neither Jews nor Christians make any mistake in believing that the prophets spoke by divine inspiration, although they [the Jews] are wrong in holding the mistaken opinion that the prophesied Christ is still awaited, whose identity and origin have been proclaimed in accordance with the true meaning of the prophets.[41]

This passage captures well the sort of exegetical disputes among Jews and Christians in Origen's day concerning the prophecies in their shared Scriptures. At stake was the identity of the person prophesied. Here in *Against Celsus* Origen does not explicitly link the Jewish failure to identify Jesus as the prophesied Messiah with the literal reading of prophetic passages. This is also the case elsewhere, since the refusal to identify Jesus as the prophetic referent was not always due to a literal reading of the passage in question. For instance, amidst a lengthy discussion of prophecy earlier in *Against Celsus* (1.49–1.57), Origen relays excerpts of a disputation he had with a rabbi in Caesarea over the identity of the famous suffering servant in Isaiah (Isa 52:13–53:12). His opponent contended that the passage spoke of the Jewish nation as if it were this servant, since it, like this servant, had been scattered and afflicted in the dispersion. Origen offered a counter-argument, in his estimation putting his opponent "in the greatest difficulty" when he mentioned a line apparently overlooked by the rabbi: "because of the iniquities *of my people* he [the servant] was led to death" (Isa 53:8). If the suffering servant was already the people of Israel, Origen wonders aloud, how could this people be led to death by "my people," that is, itself?[42] From Origen's perspective, this rabbi erred not because he read the passage in Isaiah too literally. Rather, he interpreted it incompletely, not taking into consideration a clause in Isaiah that conflicted with the proposed interpretation of the servant as the nation of Israel.

Yet in other passages Origen clearly directed the charge of literalism against Jewish prophetic interpretation. There were circumstances when his opponents denied Jesus as the prophetic referent because (at least as Origen saw it) they were insisting on an overly scrupulous, literal rendering of the prophetic text. For instance, in *On First Principles* he writes that the Jews "have not

---

[40] CC 3.1/SC 136, 14.14–15.   [41] CC 3.4/SC 136, 20.7–17.   [42] CC 1.55.

believed in our Savior because they think that they are complying with the wording [τῇ λέξει... κατακολουθεῖν] of the prophecies concerning him."[43] Origen then illustrates this ostensibly close reading. And they

> do not actually [αἰσθητῶς] see him "proclaiming release to captives" [cf. Isa 61:1; Lk 4:18] nor building what they truly [ἀληθῶς] think is the "city of God" [cf. Ps 45(46):5] nor "destroying the chariots of Ephraim and the horse from Jerusalem" [Zech 9:10], nor "eating butter and honey, and choosing the good before he knew or preferred the evil" [cf. Isa 7:15]. Further, they think that it is the wolf, the four-footed animal, which is said in prophecy to be going to "feed with the lamb, and the leopard to lie down with the kid, and the calf and bull and lion to feed together, led by a little child, and the ox and the bear to pasture together, their young ones growing up with each other, and the lion to eat straw like the ox" [cf. Isa 11:6, 7].[44]

Such an approach to prophecy, Origen concludes, reflects how Scripture among the Jews "is not understood in its spiritual sense [κατὰ τὰ πνευματικὰ], but is interpreted according to the bare letter [πρὸς τὸ ψιλὸν γράμμα]."[45] There is another, similar passage in the *Commentary on Romans* where Origen refers to a prophecy in Isaiah that the Messiah would build a city and call back the captivity (Isa 45:13). He remarks that many among the Jews deny Jesus fulfilled this prophecy because he did not actually build a city of God or call the people back from a literal captivity. This is the case, he adds, because they do not

> understand intelligibly [*intellegibiliter*] the things that have been set out for them. For Christ was prophesied as one who was going to do these things not visibly but intelligibly, that is, spiritually [*Non enim visibiliter haec sed intellegibiliter, hoc est spiritaliter*]. For he truly [*vere*] did build the city of God, but out of living stones from which he raised up sons of Abraham. Out of them he built the Church of God. And he converted the captivity of those people whom the devil was holding captive in sins.[46]

Here again, a literal examination of ancient prophecies pointed away from Jesus as the anticipated Messiah. This, then, was the other variety of literalism that Origen consistently reproached in the Jewish community: its denial that Jesus was the Messiah promised beforehand by the law and prophets.[47]

The foregoing analysis confirms that Jewish literalism in Origen's day was less a challenge to philological integrity than it was to Christian identity in the form of two particularly contentious literal interpretations. We can briefly

---

[43] PA 4.2.1/GK 696, 306.3–5—transl. mine.

[44] PA 4.2.1/GK 696, 306.5–14—transl. mine.

[45] PA 4.2.2/GK 700, 308.8–11.

[46] Comm Rom 8.8.10/Bammel, 679.135–140. Also see CC 2.38.

[47] There are only a handful of passages scattered throughout the corpus where Origen censures other literal readings in the Jewish community. For corporeal understandings of God derived from a literal understanding of certain OT passages, see Hom Gen 3.1; 3.2 and PA 1.1.1–2. For taking the promised eschatological blessings literally, see Hom Lev 16.1.3 and 16.2.2. These instances of literalism were not, however, exclusive to the Jewish community.

expand upon this thesis by noting that this variety of literalism was an extension (as he saw it) of what had already transpired in Jesus' day. At stake, then, in this debate about Jewish exegesis was not simply a denial of *present* Christian identity, but also *past*, since the literal interpretation of the law and prophets was deeply implicated in the historical figure of Jesus himself: in the rejection of his ministry, including his exegetical tutelage, and, ultimately, in his crucifixion. Origen repeatedly highlights, for instance, the conflict between Jesus and the Jewish leaders of his day concerning the correct reading of the law.[48] In his *Homilies on Genesis*, he refers to the dispute about Jesus and his disciples plucking heads of grain in the fields on the Sabbath (Lk 6:1). Origen notes how Jesus' behavior on the Sabbath reflected an approach to the law that opened up its true spiritual sense. The Pharisees who confronted Jesus, on the other hand, castigated his behavior since they "put an earthly and fleshly interpretation on the Law" and stopped up its "spiritual and mystical interpretation."[49] Or again, in his *Commentary on Matthew* when Origen reaches Jesus' saying that it is "not that which enters in the mouth that defiles a man, but that which proceeds out of the mouth" (Matt 15:11), he remarks that Jesus' contemporaries rejected the allegorical approach to the "books of Leviticus and Deuteronomy" that his teaching embodied.[50] As Origen saw it, most of Jesus' contemporaries read the law and prophets in such a way that these writings did not point toward him in a salutary fashion, but rather away from and against him. Thus literal exegesis was instrumental in the rejection of his ministry and, eventually, his very person.[51]

This portrait of Origen's critique of Jewish literalism puts us in an advantageous position for revisiting the numerous confusions surrounding this topic. As I have argued, talk of Jewish literalism for Origen was invariably intended *not* as a summary description of all the exegesis that flourished within the Jewish communities of his day. Rather, he voiced a focused critique. He censured Jewish literalism when it had, in the past, promoted the rejection of Jesus as the Messiah; and again, he censured it in his own day when it advanced teachings and practices at odds with most forms of Christianity,

---

[48] References to Jewish interpreters of Scripture at the beginning of the new dispensation (particularly the Pharisees, Sadducees, scribes, and lawyers) are consistently critical. On their ignorance of the spiritual sense, see Hom Gen 15.7; Comm Matt 11.14, 12.5, 16.3, 17.2; PA 2.4.3; Phil 2.2. In particular, see Comm Matt Ser 10, 13, 14, 23, and 27 where the Pharisees and scribes did not have access to the spiritual sense of Scripture.

[49] Hom Gen 13.2/GCS 6, 114.26–28.

[50] Comm Matt 11.12/GCS 10, 52.28–30.

[51] For additional passages on the literalism in Jesus' day that rejected his exegetical tutelage and was instrumental in his death, see Hom Ex 5.1; Hom Jer 12.13.1; Comm Matt Ser 27; PA 4.2.1; CC 2.8, 3.1, 3.28.

invariably the observance of Jewish customs and the denial that Jesus was the prophesied Messiah.

When we keep this precise critique in mind, it helps us unravel the puzzles associated with Origen's denunciation of Jewish literalism. To begin with, since this exegetical project was less a challenge to philology than it was to Christian identity (both past and present), we begin to appreciate why Origen strongly implicated this approach to Scripture in the division between Jews and Christians. Admittedly, at first glance the claims he made about two religious communities divided simply by their exegetical approach to the law and prophets appear inflated. However, the particular variety of Jewish literalism Origen had in mind certainly contributed to the existence of two distinct communities, since it promoted a distinctive Jewish way of liturgical and ceremonial life, and simultaneously challenged the central Christian conviction that Jesus was the prophesied Messiah.

Moreover, as I have also emphasized above, by targeting two *specific* literal readings, Origen created ample space for the selective retrieval and integration of Jewish exegesis into his own interpretive activity. So long as what he borrowed did not undermine central Christian convictions, there would have been no difficulty in adapting Jewish exegetical traditions for his own purposes, as in fact he often did.[52] Related to this, the critique of these specific literal readings would also not have precluded Origen himself from offering his own literal interpretations of Scripture, including those Scriptures shared with the Jews. It would be moving far beyond the evidence to conclude from his criticism of Jewish literalism that he was in principle opposed to discovering the literal referents of scriptural passages. In fact, the evidence from Origen's exegetical corpus clearly attests that he felt the freedom to offer such interpretations of Scripture, so long as they did not lead to the denial of Christian convictions.[53] Moreover, it becomes particularly clear in light of Origen's pinpoint critique that he was not mired in self-contradiction when he acknowledged (as he did) the simultaneous presence of allegory within Jewish circles. The bafflement expressed by De Lange, Harl, and Stroumsa over his charge of literalism seems to rest largely on the assumption that Origen's critique of Jewish exegesis as literalist was intended to be a description of all Jewish exegesis. But this appears not to have been the case.

And what, finally, are we to make of the observation with which this chapter began, that Origen customarily identified a whole range of exegetical deficiencies

---

[52] See the passages listed in n. 26. This judicious approach to Jewish exegesis fits the general pattern of how Origen assessed Gnostic exegesis and Greco-Roman learning (as already discussed in previous chapters). While these were often suspect, they were not always so, and in such circumstances they could be used for the purposes of his own exegesis. Recall his advocacy of a discriminating stance toward Gnostic exegesis (Hom Num 9.1.2) and Greco-Roman learning (Hom Gen 11.2 and Hom Lev 7.6.7).

[53] See n. 27 above.

in the biblical scholarship of the Gnostic heterodox, but in the case of Jewish exegesis, the only consistent charge he leveled was that it was literalist? The answer to this question appears to hinge on the actual interpretations to which Origen took exception in the Jewish and Gnostic exegetical communities. What most worried him in the former were interpretations that either denied Jesus was the prophesied Messiah or insisted upon the factual observance of the law's cultic prescriptions. As we have seen, for Origen both of these readings could be easily traced back to a literal exegesis of the biblical texts in question. There was simply no need to introduce other explanations for these troubling interpretations. Yet as we saw in the previous chapter, this was not the case with the two principal Gnostic interpretations with which Origen took issue. Neither a dualistic account of God nor a deterministic theory of human nature could be, or in fact was, easily explained by a reliance simply on the literal interpretation of Scripture. It appears, then, that at least one of the reasons why literalism became a convenient shorthand for Jewish and not Gnostic exegetical deficiencies was because there was such an obvious link in the former, but not the latter, between the search for the literal referent and the particular interpretations that proved so troubling.

LITERALISM AND EBIONITE EXEGESIS

In Origen's day, a fragmentary version of Jewish literalism also surfaced within the larger Christian community, particularly within his own congregations in Caesarea, a city with a thriving Jewish community. There are passages scattered throughout his homilies where we find him admonishing the laity for their adherence to some aspect or another of Jewish ceremonial life. In his *Homilies on Leviticus*, for instance, Origen makes a passing, critical remark about those in his Sunday congregation who attended a Jewish synagogue the previous day.[54] Or again, in his *Homilies on Jeremiah*, he reprimands women in his congregation who hold to the feast of unleavened bread.[55] Passages such as these confirm that not everyone agreed on where the boundaries between Judaism and Christianity ought to be located.[56] Much to his consternation,

---

[54] Hom Lev 5.8.3.

[55] Hom Jer 12.13.1 (as well as Hom Lev 10.2). On this theme, see N. de Lange, *Origen and the Jews*, 36, 86–87 and R. E. Heine, *Origen: Scholarship in the Service of the Church*, 172–176.

[56] For orientation to this complex theme, see J. D. G. Dunn, *The Partings of the Ways: Between Christianity and Judaism and their Significance for the Character of Christianity*, 2nd edn. (London: SCM, 2006); A. H. Becker and A. Y. Reeds, eds., *The Ways that Never Parted: Jews and Christians in Late Antiquity and the Early Middle Ages* (Tübingen: Mohr Siebeck, 2003); D. Boyarin, *Border Lines: The Partition of Judaeo-Christianity* (Philadelphia: University of Pennsylvania Press, 2004).

some of Origen's congregants perpetrated half (as it were) of the Jewish literalism he censured: while accepting Jesus as the prophesied Messiah, they nevertheless practiced several of the ceremonial precepts advocated in the Jewish law, validating this Jewish way of living with a literal interpretation of the relevant passages in the Torah. From Origen's perspective, these figures straddled clear boundaries.[57]

The scholarly literature today often designates these Christians as "Jewish Christians" or representatives of "Jewish Christianity."[58] As is the case with the label "Gnosticism," here too we face a number of challenges. Most concern how we ought to define these expressions, and whether we ought even to speak of Jewish Christianity as a singular movement.[59] There is, moreover, also the

---

[57] It is not clear whether Origen saw these figures primarily as Jews who had one notable Christian conviction (belief in Jesus as Messiah), or primarily as Christians who, like others within the broad Christian ambit, entertained heterodox convictions (so also N. de Lange, *Origen and the Jews*, 36, who thinks Origen does not tip his hand either way). The image of straddling boundaries seems appropriate, since Origen appears to have located these figures in both camps. There are, for instance, passages where he explicitly associates the Ebionites, believers in Jesus who accept parts of the Jewish law, with troubling Christian sects: Hom Lk 17.4 and Comm Rom 3.11.2 (where, like the Marcionites, some of them reject the virgin birth); Comm Titus/SC 464, 82.22–23 (like the Valentinians, they deny the virgin birth); CC 5.65 (like the Encratites, they do not accept Paul's letters); note esp. CC 2.1–3 (where Origen chastises Celsus for being unaware of the variety of approaches to the Jewish customs within the larger Christian church, and includes the Ebionites within the Christian fold). On the other hand, there are passages that just as clearly locate these figures in the Jewish world: Lk Frg 212 (where they are "Jewish Ebionites"); CC 5.61 (where they live like Jews in accordance with the Jewish law); Comm Matt 11.12 (where they "differ not much" from Jews by birth). There is a passage in his *Commentary on Matthew* that illustrates well how Origen thought of these figures sitting on both sides of the fence: they "choose to live like Jews in a bodily fashion alongside living in a Christian manner" (Comm Matt 12.5/GCS 10, 76.10–14).

[58] See F. J. Klijn and G. J. Reininck, *Patristic Evidence for Jewish-Christian Sects* (Leiden: Brill, 1973) for an anthology of early Christian literature on these figures. Scholarship on these groups is substantial. Readers can consult with profit: F. J. A. Hort, *Judaistic Christianity: A Course of Lectures* (Cambridge: Macmillan, 1894); H. J. Schoeps, "Ebionite Christianity," *JTS* 4 (1953): 219–224; R. A. Kraft, "In Search of 'Jewish Christianity' and its 'Theology': Problems of definition and methodology," *RSR* 60 (1972): 81–92; A. F. J. Klijn, "The Study of Jewish Christianity," *NTS* 20 (1973): 419–431; M. Simon, *Verus Israel: A Study of the Relations between Christians and Jews in the Roman Empire (132–425)* (Oxford: Oxford University Press, 1986); J. E. Taylor, "The Phenomenon of early Jewish-Christianity: Reality or scholarly invention?" *VC* 44 (1990): 313–334; S. C. Mimouni, *Le judéo-christianisme ancien: essais historiques* (Paris: Cerf, 1998); S. C. Mimouni and F. Stanley Jones, eds., *Le judéo-christianisme dans tous ses états* (Paris: Cerf, 2001); P. J. Tomson and D. Lambers-Petry, eds., *The Image of the Judaeo-Christians in Ancient Jewish and Christian Literature* (Tübingen: Mohr Siebeck, 2003); and recently (with full bibliography), O. Skarsaune and R. Hvalvik, eds., *Jewish Believers in Jesus: The Early Centuries* (Peabody, MA: Hendrickson, 2007).

[59] There is a good deal of fluidity in the modern definitions of these (and other related) expressions, as well as justified skepticism about whether we ought to be speaking of a singular movement, "Jewish Christianity," or of a plurality of movements that are somehow related, i.e. "Jewish Christianities." For a helpful survey of various definitions in circulation today, see J. C. Paget, "Jewish Christianity," in *Cambridge History of Judaism*, vol. 3, ed. W. Horbury, W. D. Davies, and J. Sturdy (Cambridge: Cambridge University Press, 1999), 733–742. Also note the ambiguities of the designation "Jewish Christian" in the French, German, and English

matter of the labels themselves. While "Jewish Christian" and "Jewish Christianity" are often considered neologisms only reaching back to the early seventeenth century,[60] there are in fact a handful of passages in the ancient literature that speak of "Jewish Christians."[61] In the case of Origen, we find close approximations to this terminology. On several occasions he speaks of "Jewish believers in Jesus" who accept Jesus as the Messiah yet embrace some of the precepts of the Jewish law.[62] On at least two occasions he explicitly identifies these figures as "Ebionites."[63] There are scattered references to these Christians in his corpus. While they accepted Jesus as the Messiah,[64] they themselves split into two groups over the issue of Jesus' birth: one sect accepted the virgin birth while the other argued he was the son of Joseph and Mary.[65] They rejected Paul's letters and elements of his teaching.[66] Of particular importance to Origen was their historical interpretation and literal observance of a number of the precepts in the Jewish law.[67] Because of this close affinity with the Jewish exegetical approach to the Scriptures and way of life, he did not hesitate to speak of them as "Jewish Ebionites [Ἰουδαῖοι

languages: M. Simon, "Problèmes du Judéo-Christianisme," in *Aspects du judéo-christianisme. Colloque de Strasbourg, 22–25 avril 1964* (Paris: Presses Universitaires de France, 1965), 1–17. For a helpful overview of several of the issues surrounding this theme, see the introductory essays in two recent volumes on the theme of Jewish Christianity: M. Jackson-McCabe, "What's in a name? The problem of 'Jewish Christianity,'" in *Jewish Christianity Reconsidered: Rethinking Ancient Groups and Texts*, ed. M. Jackson-McCabe (Minneapolis: Fortress Press, 2007), 7–38; O. Skarsaune, "Jewish believers in Jesus in antiquity—Problems of definition, method, and sources," in *Jewish Believers in Jesus*, 3–21.

[60] For a discussion of the history of these expressions (and their definitions) in modern scholarship, see J. C. Paget, "The definition of the terms 'Jewish Christian' and 'Jewish Christianity,'" *Jewish Believers in Jesus*, 30–48.

[61] See O. Skarsaune, "Jewish believers in Jesus in antiquity," in *Jewish Believers in Jesus*, 5–7.

[62] In CC 2.1 Origen speaks, for instance, of "Jewish believers [τοὺς ἀπὸ Ἰουδαίων πιστεύοντας]" (SC 132, 276.14); "Jewish believers in Jesus [οἱ ἀπὸ Ἰουδαίων εἰς τὸν Ἰησοῦν πιστεύοντες]" (SC 132, 276.18–19); later, in CC 2.4 he again refers to "believers from the Jewish people [πρὸς τοὺς ἀπὸ τοῦ λαοῦ πιστεύσαντας]" (SC 132, 288.1–2). Also see Eusebius' citation from book one of Origen's *Commentary on Matthew* where the latter refers to Matthew's gospel being written "for the believers from Judaism [τοῖς ἀπὸ Ἰουδαϊσμοῦ πιστεύσασιν]" (HE 6.25.4/ GCS 9.2, 576.10–11). Later in the *Commentary* Origen again speaks of "those among the Jews who believe in Jesus [τῶν ἀπὸ Ἰουδαίων πιστευόντων εἰς τὸν Ἰησοῦν]" (Comm Matt 16.12/GCS 10, 511.25–26).

[63] See CC 2.1 and Comm Matt 16.12.

[64] Hom Gen 3.5; Comm Matt 11.12; CC 2.1, 5.61.

[65] See Hom Lk 17.4 and Comm Titus/SC 464, 82.22–23 where they are said to deny the virgin birth (also see Eusebius, HE 6.27). In other passages, Origen acknowledges a debate in their circles about this issue: see Comm Matt 16.12 and CC 5.61.

[66] Hom Jer 19.12; Comm Matt Ser 79; CC 5.65.

[67] Sometimes, as in CC 2.1 and 5.61, Origen offers a blanket description of the Ebionites' adherence to the Jewish law: "they still want to live according to the law of the Jews like the multitude of the Jews" (CC 5.61). In other places he is more specific about how they live according to the (literal) Jewish law: they practice circumcision (Hom Gen 3.5); they maintain the distinction between pure and impure foods (Comm Matt 11.12); they celebrate the Passover and Feast of Unleavened Bread (Comm Matt Ser 79).

'Εβιωναῖοι],"[68] or as those who "want to live according to the law of the Jews like the multitude of the Jews,"[69] or even as those "who differ not much from them [Jews by birth]."[70] As a general rule, Origen has the Ebionites in mind when he censures Christians who accepted Jesus and yet still held literally to some facet of the ceremonial or liturgical law.[71]

The Ebionites approached a handful of passages in the law much as did the Jews, and so it is against these Christians, as well as others who shared similar convictions, that Origen aimed his critique of their literalist exegesis. In his twelfth *Homily on Jeremiah*, Origen, taking his cue from the reference to hearing "in a hidden way" (Jer 13:17), distinguishes between two competing interpretations of the law, one visible and the other hidden. He begins by addressing how the Jews interpret the law in a visible, outward, or literal way when they practice physical circumcision or celebrate the Passover. But then he immediately turns to otherwise anonymous women in his congregation who, he claims, also hear the law in this way. While it is advisable to interpret the passages detailing the feast of unleavened bread "in a hidden manner [κεκρυμμένως]," these women celebrate it "in a visible manner [φανερῶς]," as if it were corporeal.[72] In so doing, he preaches, "they go back 'to the poor and weak elementals' [cf. Gal 4:9], as if Christ had not yet appeared, who perfects us and leads us over from the elementals of the Law to the perfection of the Gospel."[73] These literal appropriations of select precepts in the Jewish law, Origen contends, disregard the advent of the Christ.

---

[68] Lk Frg 212/GCS 9, 319.3.

[69] CC 5.61/SC 147, 166, 29–30.

[70] Comm Matt 11.12/GCS 10, 52.30–31.

[71] There is an important qualification of this rule. There is at least one passage where Origen refers to Christians who accept Jesus and some facet of the literal law, but tellingly does not equate them with the Ebionites. As he notes in his *Homilies on Genesis*, there are those who have "accepted the name of Christ but nevertheless believe that the rule of carnal circumcision has to be accepted, like the Ebionites and any others who err with them in similar poverty of understanding" (Hom Gen 3.5/GCS 6, 44.19–22). Here Origen speaks of the Ebionites as if they do not exhaust the category of those who accept Jesus as Messiah and still hold to the literal precepts in the law. We ought to be cautious, then, about hurriedly designating such Christians in Origen's writings as Ebionites.

[72] Hom Jer 12.13.1/SC 238, 46.23–27. In the next line of this passage Origen notes that some of these same women "do not bathe the day [οὐ λούονται τὴν ἡμέραν] of the Sabbath" (SC 238, 46.30–31). This cryptic passage probably refers to Christian women who, following Jewish practice, abstained from entering a bath-house on the Sabbath. In so doing, Origen remarks, they fail to bathe or wash this day clean which they would do were they to adhere exclusively to the Christian Sabbath. See as well Origen's comments on Ps 118:38 (SC 189, 256.14–15) and R. E. Heine, *Origen: Scholarship in the Service of the Church*, 175.

[73] Hom Jer 12.13.1/SC 238, 46.31–34. The reference here to Christ leading people over from the law to the gospel is suggestive of another element in Origen's anti-Ebionite polemic. Note esp. Comm Matt Ser 79 where he acknowledges the Ebionite argument that for Christians to be imitators of Christ, they need to do as Jesus did: celebrate the Passover and Feast of Unleavened Bread. Origen replies there, as here in the *Homilies on Jeremiah*, with a passage from Galatians 4. While Jesus was admittedly born "under the Law [Gal 4:4]," this fact was not designed to keep

There is a passage in his *Commentary on Matthew* where Origen mentions the Ebionites by name, developing his contention that their exegesis amounts to a rejection of Jesus' exegetical tutelage. He reaches the text where Jesus contends that it is "not that which enters in the mouth that defiles a man, but that which proceeds out of the mouth" (Matt 15:11). Origen draws an exegetical lesson from this teaching:

> We are clearly taught in these words by the Savior that when we read in the books of Leviticus and Deuteronomy about the commands concerning clean and unclean foods—because we transgress these the bodily Jews and Ebionites who differ little from them level charges against us—we are not to think that the intent of Scripture is the obvious meaning about these things [μὴ νομίζειν τὸν σκοπὸν εἶναι τῇ γραφῇ τὸν πρόχειρον περὶ τούτων νοῦν].[74]

When Jesus insisted that no one was defiled who ate the foods traditionally declared unclean in Judaism, he was implying an eschewal of the literal interpretation of the Torah's injunctions about clean and unclean foods, the very sort of interpretation offered by the Ebionites of Origen's day. They flirted only with the surface sense of the food laws in Leviticus and Deuteronomy, missing thereby the deeper sense of these passages. A few sections later in this *Commentary*, Origen revisits Ebionite exegesis when he reaches the verse: "Watch out, and beware of the yeast of the Pharisees and Sadducees" (Matt 16:6). Origen interprets this yeast as the teaching of the law "according to the bare letter," and after juxtaposing it with the "new and spiritual" teaching of Jesus, he turns to his contemporary Ebionites: "And we might fittingly apply this passage to those who choose to live like Jews in a bodily fashion alongside living in a Christian manner [τοῖς μετὰ τοῦ Χριστιανίζειν αἱρουμένοις τὸ σωματικῶς Ἰουδαΐζειν]. For these neither see nor heed the leaven of the Pharisees and Sadducees, but contrary to the will of Jesus who forbade it, eat the bread of the Pharisees."[75]

One final passage from *Against Celsus* deserves close attention since it contains Origen's lengthiest discussion of the Ebionites, detailing how their literal adherence to the law entailed a denial of Jesus' loftier interpretations of this law. Origen opens book two by replying to the charge Celsus' literary Jew levels against "those of the Jewish people who have believed in Jesus."[76] According to the accusation, these Jews were deluded by Jesus into abandoning their traditional laws for the sake of another way of life. This charge probably took Origen by surprise, since he begins his response to Celsus by noting how his critic plainly overlooked the Ebionites. "He failed to notice that

---

those who were under the law permanently there, but rather to lead them away from the literal law to the spiritual law or gospel.

[74] Comm Matt 11.12/GCS 10, 52.28–53.4—transl. mine.
[75] Comm Matt 12.5/GCS 10, 76.10–14—transl. mine.
[76] CC 2.1/SC 132, 276.6–7.

Jewish believers in Jesus have not left the law of their fathers. For they live according to it, and derive their name from the poverty of their interpretation of the law."[77] Origen continues, offering an etymology of these Ebionites: "The Jews call a poor man Ebion, and those Jews who have accepted Jesus as the Christ are called Ebionites."[78] Origen then bolsters his response to Celsus by offering two other examples of Jews who followed Jesus, yet nevertheless maintained the customs of the Mosaic law: the apostles Peter and Paul. In the case of Peter, Origen cites the passage from Acts 10 where the apostle received a vision commanding him to kill and eat what was ritually unclean in preparation for his conversation with Cornelius who was "not an Israelite according to the flesh"—that Peter needed such a vision demonstrated that he was "still keeping the Jewish customs about clean and unclean things."[79] And even the apostle Paul, Origen notes, spoke of becoming a Jew to the Jews so that he might more effectively evangelize them (1 Cor 9:20). Origen recalls that Paul brought an offering to the altar in Jerusalem so that "he might persuade the Jews that he was not an apostate from the law [Act 21:26]."[80]

Having rebuffed Celsus' assertion that Jewish believers abandoned their ancestral laws at Jesus' instigation, Origen's argument takes a distinct, yet hardly surprising, turn. He immediately seeks to distance himself from the Ebionites since, while useful in refuting Celsus, they were decidedly less helpful on another front. Elsewhere in his writings, as here, Origen was explicitly critical of the way in which they adhered to their ancestral laws. (That he has little sympathy for their approach to the law here in *Against Celsus* is evident from his brief, pointed reference to their name: they are appropriately designated "Ebionites" because of their impoverished literal interpretation of the law.) Yet Origen faces a delicate task in turning his argument. He has just invoked two instances of the apostolic approach to the law that confirm, and perhaps even set a precedent for, the Ebionite approach. Now he seeks to chart a different course that advocates the allegorical or spiritual interpretation of the law. He must, then, somehow exonerate these apostles from their originally deficient literal interpretation of the law, while at the same time insist upon his criticism of those in the Christian ambit of his day who continue to read the law literally as Peter and Paul had once done. Moreover, Origen must also demonstrate that Christians who approach the law allegorically have not unwittingly opened themselves up to Celsus'

---

[77] CC 2.1/SC 132, 276.18–21—Chadwick slightly altered.

[78] SC 132, 276.21–278.23. Here the name refers to their poverty of their (literal) interpretation of the law. Elsewhere Origen speaks of the "poverty" of their thought (PA 4.3.8/GK 752, 34.1; Hom Gen 3.5), or the "poverty" of their faith in Jesus (Comm Matt 16.12/GCS 10, 513.2).

[79] CC 2.1/SC 132, 278.41–43. And a few lines later Origen describes Peter prior to his vision as "still a Jew" who was "still living according to the traditions of the Jews, despising those outside Judaism."

[80] CC 2.1/SC 132, 280.63–64.

initial critique, that followers of Jesus are a rebellious lot who have cast aside the Jewish law.

Origen signals the shift in his argument by remarking that he does "not think it out of place to quote a certain utterance of Jesus' gospel, and to explain it."[81] He turns to the passage in question where Jesus says: "I have still many things to say to you, but you cannot bear them now; but when he, the Spirit of Truth, is come, he shall guide you into all the truth [Jn 16:12-13]."[82] Origen wonders what teaching Jesus might have held in reserve from his disciples who could not during the time of his teaching ministry bear it. He proposes the following interpretation of Jesus' words:

> This is my view. Perhaps because the apostles were Jews and had been brought up in the literal interpretation of the Mosaic law [συντραφεῖσι τῷ κατὰ τὸ γράμμα Μωϋσέως νόμῳ], he had to tell them what was the true law, and of what "heavenly things" the Jewish worship was "a pattern and shadow" [Heb 8:5], and what were "the good things to come" of which "a shadow" [Heb 10:1] was provided by the law about meat and drink and feasts and new moons and Sabbaths [Col 2:16]. These were the "many things" which he had to tell them.[83]

A few lines later Origen clarifies: "By 'many things' he [Jesus] means the interpretation and knowledge of the law according to the spiritual sense [κατὰ τὰ πνευματικὰ]."[84] So, turning back to Peter's vision, Origen notes how before Peter received his vision of the unclean animals, "he had not yet learnt from Jesus to ascend from the letter of the law to its spiritual interpretation [ἀναβαίνειν ἀπὸ τοῦ κατὰ τὸ γράμμα νόμου ἐπὶ τὸν κατὰ τὸ πνεῦμα]."[85] However, after Jesus' passion and resurrection the "Spirit of Truth" finally approached Peter in a vision and guided him out of his "superstition" about the traditional distinction between clean and unclean foods, and into the "doctrine about true and spiritual meats."[86]

This line of argument serves several purposes. First, it is explicitly intended to absolve Peter of the charge of literalism that, as we already have seen in this chapter, Origen repeatedly directs against the Jews and Christians of his own day. Prior to the Spirit's instruction about how to interpret the Mosaic law suitably, Peter was legitimately unaware about its spiritual

---

[81] CC 2.2/SC 132, 282.3-4.
[82] CC 2.2/SC 132, 282.5-8.
[83] CC 2.2/SC 132, 282.11-18.
[84] CC 2.2/SC 132, 284.33-34—transl. mine. Note also how this identification of the "many things" Jesus wished to teach with the spiritual interpretation of the law is facilitated by the exegetical terminology Origen sees in John's gospel. Jesus will send the Spirit of ἀλήθεια, which by implication is not the Spirit of a τύπος. In Origen's day, the distinction between a figure (τύπος) and that which the figure figures (its ἀλήθεια), was already well established. This Spirit will help Jesus' followers discern the ἀλήθεια of scriptural figures.
[85] CC 2.1/SC 132, 278.25-27.
[86] CC 2.2/SC 132, 284.49-50.

interpretation.[87] At the same time, this argument also takes aim at the Ebionites. It is hard to miss Origen's swipe at their "poor" interpretation of the law. While Peter had an excuse for reading the law literally—Jesus' method of spiritual interpretation had not yet been imparted to him—this new approach to Scripture was sufficiently known by Jesus' followers in the subsequent Christian community that it left the Ebionites without excuse.

This argument also casts new light on Origen's initial rejoinder to Celsus. Contrary to this critic's claim, there are Jewish believers who have obviously kept their ancestral traditions. However, it is now clear that he thinks they have kept these traditions unacceptably since they interpret them literally. There are other Christians, Origen continues, who seek to discern the true, spiritual sense in the law, and in so doing, abandon only a *literal* adherence to the law. But this does not mean they are guilty of abandoning the "law of their fathers" as Celsus' Jew initially insisted. Origen secures this point by turning to the bane of the Ebionites, the apostle Paul, and notes how he explicitly invoked the law allegorically in his letters.[88] It is simply not true, Origen concludes this extended discussion of the Ebionites in *Against Celsus*, that Christians who interpret the law spiritually, as Paul did, despise it. On the contrary, they are the only ones who do justice to the ancestral law of the Jews. Indeed, "for Christians the introduction to the faith is based on the religion of Moses and the prophetic writings." However, Origen continues,

> the next stage of progress for beginners consists in the interpretation and exegesis of these. They seek the mystery "according to revelation," which has been kept in silence through times eternal, but now is manifested by the prophetic utterances and by the appearing of our Lord Jesus Christ [Rom 16:25–26]. It is not true, as you [Celsus] say, that as if progressing in knowledge they despise what is written in the law, but they accord it greater honour by showing what a depth of wise and mysterious doctrines is contained by those writings.[89]

For Origen, thus, the Ebionites and others with similar convictions in the Christian community practiced a limited version of the literalism that flourished in Jewish exegetical circles. While recognizing Jesus as the prophesied Messiah, they nevertheless insisted upon regarding several of the law's precepts literally. The common strand running through Origen's critique of their

---

[87] Of course, this exoneration of Peter opens the question of whether Jesus' contemporaries like the Pharisees could be legitimately blamed for their approach to the law (see n. 48 above).

[88] The two Pauline passages Origen cites in CC 2.3 are Galatians 4:21–24 (where the apostle refers to Hagar and Sarah in Genesis as allegories) and 1 Corinthians 9:8–10 (where he refers to the muzzled ox in Deuteronomy as relevant for "our sake").

[89] CC 2.4/SC 132, 288.8–290.18. Recall the point made above in Origen's critique of the Jewish exegesis of the law where he insisted (as he does here) that Christians who allegorize its ceremonial precepts are not rejecting the law, but rather keeping it, and indeed, keeping it properly since they adhere to its loftier sense.

exegesis is that it constituted a rejection of their Messiah's and the apostolic exegetical counsel.

ALLEGORICAL INSIGHT: THE EXEGETICAL TUTELAGE OF JESUS AND PAUL

Just as Origen's critique of Gnostic exegesis illumined his account of Scripture's ideal interpreter, so here as well. His encounter with Jewish and Ebionite exegesis highlights another defining feature in his profile of Scripture's ideal interpreter. The correct interpretation of the law and prophets within the new Israel ought to take its cues from Christianity's founder, Jesus, and its chief apostle, Paul. With such a portrayal of Scripture's ideal interpreter, the thesis for which I am arguing in this project finds further confirmation. Origen deliberately contextualized interpreters of Scripture within the drama of the Christian faith. As we have seen in this chapter, the exegetical enterprise afforded these Christian philologists an occasion to express various facets of their existing Christian commitment, and this certainly included their loyalty to the exegetical precedent set by Jesus and Paul. I draw this chapter to a close by examining this exegetical precedent more closely.

For Origen, the point of departure was Jesus who "explained the mysteries" in Israel's Scriptures.[90] The ideal interpreter turned to him for guidance in deciphering the spiritual sense in the law and prophets. Origen repeatedly makes this point with the help of 2 Corinthians 3:14–16, where Paul wrote of the Jews whose minds were occluded by a veil when they read Moses, yet how this veil was removed from anyone who turned to Jesus. In *On First Principles* Origen famously contends that it was only "after the advent of Jesus that the inspiration of the prophetic words and the spiritual nature of Moses' law came to light. For before the advent of Christ it was not at all possible to bring forward clear proofs of the divine inspiration of the old scriptures."[91] Indeed, Origen continues, "the light which was contained within the law of Moses, but was hidden away under a veil, shone forth at the advent of Jesus, when 'the veil was taken away' [cf. 2 Cor 3:15] and there came at once to men's knowledge those 'good things' of which the letter of the law held a 'shadow' [cf. Heb 10:1]."[92] Again, in his *Homilies on Ezekiel*, Origen makes a similar claim when he comments on Ezekiel's vision of the new, divinely infused temple, whose gate was closed (Ez 44:1–3). This temple symbolized the divinely inspired Scripture, and its closed gate pointed to the obstacles that hindered those who

---

[90] Comm Jn 1.33/GCS 4, 11.1–7.
[91] PA 4.1.6/GK 686, 301.13–688, 302.1.
[92] PA 4.1.6/GK 688, 302.7–10.

wished to penetrate the deeper sense of Scripture. When was this Scripture opened, and by whom?

> As long as my Lord had not come, the law was closed, the prophetic words were closed, the reading of the Old Testament was veiled, and "until this day when Moses is read, a veil lies over the hearts of the Jews" [cf. 2 Cor 3:14, 15]...But we "are converted to the Lord," so that when the veil is removed, we may say: "But we all with unveiled faces that behold the glory of the Lord are being transformed into the same image from glory to glory" [2 Cor 3:16, 18].[93]

More often than not Origen associated Jesus' exegetical tutelage with deciphering the Mosaic legislation. During his ministry, Jesus' teachings and actions challenged the literal observance of several of the liturgical and ceremonial prescriptions in the Torah.[94] This ministry embraced an exegetical approach to the law that Origen wished to espouse. For instance, in a passage already noted above from his *Homilies on Numbers,* he admits that there are those within the church who struggle with the precepts of the Jewish cult as outlined in the books of Leviticus and Numbers, such as the rites of sacrifice, or the observation of the Sabbath. When his congregants hear passages read in the church that advocate these practices they are offended and exclaim: "What need is there for this to be read in the church? What good are Judaic precepts to us and the observances of a rejected people?"[95] Origen responds by arguing that Moses is denigrated if Christians do not strive to understand how his "law is spiritual" (Rom 7:14). And they ought to strive, he continues, in the following manner: "'Let us be converted to the Lord' so that he may 'remove the veil' of the letter for us [2 Cor 3:16], so that the face of Moses may not seem ugly to us, but glorious and lovely, so that we may not merely disparage him, but also confer upon him praise and glory for the greatness of his meanings."[96] Elsewhere in his writings we find Origen making the same point about how Jesus helps with these difficult "Judaic precepts." For instance, in his response to Celsus' charge that Jesus was profane when he challenged the literal observance of the Mosaic law, Origen offers a sweeping reply: "Was it profane to abandon physical circumcision, and a literal Sabbath and literal feasts, literal new moons, and clean and unclean things, and rather to turn the mind to the true and spiritual law, worthy of God?"[97] Jesus' ministry offered a lens for assessing the law correctly.[98]

---

[93] Hom Ez 14.2.3/GCS 8, 452.16–23.

[94] For passages where Origen discusses Jesus' approach to the law, see the passages listed at nn. 48–50 above.

[95] Hom Num 7.2.4/GCS 7, 40.19–23.

[96] Hom Num 7.2.4/GCS 7, 40.27–41.2.

[97] CC 2.7/SC 132, 18–22.

[98] Recall CC 2.1–3 (discussed above in Origen's assessment of the Ebionites) where Jesus' exegetical ministry continued after his resurrection when, through the Holy Spirit, he taught his disciples "the interpretation and knowledge of the law according to the spiritual sense" (CC 2.2/

Yet it was Paul who took up the mantle of Jesus' exegetical tutelage in the nascent church. In response to Celsus' challenge that the Scriptures were "incapable of being interpreted allegorically," Origen swiftly replies: "We will quote a few examples out of a great number in order to show that Celsus falsely accuses the Bible to no purpose when he says that it cannot be interpreted allegorically."[99] Origen then proceeds to cite a number of passages in Paul's letters where he allegorized episodes in the law: the reference in Deuteronomy to not muzzling the oxen was written, according to Paul, "for our sake" (1 Cor 9:9–10); the passage in Genesis about a man leaving his father and mother to cleave to his wife refers to the mystery of Christ and his church (Eph 5:31–32); and episodes from the Hebrew exodus out of Egypt point likewise to Christ and the church (1 Cor 10:1–4). Throughout his entire career, Origen repeatedly invoked Paul's name as the practitioner and guide par excellence to the allegorical interpretation of Israel's Scriptures.[100] Perhaps Origen's clearest statement on the authority of Paul for the reading of the Old Testament can be found in the opening lines of his fifth *Homily on Exodus*. Here he offers a panegyric on the apostle, whose precedent in the interpretation of the Jewish law Origen wishes to follow. He is a disciple of Paul, and not the synagogue, when it comes to the interpretation of the law:

> The apostle Paul, "teacher of the Gentiles in faith and truth" [cf. 1 Tim 2:7] taught the Church which he gathered from the Gentiles how it ought to interpret the books of the Law. These books were received from others and were formerly unknown to the

---

SC 132, 284.33–34). Additional passages where Jesus instructs in the interpretation of the law: Hom Gen 13.2, 15.7; Hom Ex 7.1; Comm Matt 11.14; CC 2.76.

[99] CC 4.49/SC 136, 310.16–312.36.

[100] The verses where Paul either illustrates or commends the allegorical exegesis of the OT include: Rom 2:28–29 (PA 4.3.6; Hom Gen 3.4; Comm Rom 2.11.4), Rom 7:14 (Hom Gen 6.1, 11.1; Hom Ex 10.2; Hom Lev 16.1.3; Comm Matt 12.5; Comm Rom 2.13.19; PA, preface 8, 4.2.4; CC 7.20), Rom 9:8 (PA 4.3.6, 4.3.8), 1 Cor 5:8 (Hom Josh 2.1; Hom Jer 14.16.3; Comm Matt 12.5; Comm Jn 10.90), 1 Cor 9:9 (PA 4.2.6; Hom Lev 8.5.3; Hom Josh 9.8), 1 Cor 10:3–4 (Hom Ex 5.2; Hom Lev 7.4.2; Hom Num 7.2.2; Hom Jer 16.2.2; Comm Jn 6.227–228; CC 4.49; PA 4.2.6), 1 Cor 10:11 (CC 4.43; PA 4.2.6; Hom Lev 10.1.2, 15.3.2; Hom Josh 3.1; Comm Jn 1.34), 1 Cor 10:18 (Hom Ex 1.2, 8.2; Hom Jud 7.2; PA 4.1.4, 4.2.6, 4.3.6), 2 Cor 3:6 (Hom Gen 3.4; Hom Ex 7.1; Comm Matt 11.14, 15.2; Comm Jn 5.3, 5.8, 13.110, 13.140; Comm Eph 12; esp. CC 7:20), 2 Cor 3:7–8 (Hom Ex 12.1; Comm Rom 3.11.3; CC 7.20), 2 Cor 4:7 (Hom Ex 7.1; Comm Jn 1.24; PA 4.3.14), Gal 4:21–24 (Hom Gen 7.2, 10.1, 10.5; Hom Josh 9.8; Comm Rom 2.13.19; CC 4.44; PA 4.2.6), Eph 5:31–32 (CC 4.49; PA 4.3.7; Hom Gen 2.6, 9.2; Comm Matt 14.17), Phil 3:2–3 (Hom Gen 3.4; Hom Jer 5.14.1; Comm Rom 2.11.4, 2.12.1), Col 2:16ff (Hom Lev 7.4.2; Hom Num 27.8; Comm Matt 10.11, 12.5; CC 2.2, 2.7), Heb 8:5 (PA 4.2.6, 4.3.12; Comm Jn 10.85, 10.91), 10:1 (Hom Lev 8.5.3, 10.1.2; CC 2.2; Comm Matt 10.11; Comm Jn 1.39; PA 4.2.4, 4.2.6). Recall also how 1 Cor 2:13 could also be used to justify allegorical exegesis (see Chapter 3 and the discussion around clarifying unclear passages of Scripture with clearer ones). On Origen's view of Paul, see W. Völker, "Paulus bei Origenes," *Theologische Studien und Kritiken* 102 (1930): 258–279; H. de Lubac, *History and Spirit*, 77–86; R. P. C. Hanson, *Tradition*, 101–104; F. Cocchini, *Il Paolo di Origene: Contributo alla storia della recezione delle epistole paoline nel III secolo* (Rome: Edizioni Studium, 1992), 137–148.

Gentiles and were very strange. He feared that the Church, receiving foreign instructions and not knowing the principle of the instructions, would be in a state of confusion about the foreign document. For that reason he gives some examples of interpretation that we also might note similar things in other passages, lest we believe that by imitation of the text and document of the Jews we be made disciples. He wishes, therefore, to distinguish disciples of Christ from disciples of the Synagogue by the way they understand the Law. The Jews, by misunderstanding it, rejected Christ. We, by understanding the Law spiritually, show that it was justly given for the instruction of the Church.[101]

In this remarkable passage Origen distinguishes (as we have already seen above) "disciples of Christ" from the "disciples of the Synagogue" simply in terms of their respective approaches to the law. The latter, he contends, "misunderstand" the law as they are still beholden to principles of exegesis that do not uncover its spiritual message. The former, however, take their cues from the apostle Paul and learn how to read this foreign Jewish collection of writings spiritually, thereby appropriating the law for the instruction of the church.

Of course, when Jesus and Paul pointed to the deeper sense of the law and prophets, they were not highlighting something that the authors of these Scriptures did not already know. To the certain consternation of Ebionite and Jewish exegetes, Origen contended that Moses and the prophets already discerned the deeper, spiritual sense of their writings that Christians would later recover. For instance, Origen explains to Celsus that Christians value Israel's Scriptures without falling into the "mythologies of the Jews," because they "are educated by mystical contemplation of the law and the prophets." He continues, arguing that it is the prophets themselves who knowingly introduce another sense into their writings: "[t]he prophets also do not limit the meaning of their sayings to the obvious history and to the text and letter of the law. For in one place, when about to recount supposed history, they say: 'I will open my mouth in parables, I will utter dark sayings of old' [Ps 77(78):2]."[102] Elsewhere he could make the same point quite ingeniously. In his *Commentary on Romans*, Origen contends that the Jews of his day do not possess the Scriptures because they do not discern within them their specifically Christian sense, their "glory," "power," or "sense of Christ." Rather than make this point by dwelling on Paul's claim that the letter kills (2 Cor 3:16), Origen argues that already Moses, the great leader of Judaism and author of its law, corroborated the apostle's claim. Moses conveyed this point through a symbolic gesture. The tablets of the law represented the letter of the law, and when Moses broke these tablets he conveyed already on Mt. Sinai that the law's letter should be similarly destroyed.

---

[101] Hom Ex 5.1/GCS 6, 183.11–21.
[102] CC 2.6/SC 132, 294.9–13. For very similar passages about the prophets' insight into the deeper sense of their writings, see CC 1.50 and 4.49.

Suppose the Jews are unwilling to accept the opinion of our Apostle which says that the letter of the law kills [cf. 2 Cor 3:6]. Perhaps they think injury is done to the law if it would seem to be spurned according to the letter. Let us then turn back to Moses himself and see how highly he esteemed the letter of the law. When he had received the stone tablets inscribed by the finger of God [Ex 31:18], he conferred so little honor upon the letter of the law that he threw down the tablets from his own hands and shattered to pieces what had in fact been written by the finger of God [Ex 32:19]. Yet he was not branded as being guilty of impiety because of this act. You see, then, that it is not Paul alone who spurns the letter of the law, but well before him Moses had also spurned and rejected and broken up the letters of the law. In so doing he was without doubt even then showing that the glory and power of the law was not contained in the letters but in the Spirit.[103]

There are numerous passages in his writings where Origen credits insight into the spiritual sense of Israel's Scriptures to the authors of these writings, or indeed, to other holy Jews prior to the coming of Jesus.[104]

In this chapter I have argued that Origen's critique of Jewish literalism, as well as its restricted counterpart in the Christian community, went far beyond a mere procedural assessment of philology. At its core, this critique concerned central Christian practices and beliefs. What elicited Origen's censure was a handful of literal interpretations that squarely confronted and undermined central Christian convictions, namely the denial that Jesus was Israel's prophesied Messiah and the continuance of Jewish liturgical and ceremonial customs. The Ebionites committed the latter fallacy, the Jews both. These varieties of literalism could, moreover, be implicated in varying degrees in the rejection of Jesus' and Paul's exegetical instruction. For Origen, then, this encounter with Jewish and Ebionite exegesis accentuated another feature in his profile of Scripture's ideal interpreter. These interpreters avoided the pitfalls of Jewish literalism when they "turned to the Lord" (2 Cor 3:16) and his apostle Paul for insight into their interpretation of the law and prophets. In this way, Christian conviction transformed the exegetical enterprise.

---

[103] Comm Rom 2.14.12/Bammel 2.10(14): 122–133. Also see Hom Jer 14.12.3.

[104] Though Origen was convinced that, by the time of Jesus, most interpreters of these Scriptures in Judaism failed to grasp this spiritual sense (see n. 48). For references to the authors of Israel's Scriptures knowing the deeper sense of their own writings, see esp. Comm Rom 2.14.6–8, as well as Hom Gen 13.2; Comm Matt 17.2; Comm Jn 6.15–31, 13.314–319; CC 2.6, 5.44, 5.46, 6.78. Note also CC 7.20 where Origen writes: "We maintain that the law has a twofold interpretation, one literal and the other spiritual, as was also taught by some of our predecessors." He immediately turns to Ezekiel to justify the spiritual interpretation of the law, but then corrects himself: it is "not so much we as God, speaking in one of the prophets, who described the law literally understood as 'judgments that are not good' [Ez 20:25] . . . and in the same prophet God is represented as saying that the law spiritually understood is 'judgments that are good' [Ez 20:11]" (SC 150, 60.8–13).

8

Conduct: Moral Inquiry

In the second part of this study I have argued that Origen located the ideal interpreter of Scripture within the Christian drama of salvation, and that he did so in several different ways. The best of this interpreter's learning, including the discipline of philology, was not foreign to Christianity, but rather enjoyed divine provenance and ushered the interpreter into communion with God (Chapter 4). The commitment to embark upon a scholarly examination of Scripture manifested an obedience to Jesus' command to "search the Scriptures," marked the mind's abandonment of the world as it pursued the things of God, and signaled the attempt to grasp Christianity more profoundly by augmenting a simple faith with a first-hand acquaintance with its Scriptures (Chapter 5). In the last two chapters I explored several of Origen's guidelines for interpreting Scripture well. His critique of Gnostic exegetes revealed the importance of adhering to the church's rule of faith and interacting discerningly with Greco-Roman learning (Chapter 6). His account of Jewish and Ebionite exegesis indicated how central Jesus' and Paul's exegetical tutelage was for reading the law and prophets well (Chapter 7). In this chapter I continue to trace the contours in Origen's profile of the ideal exegetical life by turning to a new topic: how the moral character and conduct of the Christian philologist influenced scriptural interpretation. With this topic, then, I further confirm the overarching thesis of this project, that the ideal interpreter of Scripture for Origen was a participant in the Christian drama of salvation.

One of Origen's oft-repeated maxims was that only those who were "worthy" or "pure"—that is, only those who had made some moral progress on the itinerary of the Christian faith—could interpret the Scriptures well.[1] I touched

---

[1] For literature on Origen's account of the moral life, see W. Capitaine, *De Origenis Ethica* (Munster: Aschendorff, 1898); W. Völker, *Das Vollkommenheitsideal des Origenes: Eine Untersuchung zur Geschichte der Frömmigkeit und zu den Anfängen christlicher Mystik* (Tübingen: J. C. B. Mohr, 1931); G. Bardy, "Les idées morales d'Origène," *Mélanges des Science Religieuse* 13 (1956): 23–38; P. Nemeshegyi, "La morale d'Origène," *Revue d'ascétique et de mystique* 37 (1961): 409–428; G. Gruber, *ΖΩΗ—Wesen, Stufen und Mitteilung des wahren Lebens bei Origenes* (Munich: Max Hueber, 1962); B. J. M. Bradley, *Arete as a Christian Concept: The Structural Elements of Origen's Doctrine* (Thesis. University of Cambridge, 1976); J. Dillon,

upon this intersection between exegesis and morality when I explained how, for Origen, the decision to embark upon a life of scriptural study marked a watershed in the interpreter's moral growth, since inquiry into loftier matters replaced a disordered preoccupation with the physical world. Yet this was not the only way in which the moral life surfaced in biblical interpretation. As imperative as it was *that* interpreters directed an interest toward Scripture, what followed was equally important: *how* interpreters directed their interest. In this chapter I examine this latter theme in detail, exploring the various ways in which interpreters-at-work were moral agents for Origen. What character and conduct informed scriptural interpretation, and how precisely did these commitments shape the exegetical enterprise? In this chapter we will also encounter the familiar autobiographical refrain that frequently attends Origen's account of Scripture's ideal interpreter. He not only advocated moral inquiry into Scripture, but was also seen as a "friend and guide to the virtues (φίλος τῶν ἀρετῶν καὶ προήγορος)," who sought to embrace this principled pattern of inquiry for himself.[2]

MORAL CONDITIONING

In his weighty tome *Origène et la "Connaissance Mystique*," Henri Crouzel succinctly remarked that for Origen "the most important subjective condition for knowledge is the moral and ascetic life."[3] There is ample evidence that confirms that this principle held for the project of scriptural exegesis as well.

"Plotinus, Philo and Origen on the grades of virtue," in *Platonismus und Christentum: Festschrift für Heinrich Dörrie*, ed. H.-D. Blume and F. Mann (Munster: Aschendorffsche Verlagsbuchhandlung, 1983), 92–105; R. Wilken, "Alexandria: A school for training in virtue," in *Schools of Thought in the Christian Tradition*, ed. P. Henry (Philadelphia: Fortress Press, 1984), 15–30; E. Schockenhoff, *Zum Fest der Freiheit: Theologie des christlichen Handelns bei Origenes* (Mainz: Matthias-Grünewald, 1990); J. J. Alviar, *Klesis: The Theology of the Christian Vocation According to Origen* (Dublin: Four Courts, 1993); F. Cocchini, "Il progresso spirituale in Origene," in *Spiritual Progress: Studies in the Spirituality of Late Antiquity and Early Monasticism*, ed. M. Sheridan and J. Driscoll (Rome: Centro studi S. Anselmo, 1994), 29–45; L. F. Pizzolato and M. Rizzi, eds., *Origene maestro di vita spirituale/Origen: Master of Spiritual Life (Milano, 13–15 Settembre 1999)* (Milan: Vita e Pensiero, 2001); L. Larson, "Virtue," *WHO*.

[2] According to the testimony of Origen's Caesarean pupil, Gregory, in the *Address of Thanksgiving* (12/SC 148, 156.15). A recurring theme in this treatise is that Origen not simply taught but also lived the moral or virtuous life (see esp. 9/SC 148, 144.12–14; 9/SC 148, 146.56–148.2; 11/SC 148, 150.1–22). See also R. Wilken, "Alexandria: A school for training in virtue," 23–25.

[3] *Connaissance*, 409 (he elaborates on this theme, including its philosophical precedent, on 409–428). For passages in Origen's corpus that express this sentiment, see Hom Gen 14.4; Hom Ex 3.3; Hom Num 5.1.2; Hom Josh 12.2; Comm Song of Songs 1/GCS 8, 107.1–11; Comm Matt 12.14, 17.3; Hom Lk 3.4; Comm Rom 1.1.4, 2.14.19; PA 1.1.9, 1.3.8, 2.7.2, 3.3.3; CC 2.24, 3.34, 3.59–62, 6.4, 6.13, 6.17, 6.77, 7.39, 7.44; Phil 1.28.

Origen frequently contended that for interpreters to glean knowledge from Scripture, they first had to evince a robust commitment to the moral standards advocated in Christianity. Such commitment was not merely useful, but actually necessary for the interpreter's exegetical success. Sometimes Origen expressed this counsel negatively, cautioning against the consequences of a morally deficient life for the would-be interpreter. There is a passage in his first *Homily on Leviticus*, for instance, where he contends that the interpreter's "stains of sins" prevent an appreciation for the wonders of the Scriptures:

> Therefore we must entreat the Lord himself, the Holy Spirit himself so that he might deign to remove every cloud and all darkness which, hardened by the stains of sins, obscures the vision of our heart in order that we might be able to behold the spiritual and wonderful knowledge of his Law, according to him who said, "Unveil my eyes and I will observe the wonders of your Law [Ps 118:18]."[4]

It is these otherwise unspecified blemishes that obscure the mind's vision, preventing it from gazing upon the glorious truths inscribed in God's law. Conversely, there are numerous passages where Origen lauds the virtuous life as an indispensable condition for reading Scripture well. In his first *Homily on the Song of Songs* he spells out the moral requirements for becoming "worthy of spiritual mysteries" woven throughout the Scriptures. "It is necessary," he preaches, "for the one who knows how to hear the Scriptures spiritually, or certainly for one who does not know how but desires to know how, to contend with all his effort so as not to be turned back to flesh and blood." Origen proceeds by clarifying that he does not mean such an interpreter has despised literal flesh and blood, but rather "money and possessions and the very earth and heaven." If such an interpreter works industriously to renounce these interests, "it is possible to become worthy of spiritual mysteries."[5]

Admittedly, these exhortations to the importance of ethical conduct for proper scriptural interpretation can easily come across as pious commonplaces. After all, Origen often makes these claims sweepingly, with little articulation of the particular virtues that might be most relevant for biblical scholarship. Even more conspicuous is that he usually does not explain *how* or *why* ethical conduct should ever matter for biblical scholarship in the first place. We could be excused for initially thinking that a profound connection between morality and exegesis does not exist in his writings.[6] Yet when we delve more deeply into Origen's

---

[4] Hom Lev 1.1.4/GCS 6, 281.18–23.

[5] Hom Song of Songs 1.2/GCS 8, 31.2–7, 31.11–15. Also see Hom Jer 5.8.2 for a similar reflection on "dishonorable works" and how they occlude the meaning of Scripture; in Hom Ez 3.1.2 Origen disqualifies those who are preoccupied with the "affairs of the world," "worldly cares," or "the hunger to have more" from grasping the message in Scripture.

[6] H. de Lubac, for instance, offers only a very brief discussion of Origen's moral requirements for proper exegesis, and does not explain why these requirements actually mattered for Origen (*History and Spirit*, 365–366).

moral thought, we discover explicit rationale for why he thought the interpreter's moral commitments were indispensable for unraveling the many challenges surrounding scriptural scholarship. One of these reasons was that interpreters who embraced the Christian moral life came to the Scriptures with expectations that were harmonious with and thus conducive to extracting their message. Or expressed negatively, those who were deficient in this way of life invariably distorted the message in these writings because they made it conform to a pattern of conduct incompatible with their original moral tenor.

For Origen, those embarking upon the path of scriptural scholarship were invariably unprepared for the message Scripture's authors sought to convey. As we have already seen, part of this lack of preparation concerned education: did these budding interpreters possess the basic literary competence necessary for deciphering these writings?[7] But this lack of preparation also extended into the moral sphere. Scripture was a collection of writings overflowing with the profound moral convictions of its authors—not simply the convictions of Moses, the prophets, evangelists and apostles, but also those of the divine authors who helped compose these Scriptures.[8] Thus an incongruity often existed between the life and message of the scriptural authors on the one hand, and the desires, inclinations, and thoughts of would-be interpreters on the other. Those who failed to exemplify the sort of character and conduct advocated in the Christian Scriptures often forcibly read into these writings the discordant patterns of living that they espoused.[9]

Thus we regularly find Origen alert to interpreters of baser character, warning them against approaching Scripture while still harboring expectations about its message that were little more than extensions of their own ignoble disposition. These warnings are especially acute when Origen confronts passages in these

---

[7] Recall the discussion in Chapters 2 and 3 where Origen advocated that interpreters achieve a scholarly expertise adequate for a learned comprehension of the Scriptures.

[8] See in particular the section entitled "Authorial intent" in the next chapter.

[9] It is important to note that when Origen calls for a moral correspondence between the interpreter and Scripture's authors, this particular exegetical counsel distinctly echoes his discussion of the mind's more expansive quest to know God. This quest cannot transpire happily, he similarly insists, unless the mind achieves some sort of conformity to God. In *Against Celsus* Origen finds himself in a debate about "knowing and seeing" God and clarifies that the only sort of mind that can know God is the mind that has come to resemble this God: "And that which sees God is a pure heart, from which evil thoughts no longer proceed, nor murders, nor adulteries, nor fornications, nor thefts, nor false witnessings, nor blasphemies, nor an evil eye, nor any other evil deed. That is why it is said: 'Blessed are the pure in heart, for they shall see God' [Matt 5:8]" (CC 7.33/SC 150, 88.11–13, 88.13–90.19). In passages such as these, Origen repeatedly emphasizes the importance of Christian character and conduct broadly construed for the deeper knowledge of God (also see CC 3.59–62 and 6.69). The topic we are examining here—that interpreters strive for a moral resemblance with the life and message of Scripture's authors—does not simply mirror the theme of the mind's quest to know God. It is more precisely an individual episode in this larger drama of salvation. The pattern that holds for the mind's sweeping quest for God holds also for the interpreter's need to emulate Scripture's ultimate author, God.

Scriptures that on the surface admit troubling moral interpretations. In *On First Principles,* for instance, he discusses the future eschatological state of souls and is eager to dismiss any scriptural interpretation that would have heaven populated with humans of flesh and blood who will marry, have children, and reside in a bejeweled Jerusalem. While there are passages in Scripture that conceivably admit such corporeal readings, it is only those interpreters who are *already* captivated by the pleasures of the corporeal world who would dare offer such readings. Those who "seek after the outward and literal meaning of the law, or rather, give way to their own desires and lusts, disciples of the mere letter, consider that the promises of the future are to be looked for in the form of pleasure and bodily luxury."[10] Those, in other words, who are already beholden to sexual and material pleasure offer scriptural interpretations that follow such preoccupations. Such interpretations, Origen adds, are out of step with the true "figurative and spiritual" sense of the Scriptures and, as a result, these readers "extract from them nothing that is worthy of the divine promises."[11]

Not surprisingly, this same concern for the interpreter's moral formation surfaces in the prologue to Origen's *Commentary on the Song of Songs.* The patently erotic sense of this book makes him apprehensive, since those who live according to the "molestations of flesh and blood" and who have a desire for "material nature" will not think to look beyond this book's literal sense to its pure and chaste message:

> But if anyone should approach [it, i.e. Song of Songs], who is a man only according to the flesh, to such a one there emerges from this Scripture no little amount of hazard and danger. For this one, not knowing how to hear the words of love purely and with chaste ears, will bend the whole manner of his hearing away from the inner to the outward and carnal man . . . For this reason, therefore, I advise and counsel everyone who is not yet free of the molestations of flesh and blood and has not withdrawn from the affection for material nature, to refrain completely from reading this little book and the things that are said in it.[12]

Here again, it is the interpreter who lives "according to the flesh" who distorts the sense of this book by conforming its message ("bending" it) to his own preoccupations. In both of these passages we see how, for Origen, interpreters who have failed to undergo an adequate moral formation are adversely prejudiced when they approach the lofty message in Scripture. Their expectations about its message deviate from, and thus also easily distort, the message Scripture's authors sought to convey.

Expressed affirmatively, however, interpreters who lived or aspired to the Christian moral life found themselves well positioned for studying Scripture insightfully. These interpreters achieved in their lives a degree of conformity

---

[10] PA 2.11.2/GK 440, 184.5–9.   [11] PA 2.11.2/GK 442, 186.3.
[12] Comm Song of Songs prol./GCS 8, 62.12–16; 19–22.

with Scripture's message, and by extension, with the lives and ideals of the authors who composed this message. Origen famously voices this principle in the first book of his ambitious *Commentary on John*. There he is grappling with the problem of who can understand John's difficult gospel well. He begins his proposal in a straightforward manner: to understand this gospel would-be interpreters need to resemble its author, John. The meaning of John's gospel, Origen writes, "no one can understand who has not leaned on Jesus' breast [Jn 21:20] nor received Mary from Jesus to be his mother also [Jn 19:26]."[13] But what exactly about John's life does the interpreter need to imitate or resemble? Origen answers by curiously insisting that for interpreters to become like this author, they actually need to become like Jesus: "But it is necessary for the one who will be another John to become so great that, like that John, he be shown by Jesus to be a Jesus."[14] Here Origen is cryptically alluding to Jesus' statement to his mother Mary about John: "Behold your son" (Jn 19:26). While on the cross, Jesus did not say of John, "Behold this man is *also* your son," as if John was another of Mary's sons. Rather, in saying "Behold, your son," Jesus was announcing John's profound Christ-likeness to his mother: "This is Jesus whom you bore." Origen further ruminates that Jesus could only have right-fully called John another Jesus because, with Paul, he knew that "everyone who has been perfected 'no longer lives,' but 'Christ lives in him'" (cf. Gal 2:20). It was, then, only because "Christ lives" in the perfected John that Jesus uttered, "Behold your son, the Christ."[15] In Origen's mind, thus, the qualifications required of interpreters of John's gospel were nothing less than bringing their lives into compliance with John's life. Yet since his life had become so perfected and "so great" that Christ had come to live in him, render him Christ-like, and call him, accordingly, Mary's son, interpreters of John's gospel were ultimately called to the imitation of Christ.[16]

There are a number of other passages where Origen forges a similar (though less labyrinthine) link to the one he makes here in the *Commentary on John*. He repeatedly accentuates the need for interpreters to undergo a transform-ation in their character so that they resemble more closely the life and message of the authors they were attempting to interpret.[17] Implicit in these passages is Origen's conviction that interpreters were often inadequate to the moral

---

[13] Comm Jn 1.23/GCS 4, 8.16–18. Also see Hom Ez 6.4.3 for Origen's interpretation of reclining on the breast of Jesus.

[14] Comm Jn 1.23/GCS 4, 8.18–20—transl. mine.

[15] Comm Jn 1.23/GCS 4, 9.1–3.

[16] In arguing that interpreters need to become Christ-like, Origen was probably thinking not only about their conformity to the author of the gospel (as we have seen), but also of their conformity to this gospel's *theme*: Jesus himself. See also Hom Ez 3.1.2.

[17] See Hom Gen 7.2 and 10.5 (where Origen cites 1 Cor 2:14: "The sensual man does not perceive the things that are of the Spirit of God"); Hom Num 27.7; Hom 1.2 Ps 36; Hom Ez 3.1; Comm Matt 12.36–38; Comm Jn 10.300; Comm Rom 7.17.4; Phil 15.19; PA 2.11.2.

contours of the scriptural message. Such interpreters invariably twisted its sense to make it mirror their own concerns. To remedy this situation Origen argued that interpreters needed, instead, to mirror the lives and ideals of the authors they were examining, so that the emerging moral congruity created expectations commensurate to Scripture's message. Those who underwent such a moral formation were well conditioned to anticipate the true sense of the Scriptures.

Yet this was not the only way in which Origen understood the moral life to shape the exegetical enterprise. For him, scholarly competence both harnessed to the sort of exegetical guidelines highlighted in the previous two chapters, and embraced by someone who cultivated an admirable moral profile, did not always suffice in yielding valid interpretations of Scripture. In keeping with his rigorous philological training, Origen frequently emphasized the linguistic difficulties that lurked on the scriptural page. One of the hallmarks of his account of these writings was that they were opaque documents whose meaning was not readily discernible to interpreters. This is a leading motif in book four of *On First Principles*, his most extensive treatment of Scripture and its interpretation. Here, as elsewhere, Origen repeatedly alerts his readers to the indecipherable quality of the Scriptures—they are full of difficulties, impossibilities, irrationalities, riddles, parables, and enigmas.[18] Laden, then, as the Scriptures were with these obstacles, they often had a deleterious effect on unsuspecting interpreters, thwarting their quest for understanding. In this situation, Origen called for a heightened moral response that went well beyond embracing a morality that shaped the interpreter's expectations about the scriptural message.

In what follows I will argue that there were three distinct facets of this moral response: the interpreter's exegetical virtues, the exercise of trust, and the practice of prayer. Some interpreters needed to be emboldened to apply themselves more inquisitively, attentively and diligently to vexing scriptural passages—to exercise what I will call exegetical virtues when studying Scripture. Still others needed to cultivate an enduring trust that a helpful message resided in Scripture. These were interpreters who were thwarted by difficult passages that had, in turn, triggered discouragement or even abandonment of inquiry. Finally, other interpreters still needed to turn in prayer to God for help in deciphering what appeared undecipherable. Each of these facets of the interpreter's moral life played a leading role within the exegetical enterprise. And as we will see below, on a number of occasions Origen's discussion of these topics turned autobiographical as he referred to his own often futile attempts to offer this heightened moral response.

---

[18] See PA 4.1.7, 4.2.2–3, 4.2.8–9, 4.3.1–5. This theme surfaces elsewhere: Hom Gen 2.6; Hom Lev 6.3, 7.5, 10.2; Hom Num 25.3; Hom 3.9 Ps 37; Comm Matt 14.5, 15.1–2; Comm Jn 2.172–173; Comm Rom 1.10; Phil 2.1, 2.5; CC 6.17, etc.

EXEGETICAL VIRTUES

In the following paragraph from his *Commentary on Romans* Origen offers an illuminating introduction to the exegetical virtues. Here he provides an unusually rich description of the dispositions interpreters ought to espouse if they wish to unlock the riddles in Scripture. He writes:

> Therefore, if there is some secret and hidden thing of God we long to know . . . let us faithfully and humbly inquire into the more concealed judgments of God that are sown in the Holy Scriptures. Surely this is also why the Lord was saying, "Search the Scriptures [Jn 5:39]!" since he knew that these things are opened not by those who fleetingly listen to or read [the Scriptures] while occupied with other business, but by those who with an upright and sincere heart search more deeply into the Holy Scriptures, by constant effort and uninterrupted nightly vigils. I know well that I myself am not one of these. But if anyone seeks in this way, he will find.[19]

Origen highlights the need to examine Scripture "faithfully and humbly," to search it with an "upright and sincere heart," and to do so not "fleetingly," distracted by other affairs, but rather vigilantly and with "constant effort." Interestingly, toward the end of this passage there is also an autobiographical remark in which he laments his deficit when it comes to reading Scripture in such a principled manner. When it comes to the exegetical virtues, self-referential comments (and often self-effacing comments, as here) occur with some frequency in Origen's writings. Among other things, such remarks testify to the high regard in which he held these moral qualities for interpretive activity. In what follows, I will offer a compendium of the virtues (and corresponding vices) that Origen thought colored the very act of scriptural inquiry. While he employed a vast moral lexicon, most of these terms signified virtues that can be conveniently grouped under four headings: inquisitiveness, open-mindedness, watchfulness, and exertion.[20]

1. Ideal interpreters were *inquisitive*. Origen draws book four of *On First Principles* to a close by encouraging the reader who "is more curious [*curiosius*] and persists in asking for an explanation of every detail" to pursue the

---

[19] Comm Rom 7.17.4/Bammel, 626.25–34. In book four of *On First Principles* we find another particularly rich description of the virtuous pattern of scriptural inquiry. The ideal reader is depicted variously in the course of a few lines as obedient to the Savior's precept, "Search the Scriptures" (Jn 5:39), being precise, investigating carefully, reading the divine books reverently, believing them to be divine writings, and, at the end of this list, exercising much attention (PA 4.3.5/GK 744, 330.14–746, 331.17).

[20] While there is discussion of the virtues in Origen's theology (see the literature in n. 1) the relevance of this topic for his understanding of the scriptural interpreter has been woefully underdeveloped, if not overlooked. For instance, in a section of H. de Lubac's chapter "The effort to understand" there is only an incomplete account of what will follow here (*History and Spirit*, 365–372). R. P. C. Hanson is all but silent on this issue in *Allegory and Event*. In W. A. Bienert's *"Allegoria" und "Anagoge"* there is a strangely reductionistic position about the moral qualifications of the interpreter: "The sole presupposition for a true understanding of Scripture is faith" (48).

deeper allegorical interpretation of Scripture with Paul as a guide.[21] Origen expresses this theme elsewhere. In his *Commentary on Matthew*, for instance, he exhorts those who listen to Scripture "more inquisitively [περιεργότερον]" to make further inquiry into the gospel text.[22] Such interpreters are taken by an eagerness or love of learning (φιλομάθεια). Origen concludes his *Letter to Africanus* with the remark that further study of the history of Susanna requires "someone who has studied the divine writings with a love for knowledge [φιλομαθῶς] and competence."[23] In an excursus on the reliability of the names in Scripture, he writes: "We will present a few things, therefore, that those who are eager for learning [τοὺς φιλομαθεῖς] might become more attentive about these matters."[24]

Origen often criticized his exegetical adversaries for their failure to cultivate reading virtues. This included a lack of inquisitiveness. In a fragment from the second book of his *Commentary on Matthew* he censures the Gnostic inability to detect the one melodic meaning that runs throughout the Old and New Testaments. He describes keen students of Scripture as those who learn to discern its harmonious meaning, and twice refers to them as those "who desire to learn [τοῖς μανθάνειν ἐθέλουσι]"[25] and "truly love to learn [τοῖς ... γνησίως φιλομαθοῦσιν]."[26] Numenius the Pythagorean wins Origen's approval because he, unlike Celsus, had a greater desire "to examine even our writings with an eager desire for knowledge [φιλομαθῶς]."[27] Even Heracleon comes in for scrutiny. He misinterpreted the significance of "Capharnaum," and Origen counsels in reply that the "one eager for knowledge in Christ [ἐν Χριστῷ φιλομαθεῖ]" ought to see what all four gospels have to say about this city so as to avoid a bad reading.[28]

2. The inquisitive interpreter ought also to be *fair* and *open-minded*. In *Against Celsus* Origen responds to his opponent's skepticism about the

---

[21] PA 4.3.14/GK 774, 345.10. Also see PA 2.8.3.

[22] Comm Matt 14.14/GCS 10, 315.19–20. As É. Junod has noted, for Origen this Greek family of terms took on the positive sense of curiosity, as well as the pejorative sense of an excessive or meddlesome interest (see his instructive discussion of περιεργάζω, περιεργία, and περίεργος in SC 226, 196–198, n. 2). In his *Commentary on John*, for instance, Origen keeps close watch on himself, deliberating if he is not, in fact, only expressing a prying interest in Scripture. After patching together several possible interpretations of the reference to Judas departing immediately after receiving the morsel from Jesus (Jn 13:30), Origen encourages his readers to give closer attention to the peculiarities of the verse, "unless", he cautions, "I am inquiring superfluously [εἰ δὲ μὴ περιέργως ζητῶ]" (Comm Jn 32.303/GCS 4, 467, 16—transl. mine). For other examples where he warns against such a meddlesome interest in Scripture, see Hom Jer 7.3.3; Comm Matt 16.2; Comm Jn 32.294.

[23] LA 23/SC 302, 572.4–5—transl. mine.

[24] Comm Jn 6.213/GCS 4, 150.25–26.

[25] Phil 6.2/SC 302, 310.19.

[26] Phil 6.2/SC 302, 310.25.

[27] CC 4.51/SC 136, 316.26–27.

[28] Comm Jn 10.62/GCS 4, 182.12–13. For other references to the reader who is eager to learn, see Hom Gen 12.5; Hom Ex 4.4; PA 3.1.22; perhaps CC 5.62.

historicity of the events surrounding Jesus' baptism, since no one other than Jesus witnessed the Holy Spirit descend on him and heard the voice pronouncing him God's Son (Matt 3:16–17; cf. Jn 1:32). Origen replies that it is difficult, if not impossible, to establish with complete certainty whether a story records what actually happened. However, Origen counsels, "Anyone who reads the stories with a fair mind [Ἀλλ' ὁ εὐγνωμόνως ἐντυχάνων ταῖς ἱστορίαις] will search out carefully what is fictitious ... and what ought to be accepted as historical." Such interpreters, he continues, "need an open mind and considerable study [εὐγνωμοσύνης χρεία ... καὶ πολλῆς ἐξετάσεως]" when examining the gospel accounts of Jesus' life.[29]

Not surprisingly, Celsus often came in for criticism here. "If Celsus had read the Bible impartially [ἀδεκάστως], he would not have said that our writings 'are incapable of being interpreted allegorically.'"[30] Again, Celsus would never have claimed to know all the Christian beliefs if he had actually read the difficult passages in Scripture, "and if he had read with an open mind [ἀναγνοὺς εὐγνωμόνως] and a desire to enter into the meaning of the words."[31] Origen also leveled this critique against the Gnostics whom he repeatedly accused of reading Scripture inconsistently. Statements in the Old Testament that pointed to the goodness of God or those in the New Testament that referred to God's ostensible cruelty were conveniently overlooked or allegorized away since they contradicted Gnostic convictions. In *On First Principles*, for instance, he notes how his opponents "hunt out" passages in the Old Testament that suggest "the cruelty of the Creator." Yet when they come to a passage in the New Testament (such as Mk 4:12 where Jesus says, "seeing they may not see and hearing they may not understand, lest they should turn and it should be forgiven them"), his opponents "do not deal in a similar way, nor even fairly [οὐδὲ εὐγνωμόνως], but pass over statements closely resembling those that they consider open to criticism in the Old Testament."[32]

---

[29] CC 1.42/SC 132, 188.19–20 and 27–28. Origen often conveyed the open and fair reading of Scripture with the term εὐγνωμόνως: it refers to doing something in a reasonable, fair, or considerate spirit (*Lampe*, s.v. "εὐγνωμόνως," and "εὐγνωμοσύνη"). The gloss in *Lampe* is instructive: the "fundamental meaning seems to imply an honest acknowledgment of facts" (*Lampe*, s.v. "εὐγνωμοσύνη," 1). Also see CC 1.53, 1.62, 6.46, 8.48 and Comm Cor 31 where this disposition is predicated of the ideal reader.

[30] CC 4.49/SC 136, 308.1–3.

[31] CC 1.12/SC 132, 108.13–14. Similar charges are leveled against Celsus in CC 1.42, 2.37, 2.62, 3.64, 3.74, 4.35, 4.52, 5.53, 6.16.

[32] PA 3.1.16/GK 520, 224.10–522, 225.1—Butterworth renders the adverb in question "candidly." There are numerous criticisms of Gnostic inconsistency in Origen's writings. Sometimes he charges them, as he does here, with overlooking passages in the NT that they would otherwise attack were they in the OT; at other times, he criticizes them for overlooking passages in the OT that would challenge their conception of the Creator. See Hom Josh 12.2; Comm Matt 17.18; Hom Lk 16.5–6; Comm Jn 13.106–8; Comm Rom 3.7.4; Comm Eph 25; CC 7.25; PA 2.4.4, 2.5.3–4, 3.1.16.

3. *Watchfulness* arguably ranked foremost among Origen's reading virtues. Several Greek terms evoke the intentional, focused concentration ideal readers needed to direct toward Scripture. Such interpreters were observant (τήρησις). In his response to Celsus' charge that what Christians have to say about Jesus is "nothing more worthy of attention than the goats and dogs of the Egyptians," Origen wryly suggests that an "observance [περὶ τῆς ... τηρήσεως] of everything written in the gospels"[33] would clear up the matter. When Origen is parsing Jesus' anguish in Gethsemane, attempting to decipher which sayings ought to be attributed to his divinity and which to his humanity, the philologist counsels that readers "observe the order [τὴν τάξιν ... τηρῆσαι] of the sayings attributed to Jesus."[34] Or in the midst of his enumeration of all the impossibilities and irrationalities in Scripture, including the gospels, Origen remarks hyperbolically: "And the careful reader will observe [τηρῆσαι] thousands of other passages like this in the gospels" where events that could not possibly have happened are recorded as if they did.[35] Origen repeatedly advocates the close observance of the text.[36]

Closely related, and with far more frequency, Origen urges interpreters to an attentive reading of Scripture.[37] "[L]et us pay close attention to the text,"[38] he preaches before his congregation. After an exhortation to interpreters that they leave no passage of Scripture unexamined, scrutinizing it with the same sort of care that a botanist devotes to a garden of herbs, he draws his remarks to a close: those who "attend to the reading" should not let a single letter of Scripture pass by without examination or scrutiny.[39] For those without an appreciation for horticultural labor, Origen develops a fascinating eucharistic analogy in his *Homilies on Exodus*. He issues a challenge to his congregation:

> You who are accustomed to take part in divine mysteries know, when you receive the body of the Lord, how you protect it with all caution and veneration lest any small part fall from it, lest anything of the consecrated gift be lost. For you believe, and correctly, that you are answerable if anything falls from there by neglect [*per negligentiam*]. But if you are so careful to preserve his body, and rightly so, how do you think that there is less guilt to have neglected God's word [*verbum Dei neglexisse*] than to have neglected his body?[40]

---

[33] CC 3.21/SC 136, 48.1–2.   [34] CC 2.25/SC 132, 352.12–13.

[35] PA 4.3.1/GK 734, 325.2.

[36] See Comm Matt 10.22, 11.8, 14.4; Comm Jn 1.133, 6.51, 13.448; Phil 8.1, 11.2; On Martyr. 34.1; CC 5.59; LA 21.

[37] This virtue is conveyed through a rich terminology, including: προσοχή (προσέχω), σχολή, ἐπιστρεφής, ἐφίστημι, ἐπίστασις. Also note the combination of ἐπερείδω and διάνοια: "to attend to" (Comm Jn 1.282; CC 5.42).

[38] Hom Jer 18.6.2/SC 238, 196.10.

[39] Phil 10.2/SC 302, 370.26—transl. mine.

[40] Hom Ex 13.3/GCS 6, 274.7–13. For a useful discussion of the sorts of analogies Origen draws with the eucharist, see L. Lies, *Wort und Eucharistie bei Origenes: Zur Spiritualisierungstendenz des Eucharistieverständnisses* (Innsbruck: Tyrolia-Verlag, 1978), 217–258. For a quick discussion of

We find numerous references to the attentive examination of Scripture in Origen's writings. None, however, announce this theme as clearly as the concluding section of his *Letter to Gregory*, where Origen alludes to Paul's own advice to Timothy: "devote yourself to reading [πρόσεχε τῇ ἀναγνώσει]" Scripture (1 Tim 4:13). Drawing upon this verse, Origen exhorts Gregory to similar attentiveness of Scripture. Within the space of a few lines the verb προσέχω surfaces four times, and the noun, προσοχή, once:

> Now you, my lord and son, attend principally to the reading of the divine writings [προηγουμένως πρόσεχε τῇ τῶν θείων γραφῶν ἀναγνώσει] [cf. 1 Tim 4:13]—do attend [ἀλλὰ πρόσεχε]. For we who read the divine writings are in need of great attentiveness [Πολλῆς γὰρ προσοχῆς], lest we say or think something too rashly about them. And devoting yourself to the reading of the divine books [Καὶ προσέχων τῇ τῶν θείων ἀναγνώσει] with a disposition faithful and pleasing to God, knock at its closed door and it will be opened to you by the doorkeeper of whom Jesus said: "To this one the doorkeeper opens" [Jn 10:3]. And as you apply yourself to this divine reading, seek correctly with an unshaken faith in God the meaning of the divine writings hidden from the multitude. Do not be satisfied with knocking and seeking, for prayer is most necessary for understanding the divine books.[41]

In this passage, admonition to attentiveness is surrounded by several other dispositions that characterize the worthy reader of Scripture. (Two in particular will be examined more closely in the next sections of this chapter: that readers ought to interpret Scripture with an "unshaken faith in God" and, when necessary, accompany this inquiry with prayer.) For Origen, attentiveness was an essential characteristic of the interpreter of Scripture.[42]

This disposition also implied the exercise of care (ἐπιμελεία) when studying the Bible. "And he who approaches the prophetic words with care and attention [μετ' ἐπιμελείας καὶ προσοχῆς]," Origen writes, will become convinced, particularly after the advent of Christ, that the prophets were inspired by God and speak of Christ.[43] In a Greek fragment from the *Commentary on Romans*, Origen wrestles with Paul's two seemingly different uses of the term "law" in one passage in this letter: "Therefore it is necessary that the one reading the divine Scripture carefully [ἐπιμελῶς τὸν ἀναγινώσκοντα]" observe that Scripture is full of homonyms, as in the case of this verse where the term

Origen's analogies between Scripture, the eucharist, and the church, see H. de Lubac, *History and Spirit*, 406–426.

[41] LG 4/SC 148, 192.80–194.91—transl. mine. For other citations, paraphrases or allusions to 1 Tim 4:13 when Origen wishes to enlist apostolic precedent for the attentive examination of Scripture, see Comm Matt 10.15 and esp. CC 3.20. In the latter passage Origen commends Celsus to an "attentive reading [τῇ μετὰ τοῦ προσέχειν ἀναγνώσει] of Paul's letters. The bite in this suggestion—the expression comes from Paul's own exegetical advice to Timothy—would have not have been lost on Origen's Christian readers (CC 3.20/SC 136, 48.11–12).

[42] Other references to the attentive reading of Scripture: Hom Ex 9.1, 13.3; Hom Lev 13.1.1; Hom Num 17.4.5; Hom 2.1 Ps 36; Lk Frg 183, 186; Comm Jn 1.156, 6.213; PA 4.3.5; CC 7.60; Phil 3.

[43] PA 4.1.6/GK 688, 302.3–4.

"law" can be used to refer to the "law of nature," or the "law of Moses."[44] Or again, in his *Commentary on John*, after distinguishing the questions that the priests and Levites asked John the Baptist from those posed by the Pharisees (cf. Jn 1:19, 24), Origen counsels: "the one who will read Scripture accurately must exercise care everywhere [πανταχοῦ ἐπιμέλειαν τὸν ἀκριβῶς ἐντευξόμενον τῇ γραφῇ ποιητέον], to observe, when necessary, who is speaking and when it is spoken, that we may discover that words are appropriately matched with characters throughout the holy books."[45]

Related to this ideal of careful inquiry was the virtue of an exacting or precise manner of study (ἀκρίβεια, etc.). "Nevertheless, the exact reader ['Ο μέντοι γε ἀκριβὴς] will hesitate in regard to some passages,"[46] Origen remarks, when trying to make a delicate decision about whether an incident narrated in Scripture actually transpired, or whether a law promulgated was meant to be literally observed or not.[47] In book one of his *Commentary on John*, he begins his lengthy exposition of its opening verse by remarking that it is not only the Greeks who thought the noun ἀρχή (usually translated as "beginning") had multiple meanings. If someone were to study this term by gathering together all its uses in Scripture and "by examining it precisely [ἀκριβῶς ἐξετάζων]," this one would discover (as Origen will proceed to do) how polysemic this noun is even within Scripture.[48] Or again, in *On Martyrdom* Origen reaches Jesus' words in Gethsemane: "Father, if it be possible, let this cup pass from me" (Matt 26:39). He acknowledges that "someone who does not accurately understand the intent of Scripture [μὴ ἀκριβώσαντα τὸ βούλημα τῆς γραφῆς]"[49] will think that Jesus acted like a coward here. However a precise distinction between "let *this* cup pass from me," and "let *the* cup pass from me," will show that this was not the case.[50]

Not surprisingly, Origen set the careful and precise interpretation of Scripture against readings that were rash. "In the Scripture will be found," he writes in a fragment from *On the Passover*, "many such things which, to those who

---

[44] Phil 9.3/SC 302, 356.15–16. The passage in question is Romans 3:21.

[45] Comm Jn 6.53/GCS 4, 117.16–20—Heine slightly modified. There are numerous additional references to carefulness in reading Scripture: see Hom Lev 13.1.2; Comm Matt 14.6, 14.14; Comm Jn 1.199, 6.251, 13.42, 13.144; Comm Eph 13; PA 4.3.5; CC 6.52; Phil 11.1, 14.2.

[46] PA 4.3.5/GK 744, 330.14.

[47] Shortly thereafter in the same passage he writes that "it is necessary for the one reading exactingly [διὰ τοῦτο δεῖ ἀκριβῶς τὸν ἐντυγχάνοντα]," and there follows a list of suggestions for how to negotiate the impossibilities of Scripture (PA 4.3.5/GK 756, 331.2–3).

[48] Comm Jn 1.90/GCS 4, 20.3.

[49] On Martyr. 29/GCS 1, 25.4–5.

[50] For other references to reading precisely, see: Hom Jer 5.14.2; Comm Jn 1.24, 1.90, 2.64, 6.53, 6.207, 6.265, 10.91, 13.26, 13.30, 13.37; PE 31.3; PA 4.2.3, 4.3.1, 4.3.2; On Martyr. 13; CC 6.50. M. Harl makes an important point on *akribeia* in Origen's writings: "His principal affirmation is that the labor of the exegete ought to correspond in rigor to the rigor of the composition of the text" (SC 302, 126). She references Phil 2.4–5 where Origen refers to God's ἀκρίβεια in forming the world and Scripture (SC 302, 257–258). For additional passages on Scripture being composed in such a manner, see Chapter 3, n. 73 above.

read cursorily [παρέργως], will seem to be identical, but which, to those who read with care and attention, will reveal their differences."[51] The *simpliciores* are often accused of reading Scripture hastily. For example, they do not detect the spiritual sense of Scripture, "sometimes owing to the lack of thorough training, sometimes owing to rashness [διὰ τὴν προπέτειαν] . . ."[52] Celsus is similarly accused: had he had "the patience and endurance to give his attention" to the Pentateuch and prophets "he would not have recklessly [εὐχερῶς] accused of being silly and of having no secret meaning the account written of these matters either by Moses, or as we would say, by the divine Spirit in Moses . . . "[53] The Gnostics too are accused of this way of reading: the difficult texts in Scripture seem to cause them to go astray and "they accuse God thoughtlessly and with rashness [μετὰ προπετείας] from the writings which they do not understand."[54] But this counsel was not only directed against Origen's exegetical opponents. As we saw above in the *Letter to Gregory*, he directed it to his addressee, and he was also alert to the danger of his own potential impulsiveness: "But since it is necessary to examine Scripture with integrity, not rashly [προπετῶς] flattering oneself to have understood because one has grasped the bare letter . . . "[55]

4. We turn, finally, to those passages where Origen testified to the importance of *exertion* when interpreting Scripture.[56] "To interpret what follows is

---

[51] Pascha 12/Witte, 102.9. The adverb παρέργως is the antonym of ἀκριβῶς.

[52] PA 4.2.2/GK 704, 310.2–3. Other texts on the *simpliciores'* rashness: Hom Lk 17.2; CC 6.62, 8.14.

[53] CC 4.55/SC 136, 318.20–24—Chadwick modified. Other references to Celsus' rashness at CC 3.20, 6.16, 8.53.

[54] Phil 1.29/SC 302, 214.21–23. Other texts on Gnostic rashness in reading Scripture include Phil 1.28, 14.2; LG 4. An extraordinary passage (PE 29.10) should be recalled, however, where Origen remarks that the Gnostics do *not* seem to be negligent in the reading of Scripture.

[55] Comm Jn 5.2/GCS 4, 101.8–10—transl. mine. Also see Hom Gen 7.6; Hom Ex 12.4; Hom Josh 8.2.

[56] For other discussions of this theme, see H. de Lubac, *History and Spirit*, 361–374; M. Harl, SC 302, 132–133, 145–147 and G. af. Hällström, *Fides Simpliciorum*, 28.

The vocabulary Origen avails himself of when he wishes to signal the studious examination of Scripture includes: ζητέω (ζήτησις, ζητητικός), "to seek, inquire, search out, investigate, examine" (PA 4.3.1/GK 732, 324.4–7; Comm Jn 5.5/GCS 4, 102.27; PE 29.1/GCS 2, 381.26, etc.); ἐξετάζω (ἐξέτασις, ἐξεταστικός, ἐξεταστικῶς), "to scrutinize, examine" (Comm Jn 5.2/GCS 4, 101.3–12; Phil 10.2/SC 302, 370.25–27; CC 5.53/SC 147, 148.14–15, etc.); ἐρευνάω/ἐραυνάω (ἔρευνα), "to search, explore, inquire" (Comm Jn 1.157/GCS 4, 30.15, 32.68/GCS 4, 435.17–18; CC 6.37/SC 147, 268.22–27; LA 9/SC 302, 534.1, etc.); and βασανίζω (βάσανος, ἀβασανιστός), "to investigate, examine closely" (CC 1.55/SC 132, 226.29–228.31; PA 4.2.9/GK 728, 322.8–10; PA 4.3.5/GK 744, 330.14–746, 331.3, etc.). Also note the following terms: σκοπέω, "to examine" (Hom Jer 20.3.1/SC 238, 260.8–11); φιλολογέω (φιλολογία), "to love learning, study" (both the noun and verb used in P. Nautin, *Lettres et Écrivains Chrétiens*, 250.3–251.15); περιεργάζομαι, "to make inquiry" (Comm Jn 13.125/GCS 4, 244.28); γυμνάζω (γυμνασία), "to investigate" (Lk Frg 186/GCS 9, 305.6–10); ἐξιχνεύω, "trace out the meaning of" (PA 4.3.5/GK 746, 331.4–8); μελετάω, "to attend to, study" (Comm Matt 10.15/GCS 10, 18.29–19.1); ἐφοδεύω, "examine, pass in review" (Comm Jn 13.130/GCS 4, 245.19–21).

laborious."[57] "I do not know if anyone can be renewed who is lazy in respect to the Holy Scriptures."[58] Those who give themselves "to the toil of examining" what is written in Scripture will discern where the law legislates impossibilities, and where it does not.[59] Not surprisingly, Origen drew upon one of his leading images for the spiritual life, the athletic contest or struggle, to describe the worthy interpreter's effort at interpretation.[60] This theme emerges with particular clarity in his *Homilies on Samuel* where he comments on the vexing passage about the necromancer who seemingly summoned Samuel from the dead at Saul's behest (1 Sam 28:3–25). Origen begins his interpretation of this troubling passage by relaying another reading that claims the witch actually lied when she said she had summoned Samuel. However, Origen immediately registers his dissatisfaction with this reading: "The one who does not want to accept the struggle [ἀγῶνα] that Samuel was truly summoned will say these things."[61] A few paragraphs later he again writes: "For, it seems that in order not to experience the struggle [μὴ ἀγῶνα ἔχειν] surrounding so many other matters that could be examined in this passage, that [the regnant interpretation] says: 'it is not Samuel; the demon is lying . . . '"[62] There are several other passages where this agonistic motif surfaces in exegetical contexts.[63]

Origen will often couch the need for hard work at interpreting Scripture in scriptural language. Note in particular how the following verses repeatedly illustrate for him the laborious nature of biblical exegesis: Mt 7:7–8, "Ask and it will be given to you; seek and you will find; knock and the door will be opened to you . . ." (Hom Ex 9.1; Hom Lev 6.1.1; Comm Jn 10.131; Comm Rom 7.17.4; LG 4; CC 6.7), Ps 1:2, "and on his law he meditates day and night" (Hom Gen 11.3; Hom Josh 17.3, 19.4; Hom Lk 39.2; Comm Rom 9.2.14; PE 29.9), 2 Cor 3:16, "But when anyone shall turn to the Lord, the veil shall be removed" (Hom Ex 12.2, 12.4), and Matt 20:30, where two blind men petition Jesus, "Lord, let our eyes be opened" (Hom Gen 7.6, 15.7; Comm Matt 16.11).

[57] Comm Matt 13.17/GCS 10, 223.6–8.

[58] Comm Rom 9.1.12/Bammel, 717.134–135.

[59] PA 4.2.9/GK 728, 322.8–10. For other discussions of the need for effort when studying Scripture, see Comm Jn 10.62, 10.104, 10.263, 13.447; PA 4.3.4, 4.3.5, 4.3.14; Phil 14.2; CC 7.60.

[60] On the theme of struggle or combat in the moral life, see Hom Gen 9.3; Hom Ex 4.9; Hom Lev 16.1; Hom Num 26.2; Hom Jd 9.2; Hom 4.2 Ps 36; Comm Rom 5.3; PA 1.6.3, 2.11.5–7, 3.2.4–7; On Martyr. 5; PE 32, etc. For more on this moral theme, see E. Schockenhoff, *Zum Fest der Freiheit*, 258–265.

[61] Hom Sam 5.4/SC 328, 180.1–2—transl. mine.

[62] Hom Sam 5.6/SC 328, 186.5–8—transl. mine.

[63] Other references to ἀγών or ἀγωνίζομαι when interpreting Scripture include: Hom Josh 1.7, 16.5; Ps Frg/PG 12.1148; Hom Jer 19.11.2; Phil 2.2. Of particular interest, note how the agonistic theme surfaces in Origen's eighteenth and nineteenth *Homilies on Luke*. Here he is commenting on Mary and Joseph's search for Jesus, how they found him in the temple, and in particular, how they were "seeking" him while "sorrowing" (Lk 2:46–48). Origen turns to his audience, and exhorts them, like Mary and Joseph, to seek Jesus, not in the temple but in the Scriptures. "He who seeks Jesus should do so not carelessly, not laxly, not halfhearted [*non neglegenter, non dissolute, non transitorie*], as some seek him and cannot find him" (Hom Lk 18.5/GCS 9, 113.17–19). This person ought, rather, to seek Jesus in the difficult passages of Scripture and be willing to suffer on this journey: "Sometimes you read the Scriptures and in them seek their meaning with a certain sorrow, and even pain . . . You cannot discover what is true" (Hom Lk 19.5/GCS 9, 116.16–117.4).

Origen famously called attention to the labor associated with gathering clearer passages scattered throughout the Scriptures to help interpret a difficult passage. He recounts that "most pleasing tradition handed down by a Hebrew" in which the Scriptures are likened to a house with many locked rooms, and next to each room lies a key, yet the key does not fit its door. He writes: "It is a great labor, both to discover the keys and to match them to the rooms which they are able to open."[64] Another situation that called for particular effort was the quest for the deeper sense of Scripture. Referring to the prophets, Origen argues that they often communicated in a twofold manner. Some of their words were spoken "without any obscurity" so that these morally beneficial words could be understood by a wide class of readers; other words, however, expressed "more mysterious and esoteric truths" through riddles and allegories. "Their purpose," Origen continues, referring to the prophets, "was that those who are not afraid of hard work [οἱ μὴ φυγοπονοῦντες] but will accept any toil [πάντα πόνον] to attain to virtue and truth might find out their meaning by study, and after finding it might use it as reason demands."[65]

We can conclude this discussion on effort by noting those passages where Origen spoke with autobiographical candor about the effort he himself exerted in studying Scripture.[66] In a fragment from a letter to an otherwise unknown

---

[64] Phil 2.3/SC 302, 244.9–10—transl. mine.

[65] CC 7.10/SC 150, 38.23–25.

[66] It is interesting to recall here that much of Origen's reputation in antiquity revolved around his arduous study of Scripture. His main biographer, Eusebius, made Origen's toiling exegetical labors one of the leitmotifs in the *Ecclesiastical History*. Origen was, for instance, diligent as a youth in studying Scripture with his father (HE 6.1.8–10); after giving up his instruction in Greek literature he devoted himself tirelessly to Scripture (6.3.7–13); he taught Scripture day and night in Alexandria (6.8.6); he labored in the compilation of the *Hexapla* (6.16.1–4). Nor was Eusebius alone in expressing this sentiment about Origen. He passes along Porphyry's sentiments about Origen's industry and learning when it came to the interpretation of the Hebrew Scriptures (6.19.1–9). Jerome as well spoke effusively of Origen's zeal for the Scriptures. See *On Illustrious Men* 54.6–7 for his admiration of Origen's linguistic abilities and work on the *Hexapla*; *Letter* 84.8 for his memorization, daily study, and numerous homilies and commentaries on Scripture; and especially *Letter* 33 where he offers a list of Origen's writings and praises him for his zeal for Scripture.

Pamphilus and Eusebius were probably the first to refer to Origen as "Adamantius" in their *Apology for Origen*. In Photius' entry on their work in his *Bibliotheca* he says (likely relaying the sentiments of the *Apology*) that Origen was punningly called Adamantius "because his arguments were linked together like adamantine chains [ἀδαμαντίνοις δεσμοῖς]" (*Bibliotheca* 118/Henry 92b, 24). His name, Ἀδαμάντιος, played on the adjective ἀδαμάντινος, which is derived from ἀδάμας, "the hardest substance," such as steel or diamond. Jerome also detected the pun, though took it in a different direction, referring not to the character of Origen's arguments, but rather to the way in which he studied Scripture. Likening Origen to the prolific Roman historian Varro, he says that Origen's "zeal for the study of Scripture has fairly earned for him this latter name" (*Letter* 33.3). However, special significance was not always attached to this name. In his *Ecclesiastical History* Eusebius again refers to Origen as Ἀδαμάντιος, though this time he simply says that "this was also Origen's name" (HE 6.14.10/GCS 9.2, 552.9). Jerome too declined to offer a gloss on this name in *On Illustrious Men* (54.1). On this designation, see P. Nautin, *Origène*, 47,

third party, he softly laments the painstaking labors associated with the correction of manuscripts. Speaking of his patron, Ambrose, Origen writes:

> Although he thinks that I am industrious and exceedingly thirsty for the divine word [νομίζων με φιλόπονον εἶναι καὶ πάνυ διψᾶν τοῦ θείου λόγου], he has put [me] to shame with his own zeal and his love for the sacred disciplines . . . For it is neither possible to eat without conversation, nor, after having eaten, to take a walk and allow the body to rest awhile, but even during these times we are compelled to study and to correct the copies; nor indeed are we allowed to go to bed for the whole night in order to care for the body, since study extends deep into the night. If I were permitted to say, [we do] these things from day break until the ninth, and at times, even the tenth hour. For all those who desire to labor [πάντες γὰρ οἱ θέλοντες φιλοπονεῖν] devote these periods of time to the examination of the divine words and their readings.[67]

Nor was Origen averse to voicing his grievances about the labors of biblical scholarship directly to Ambrose. He does so in a particularly mischievous passage in the fifth book of his *Commentary on John*. He opens this book by informing his patron that he has, if for only a moment, entertained the thought of authoring fewer volumes (the first four books of this *Commentary* had not taken Origen beyond the first chapter of John's gospel). A reduction of his labor would help him avoid all the "toil" of authorship. But more importantly, it would help him circumvent the danger that Scripture threatens those who produce many books. Origen is quick to point out Solomon's admonishment: "My son, beware of making many books; there is no end and much study is tiring for the flesh" (Ecc 12:12). It appears, Origen remarks to his patron, that "we" have violated this command by producing so many books. And if this note of caution does not suffice, Origen reminds Ambrose of another disconcerting passage in Solomon's corpus: "In a multitude of words you will not escape sin, but you will be wise if you restrain your lips" (Prov 10:19).[68] Presumably with Ambrose's full attention, Origen relaxes some of the tension he has created. Perhaps there is a deeper sense in both of these passages that might exonerate industrious publishers?[69] The prolixity Solomon warns against, he proposes, does not concern those who author (and sponsor) many books, so long as what they write is in keeping with the single truth.[70] As these and other passages testify, scriptural exegesis for Origen was a rigorous and demanding exercise.[71]

---

n. 15 and M. Lacore, "L'Homme d'acier-ἀδαμάντινος ἀνήρ de l'Anonyme de Jamblique à Platon," *Revue des études grecques* 110 (1997): 399–419.

[67] P. Nautin, *Lettres et Écrivains Chrétiens*, 250.3–251.15—transl. mine. See also the discussion of this passage in the section on text criticism in Chapter 3 above.

[68] Comm Jn 5.4/GCS 4, 102.10–11.

[69] Comm Jn 5.2.

[70] Comm Jn 5.5.

[71] Other texts on the labor of biblical exegesis, often directed against the *simpliciores*: Hom Gen 7.5; Comm Song of Songs 3; Hom Isa 5; Lam Frg 8; Comm Matt 16.20; DH 13; CC 5.16, 5.62, 6.37, 7.60; PA 2.11.1–2, 4.2.9, 4.3.5; Phil 12.2; LA 9.

In this section I have discussed a largely neglected facet in Origen's portrait of the ideal interpreter of Scripture. This collection of writings often presented readers with challenges that necessitated a distinct moral response. Those who wished to study these writings well needed to espouse heightened levels of inquisitiveness, open-mindedness, attentiveness, and effort.[72] Yet sometimes even the most virtuous interpreters could not push past the impasse that the Scriptures presented. These interpreters began to experience a crisis of doubt about whether these writings even possessed an intelligible, useful meaning. In such a circumstance Origen did not persist in his insistence that these interpreters exercise the virtues cataloged above. Rather, he called for a particular sort of faith that would reinvigorate the stalled exegetical enterprise.

FAITH

In Chapter 5, I discussed Origen's conception of spiritual growth as a movement from faith to reason. As we saw there, he invariably spoke of faith critically in exegetical contexts. Christians who practiced faith (and not reason) or held an irrational faith (as opposed to a reasonable faith) were those who had failed to examine Scripture carefully for themselves. These—usually the *simpliciores*—were still mired in an unquestioning acceptance of others' interpretations of Scripture. For Origen, however, the rigorous, first-hand examination of Scripture was a quintessentially rational activity and, thus, a hallmark of advanced Christianity. It is at first glance puzzling, then, that on several occasions we find him commending the act of faith in exegetical contexts. Indeed, as we will see in this section, Origen spoke favorably of the faith of those who had *already committed* themselves to a reasoned examination of Scripture. What sort of faith did he have in mind?

Origen was keenly aware of how Scripture's difficulties frequently discouraged interpreters from continuing their exegetical labors. Sometimes interpreters became so perplexed by these writings that they abandoned all hope for an intelligent interpretation, often casting doubt on whether Scripture had

---

[72] As we have also seen, Origen enumerated a series of corresponding vices that plagued, or so he thought, his opponents' approach to the biblical text. Very little in this discussion surprises, though one point merits attention: the fact that Origen rarely castigates the Jews for the sorts of moral deficiencies that he frequently attributes to the exegesis of Celsus, the Gnostic heterodox, or even the *simpliciores*. This telling refusal to label the exegesis in Jewish communities as rash, inattentive, or lethargic is probably best explained by Origen's numerous first-hand encounters with Jewish exegetes (see "Origen among the Jews" in the previous chapter). Presumably from these encounters he would have quickly gathered how careful their approach to Scripture was. They might have been flawed (from his perspective) in their literal adherence to the Jewish cult and denial that Jesus was the prophesied Messiah, but Origen would have had difficulty reproaching the earnestness and care with which they studied Scripture.

even been authored intelligently in the first place. In book four of *On First Principles*, Origen tackles this fundamental doubt in the divine authorship of Scripture with a fascinating analogy. He was aware that there were those who doubted the "divine origin" of the Scriptures because "in every passage of the Scriptures the superhuman element of the thought does not appear obvious to the uninstructed."[73] Yet, he continues, this sort of doubt is hardly surprising, since the Scriptures are analogous to the cosmos: while both take their origin from God, both are nevertheless riddled with challenges, even—indeed, especially—for the person who believes in God. "For in regard to the works of that Providence which controls the whole world, while some show themselves most plainly to be works of Providence, others are so obscure as to appear to afford grounds for disbelief in the God who with unspeakable skill and power superintends the universe."[74] As this passage unfolds, Origen concedes that God's skillful plan is more apparent in the movements of celestial bodies than in events below on earth, and clearer again in the cases of animals than in the distressing, immoral affairs of humans. "But," he insists,

> just as Providence is not abolished because of our ignorance, at least not for those who have once and for all rightly believed in it [παρὰ τοῖς γε ἄπαξ παραδεξαμένοις αὐτὴν καλῶς], so neither is the divine character of Scripture, which extends through all of it, abolished because our weakness cannot discern in every sentence the hidden splendour of its teachings, concealed under a poor and humble style.[75]

Just as belief in Providence is not eradicated because of events that challenge the notion of God's goodness and superintendence, so too is belief in Scripture's "divine origin" not abandoned because some passages provide no immediate evidence for a favorable interpretation.[76]

---

[73] PA 4.1.7/GK 688, 302.14–690, 303.2.

[74] PA 4.1.7/GK 690, 303.4–6.

[75] PA 4.1.7/GK 690, 303.12–692, 304.3.

[76] PA 4.1.7/GK 688, 302.12–13. This belief in the underlying divine authorship of the Christian Scriptures is widely attested in his writings. While there are disputes among Christians on how to interpret their Scriptures, Origen explains to Celsus, the Scriptures are nevertheless "universally believed to be divine [τοὺς ἅμα πᾶσι πιστευθέντας εἶναι θείους λόγους]" (CC 3.12/SC 136, 36.30–31). Or again, in an excerpt from his thirty-ninth *Homily on Jeremiah* anthologized in the *Philocalia*, Origen writes: "Now it is fitting to believe [Πρέπει . . . πιστεύειν] that the holy writings have no tittle empty of the Wisdom of God." The Scriptures, he continues, are from the fullness of God and exhale this fullness "to those having eyes that see the things of the fullness and ears that hear the things of the fullness" (Phil 1.28/SC 302, 202.19–20, 27–29—transl. mine). Origen opens book four of *On First Principles* with the contention that it is the Scriptures, both the Old and New Testaments, "which we believe to be divine" (PA 4.1.1/GK 668, 292.11). Here he echoes the preface to this work where he listed the articles in the church's rule that alone "are to be believed as the truth [*illa sola credenda est veritas*]" (PA pref.2/GK 84, 8.27–28). The second to last article is on the Scriptures, that Christians ought to believe they "were composed through the Spirit of God and that they have not only that meaning which is obvious, but also another which is hidden from the majority of readers" (PA pref.8/GK 94, 14.7–8). Also see CC 3.11–12 on the Scriptures being believed to be divine.

When Origen spoke of the salutary role of faith in biblical exegesis, he invariably had the confused interpreter in mind. He entreated the reader confronted with a challenging text to persist with inquiry, trusting that the passage in question had been divinely authored and had an intelligent sense, even if that sense was not immediately noticeable. There are several passages where Origen urges the baffled interpreter to this sort of trust. In the *Letter to Gregory*, for instance, he concludes with an exhortation to "seek correctly and with unshakable faith in God [μετὰ πίστεως τῆς εἰς θεὸν ἀκλινοῦς] the sense of the divine Scriptures hidden from the many."[77] In another short passage anthologized in the *Philocalia* Origen offers a similar reflection on the role of faith in biblical scholarship. After expressing his confidence that God's Word authored all of Scripture, he admits that there are difficult passages in Scripture that cause readers to stumble. Nevertheless, he writes: "Do not lose hope [Μὴ ἀπελπίσῃς] that this stone of stumbling and this rock of scandal contain meanings, so that that which is written might come to pass: 'The one who believes will not be put to shame' [Isa 28:16]. Believe first [Πίστευσον πρῶτον] and you will discover under what was thought to be a scandal great and holy help."[78] We see this nexus, between the interpreter's difficulty with Scripture and the need for trust, very clearly in a Greek fragment from Origen's twentieth *Homily on Joshua*. He finds himself perplexed by the significance of the dozens of place names of the towns that were to be given to Caleb and the tribe of Judah in Canaan (Josh 15:13–62). Origen consoles his congregants (and perhaps also himself), who have difficulties in grasping the deeper sense of these names:

> Let us not became faint-hearted when we read the Scriptures which we do not understand, but let it be for us according to our faith [cf. Mt 9:29], which indeed we believe, that all Scripture being inspired is helpful [cf. 2 Tim 3:16] [ἀλλὰ γενηθήτω ἡμῖν κατὰ τὴν πίστιν ἡμῶν, ἣν καὶ πιστεύομεν, ὅτι πᾶσα γραφὴ θεόπνευστος οὖσα ὠφέλιμός ἐστιν]. For one of two things is necessary for you to admit concerning all the Scriptures: either that they are not inspired because they are not helpful (as an unbeliever would maintain) or, as the believer accepts, that since they are inspired they are useful [ἢ ὡς πιστὸς παραδέξασθαι ὅτι ἐπεί εἰσιν θεόπνευστοι ὠφέλιμοί εἰσιν].[79]

For Origen, the circumstance in which faith ornamented the exegetical life was invariably the same: interpreters, himself included, were confounded by

---

[77]	LG 4/SC 148, 192.87–89.

[78]	Phil 1.28/SC 302, 202.30–36—transl. mine. This text is also anthologized at Phil 10.1/SC 302, 366.1–7. For a discussion of the disputed provenance of these texts, see M. Harl, SC 302, 372–374.

[79]	Phil 12.2/SC 302, 392.8–15—transl. mine. What is particularly interesting is how Origen goes on in this text to insist that even if readers cannot understand a difficult passage, they should still believe that the Scriptures are inspired since they can even benefit readers who do not understand them. For other places where Origen speaks of the role of faith when confronted with challenging passages in Scripture, see Hom Sam 5.2 and 5.4; PA 4.3.5.

exegetical aporia and needed to exercise trust in God that the passages in question carried an edifying sense, even if it was far from evident what this message actually was. This trust buoyed the interpretive enterprise. Clearly, then, Origen could speak of faith in two decidedly different ways in exegetical contexts. As we saw in Chapter 5, it often disapprovingly signaled the refusal to engage in careful scriptural scholarship and continue in a blind assent to someone else's idea of the Scriptures' teachings. But as we have also seen in this chapter, faith could refer commendably to a trust placed in God by those *already* studying the Scriptures. Whatever difficulties interpreters should encounter, their faith spurred them on so that "by putting away all hesitation and indecision, they might devote themselves with their whole souls to the words of God."[80]

DIVINE AID

The discussion up until this point can give the impression that the exegetical process for Origen was a largely autonomous affair. After all, confronted with the various difficulties in Scripture, the interpreter rose to this challenge by cultivating a worthy moral disposition, by threading exegetical virtues into the act of inquiry, and by anchoring this effort in a persistent trust that Scripture contained an intelligible sense. Yet we are left with a misleading impression if we think independent inquiry fully captured how Origen thought about or practiced scriptural interpretation. Sometimes the difficulties presented by Scripture were so acute that readers, despite all these efforts, were left confounded. Such a situation called for divine aid.[81] Origen often spoke of the divine gift of comprehension for interpreting Scripture well. Exegetical insight came from God[82] or the Holy Spirit,[83] but more often than not, he highlighted the revelatory work of the Word or Jesus Christ in facilitating

---

[80] PA 4.1.7/GK 688, 302.13–14 (subject rendered as plural in translation). For a very similar passage, see Phil 2.5.

[81] In Origen's theology divine aid for exegetical inquiry was simply one particular instance of the grace available for any sort of intellectual endeavor. See Hom Gen 3.1, 13.3; Comm Matt 14.6; Hom Lk 3.1–2; Comm Jn 1.246; Phil 1.28; PE 1.1, 18.1; PA 2.9.4; CC 2.71, 3.34, 3.61–62, 4.95, 6.4, 6.13, 6.65–69, 7.42.

[82] See Hom Num 13.1.1, 13.4.1; Hom Josh 17.3; Hom Lk 38.1; Comm Rom pref.2; PA 4.3.11; CC 4.50. Also see Origen's citations of 1 Cor 2:16, followed by verse 10 ("We have the mind of Christ . . . that we may know the things freely given to us by God"), which signal God's help in exegesis: Hom Lev 5.6.2; Comm Jn 1.24, 10.172; PA 4.2.3.

[83] See Hom Gen 9.1; Hom Lev 6.6.6, 13.6.2; Hom Num 12.2.4; Hom Josh 8.1; Comm Jn 1.89; Comm Rom pref.2; Comm Cor 11; PA pref.3, pref.8, 1.1.2, 2.2.2, 2.7.2, 4.2.3; CC 1.44, 3.18–19. Origen frequently refers to the Holy Spirit's aid in the language of 1 Cor 2:10 ("the Spirit searches even the depths of God"): Hom Ez 11.3.3; Comm Matt 14.11, 15.31, 17.33; Comm Jn 2.6; Comm Cor 10; PA 4.2.7, 4.3.14; CC 6.17.

interpretation.[84] All of these divine agents—especially in their capacity as authors—were willing to offer floundering interpreters exegetical aid. These had, after all, already shared in the task of composing the very Scriptures interpreters desired to unlock.[85]

It is remarkable that Origen frequently spoke of his exegetical project as anything but an autonomous affair in which he wrestled with the text in isolation from its divine authors. Interpretation transpired, rather, within a relationship. "I confess," he preaches, "that I by myself am not able to discuss these words, but I need . . . the appearance of the power of Jesus, in the way he

---

[84] The rationale for privileging the Word rests in Origen's fundamental understanding of the Word as the communicator or revealer of God to creatures. For a quick overview of the revelatory work of the Word or Jesus Christ in exegesis, see H. de Lubac, *History and Spirit*, 361–365; for a more substantial discussion, consult M. Harl, *Origène et la fonction révélatrice du Verb Incarné* (Paris: Éditions du Seuil, 1958). J. Daniélou, however, reduces divine aid in exegesis too narrowly to Christ (*Origen*, 157–160)—see the two previous notes. For passages in Origen's writings where the Word, Wisdom, Lord, or Jesus aids the reader of Scripture, see Hom Gen 6.1, 7.6, 15.7; Hom Ex 2.4; Hom Lev 13.2.1; Hom Josh 12.2; Hom Is 5.2; Hom Ez 11.3.3; Comm Matt 14.11, 16.11; Comm Jn 2.47; 1 Thess Frg/PG 14.1302b; Phil 1.28, 1.29; CC 2.24, 3.33, 8.4. An important Pauline text that Origen repeatedly draws upon to signal the interpreter's intimacy with Christ is 1 Cor 2:16, 12 ("We have the mind of Christ, that we may know the things freely given to us by God"). Readers need Christ's mind to understand the difficult passages in Scripture, and often the gospels: see PA 4.2.3; Hom Lev 5.6.2; Comm Hom Josh 9.8; Comm Matt 14.6, 14.11; and esp. Comm Jn 10.286.

[85] H. de Lubac puts the matter well: "The Spirit who inspired it [the Bible] at the time of its writing is also the one who now makes it understood. Or rather, there is as if a twofold inspiration; the first, for its human authors; the second, analogous one, for its readers and interpreters" (*History and Spirit*, 361). So too M. Harl: "Only the one who has inspired the sacred texts, Origen often repeats, is able to reveal their meaning; only the one who has closed the doors is able to open them . . ." (SC 302, 146).

There is, however, an important caveat to this axiom about the divine aid available to Scriptures' interpreters. In Origen's polemic against Jewish exegesis, he maintains that this divine aid was taken away from the Jews after their rejection of Jesus as Messiah. Standing within a long tradition of *contra iudaeos* literature, Origen offered what by his day was a traditional Christian location of the Jews within the history of God's plan of salvation: "Accordingly we Christians say that while it was truly characteristic of them [the Jews] to experience the favor of God and to be loved more than any others, yet this care and grace changed to us when Jesus transferred the power at work among the Jews to those Gentiles who believed in him" (CC 5.50/SC 147, 142.18–23). Invariably this judgment of Judaism and the extension of salvation to the Gentiles were elicited, Origen argued, by a lack of belief in Jesus as the promised Messiah, culminating in his crucifixion (CC 2.9, 2.38, 2.78, 4.22, etc.). This rejection of Jesus inaugurated the decisive shift in God's plan of salvation where a new Israel emerged alongside the traditional Israel (Comm Matt 14.19; Comm Jn 28.211–233; Comm Rom 3.1.3; PA 4.1.4; CC 2.78, etc.). This traditional Israel underwent a gradual demise. By acting through the Roman siege and conquest of Jerusalem and its temple in CE 70, God had punished the Jews by depriving them not only of their worship, city, and nation (e.g. CC 1.47, 2.8, 2.25, 2.34, etc.), but also by rendering them incapable of discerning the deeper sense of their writings. In several passages Origen makes this latter claim. The empowering Spirit of God that helps Christians discern the law and prophets spiritually is absent from the Jews (PA 2.7.2); the sense of the Scriptures has been taken away from the Jews in accordance with Matthew 21:43 ("The kingdom of God will be taken away from you and given to a people that produces the fruits of the kingdom") (Hom Jer 14.12.3; Comm Rom 2.14.12–14).

is Wisdom, in the way he is the Word, in the way he is the Truth, so that his appearance might illumine the countenance of my soul."[86] There are other passages like these scattered throughout his writings where Origen testifies to his own encounter with Scripture's divine authors when attempting to unravel the mysteries in the writings they helped produce. In a fragment from his *Homilies on Luke*, he remarks that Jesus' disciples often did not understand their master's teachings until he explained them at a later time. "We, too, often," Origen adds, "when we carefully study the Scriptures and do not understand them, look up, as it were, with fixed attention as, for a moment, the Word shines 'in our hearts to illuminate the knowledge of his glory' [2 Cor 4:6; cf. 2 Cor 4:4]; and he is Christ."[87] And there is a particularly vivid passage in his *Commentary on the Song of Songs* where Origen expounds upon the verse, "Behold, here he comes, leaping upon the mountains, skipping over the hills" (Song 2:8). The allegorical identity of this approaching figure is the Word of God. The passage merits generous citation:

> Now every soul—if such there is who is constrained by love for the Word of God—if at any time it is in the thick of an argument about some passage—and everyone knows from his own experience how when one gets into a tight corner like this, one gets shut up in the straits of propositions and enquiries—if at any time some riddles or obscure sayings of the Law or the Prophets hem in the soul, if then she should chance to perceive Him to be present, and from afar should catch the sound of His voice, forthwith she is uplifted. And, when He has begun more and more to draw near to her senses and to illuminate the things that are obscure, then she sees Him "leaping upon the mountains and the hills"; that is to say, He then suggests to her interpretations of a high and lofty sort, so that this soul can rightly say: "Behold: He comes leaping upon the mountains, skipping over the hills."[88]

In passages such as these, Origen cultivated an extraordinarily rich forest of images—appearance, illumination, presence and opening are only a few—to help him describe this moment of gifted insight.[89] It was, to be sure, only a fleeting moment. Sometimes this aid did not arrive, or at least, not immediately so. In his *Commentary on Matthew* he writes candidly about his struggles to make sense of scriptural passages: "And we see this daily among us when we search for some true meaning in the Scriptures. Before we find what we are looking for, we suffer from an absence of meanings, until such an absence is

---

[86] Hom Jer 19.11.2/SC 238, 220.54–59—Smith modified.

[87] Lk Frg 151/GCS 9, 287.10–14.

[88] Comm Song of Songs 3/GCS 8, 202.1–11. Also see GCS 8, 218.16–19.

[89] This divinely granted insight is a teaching (Hom Jer 19.10), interpretation (Phil 1.29), opening and explaining (Hom Gen 12.1; Comm Jn 2.47; Comm Cor 11). It is also an illumination (Lk Frg 151), making clear (Hom Jer 19.10, 19.14.1), revelation (Hom Ex 2.4, 10.4), showing (Hom Ex 2.4), inspiration (CC 7.30), participation (PA 4.2.7; Comm Matt 14.6), union or marriage (Hom Gen 10.5), vision (Hom Num 27.12), a seeing (PA 1.1.2; Hom Josh 3.1), a touching (Comm Jn 10.173), grace (Hom Josh 8.1; Comm Matt 14.12; PA 4.2.3), and coming (Hom Jer 19.10, 19.14.1; Hom Ez 11.3.3).

brought to an end in us by God who gives to the worthy 'food at the right time' [Ps 144:15]."[90] Divine insight was elusive. There is a poignant passage in his first *Homily on the Song of Songs* where Origen applies the transitory encounter between the bride and bridegroom to his wrestling with the biblical text:

> The Bride then beholds the Bridegroom; and He, as soon as she has seen Him, goes away. He does this frequently throughout the Song; and that is something nobody can understand who has not suffered it himself. God is my witness that I have often perceived the Bridegroom drawing near me and being most intensely present with me; then suddenly He has withdrawn and I could not find Him, though I sought to do so. I long therefore for Him to come again, and sometimes He does so. Then, when He has appeared and I lay hold of Him, He slips away once more; and when He has so slipped away, my search for Him begins anew. So does He act with me repeatedly.[91]

Passages such as these have led scholars to recognize how intrinsic the "mystical," "spiritual," or "religious" life was to Origen's exegetical enterprise. "Understanding Scripture is not for Origen simply an academic exercise but a religious experience,"[92] Andrew Louth writes. Marguerite Harl offers a similar sentiment, that Origen "knew his most vivid religious experiences within that particular Christian *place* which is the work of exegesis."[93]

The foregoing autobiographical fragments open a window onto the dynamic that Origen thought transpired between the interpreter of Scripture and its divine authors. This dynamic consistently emerged from within a recurring exegetical situation: the reader, despite all effort, was confounded by an obscure passage and so turned outside, as it were, for insight: from Scripture's divine authors. But as he often stressed, this divine gift only came (if it even did come) to those perplexed interpreters who positioned themselves properly before Scripture's divine authors. How, then, could interpreters propitiate these authors? As we saw above, Origen called upon a range of moral commitments that he thought facilitated successful *independent* inquiry into Scripture—a general moral disposition, exegetical virtues and the exercise of trust were ways in which interpreters took initiative in tackling challenging scriptural texts. However, a closer examination of his corpus reveals that these same moral

---

[90] Comm Matt Ser 38/GCS 11, 72.19–23—transl. mine.

[91] Hom Song of Songs 1.7/GCS 8, 39.15–22. On the inconstant divine help for interpreting Scripture, also see Comm Song of Songs 3/GCS 8, 218.8–10, 16–19. Also see the more cryptic comments at Hom Lk 18.3 and Comm Jn 6.268–272. For additional autobiographical statements about divine aid while interpreting Scripture, see Hom Lev 8.5.3 and Comm Matt Ser 38.

[92] A. Louth, *The Origins of the Christian Mystical Tradition*, 2nd edn (Oxford: Oxford University Press, 2007), 63.

[93] M. Harl, "La langage de l'expérience religieuse chez les pères grecs," *Rivista di storia e letteratura religiosa* 15 (1977): 133. Transl. B. McGinn, *The Presence of God: A History of Western Christian Mysticism*, vol. 1 *Foundations of Western Mysticism* (New York: Crossroad, 1991), 117. Also see C. W. Macleod, "Allegory and mysticism in Origen and Gregory of Nyssa," *JTS* 22 (1971): 362–379, as well as ch. 5 ("Le contact du Sauveur") in F. Bertrand, *Mystique de Jésus chez Origène* (Paris: Aubier, 1951).

commitments also contributed to the success of the exegetical enterprise by rendering interpreters fittingly *dependent*. These commitments, in other words, played simultaneously in two registers: they facilitated independent inquiry into challenging Scriptures, but when defeated by these darkened Scriptures, they also made interpreters worthy of the reception of outside divine aid.[94]

There are several passages where we find Origen emphasizing how some of the leading moral practices examined above rendered interpreters worthy of this heavenly aid. In his eleventh *Homily on Genesis*, for instance, he notes how the resurrected Jesus appears and graciously opens the Scriptures to interpreters who exercise exegetical virtues—they are attentive and persistent in their study of Scripture—and who lead a life in accordance with the divine law. Just as Jesus opened the Scriptures for his disciples on the road to Emmaus, so he also does for his disciples who labor over the Scriptures:

> You too, therefore, if you shall always search the prophetic visions, if you always inquire, always desire to learn, if you meditate on these things, if you remain in them, you too receive a blessing from the Lord and dwell "at the well of vision" [Gen 25:11]. For the Lord Jesus will appear to you also "in the way" and will open the Scriptures to you so that you may say: "Was not our heart burning within us when he opened to us the Scriptures" [Lk 24:32]? But he appears to these who think about him and meditate on him and live "in his law day and night" [Ps 1:2].[95]

There are several other passages written to this same effect. Confronted with the ethical predicament posed by the holy wars in the book of Joshua, Origen expresses his hope that the "worthy" interpreter receives the gift of exegetical insight from Jesus:

> Indeed, would that we might be worthy for the Lord Jesus to throw open the courtyard of his wisdom and bring us into the treasure vaults of his knowledge [cf. 1 Cor 12:8] and deem it fitting to reveal more fully to us and uncover more completely those things whose figures we now haltingly try to behold in part and examine "as if through a mirror and in a riddle" [1 Cor 13:12].[96]

In the preface of *On First Principles*, Origen acknowledges how interpreters need to receive perception from the Holy Spirit about the apostles' more

---

[94] When Origen speaks of interpreters becoming worthy to receive the reward of the divine gift of understanding, he is touching upon his larger anti-Gnostic polemic. He repeatedly insists that intellects do not lead lives pre-determined to either judgment or salvation. Rather, they carry responsibility for their actions, and God usually comes to the rescue of those who have already exercised the power of choice to lead righteous lives. Applied to biblical scholarship, for Origen, God does not arbitrarily reward pre-determined interpreters with exegetical insight, but rather those who have struggled to become "worthy." For an orientation to this aspect of Origen's anti-Gnostic polemic, see esp. PA 1.5 and 3.1.

[95] Hom Gen 11.3/GCS 6, 106.10–16. For other uses of Lk 24:32 in contexts where Jesus discloses the message of Scripture to the interpreter, see Hom Gen 13.3, 15.7; Hom Ex 12.4; Hom Josh 9.8; and Hom Song of Songs 2.11.

[96] Hom Josh 12.2/GCS 7, 368.19–23.

demanding statements. The apostles left the grounds of their statements "to be investigated by such as should merit the higher gifts of the Spirit and in particular by such as should afterwards receive through the Holy Spirit himself the graces of the 'word of wisdom and knowledge' [1 Cor 12:8]." These interpreters are "diligent," "lovers of wisdom," and "train themselves to become worthy and capable of receiving wisdom."[97] In passages such as these, Origen spoke of divine aid arriving *without* the interpreter's request— a worthy life and worthy inquiry already merited the gift of understanding. Yet when Origen raised the issue of divine aid for interpretation, he spoke far more frequently of the importance of *requesting* this aid. "Perhaps it is some sort of tenet," he aphorizes, "that no one receives a divine gift who does not ask for it."[98] This principle was certainly applicable to biblical scholarship. As Origen understood it, the request for divine aid, or prayer, was central to the labors of the biblical exegete.[99]

PRAYER

While his treatise *On Prayer* has surprisingly little to say about the role of prayer in biblical scholarship, Origen disperses substantial reflections on this topic throughout his commentaries, homilies (frequently in their prefaces and epilogues), and correspondence.[100] From his wider corpus we quickly gather

---

[97] PA, pref.3/GK 86, 9.4–11—Butterworth modified, following Karpp's emendation of this passage in the appendix (GK 884 at the entry "86 p. 9, 6"). Note how both in this and the preceding passage Origen draws upon 1 Cor 12:8 to depict the ideal interpreter of Scripture. This figure has graciously received the gifts of wisdom and knowledge from the Holy Spirit. Origen often uses the verse in such a capacity: see Comm Song of Songs prol./GCS 8, 77.17–23; PA pref.8; CC 1.44, 3.18.

[98] Comm Jn 13.5/GCS 4, 227.1–2—transl. mine. Also see Matt Frg 139; CC 7.42.

[99] Note Origen's important lexicographical discussion of $(\pi\rho\sigma)\epsilon\upsilon\chi\acute{\eta}$ in *On Prayer* 3.1–4.2, where he contends that this noun has two distinct senses in Scripture. There is a specialized sense of "vow" or "promise", and the more prevalent sense of "request." It is the latter sense that expresses the core element in Origen's understanding of prayer (also see PE 14.2 for the fundamentally petitionary sense of prayer).

[100] For literature on Origen's view of prayer, see W. Gessel, *Die Theologie des Gebetes nach "De oratione" von Origenes* (Munich: Schöningh, 1975); H. Crouzel, "Les doxologie finales des homélies d'Origène selon le texte grec et les versions latines," *Aug* 20 (1980): 95–107; M. Harl, SC 302, 145–148; D. Sheerin, "The role of prayer in Origen's homilies," in C. Kannengieser and W. L. Petersen, eds., *Origen of Alexandria: His World and His Legacy* (Notre Dame: Notre Dame University Press, 1988), 200–214; L. Perrone, "I paradigmi biblici della preghiera nel *Peri Euchês* di Origene: Aspetti formali e problematiche ermeneutiche," *Aug* 33 (1993): 339–368; D. Bertrand, "Piété et sagesse dans le *Peri Euchês*," in *Orig V*: 476–480; P. S. A. Lefeber, *Kreuze en verlangen. Een onderzoek naar zin en functie van het gebed in Origenes' preken en zijn tractaat Over het gebed* (Gorinchem: Narratio, 1997), esp. ch. 3, "Gebed en Schrift" (65–88); P. S. A. Lefeber, "The same view on prayer in Origen's sermons and his treatise *On Prayer*", in *Orig VII*: 33–38; L. Perrone, "Il discorso protrettico di Origene sulla preghiera. Introduzione al

his insistence that interpreters needed to cultivate a life of prayer when examining the Scriptures carefully. "It is necessary," Origen says, "to inquire carefully into the truth of doctrines, and next to ask God to reveal to us the mysteries of wisdom that have been concealed."[101] "[I]t is shown," he preaches elsewhere, "that we must not only employ zeal to learn the sacred literature, but we must also pray to the Lord and entreat 'day and night' [Ps 1:2]."[102] In his *Homilies on Genesis* he reaches the verse, "the Lord blessed Isaac his [Abraham's] son and he dwelt at the well of vision" (Gen 25:11), and wonders what this passage could signify for contemporary Christians. The "well of vision" becomes the Scriptures, and the one who dwells on the Scriptures, like Origen, has the following profile:

> if I am, nevertheless, busily engaged in the divine Scriptures and "I meditate on the Law of God day and night" [cf. Ps 1:2] and at no time at all do I desist inquiring, discussing, investigating, and certainly, what is greatest, praying to God and asking for understanding from him [*quod maximum est, orando Deum et ab illo poscendo intellectum*] who "teaches man knowledge" [Ps 93:10], I shall appear to dwell "at the well of vision."[103]

Prayer was indispensable for exegetical success. "Do not be satisfied with knocking and seeking," Origen counsels Gregory, "because prayer is indeed most necessary for understanding the divine writings [ἀναγκαιοτάτη γὰρ καὶ ἡ περὶ τοῦ νοεῖν τὰ θεῖα εὐχή]."[104]

As already intimated above, the interpreter's prayer emerged from within a specific exegetical situation: the meaning of Scripture was inaccessible. In *Against Celsus*, for instance, Origen notes how the prophets themselves inquired into the law with the help of prayer since it was at points obscure. "When praying about the law because it is obscure and in need of God to make it intelligible, they say in prayer: 'Open my eyes, and I will understand thy wonders out of thy law' [Ps 118:18]".[105] Indeed, Origen often wrote of the need for prayer when he found

---

ΠΕΡΙ ΕΥΧΗΣ," in F. Cocchini, ed., *Il dono e la sua ombra: Ricerche sul ΠΕΡΙ ΕΥΧΗΣ di Origene* (Rome: Institutum Patristicum Augustinianum, 1997), 7–32; L. Perrone, "Prayer in Origen's *Contra Celsum*: The knowledge of God and the truth of Christianity," *VChr* 55 (2001): 1–19; G. E. Rossi, *Bibel und Gebet in den Predigtepilogen bei Origenes* (Dissertation at the Friedrich-Schiller-Universität Jena, 2003).

[101] Matt Frg 139/GCS 12, 71.1–2—transl. mine.

[102] Hom Ex 12.4/GCS 6, 266.20–23—Heine modified. Origen is commenting here on 2 Cor 3:14–16 where Paul writes of the need to "turn to the Lord" to have the "veil removed." For similar interpretations of these verses, see Hom Lev 4.7.3; Hom Ez 3.1; Comm Matt 11.14; Comm Rom 6.7.18; CC 5.60.

[103] Hom Gen 11.3/GCS 6, 105.20–24—Heine modified.

[104] LG 4/SC 148, 192.83–194.93—transl. mine. The sequence Origen highlights in all these passages (the reader ought first to apply effort and, should that fail, request God for help) is found elsewhere: see esp. Comm Song of Songs prol./GCS 8, 77.17–23; CC 4.50.

[105] CC 2.6/SC 132, 294.13–16. For other references to Ps 118:18 in similar exegetical contexts, see Hom Gen 12.1; Hom Lev 1.1.4, 6.1.1; Hom Ez 2.3.4; CC 4.50.

himself in such difficult situations. In the *Dialogue with Heraclides* he is confronted with a "really vexing text" that suggests the soul is corporeal. He begins his response by "praying for assistance in reading the sacred texts (for we need assistance to keep our thought from departing from the truth)."[106] Moreover, in the face of challenging passages Origen not only prayed, but often asked his congregants to pray on his behalf. We see this at the start of his sixth *Homily on Leviticus*. A lectionary passage about priestly clothing and the ceremony of consecration of the high priest has just been read before Origen's congregation in Caesarea, but it is a challenge to offer an interpretation that goes beyond the literal sense. Thus, Origen insists:

> we must strive to explain these things not by the power of human thinking but by prayers and supplications poured out to God. In this likewise we stand in need of your aid, that God, Father of the Word, may give us the word "in the opening of our mouth" [cf. Eph 6:10] that we can consider the wonders of his Law [cf. Ps 118:18].[107]

In this passage we detect one of the few instances in Origen's larger exegetical enterprise where he enrolled his congregants not as an *audience*, but as *participants* in his project of scriptural exegesis. He turns to his congregation and asks for "your aid"—that is, their prayers on his behalf for interpreting Scripture's difficult passages well. A wider examination of Origen's corpus reveals that when he spoke of vicarious prayer for aid in deciphering Scripture, he invariably did so in his homilies (and not in his commentaries).[108] The significance of this rests largely on the distinctive situation in which he delivered his homilies. Origen's sermons were often conducted conversationally: he would draw his audience into his own exposition of Scripture by asking them questions, addressing them in the second-person singular, or, as here, requesting their prayers on his behalf.[109] Nor were such requests scripted rhetorical exercises. Especially during his early years in Caesarea, Origen often preached extemporaneously, and so even though most of his surviving sermons come down to us in heavily edited Latin translations, their largely improvisational character still shines through as we see him frequently pausing before challenging scriptural passages, gathering his thoughts and, often enough, enlisting the prayers of his congregants for help with these texts.[110]

---

[106] DH 11/SC 67, 11.11–12, 14–16—transl. mine.

[107] Hom Lev 6.1.1/GCS 6, 359.10–14.

[108] There are a number of such passages where Origen draws his congregation into the interpretive enterprise, requesting their prayers that divine aid be sent for his exegesis of a challenging passage: see Hom Gen 3.5, 9.1; Hom Ex 9.2; Hom Lev 5.2, 6.6.6, 9.1.1, 12.4.1, 14.4.1; Hom Num 26.3.5; Hom Josh 8.2, 20.4; Hom Jer 19.10; Hom Ez 4.3, 7.10, 11.2.

[109] On Origen's preaching style, see P. Nautin, "Origène prédicateur," in *Homélies sur Jérémie*, SC 232 (Paris: Cerf, 1976), 100–109; A. M. Castagno, *Origene predicatore e il suo pubblico* (Milan: Franco Angeli, 1987); J. W. Trigg, *Origen* (London: Routledge, 1998), 39.

[110] Origen's *Homily on the Witch of Endor* offers particularly clear testimony to the improvisational character of his sermons (in no small measure due to surviving in Greek). In the opening

Faced with exegetical difficulties, interpreters prayed. Yet what did they request, and of whom did they make this request? These two questions pinpoint topics of particular importance to Origen in his treatise *On Prayer*. One of his main concerns was to articulate what people ought to request (and ought *not* to request) of God in their prayers.[111] This issue proved particularly troublesome to Origen since he perceived conflicting instruction in Scripture. "Apparently, the divine Word summons us to imitate the prayers of the saints," he notes, and acknowledges that many of these prayers contained requests for material or corporeal objects (e.g. prayers for fertility, for deliverance from enemies, etc.). Yet at the same time, he also observes a seemingly conflicting, though loftier, teaching about prayer attributed to Jesus: "Seek the great things and the little things will be added for you; seek the heavenly things and the earthly things will be added for you."[112] It is this latter instruction to which Origen clearly inclines, yet he also has no interest in jettisoning the numerous prayers for material goods that he finds in Scripture. He thus proposes a resolution to his dilemma by invoking a familiar exegetical distinction between types and symbols on the one hand, and the truths or mysteries to which they point on the other.[113] The prayers for corporeal or material gifts in Scripture were types, he proposes, of the loftier realities for which Christians ought to aspire. Thus, for instance, while Esther and Mordecai prayed for deliverance from their physical enemy, Haman (cf. Esther 3:6–7, 4:16–17, 9:26–28), Christians ought to imitate this request, but need to do so in a loftier manner by seeking deliverance from their spiritual enemies. Thus they fulfill the dominical mandate to seek for "great" and "heavenly" things.[114]

It is in this context in *On Prayer* that Origen alludes to the role of prayer in biblical exegesis. Christians ought not to pray for physical wealth, "[f]or what

---

section of this homily he briefly summarizes the four pericopes in the lectionary reading and concludes that he does not have time to do justice to the whole passage. So, he turns to his bishop and asks him to choose only one of the four biblical episodes that Origen ought to expound. He then delivers a largely impromptu sermon on the necromancer who summoned Samuel from the dead. Also, recall Origen's reluctance to have stenographers take down his sermons until he was over sixty years old (Eusebius, HE 6.36.1). Eusebius does not give Origen's rationale for prohibiting the transcription of his sermons, but simply says that "he had never before allowed it." This reluctance on Origen's part might very well reflect his concerns over disseminating unpolished homilies.

[111]   See esp. PE 2.2; 8.1; 17.1, 2; 25.1, 2.

[112]   This passage does not occur in our New Testament. In *On Prayer* Origen first cites it at 2.2, and then several times thereafter (PE 14.1, 16.2; also see Comm Matt 16.28, 16.29; Lk Frg 172–173). This agraphon is also cited at CC 7.44.

[113]   See esp. PE 13.4, 14.1.

[114]   PE 13.4, with other examples. Note the ensuing discussion where Origen explains how it is that the saints mentioned in Scripture nevertheless received corporeal gifts. He proposes that these gifts were shadows of the true spiritual gifts God was bestowing upon them. Thus, for example, it was not simply Hannah's soul that bore fruit, but also her body that was transformed from sterility (PE 16.2–17.2).

comparison is there," he asks, "between corporeal wealth and the wealth with all speech and all knowledge [1 Cor 1:5]?"[115] It is the struggling interpreter's request for the wealth of knowledge that locates this plea commendably among those prayers that only seek "great" and "heavenly things."[116] Not surprisingly, when we look elsewhere in Origen's corpus for a more explicit discussion of what interpreters ought to pray, we find him insisting upon the lofty request for the gift of insight into Scripture. He preaches in his *Homilies on Leviticus*: "This passage of Scripture is most difficult to explain, but if you entreat God the Father of the Word in your prayers that he may see fit to illuminate us, when he gives this, it can be explained."[117] Or again in his *Homilies on Joshua*:

> You see that the aid of God truly is necessary so that these things can be explained; and it is utterly impossible for any man to discourse about these things unless he has been illumined by the grace of God. On that account, therefore, aid me with your prayers, and labor together with me, so that in these passages, so obscure and hidden the Lord may deign to make known the light of truth to us . . . [118]

There are dozens of passages where Origen himself requests, or requests through others, the lofty gift of knowledge for the interpretation of vexing biblical passages.[119]

And to whom, finally, is this request made? Origen briefly tackles this issue, albeit cautiously ("if" . . . "perhaps"), in a famous discussion in *On Prayer*. "Now if we are to take prayer in its most exact sense," he writes, "perhaps we should not pray to anyone begotten, not even to Christ Himself, but only to the God and Father of all, to whom even our Savior Himself prayed."[120] Origen voices his position carefully, since he acknowledges that less instructed Christians addressed their prayers to Christ (and curiously, as we will see below, he too did this).[121] However, he here notes, there are several rationale behind his tentative proposal, including most notably the fact that Jesus taught his disciples to pray only to God "Our Father in heaven" (Matt 6:5; Lk 11:1). At the same time, Origen immediately insists that because Jesus taught his followers to request anything of the Father in his name (Jn 16:23–24), and because of his intercessory role as High Priest on their behalf before God (Heb 7:20–21, etc.), Christians are not only permitted, but entreated to address their

---

[115] PE 17.1/GCS 2. 338.27–339.1.

[116] Note also that recourse to prayer accompanies not just difficult exegetical endeavors, but also other intellectual challenges: see PA 2.9.4; CC 4.1, 5.1, 7.1, 8.1; PE 2.6, etc.

[117] Hom Lev 12.4.1/GCS 6, 460.8–11.

[118] Hom Josh 20.4/GCS 7, 422.15–20—Bruce modified.

[119] See Hom Gen 2.3, 7.6; Hom Ex 9.2; Hom Lev 6.6.6, 9.1.1, 13.1.2; Hom Num 13.4.2; Hom Josh 17.3; Hom Ez 1.4, 7.10; Hom Lk 35.1, etc.

[120] PE 15.1/GCS 2, 333.26–334.1. The discussion runs from PE 14.6 to 16.1. For other related statements on the addressee of prayer, see CC 3.34; 5.4–5, 11; 7.51; 8.13.

[121] See PE 16.1.

prayers to God the Father *through* (not *to*) Jesus their High Priest and Advocate.[122] As indicated above, when we scan Origen's own writings we see that he himself did not always hold to the distinction he advocates here in *On Prayer*. When offering prayers in exegetical contexts, he variously addressed his petitions for help to "God," but also to the "Word," "Jesus," "Lord," and perhaps even on a handful of occasions, to the "Holy Spirit."[123]

In this chapter I have advanced the central thesis of this project one step further by detailing the many intersections between scriptural exegesis and the moral life for Origen. While the commitment to embark upon a life of scriptural study was itself already a mark of moral advancement (Chapter 5), it has also become clear in the preceding pages that the interpreter's moral commitments colored the very task of deciphering Scripture. The interpreter-at-work was a moral agent. The character and conduct of this interpreter— provided he was "worthy" or "pure"—helped form expectations about the scriptural message conducive to extracting its lofty sense. When challenged by difficult passages, this interpreter was exhorted to study Scripture with a range of exegetical virtues, and should discouragement over an unyielding passage follow, to exercise an abiding trust that an underlying sense resided in Scripture. The "pure" life, exegetical virtues, and the exercise of faith all facilitated independent scriptural study. But they also rendered the interpreter worthy of divine aid when Scripture proved impenetrable. To an interpreter who cultivated such a moral profile, especially one who prayed for this divine aid, God, the Word, and the Holy Spirit were willing to offer exegetical aid.

In the next chapter I turn to the message Scripture's authors sought to convey and its interpreters, in turn, to discover. What was this message? And how did it play a role in the interpreter's salvation?

---

[122] PE 15.4/GCS 2, 335.19–22 (where the distinction is between praying "to" the High Priest and Advocate [dative case] and "through" [signaled by the preposition διά]).

[123] For references to prayers directed to "God, Father of the Word" see Hom Gen 12.1, 13.1; Hom Lev 12.4.1; Hom Josh 8.2; simply to "God" see Hom Num 13.4.2; Hom Lev 6.1; Hom Josh 17.3; Hom Ez 1.4, 7.10; Comm Rom pref.2; CC 4.50; to the "Word" see Hom Num 26.3.5; to "Jesus" see Hom Gen 7.6; Hom Ex 2.4; Hom Lev 5.5.2; Hom Jud 8.5; Hom Jer 19.10, 19.15.1; to the "Lord" see Hom Gen 6.1, 7.1, 12.4; Hom Ez 4.3; Hom Lev 1.1.4, 6.6.6, 13.2.1; Hom Num 26.3.4 (note, however, that "Lord" is often an ambiguous designation in Origen's theology where it can refer to either God or Jesus, and sometimes both, as in Hom Ex 10.4). Note also the curious reference in Hom Lev 1.1.4 to entreating "the Lord himself, the Holy Spirit himself" (perhaps also Hom Num 27.1.7). If Origen could justify invoking Christ in his prayers because of his intercessory role, then a similar justification held for calling upon the Holy Spirit, since Origen speaks at length in *On Prayer* (2.3–4; 14.5) about the Spirit's role in praying to God on our behalf. References to prayer to the Holy Spirit are, nevertheless, rare in Origen's corpus. On angels hearing our prayers and mediating them: CC 8.34, 8.36, 8.64. In short, Origen was not settled on the issue of the recipient of prayer.

9

Message: Saving Knowledge

In the second part of this study I have argued how biblical scholarship for Origen afforded Christian philologists an occasion through which to express any number of loyalties, doctrines, practices, and relationships characteristic of the Christian faith. Yet, as I demonstrated in the previous chapter, these interpreters did more than *express* these various facets of faith while examining Scripture. Exegetical activity also became a moment for their *reception* of divine aid. Scriptural interpretation was, in other words, an occasion to perform the faith as well as to welcome resources that strengthened this faith. Scripture for Origen was a resource—and arguably the privileged resource—that expedited Christians along their journey toward salvation. "Who would dare to say," he asks in his *Homilies on Numbers*, "that what is written 'by the Word of God' [Num 33:2] is of no use and makes no contribution to our salvation, but merely narrates an event that happened, and which, to be sure, passed on by back then, but now pertains in no way to us when it is related? This opinion," he quickly dismisses, "is impious and foreign to the catholic faith."[1] Scripture, Origen concisely remarks elsewhere, was written "for the cure of the soul [ἐπὶ τὴν θεραπείαν τῆς ψυχῆς]."[2] Arguably the cornerstone of Origen's elaborate account of Scripture was that this collection of writings was "useful" or "beneficial," serving as an instrument in the divine plan of salvation for those who read and heard it well.[3]

This extraordinarily rich doctrine of Scripture has been a perennial topic in modern Origenian scholarship.[4] The task in this chapter is certainly not to

---

[1] Hom Num 27.2.1/GCS 7, 258.13–18. Also see Hom Ex 2.3.

[2] Comm Jn 10.174/GCS 4, 201, 26–27. Also see Hom Jer 14.1.2.

[3] The terms Origen most frequently uses to convey the "useful," "serviceable," or "beneficial" character of Scripture are χρήσιμος (Hom Sam 5.2/SC 328, 174.4, 8; CC 7.10/SC 150, 36.16–17) and ὠφέλιμος, ὠφέλεια (CC 1.18/SC 132, 122.19–20; CC 7.29/SC 150, 80.14–15; PA 4.2.6/GK 714, 315.4–5; Phil 12.2/SC 302, 392.8–15). For the Latin expressions (utilitas, utilis), see Hom Num 22.1/GCS 7, 204.20–21; Hom Josh 20.2/GCS 7, 419.9–11; Hom 3.6 Ps 36/Prinzivalli, 126.3.

[4] The literature on Origen's doctrine of Scripture is large. See esp. A. Zöllig, *Die Inspirationslehre des Origenes: Ein Beitrag zur Dogmengeschichte* (Freiburg: Herder, 1902); E. Stuiber, "Einiges zur Schriftauffassung des Origenes," *IKZ* 13 (1923): 145–169; H. de Lubac, *History and Spirit*, 337–348; J. Daniélou, *Origen*, 139–173; R. P. C. Hanson, *Allegory and Event*, 187–258;

address the numerous facets of this many-sided doctrine, but rather to examine the one issue that is relevant to Origen's portrait of the scriptural interpreter: how did he think Scripture served as a catalyst for this interpreter's salvation? To help answer this question, I will address the following themes: Origen's conception of Scripture's authorship, and in particular, authorial intent; the central message these authors conveyed in Scripture; and finally, briefly, the effects this message had on its readership. This focused inquiry into Origen's view of Scripture will provide additional detail for the emerging portrait of his scriptural interpreter and, in turn, advance the central argument in this book: that the interpreter of Scripture was a participant in the Christian drama of salvation.

AUTHORIAL INTENT

Origen usually demarcated the writings he deemed scriptural from other literature by modifying the former with the adjectives "divine," "holy," or "sacred."[5] Such lofty qualifiers were rooted in a conviction about the provenance of these writings: he believed (and argued) that the church's Scriptures enjoyed not simply a human, but also a divine, authorship.[6] "We have believed," he writes, referring to a passage from 1 Samuel, "that the author of these words is not [only] a man, but rather that the Holy Spirit is the author who moved men."[7] The New Testament epistles contain "the understanding of wise men who have been aided by Christ."[8] Or again: "We believe that the gospels were accurately written also by the Holy Spirit who was assisting."[9] As these and many other passages indicate, for Origen the Scriptures were the

---

R. Gögler, *Zur Theologie des Biblischen Wortes bei Origenes*, 282–364; H. von Campenhausen, *The Formation of the Christian Bible*, transl. J. A. Baker (Philadelphia: Fortress Press, 1972), 307–318; E. Nardoni, "Origen's concept of Biblical inspiration," *The Second Century* 4 (1984): 9–23; H. Crouzel, *Origen*, 61–84; K. J. Torjesen, *Hermeneutical Procedure*, 108–147; H. J. Vogt, "Die Lehre des Origenes von der Inspiration der Heiligen Schrift: Ein Vergleich zwischen der Grundlagenschrift und der Antwort auf Kelsos," *ThQ* 170 (1990): 97–103; idem, *Origenes als Exeget*, ed. W. Geerlings (Paderborn: Ferdinand Schöningh, 1999), 179–185; E. A. Dively Lauro, *The Soul and Spirit of Scripture Within Origen's Exegesis*, 37–130.

[5] For instance, the adjective θεῖος ("divine") at PA 4.1.1/GK 668, 292.11; 670, 293.2, 3; Comm Jn 1.14/GCS 4, 6.10–11; CC 1.6/SC 132, 92.28. The adjective ἅγιος ("holy") at Comm Jn 6.217/GCS 4, 151.14. The adjective ἱερός ("holy," "sacred") at CC 4.99/SC 136, 434.39; 5.5/SC 147, 24.17–18.

[6] Note that the divine authorship of Scripture was an article in Origen's rule of faith (at PA pref.8). His most extended argument for divine inspiration occurs later in this work at PA 4.1.1–7.

[7] Hom Sam 5.4/SC 328, 180.14–16—transl. mine.

[8] Comm Jn 1.15/GCS 4, 6.19–20.

[9] Comm Matt 16.12/GCS 10, 510.14–16—transl. mine.

result of a collaborative effort, the means by which divine and human authors communicated with their readers.[10]

At various points in his career Origen vigorously argued that Scripture's human authors were not mere ciphers or passive instruments through which the divine inspiring agent communicated, but rather authors who actively and willingly participated in the writing of Scripture.[11] Nevertheless, he relied heavily on Scripture's divine authorship for determining the "will," "intent," or "aim" of this collection of writings.[12] His perspective on the authorial intent of Scripture's divine authors was largely formed by the doctrine of divine providence. This teaching provides the framework for assessing the function of Scripture: God's particular action in Scripture was a particular instance of God's larger providential action in the cosmos as a whole. This relationship between divine providence and scriptural authorship surfaces repeatedly in his writings, but perhaps nowhere as clearly as in his third *Homily on Genesis*. Here Origen begins by offering a concise definition of providence:

---

[10] When we canvass Origen's wider corpus we usually find him attributing divine authorship to God, at other times to the Word (or Jesus Christ), and still at other times to the Holy Spirit. On God as the inspiring agent, see Hom Jer 10.1.1, 16.6; Hom Lk 3.1; PA 4.1.6, 4.1.7; CC 2.6, 7.3; Phil 1.28. On the Word illuminating Scripture's human authors, see Hom Lev 1.1.1; Hom Isa 1.5; Hom Jer 9.1.1; Comm Matt 12.43, 16.12; Comm Jn 1.15, 1.37, 2.10, 6.24, 20.398; Comm Rom 2.14.21. And the Holy Spirit helping author these Scriptures: PA pref.4, pref.8, 1.3.1; CC 4.17. There is also a rare reference to the angelic role in divine authorship at PA 3.3.4 (for a related passage, also see Hom Lk 3.2). Occasionally, there are also references to divine authorship where Origen is vague about the particular author he has in mind. For example, the Scriptures are composed by "heavenly grace" (PA 4.1.6), "divine inspiration" (CC 3.4; 5.60) and have a "divine origin" (PA 4.1.7); they are authored by a "divine Spirit" (CC 7.3), the "Spirit of Christ" (CC 6.19; Comm Rom 6.13.8, 7.1), or the "Spirit of God" (Hom Gen 3.2; Comm Rom 6.13.8). R. P. C. Hanson's claim that Origen's conviction that "the Holy Spirit is *ultimately* the author of Scripture" is, in light of the above texts, unfounded (italics mine, *Allegory and Event*, 193).

Note also that Origen customarily identifies only one of these illumining agents (God, Word, or Holy Spirit) when he wishes to signal the divine authorship of Scripture. Much less frequently does he refer to two of them working in concert, and only on a handful of occasions are all three collaborating in their authorship of Scripture. See in particular two passages in book four of *On First Principles* where Origen refers to all three divine inspiring agents working together (PA 4.2.2/GK 700, 308.12–14 and PA 4.2.7/GK 720, 318.9–10). For a discussion of these passages, see my essay, "Why does Origen refer to the Trinitarian authorship of scripture in Book 4 of *Peri Archon*?" *VC* 60 (2006): 1–8.

[11] See esp. Hom Ez 6.1; Comm Matt 12.40; PA 3.3.4; CC 7.3–4. For literature on Origen's view of the process of divine inspiration, see H. de Lubac, *History and Spirit*, 342–344; R. P. C. Hanson, *Allegory and Event*, 194–196; esp. E. Nardoni, "Origen's concept of biblical inspiration," *The Second Century* 4 (1984): 9–23.

[12] References to authorial "aim" ($\sigma\kappa o\pi\acute{o}\varsigma$) include: PA 4.2.7/GK 720, 318.8–9; 4.2.9/GK 726, 321.11–12; 4.3.4/GK 740, 328.11–12; Comm Jn 5.6/GCS 4, 103.3–5; 10.19/GCS 4, 175.11–13. Important references to "intent" ($\beta o\acute{v}\lambda\eta\mu a$) include: Hom Jer 1.2/SC 232, 198.3–5; 3.1/SC 232, 250.3–4; 4.1/SC 232, 254.2–3; 14.3/SC 238, 70.31–32; 19.11/SC 238, 220.54; Comm Jn 10.286/ GCS 4, 219.9; 13.379/GCS 4, 285.26–29; 13.367/GCS 4, 284.10; CC 6.19/SC 147, 226.14–15; 7.29/ SC 150, 80.14–15; 7.59/SC 150, 150.4. On $\beta o\acute{v}\lambda\eta\sigma\iota\varsigma$, see Comm Jn 10.68/GCS 4, 183.11–12. For an important discussion in the Latin corpus, see Hom Ez 2.2.3 (and for the Latin terms that express authorial intent, see H. de Lubac, *History and Spirit*, 344, n. 44).

> As we profess that God is incorporeal and omnipotent and invisible, so we confess with a sure and immovable doctrine that he cares about [*curare*] mortal affairs and that nothing happens in heaven or earth apart from his providence [*providentia*] . . . For providence is that by which he attends to and manages and makes provision [*procurat et dispensat et providet*] for the things which happen.[13]

In this passage Origen claims that Christians do not simply believe in an omnipotent God who stands at a distance from his creation. Rather, this God is actively engaged in the affairs of the cosmos. "Cares about," "attends to," "manages," and "makes provision" are the four verbs Origen uses in this passage to characterize this providential action.[14] As this homily continues, he tellingly specifies one of the ways in which God expresses providential care for humans: by communicating a beneficial message to them. "In accordance with this profession, therefore, that God is the provider and manager of all things, it follows that he makes known what he wishes or what is advantageous for men. For," Origen concludes, "if he should not make these things known he will not be the provider for man nor will he be believed to care for mortal affairs."[15] The Scriptures are a particular instance of the divine philanthropy, of God's larger providential action for the welfare of humanity.[16]

Where Origen makes this link between divine providence and scriptural authorship, he often advances his argument further by specifying the aim or purpose behind God's providential arrangement of Scripture. What *particular* benefit does God intend to convey through the smallest detail of the scriptural text, and indeed, throughout all the writings that constitute Scripture? In the passage from the *Homily on Genesis* examined above, he refers to a message that is "advantageous" to its readership. Yet Origen is often more specific. As we will see in the following three passages, Scripture was composed with salvific intent. Arguably his best-known statement on

---

[13] Hom Gen 3.2/GCS 6, 39.20–40.4. As in this passage, so also in Comm Jn 2.31 and PA 1.4.3, 2.1.1–3, Origen closely associates belief in God with belief in providence. Indeed, the noun πρόνοια for Origen is often synonymous with θεός (PA 4.1.7/GK 690, 303.4; Phil 10.2/SC 302, 368.18, and s.v. πρόνοια, Lampe, B.2.v for additional passages). On the theme of providence in Origen's thought, see H. Koch, *Pronoia und Paideusis: Studien über Origenes und sein Verhältnis zum Platonismus* (Berlin: W. de Gruyter, 1932).

[14] He also juxtaposes "providence" with "oversight" (ἐπισκοπή) at CC 6.71/SC 147, 358.8–9, and "superintendence" (οἰκονομία) at PA 4.2.4/GK 708, 312.7–710, 313.11.

[15] Hom Gen 3.2/GCS 6, 40.5–8.

[16] There are other passages where Origen speaks of the divine authorship of Scripture as an instance of God's larger providential activity. In *Against Celsus*, for instance, he explicitly identifies God's inspiration of the prophets as an expression of providence since "[t]hey were chosen by providence [αἱρεθέντες ὑπὸ τῆς προνοίας] to be entrusted with the divine Spirit . . . (CC 7.7/SC 150, 30.1–4). In his *Commentary on John* Origen speaks of the Scriptures as supervised or arranged by a providential God: "'But we have the mind of Christ [1 Cor 2:16],' that we might understand spiritually each of the things which have been said, in accordance with the will of him who supervised [οἰκονομήσαντος] that these things be written" (Comm Jn 10.286/GCS 4, 219.8–10—Heine modified). Or again: "The Word of God has arranged the Scriptures [ὁ τοῦ θεοῦ λόγος ᾠκονομηκέναι τὰ ἀναγεγραμμένα] . . . " (CC 4.71/SC 136, 360.9–10).

biblical interpretation is found in book four of *On First Principles* where Origen famously contends for a threefold manner of scriptural interpretation. He fashions an analogy between Scripture's three senses and the flesh, soul, and spirit of a person:

> It is necessary, therefore, to register the meaning of the holy writings in a threefold way upon one's own soul, so that the simpler one may be edified [οἰκοδομῆται] by the, as it were, flesh of Scripture—this is how we call the obvious interpretation—while the one who has made some advancement [may be edified] by its soul, so to speak, and the one who is perfect—and who is like those mentioned by the apostle: "We speak wisdom among the perfect; yet a wisdom not of this world, nor of the rulers of this world, which are coming to naught; but we speak God's wisdom in a mystery, even the wisdom that has been hidden, which God foreordained before the worlds unto our glory" [1 Cor 2:6, 7]—[this one may be edified] by the "spiritual law" containing "a shadow of the good things to come" [cf. Rom 7:14 and Heb 10:1].[17]

Most scholars have labored over the details of the particular senses (and their number) in this passage and argued over whether Origen consistently applied what he says here to his exegetical practice. Yet this overlooks his basic point. His underlying interest in this passage is to announce the *purpose* of these various senses in Scripture. Its flesh, soul, and spirit, he says, are unified by a shared end: in their own way each "builds up" or "edifies" (οἰκοδομέω) three sorts of readers, the simple, those who have made "some progress," and those who are "perfect." He underscores this point as he draws the passage to a close. Origen speaks of Scripture's authorship in explicitly providential language (it is "arranged" by God), and specifies the sort of divine care God extends to readers through this collection of writings: "For just as a person consists of body and soul and spirit, so in the same way does the Scripture, which has been arranged [οἰκονομηθεῖσα] by God to be given for humanity's salvation [εἰς ἀνθρώπων σωτηρίαν]."[18] The Scriptures are an instrument of divine providence, intended to advance the salvation of its readers and hearers.

We find this same link between the Scriptures and salvation elsewhere. Later in book four of *On First Principles*, Origen explicitly speaks of the "aim" (σκοπός) of the Spirit who, together with God and the Word, enlightened the prophets and apostles with unspeakable mysteries. This scriptural message was communicated "by the providence of God [προνοίᾳ θεοῦ]," he continues, "so that the one who can be taught, 'by searching out' and giving himself 'to the depths' [cf. 1 Cor 2:10] of the meaning of the words, might become partaker of all the teachings of his [the Spirit's] counsel." After all, Origen adds, it is not possible for people "to attain perfection [τῆς τελειότητος τυχεῖν]

---

[17] PA 4.2.4/GK 708, 312.7–710, 313.1—transl. mine.

[18] PA 4.2.4/GK 710, 313.1–4—transl. mine. Among recent scholars, E. A. Dively Lauro, *The Soul and Spirit of Scripture within Origen's Exegesis* directs clearest attention to the soteriological intent behind the composition of Scripture (esp. 47–50, 78–85).

except through the rich and wise truth about God."[19] Again it is the Scriptures that advance the salvation of those who read them well (or hear them properly expounded).[20]

There is, finally, another important text where Origen forges this same link between God's authorship of Scripture and his providential concern to advance the salvation of its readers. In a fragment from his *Commentary on the Psalms* preserved in the *Philocalia*, Origen touches upon an analogy he occasionally draws between Scripture and creation. This analogy succeeds for him since Scripture and creation are both ultimately sourced in the same providential God and thus both reveal (at times, admittedly, only dimly) this God's workmanship, superintendence, and philanthropic concern. In this passage from the *Commentary* Origen notes that Jesus commands "not one letter, not one stroke of a letter, will pass from the law" (Matt 5:18) and thus, that Scripture's interpreters ought to heed each and every detail of Scripture in search of its hidden wisdom. Yet it is not only Scripture that merits close attention. For the "divine skill" ($\dot{\eta}$ $\theta\epsilon\dot{\iota}a$ $\tau\dot{\epsilon}\chi\nu\eta$) is apparent throughout the creation, not only in celestial bodies but also in terrestrial bodies where "this skill indwells" ($\dot{\epsilon}\nu\upsilon\pi\dot{a}\rho\chi o\nu\tau o s$ $\tau o\hat{\upsilon}$ $\tau\epsilon\chi\nu\iota\kappa o\hat{\upsilon}$).[21] Origen continues, returning to Scripture:

> For in similar fashion to all this, so we think about all the things written down by the inspiration of the Holy Spirit, that sacred Providence bestowed a superhuman wisdom [$\dot{\omega}s$ $\tau\hat{\eta}s$ $\dot{\epsilon}\pi\iota\delta\iota\delta o\dot{\upsilon}\sigma\eta s$ $\tau\dot{\eta}\nu$ $\dot{\upsilon}\pi\epsilon\rho\dot{a}\nu\theta\rho\omega\pi o\nu$ $\sigma o\phi\dot{\iota}a\nu$ $\dot{\iota}\epsilon\rho\hat{a}s$ $\pi\rho o\nu o\dot{\iota}a s$] on people through these writings, sowing (so to speak) saving oracles [$\lambda\dot{o}\gamma\iota a$ $\sigma\omega\tau\dot{\eta}\rho\iota a$], traces of wisdom, into each letter as far as is possible.[22]

In this passage, as in the others examined above, Origen unmistakably maps his understanding of Scripture's function onto the larger doctrine of divine care. Just as God's providential skill is evident throughout the many works of creation, so too has this "sacred Providence" left traces of "superhuman wisdom" in the Scriptures of which it too is a source. Origen spells out the philanthropic intent behind this divine authorship: to come to the aid of Scripture's readers by sowing "saving oracles, traces of wisdom" into even the smallest details of the text. In each particular passage, and indeed

---

[19] PA 4.2.7/GK 722, 319.1–3, 4–5.

[20] This motif surfaces several other times in book four of *On First Principles*. For instance, earlier in this book Origen comments on the salvific quality of the gospels. He refers to Jesus Christ as the "introducer of Christianity's saving teachings [$\tau o\hat{\upsilon}$ $\epsilon\dot{\iota}\sigma\eta\gamma\eta\tau o\hat{\upsilon}$ $\tau\hat{\omega}\nu$ $\kappa a\tau\dot{a}$ $\chi\rho\iota\sigma\tau\iota a\nu\iota\sigma\mu\dot{o}\nu$ $\sigma\omega\tau\eta\rho\dot{\iota}\omega\nu$ $\delta o\gamma\mu\dot{a}\tau\omega\nu$]" (PA 4.1.1/GK 670, 293.7–8). Later he writes that in Jesus "God has really become man and delivered to men the doctrines of salvation [$\sigma\omega\tau\eta\rho\dot{\iota}a s$ $\delta\dot{o}\gamma\mu a\tau a$]" (PA 4.1.2/GK 676, 294.4–5).

[21] Phil 2.4/SC 302, 246.9–19.

[22] Phil 2.4/SC 302, 246/19–24—transl. mine. For another passage where Origen offers a very similar analogy between God's providential action in the cosmos and Scripture, see PA 4.1.7. Other passages where this relationship is explored more briefly: Hom Num 27.1; Phil 10.2.

throughout all of Scripture, its divine authors conveyed a message with salvific intent.[23]

When we canvass Origen's wider corpus, we notice how he often evokes the redeeming function of Scripture with vivid imagery. He is especially partial to images drawn from the realms of nutrition and medicine. He opens his twenty-seventh *Homily on Numbers* with an elaborate analogy between Scripture and food. When God created the world, he created an assortment of foods for people of every constitution. "And so, each individual, whether owing to age or strength or the health of his body, longs for food suitable to himself and corresponding to his strength." Moreover, Origen continues, "the true food of a rational nature is the Word of God." This food, however, is not to the exclusion of Scripture, the written word of God. In a pun on "word" (*verbum* in Rufinus' translation, λόγος in the original Greek), he concludes: "so also each individual, insofar as he perceives himself healthy and strong, takes in all these things, which are the words of God, and in which there is different food according to the capacity of the souls."[24] Origen draws upon other nutritional analogies. In a passage from his *Commentary on Ezekiel*, he likens Scripture to pastures with flowing waters. Readers are like sheep that feed and water on such "profitable" pastures that have "saving power."[25] The Scriptures are also like an almond. Commenting on the rod of Aaron that sprouted buds, blossoms, and ripe almonds (Num 17:8), Origen dons his botanical cap and notes that an almond has three parts: it has a bitter shell which yields to a second layer that, in turn, protects its nutritious center, the third layer: "with its third layer it feeds and nourishes the one who eats it."[26] He continues, drawing a parallel with Scripture: it too has a bitter shell, a second layer, and a healthful center. "But," he concludes, "in the third place you will find hidden and concealed in the [law and the prophets] the meaning of the mysteries 'of the wisdom and knowledge of God' [Col 2:3] by which the souls of the saints are nourished and fed, not only in the present life but also in the future."[27]

There are other passages where the imagery shifts and Origen stresses the medicinal or healing value of Scripture. In his twenty-seventh *Homily on*

---

[23] Other passages where Origen speaks explicitly about the soteriological function of Scripture: Phil 6.2, 11.1.

[24] Hom Num 27.1.1–2 and 27.1.5/GCS 7, 255.22–256.1 and 257.10–12. For similar passages, see: CC 4.18 and PE 27.4–5 (which includes the same pun on λόγος).

[25] Phil 11.1/SC 302, 380.4–13. Similar imagery in Hom Num 17.4.2–4.

[26] Hom Num 9.7.3/GCS 7, 63.22.

[27] Hom Num 9.7.3/GCS 7, 64.7–10. Additional passages where Origen likens Scripture to nourishment: Hom Gen 16.4; Hom Lev 16.5.4; Hom Josh 20.1–2; Hom 1.4 Ps 36; Hom 3.10 Ps 36; Hom Jer 18.4; Comm Matt Ser 38; Comm Jn 1.208; Pascha, 26–31. Note esp. Hom Lev 1.4.2–4 where the sacrificial animal is likened to Scripture and the Levitical priest to the Christian allegorical interpreter. As the ancient Hebrew priests pulled the skin off the sacrificial animal, so this interpreter pulls away the veil of the obscuring letter, revealing the deeper spiritual sense of Scripture with which he nourishes or feeds Christians.

Numbers, he compares Scripture to a beehive: "Scripture describes the bee as a praiseworthy creature. Kings and commoners make use of its labors for their health. This is rightly understood of the words of the prophets and the apostles and of all who wrote the sacred books."[28] The Scriptures are like a garden of herbs. In a passage anthologized in the *Philocalia*, Origen acknowledges difficult verses in Scripture that do not immediately lend themselves to suitable interpretation, but nevertheless exhorts interpreters to believe that there is nothing superfluous in Scripture:

> And as with herbs, each has a power either for the healing of bodies [εἰς τὴν ὑγίειαν τῶν σωμάτων] or for something else, and it is not all who know for what each of the herbs is useful [ἐστὶ χρήσιμος]. But if some have obtained this knowledge, these busy themselves with herbs so as to know when a particular herb ought to be used, and where it is to be applied on bodies, and how when prepared it benefits the user. So too the saint is a sort of spiritual botanist who collects from the sacred writings every iota and every letter that surfaces and discovers the power of the word and for what it is useful [εἰς ὅ τι ἐστὶ χρήσιμον], and that nothing is superfluous in what is written.[29]

Even more clearly in the opening lines of his first *Homily on Psalm 37* he notes how God has given medicine and natural remedies to heal bodies, but God has also:

> prepared remedies for the soul [*animae medicamenta praeparavit*] in the words He has sown and scattered throughout the divine scriptures, so that those who are brought low by some illness, as soon as they sense the first inkling of sickness or perceive the prick and pain of a wound... they might seek out an appropriate and fitting spiritual discipline for themselves, drawn from God's precepts, which might bring them healing.[30]

With the help of images drawn from the fields of nutrition and medicine, Origen sought to make vivid for his readers and congregants the aim or purpose behind Scripture.[31] Its divine authors intended nothing less than to advance human salvation through this diverse collection of writings.

---

[28] Hom Num 27.12.12/GCS 7, 278.8–14.

[29] Phil 10.2/SC 302, 368.1–12—transl. mine. See PA 4.3.11 where the Scriptures are again likened to a field of plants.

[30] Hom 1.1 Ps 37/Prinzivalli, 256.11–248.21. Additional passages where Scripture is presented as medicinal: Hom Gen 16.4; Hom Josh 20.2; Hom Jer 2.2, 14.1.1–2, 20.3.2; Hom Ez 2.1, 3.7. Note also how passages like these about the healing written Word of God distinctly echo Origen's statements about the healing *divine* Word of God: see, for instance, CC 4.15; PA 2.5.3; esp. Hom Lk 8.1 where the link between Jesus and Scripture, both healers, is made.

[31] And there are other images as well. Origen speaks with some frequency of the Scriptures "building up" or "edifying" their readers. For instance, responding to the commandments not to kill, commit adultery, or steal, he asks: "What need is there to search in these commandments for an allegorical sense, when even the letter edifies [*cum aedificet etiam littera*]?" (Hom Num 11.1.8/GCS 7, 77.11–12). For similar imagery drawn from the realm of construction or crafts-manship, see: Hom Gen 2.6, 10.5; Hom Ex 2.4, 4.5; Hom Lev 1.1.5, 3.2.2, 7.1, 14.1; Hom Num 14.1, 20.1; Hom Josh 8.6, 20.1; PA 4.2.4.

ONE MESSAGE

If the scriptural message was composed with the intent of advancing the salvation of its readers, how many messages had to reside within this vast collection of disparate writings: the Old and New Testaments composed of the law, prophets, gospels, and apostolic writings?[32] For Origen, this question consistently yielded the same answer: there was ultimately only one message in these Scriptures. If one peered at these writings microscopically, as it were— one textual detail at a time—facets of this one message could be discerned. "Sacred Providence," he wrote, sows "saving oracles, traces of wisdom, into each letter as far as is possible."[33] As he often stressed, even the minutiae of the biblical text communicated something of this message to the reader.[34] Yet it was not simply minuscule, individual passages in the Scriptures that conveyed this one message. Viewing these writings macroscopically by taking into consideration their whole sweep, beginning with the law and running through the apostolic writings, the astute reader recognized how this one message also embraced both testaments, and indeed unified them. In the fifth book of his *Commentary on John*, Origen contends that the plurality of the scriptural writings resolved ultimately into the unity of one book in virtue of their shared, single message. The discussion begins with Origen recalling a Solomonic aphorism: "In a multitude of words you will not escape sin" (Prov 10:19). If this pithy saying is, in fact, true, what does it say about the Scriptures themselves, obviously composed by numerous books and innumerable words?[35] Origen solves his problem by making a distinction between many

---

[32] The scope of this collection was not fully defined in Origen's day. If we define a "canon" of Scriptures as (1) a list of sacred writings that was final (i.e. a list that comprehensively identified every scriptural writing, and by extension, excluded every other writing not on this list), as well as (2) a list that was accepted by a majority of Christian congregations, a canon certainly did not exist in the early third century. Origen acknowledged debates surrounding the scriptural status of several writings and made (or so it appears at least) little attempt to adjudicate these debates. Of course, to deny the existence of such a canon in his day is not to deny that the contours of a scriptural collection had already taken discernible shape by the early third century. There was widespread agreement throughout Christian congregations about a core collection of writings that made up the law, prophets, gospels, and apostolic writings. For orientation to this topic, see my essay "Scripture" in *The Routledge Companion to Early Christian Thought*, ed. J. Bingham (London: Routledge, 2009), 290–293 (with bibliography).

[33] Phil 2.4/SC 302, 246/19–24—transl. mine.

[34] For instance, ruminating on Jesus' words in Matt 5:18 that not the smallest letter will disappear from the law, Origen admonishes his readers who might think that not "every word spoken" by the prophets is significant: "do not think that anything from the Scriptures is extraneous" (Phil 10.2/SC 302, 368.21–370.24). The expression "nothing is useless" in Scripture occurs often in Origen's writings: see Hom Num 14.2, 27.1; Hom Josh 20.4; Comm Matt 16.12; Phil 10.2 (brief discussion in M. Harl, SC 302, 375–376). For other passages where Origen contends for the scriptural message residing in its smallest details, see Hom Gen 12.5; Hom Ex 1.1; Hom Josh 20.4; Comm Rom 1.8, 2.6.1, 5.10.18, 9.41.8; Phil 1.28.

[35] Comm Jn 5.4.

words that signify many conflicting teachings, and many words that always
point to the single truth. It is only the former sort of writings that run afoul of
the Solomonic aphorism: "we would say that he who utters anything hostile
to religion speaks many words." On the other hand, he continues, "he
who speaks the things of truth . . . always speaks the one Word [ἕνα ἀεὶ λέγει
λόγον]."[36] Origen applies this distinction to the Christian Scriptures that
obviously consist of numerous words. The authors of these writings ultimately
"do not speak many words since they cling to the goal which accords with
the one Word [τὸν ἕνα . . . λόγον]."[37] The Scriptures signify this one Christological message, and so "we can thus say," Origen concludes, "that all
the sacred writings are one book [ἓν βιβλίον]."[38] It is the one underlying
message running through the Old and New Testaments that turns the Scrip-
tur*es* into Scripture.

   This assertion proved controversial in Origen's day, pitting him against his
Gnostic adversaries who maintained (as he understood it) that the two testaments were in conflict since they narrated clashing accounts of two different
Gods.[39] It was, thus, a regular feature of Origen's anti-Gnostic polemic to
undergird his rival claim—that a single, overarching message unified both
testaments—by insisting upon a coherent divine authorship for all of Scripture. In his first *Homily on Ezekiel*, for instance, he reproaches the "heretics"
for "spurning the Creator." "I will recognize," Origen counters, "that everything that is written [in the Scriptures] are the words of the same God."[40]
More frequently Origen invokes the one Spirit who authored both testaments.
It is the heretics who "deny that God the Creator is the Father of Christ, and
they do not make the Old and New Testament 'one loaf' [cf. Lev 24:5, 8]." But,
Origen counters, "we say that one and the same Holy Spirit is in the Law and
the Gospels."[41] To similar effect Origen critiques Gnostic Christians in the rule
of faith that opens *On First Principles*: "It is, however, certainly taught with
the utmost clearness in the Church, that this Spirit inspired each one of the
saints, both the prophets and the apostles, and that there was not one Spirit

---

[36] Comm Jn 5.5/GCS 4, 103.2–4—Heine slightly modified.
[37] Comm Jn 5.5/GCS 4, 103.4–5—Heine slightly modified. Here Origen contrasts writings
that "speak many words" (πολυλογέω) with those that speak of the one divine λόγος. In Phil 6.1
Origen offers a different pun, though the point is still the same—while there are many words in
Scripture, they point to the one Word: "the Word is the one shepherd of the words [in Scripture]
[Εἷς δὲ ποιμὴν τῶν λογικῶν ὁ λόγος]" (Phil 6.1/SC 302, 308.15–16).
[38] Comm Jn 5.5/GCS 4, 103.7—Heine slightly modified. The force of this claim should not be
overlooked: in Origen's day, the Scriptures did not circulate as they do today, in a single codex,
but rather in multiple codices.
[39] See esp. the section in Chapter 6 above entitled "Gnostic exegesis and doctrine."
[40] Hom Ez 1.4.3/GCS 8, 328.28–29. In the rule of faith outlined in the preface to *On First
Principles* Origen writes to similar effect: "This just and good God, the Father of our Lord Jesus
Christ, himself gave the law, the prophets and the gospels, and he is God both of the apostles and
also of the Old and New Testaments" (PA pref.4/GK 88, 10.2–4). Also see: PA 2.7.1.
[41] Hom Lev 13.4.2/GCS 6, 473.19–22.

in the men of old and another in those who were inspired at the coming of Christ."[42] In these passages, as in others, Origen grounded the harmony of the one scriptural message that ran through both testaments in the same God, same Word and same Spirit who helped author both testaments.[43] Indeed, so concerned was Origen with the unity of this scriptural message that he could, on occasion, even balk at the twofold designation "Old" and "New" Testaments. In his ninth *Homily on Numbers* he remarks that the power of the gospel is also found in the law, its foundation, so that he does not give the name "Old Testament" to the law provided he understands it spiritually. "The law," Origen continues, "becomes an 'Old Testament' only for those who want to understand it in a fleshly way; and for them it has necessarily become old and aged, because it cannot maintain its strength. But," he strikingly concludes, "for us, who understand and explain it spiritually and in an evangelical sense, it is always new. Indeed, both are a 'New Testament' for us, not because of the age of time but because of the newness of understanding."[44] In passages such as these, and innumerable others, Origen asserts the unity and harmony of the scriptural message.[45]

Curiously, these passages compelled R. P. C. Hanson to conclude that Origen believed "not so much the unity as the uniformity of Scripture." The Alexandrian's view of the unity of Scripture was not like a "tapestry in which there are a multitude of different strands, and different colours and patterns woven by these strands into a single theme or picture." Rather, Hanson continued, proposing a decidedly less flattering image, "Origen's conception of the unity of scripture is more like that of the steel shell of a ship, in which a number of different but uniform plates of steel are welded into one."[46] But this claim is contestable. To begin with, to assert one profound message to which every individual passage, and ultimately all the scriptural books, testified, was *not* to deny multiple, viable interpretations of any given scriptural passage. As Hanson knew, Origen famously asserted the threefold scriptural sense in book

---

[42] PA pref.4/GK 90, 11.7–10. The anti-Gnostic thrust is clearly announced already at PA pref.2. For other passages on the same Spirit inspiring writers of the Old and New Testaments: Hom Ex 5.3; Comm Rom 6.7.19; PA 1.3.1, 2.7.1, 4.2.9.

[43] Repeatedly Origen inveighs against the Gnostics who claim the Scriptures are not harmonious: see Hom Lev 13.4.2; Hom 2.6 Ps 36; Comm Jn 2.199–201, 6.31, 10.107, 10.290; Phil 11.1–2. So also, M. Harl, SC 302, 144–145.

[44] Hom Num 9.4.2/GCS 7, 59.10–15. Other passages where Origen speaks with reluctance of the designations "Old" and "New Testaments": Comm Matt 17.12; Comm Jn 5.8; PA 4.1.1; PE 22.1. For a parallel Greek text to what he here claims in Hom Num, see his discussions about how the law and prophets ultimately become the gospel (Comm Matt 12.38, 12.43; Comm Jn 1.33, 1.36—these texts are discussed more fully below in "Contours of the message: Jesus Christ").

[45] Other passages on the unity of the testaments include: Hom Gen 10.5; Hom Lev 13.4; Comm Matt Ser 13; Matt Frg 3; Comm Jn 1.14–46, 6.24, 10.107; Phil 27.3. For two sometimes opposing discussions of this theme in Origen, see H. de Lubac, *History and Spirit*, 190–204 and R. P. C. Hanson, *Allegory and Event*, 198–205.

[46] *Allegory and Event*, 198–199.

four of *On First Principles*: in theory, any given text possessed a "flesh," "soul," and "spirit" that corresponded to the needs of readers who had progressed in varying ways on the journey of salvation.[47] These were obviously not three identical meanings, yet neither were they three competing meanings. They were, rather, distinct facets of one vast, underlying scriptural message extracted from one particular biblical passage. In principle (and in practice), many biblical texts for Origen admitted at least two different, yet related, interpretations.[48] Moreover, when we step back from the multi-faceted message that emerged from any given passage, we note occasional places where Origen spoke of a gradation in the scriptural message. As readers moved from the law and prophets into the New Testament writings, they detected not an abrupt movement between two opposing messages in two opposing testaments, but rather a transition from a simpler, sometimes less distinct, and introductory message, to a more advanced, striking and sophisticated teaching.[49] In short, rigidity or uniformity does not express well the complexity of Origen's account of the one scriptural message.[50]

Indeed, the very image Hanson *wishes* Origen to have cultivated for the unity of the Scriptures—a tapestry composed of many-colored threads— actually comes very close to the musical imagery Origen very frequently used to convey this unity: the Scriptures were an instrument that harmoniously blended various sounds together into a single melody. We find this image in the second book of his *Commentary on Matthew* where Origen is expounding on the beatitude: "Blessed are the peacemakers" (Matt 5:9). He remarks that someone can become a peacemaker "who demonstrates that the strife manifest to others in Scripture is not a strife, and who proves the

---

[47] PA 4.2.4 (cited above at nn. 17–18).

[48] See also Hom Gen 2.6, 11.3; Hom Lev 5.5.3; Hom Num 9.7 (as well as the passages discussed in E. A. Dively Lauro, *The Soul and Spirit of Scripture within Origen's Exegesis*, 94–194).

[49] Customarily, Origen will argue that the very same message exists in both testaments (though aspects of it are hidden in the law and prophets and require a deeper, nonliteral inquiry). It is true that he does not emphasize the development in revelation, but that is not surprising given his opposition to Gnostic theologians who contended (as he saw it) that the testaments proclaimed different messages, and ultimately, different Gods. Nevertheless, there are passages where he does speak of a gradation in revelation from one testament to the next: see Hom Lev 1.4; PA 3.3.1 (H. de Lubac, *History and Spirit*, 281–295, 305–306; R. P. C. Hanson, *Allegory and Event*, 210–212).

[50] Two other pieces of evidence speak against Hanson's account of Origen's view of Scripture. It is important to recall, first, how Origen frequently offered several distinct yet viable interpretations of the same scriptural passage, leaving it to his audience to decide which was best: Hom Num 21.2, 26.4, 26.7; Hom Josh 8.6; Lk Frg 171; Comm Jn 32.5–7 (see also H. de Lubac, *History and Spirit*, 160; R. P. C. Hanson, *Allegory and Event*, 245–246). If Origen thought the Scriptures conveyed a message as rigid and uniform as Hanson believes, this sort of interpretive pliability would probably not occur. Moreover, as we will see clearly in the next section of this chapter, Origen summarized this one scriptural message from several different, yet mutually informing perspectives. This too challenges the idea that Scripture's unity was an inflexible concept for him.

harmony and peace in these writings [τὴν συμφωνίαν καὶ τὴν εἰρήνην τούτων], either between the old and new writings, or the legal and prophetic writings, or the gospels with themselves, or the apostolic writings with themselves."[51] Origen continues with an exquisite musical metaphor:

> for just as the different chords of the harp and zither, each of which produces a sound unique to it that seems not to be similar to the sound of the other, are thought to be out of accord on account of the dissemblance of sounds by the uncultured who do not know the principle of musical harmony, so also with those who do not know how to listen to the harmony of God in the sacred Scriptures. These think that the Old is inharmonious with the New, or the prophets with the law, or the gospels with themselves, the apostle with the gospel or himself or the [other] apostles. But the one who has learned the music of God... this one will produce the sound of the music of God... For he knows that all Scripture is one harmonious instrument of God, producing one saving melody from different sounds for those who desire to learn, a melody that calms and hinders every action of the evil spirit.[52]

Origen never contested the vast complexity of the Christian Scriptures, characterized as they were by two testaments, numerous genres and multiple levels of meaning. However, he insisted that for the perceptive, there was ultimately only one message that Scripture's authors had woven into this collection of sacred writings. This was not a monolithic message. It was, rather, a multi-faceted one in which distinct voices blended harmoniously to sound one "saving melody." What, then, was this melody?

CONTOURS OF THE MESSAGE

The Christian Scriptures were an extraordinarily complex collection of writings, populated by myriad figures, nations, institutions and events, to say nothing of countless themes. But this did not prevent Origen from attempting to offer a summary of these writings. When he stepped back from his

---

[51] Phil 6.1/SC 302, 308.7–11—transl. mine.

[52] Phil 6.2/SC 302, 310.1–21—transl. mine (for brief commentary on this passage, see M. Harl, SC 302, 320–321). It is noteworthy that Origen here views the *written* Word of God as profoundly one in message, even though it also consists of several discrete, harmonious facets. This is precisely how he also views the divine Word of God. "The complete Word of God which was in the beginning with God is not a multitude of Words, for it is not words. It is a single Word consisting of several ideas, each of which is a part of the whole Word" (Comm Jn 5.5/GCS 4, 102.28–31). Repeatedly Origen stresses that the divine Word or Wisdom of God is one in respect to essence or substance, yet manifold in respect to "aspects" or "concepts" (ἐπινοίαι), most of which are adapted to facilitate the salvation of people: see Hom Song Songs 2.9; Comm Matt 12.37–38; Comm Jn 1.123–124, 1.200, 1.248–250, 2.39–40, 6.39; Comm Rom 5.6.7; CC 2.64–67, 4.18 (also see n. 135 below). Occasionally, Origen explicitly draws an analogy between the "one and many" structure that both Words, written and divine, share (Comm Jn 5.5).

exegetical activity to reflect, as he occasionally did, on the overarching profile of the scriptural message, he claimed that there were a handful of synopses that did justice to this message. In this section I will examine Origen's four main proposed summaries. He framed the scriptural message in terms of a *distinction*—that the Scriptures offered both ethical and doctrinal instruction; a *list*—that the church's rule of faith identified essential doctrines taught throughout all of Scripture; a *motif*—that the soul's journey to God (parts of this journey, or all of it) surfaced in various passages of the Bible; and a *figure*—that Jesus Christ was the central theme of both the Old and New Testaments. Each of these summaries differed in the specificity with which it recounted the scriptural message, as well as in the aspects of this message it highlighted. On the surface, the fact that Origen offered *plural* summaries might even appear to undermine his contention that there was, in the end, only one harmonious, "saving melody" running through both testaments. Yet as I will demonstrate, these four configurations of the scriptural message proved mutually informing, as they confirmed Origen's underlying conviction that the singular intent with which Scripture was authored coincided with its singular message: salvation.

Moral and mystical

We can begin with Origen's most abstract summary of the scriptural message. At its core, the Scriptures repeatedly advocated action and thought, twin facets of the Christian way of life. Christianity for Origen was quintessentially "practical [τὸ πρακτικόν]" and "contemplative [τὸ θεωρητικόν]," he wrote in his *Commentary on John*—it begins with the former, encapsulated by the idea of living justly, and culminates in the latter, the eschatological reflection upon God.[53] Christianity embraced "ethical teachings [τὰ μὲν ἠθικὰ μαθήματα]" as well as "esoteric and mystical doctrines [τὰ...ἀπόρρητα καὶ μυστικὰ θεωρήματα]."[54] Even Jesus hinted at this distinction. When he turned to his disciples and said, "Come and see" (Jn 1:39), Origen wonders: "Perhaps through the term 'come' he is appealing to them on the basis of the active life [ἐπὶ τὸ πρακτικὸν], and through 'see' he subjoins that there will assuredly be contemplation [τὴν...θεωρίαν]..."[55] When speaking of the Christian faith in this way, Origen was invoking a common distinction made by the philosophical and theological schools of his day: his faith espoused both

---

[53] Comm Jn 1.91–94/GCS 4, 20.6–21.2.
[54] Comm Jn 1.208/GCS 4, 37.26–32.
[55] Comm Jn 2.219/GCS 4, 95.9–11.

ethical conduct and doctrinal commitment.[56] Interestingly, even Origen's biographers saw him through the lens of this distinction.[57]

There are a number of passages where Origen speaks of the Christian faith as an inexorably practical and doctrinal affair.[58] It does not surprise, then, that when it came to the Christian Scriptures, he contended that they too spoke of these twin aspects of the faith: "If we can understand the deeper meaning of the passage [in the gospel of Luke], it begins with ethical arguments [λόγων ἠθικῶν] . . . and then with the higher mysteries [ἐποπτικῶν] . . . "[59] Origen often spoke of these moral and doctrinal facets of the scriptural message.[60] In a passage from his *Homilies on Numbers* already briefly mentioned above, he famously likens Scripture's threefold sense to the three parts of an almond, though he quickly dismisses the value of the letter (as it corresponds to the almond's bitter rind that must be thrown away). What truly matters in the law and prophets are their moral and mystical teachings. Origen develops his analogy: after discarding the rind, the interpreter "will reach the protective covering of the shell in which moral teaching or the definition of self-control [*in quo vel moralis doctrina vel ratio continentiae*] is described."[61] Thereafter, this reader "will find hidden and concealed in the [law and prophets] the meaning of the mysteries 'of the wisdom and knowledge of God' [Col 2:3] by which the souls of the saints are nourished and fed, not only in the present life but also in the future."[62] Here the moral sense

---

[56] A thesis most thoroughly developed by W. Völker, *Das Vollkommenheitsideal des Origenes*. He contended that even a cursory overview of Origen's vision of the ideal Christian life revealed that, for him, Christianity consisted of two distinct, yet interrelated, motifs: "knowledge and action, contemplation and growth in the virtues" (76). See also E. Schockenhoff, *Zum Fest der Freiheit*, 276–297; L. Perrone, "Christianity as 'Practice' in Origen's *Contra Celsum*," *Orig IX*: 293–317; R. Somos, "Christianity as practical philosophy in Origen," *Orig IX*: 327–335. For the ancient philosophical backdrop of this distinction, see esp. A. M. J. Festigiere, *Contemplation et vie contemplative selon Platon*, 4th edn (Paris: J. Vrin, 1975); N. Lobkowicz, *Theory and Practice: History of a Concept from Aristotle to Marx* (Notre Dame: University of Notre Dame Press, 1967).

[57] Eusebius claimed that "his manner of life was as his doctrine, and his doctrine as his life" (HE 6.3.7 GCS 9.2, 526.10–12). Similarly, in the *Address of Thanksgiving*, Gregory insisted on the integrity of Origen's life and thought (*Address*, 118, 123, 126, 133, 135), and highlighted how this coherence found expression in his curriculum in Caesarea where he sought to inculcate both virtue and contemplation (see esp. 150). On this twofold structure of Origen's Caesarean curriculum, see R. Wilken, "Alexandria: A school for training in virtue," in *Schools of Thought in the Christian Tradition*, ed. P. Henry (Philadelphia: Fortress Press, 1984), 15–30.

[58] See esp. Hom Ex 2.1, 13.7; Hom Num 17.4.2, 22.1.3; Hom Jud 5.6; prol. Comm Song of Songs; Hom Lk 1.5; Lk Frg 171, 209, 210; Comm Jn 19.45, 32.6; CC 4.53, 4.64, 5.15, 8.4, 8.22.

[59] Lk Frg 218/GCS 9, 321.1–3.

[60] Curiously, most scholars who have investigated the admittedly complex issue of the multiple senses of Scripture in Origen have failed to consider whether his larger view of Christianity as both an ethical and doctrinal way of life is what drives his view of Scripture having a moral and doctrinal sense. In what follows I will not delve into a detailed investigation of the issues surrounding Scripture's multiple senses. For orientation to this topic, see E. A. Dively Lauro, *The Soul and Spirit of Scripture within Origen's Exegesis*.

[61] Hom Num 9.7.3/GCS 7, 63.26–28.

[62] Hom Num 9.7.3/GCS 7, 64.7–10.

of Scripture refers, broadly, to self-control, and its deepest sense to the mysteries of God's wisdom and knowledge.

In other passages Origen offers only slightly more elaboration on the content of these respective senses. In his thirteenth *Homily on Leviticus* he comments on the shew bread that is made from fine wheat flour (Lev 24:5–9). He allegorizes the bread into Scripture, and draws a distinction between loaves made from fine wheat flour (such as the shew bread) and loaves made from regular flour:

> Every word of God is a loaf but there is a difference in loaves. For there is a certain word which can be delivered in the common hearing and which can teach the people about the works of mercy and of all kindness; and this is a loaf which will appear common. But there is another which contains secrets and speaks about the faith in God or the knowledge of things. That loaf is pure and is made from "fine wheat flour."[63]

Here the moral message (corresponding to the loaf made from regular flour) has a wider audience and concerns acts of mercy and kindness, or as Origen puts its later, concerns "the present salvation and life." The loftier doctrinal message (corresponding to the loaf made from fine wheat flour) addresses a narrower audience and concerns the knowledge of God (among other things), or, as Origen later remarks, "the mysteries and secrets of God."[64] In his second *Homily on Genesis* we again come across the distinction between the moral and mystical messages in Scripture. Origen exhorts his audience to recognize in Scripture "'the great mystery' which is fulfilled in Christ and in the Church [cf. Eph 5:32]"; but this audience is also to learn from Scripture "how to correct habits, to curtail vices, to purge the soul and draw it off from every bond of captivity, setting up in [their hearts] 'nests and nests' [Gen 6:14] of the various virtues and perfections."[65] As a final illustration, we draw brief attention to arguably Origen's most famous account of the moral and mystical senses of Scripture. In a passage already cited above from book four of *On First Principles,* he likens Scripture to a person: in principle, any given passage in Scripture has, like a person, "flesh," "soul," and "spirit."[66] A few paragraphs later, however, Origen conflates the "flesh" and "soul" of Scripture since they do not differ profoundly in terms of their content: both are "adapted to the multitude" and "edify those who cannot understand the higher meanings."[67] The "spirit" of Scripture is distinct from this moral message since it is addressed more narrowly to "the one who is perfect" and has as its great theme, following Paul, God's "'wisdom in a mystery, even the wisdom that has

---

[63] Hom Lev 13.3.4/GCS 6, 472.1–6.
[64] Hom Lev 13.3.4/GCS 6, 472.21–23.
[65] Hom Gen 2.6/GCS 6, 38.2–6.
[66] PA 4.2.4/GK 708, 312.7–712, 313.5.
[67] PA 4.2.6/GK 714, 315.12–14.

been hidden, which God foreordained before the worlds unto the glory' of the righteous [1 Cor 2:7]."[68]

Here in *On First Principles*, as elsewhere, Origen insisted that, despite all the diversity within the Christian Scriptures, their message could be summarized in terms of a prevailing distinction: they taught the mystical and moral facets of the Christian faith.[69] Stripped to its most elemental structure, the Christian pursuit of salvation called for right action and thought, and both of these dimensions were expressed in its Scriptures.

The rule of faith

Origen also offered a digest of the scriptural message in the form of a list. The church's rule of faith, itself extracted from Scripture, cataloged the essential scriptural doctrines all Christians ought to believe. This outline of the scriptural message bears a strong resemblance to the summary examined in the previous section, though with one principal difference: the rule of faith enumerated in far greater detail the specific moral and doctrinal commitments that the Scriptures advocated to those who would pursue salvation in the Christian church.

---

[68] PA 4.2.6/GK 716, 316.2–5.

[69] For additional passages where Origen makes the twofold distinction between the moral and mystical messages in Scripture, see Hom Gen 10.5; Hom Num 7.1.2, 27.1–2; Hom Ez 7.10; Comm Jn 10.174; CC 7.10. As we have seen, sometimes Origen integrates these two senses into a threefold distinction (where the historical sense is added): see Hom Gen 11.3; Hom Lev 5.5.3. For additional passages and further commentary, see H. de Lubac, *History and Spirit*, 159–171; E. A. Dively Lauro, *The Soul and Spirit of Scripture within Origen's Exegesis*, 94–194. Note esp. Dively Lauro's summary of these two higher senses at 60–76.

It is also useful to note here that while Origen frequently drew a distinction between these two aspects of scriptural doctrine, it is also clear from several of the foregoing passages that these were not separate, unrelated teachings for him. Indeed, he usually placed them on the same continuum: Christians invariably began with ethical instruction, which in turn prepared them for loftier mystical instruction. There are, moreover, even passages where Origen concedes that this twofold message is ultimately one. In his second *Homily on Genesis*, for instance, he speaks openly of the "mingled meaning" of the moral and mystical messages in Scripture (Hom Gen 2.6/ GCS 6, 37.7–8). It is, finally, important to note that this fusion of the moral and mystical senses *in Scripture* distinctly mirrors those passages where Origen speaks of the intimate relationship between the moral and doctrinal dimensions *of Christian living*. See esp. Hom Ex 13.7; Hom Lk 1.5; Lk Frg 171; CC 4.53. For helpful discussions of how the practical and theoretical facets of Christianity intertwine for Origen, see esp. W. Völker, *Das Vollkommenheitsideal*, 192–196; E. Schockenhoff, *Zum Fest der Freiheit*, 280–294. For brief discussions of how all the scriptural senses, especially the moral and mystical, point to one and the same message, see H. de Lubac, *History and Spirit*, 204–205; R. P. C. Hanson, *Allegory and Event*, 242–243; M. Wiles, "Origen as a Biblical scholar," *The Cambridge History of the Bible*, vol. 1, ed. C. F. Evans and P. R. Ackroyd (Cambridge: Cambridge University Press, 1970), 467; R. Greer and J. L. Kugel, *Early Biblical Interpretation* (Philadelphia: Westminster, 1986), 180.

Origen opens his preface to *On First Principles* by acknowledging that the Scriptures were not interpreted uniformly among Christians of his day.[70] To adjudicate between these conflicting interpretations in the heterogeneous Christian community (he has his Gnostic opponents particularly in mind) he proposes that it is "necessary first to lay down a definite line and unmistakable rule."[71] This rule is nothing other than "the teaching of the church, handed down in unbroken succession from the apostles."[72] A few lines later he specifies that this rule is more narrowly the clear apostolic preaching expressed in "plainest terms" within the church's Scriptures—what the apostles thought was most necessary to be believed they expressed most clearly.[73] This rule was, thus, drawn principally from the apostolic writings. But it is misleading to envision it as a distillation of only these writings. As Origen understood it, the rule was more accurately a précis of the *entire* scriptural message as seen through the eyes of the apostles. This stems in part from the character of the apostolic writings themselves: what the apostles conveniently expressed in clearest and plainest terms was often already latent within the Old Testament. Moreover, the apostolic writings actively integrated the law and prophets into their argument, and so an abridgement of their plain teaching implied a summary of the entire scriptural message. Furthermore, we strongly suspect that Origen intended this rule as more than an exclusive summary of the apostolic writings, since his dispute with Gnostic interpreters concerned how to assess *all* of Scripture, and not simply these particular texts. A guideline only for the interpretation of the apostolic writings would have been of limited use to Origen. The rule he lists for his readers in the opening lines of *On First Principles* was, in short, a summary of the essential teachings of the entire scriptural message.

Origen lists these teachings:

- To begin with, the Scriptures exhort belief in one God, creator and sustainer of the universe. This is the God of the righteous men in Genesis, of Moses and of all the prophets, as well as the God who sent Jesus Christ to call both Israel and the Gentiles. This God is good and just, the God

---

[70] PA pref.1–2/GK 84, 8.14–15.   [71] PA pref.2/GK 84, 8.19.

[72] PA pref.2/GK 84, 8.25–26.

[73] In PA pref.2–3 Origen speaks alternatively of the apostolic "teaching," "preaching," "doctrine," and "statements," all of which suggest that he has in mind the apostolic teaching as expressed in the New Testament writings. Later in PA 4.2.7 Origen revisits the contents of the rule that he enumerates here in the preface and explicitly describes these contents as scriptural: "the aim of the Spirit who . . . enlightened the servants of the truth, that is, the prophets and apostles, was pre-eminently concerned with the unspeakable mysteries connected with the affairs of men" (GK 720, 318.9–12). Origen proceeds to list these mysteries, and the list overlaps strikingly with the items in his rule. Note also his account of the close relationship between the apostle Paul's preaching and his literary activity at Comm Jn 1.25: "And the things which he preached and said he also wrote" (GCS 4, 9.16).

who gave both the Old and New Testaments. Without mentioning Gnostic opponents by name, it is clear that this opening article implies a critique of their view of God(s) ostensibly drawn from these same Scriptures.[74]

- There is, next, the belief in Jesus as the Christ, who was begotten by the Father, who helped create the universe, and was made man. He was born of the virgin Mary and the Holy Spirit, he suffered truly and not in appearance, and rose from the dead before he ascended into heaven.[75]

- Next, the apostles taught one Holy Spirit, who is united in dignity and honor with the Father and Son and who inspired both the prophets and the apostles.[76] Here, again, the anti-Gnostic polemic is insinuated by insisting upon the one Spirit, who inspired authors belonging to both testaments.

- Then the apostles taught about the soul and body. Of the soul, that it has an independent existence and is not fated to its actions, but rather is capable of choice and will be judged after its departure from the world according to its deeds—either rewarded with eternal life or punished in accordance with its crimes. In this life, every soul is locked in a battle with the devil and his angels, who urge, but do not force, souls to sin. There is always the possibility of leading "a wise and upright life." And of the body, that it will one day be resurrected from the dead in a state of incorruption and glory.[77] Here again we encounter an anonymous, yet trenchant, critique of the Gnostics.[78]

- Of the devil, his angels, and the other opposing spiritual powers, the only thing that is clearly taught is that they exist.[79] Later in the preface, Origen refers to the angels and good powers as those who minister to God by bringing about salvation among men and women.[80]

- Concerning the world, the Scriptures teach that it was made, began to exist at a definite time, and that because it is corruptible, it will suffer dissolution.[81]

- Finally, there is the teaching that the Scriptures were composed through the Spirit of God, and that they have both an obvious and a hidden meaning full of mysteries. Moreover, only those gifted with the grace of their author, the Holy Spirit, can discern the meaning of these Scriptures.[82]

---

[74] PA pref.4/GK 86, 9.13–88, 10.4.
[75] PA pref.4/GK 88, 10.5–90, 11.2.
[76] PA pref.4/GK 90, 11.3–10.
[77] PA pref.5/GK 90, 11.11–92, 13.11.
[78] Recall the discussion, "Gnostic exegesis and doctrine" in Chapter 6 above.
[79] PA pref.6/GK 92, 13.12–94, 13.17.
[80] PA pref.10/GK 96, 16.4–8.
[81] PA pref.7/GK 94, 14.1–5.
[82] PA pref.8/GK 94, 14.6–13.

The rule in Origen's preface to *On First Principles* offers his most detailed summary of scriptural teaching. With the exception of the doctrines about the world and Scripture, it reads largely as a digest of the main cast of characters who populate both testaments (God, Jesus, the Holy Spirit, angelic and demonic forces, and humans). It is also noteworthy, as already mentioned above, that this synopsis of Scripture largely overlaps with the summary discussed in the previous section (that the Scriptures propound moral and doctrinal instruction)—the principal difference is that the rule offers far more specificity about what particular ethical and doctrinal teachings surface in the Scriptures.[83] Nevertheless, as with the previous summary of the scriptural message, so here: Scripture's master theme is the Christian pursuit of salvation.

The soul's journey to God

Origen also crystallized the scriptural message into the motif of the soul's journey to God.[84] In his twenty-seventh *Homily on Numbers* and prologue to his *Commentary on the Song of Songs* he offers two largely overlapping itineraries for this spiritual quest. In the case of the former he contends that he has found a particular scriptural passage, and in case of the latter a set of books, that recount in outline form many of the details of the soul's long journey toward its eschatological vision of God. Here again, it is clear how this summary of the scriptural message reinforces the two preceding summaries: all three are versions of the one underlying theme of salvation in Scripture. What is distinctive about this particular summary is that it chronicles the soul's quest for salvation as a dynamic journey to God. The soul certainly wanders through the familiar moral and doctrinal territory surveyed above, but this motif expresses more clearly than the others how this quest unfolds in history, and how the soul not simply acts and knows, but also encounters God and God's Word on this journey.

In his twenty-seventh *Homily on Numbers* Origen comments on Numbers 33, which refers to the forty-two stations the Hebrews traversed on their exodus out of Egypt. This passage presents a challenge to the homilist since on the surface it conveys little more than the travel itinerary of the Hebrews on

---

[83] Though there is a decided emphasis on the latter: the rule narrates in depth the grand drama of how God, Jesus, and the Holy Spirit were overcoming the devil and opposing forces in the present world, and what role humans had in this drama. At the same time, the moral message of Scripture is not absent. Origen mentions it when he discusses the soul's capacity for choice, explaining how this soul is capable of combating evil and pursuing virtue on its journey toward God.

[84] For analyses of this important theme, see esp. G. Gruber, *ZΩH—Wesen, Stufen und Mitteilung des wahren Lebens bei Origenes* (Munich: M. Huber, 1962); K. J. Torjesen, *Hermeneutical Procedure*, 70–107; E. Schockenhoff, *Zum Fest der Freiheit*, 188–197.

their way to the promised land. However, Origen contends that this chapter must convey some benefit to its ecclesiastical recipients, and so he turns to an allegorical reading for help: "in a spiritual sense there can be seen a double exodus from Egypt, either when we leave our pagan life and come to the knowledge of the divine law, or when the soul leaves its dwelling place in the body."[85] It is to both of these departures that Moses symbolically refers in Numbers 33 when he speaks of the Hebrew departure from Egypt: first, the soul's journey in this life as it leaves behind its former ways in the world and turns to Christ, followed by the soul's second, continued journey in the next life as it leaves behind the distractions of this world and ultimately arrives at the contemplation of God.[86] A "double exodus," but ultimately only one journey, since just as the Hebrews passed through many stages on their single quest for the promised land, so too Christians progress through many stages in this life and the next as they reach out for their single goal. Ultimately, there are "many stages that lead to the Father."[87]

We can pass over Origen's meticulous allegorical interpretation of each of the stations the Hebrews passed through on their way to the promised land. For our purposes, he offers sufficient overviews of the soul's two-phased journey in the opening paragraphs of this homily. Egypt stands for "the errors of this world," "the darkness of ignorance," and is the place where people perform "the works of the devil" and "desires of the flesh." The Christian exodus commenced, Origen continues, when God "had pity on our affliction and sent the Word, his only-begotten Son, who brought us forth, snatched from the ignorance of error to the light of the divine law."[88] When people abandon the "adoration of idols" and the "worship of demons" and turn, instead, to belief in Christ who was born of the Virgin and Holy Spirit, they begin their journey of ascent.[89] Origen describes the subsequent phases of this first journey variously. It is clearly oriented along Christological coordinates, since it begins with a conversion to Christ, is marked by obedience to his commands,[90] and is ultimately characterized by an increasing likeness to Christ.[91] Origen also describes this

---

[85] Hom Num 27.2.2/GCS 7, 258.23–26.

[86] See also another description of this double exodus at Hom Num 27.6.

[87] Hom Num 27.2.3/GCS 7, 259.1–2.

[88] Hom Num 27.2.4/GCS 7, 259.16–19.

[89] Hom Num 27.3. The imagery of "ascent" is carefully chosen. Origen superimposes the Christian journey not only onto the 42-stage journey of the Hebrews out of Egypt, but also onto the 42-stage *descent* of the Word (referring to the 42 ancestors of Jesus recorded in Matthew's genealogy). "[T]here were forty-two stages in the departure of the children of Israel from Egypt; and, further, the coming of our Lord and Savior into this world is traced through forty-two generations" (Hom Num 27.3.1/GCS 7, 259.21–24). In effect, the Christian journey *retraces* the Hebrew journey in the wilderness as well as *reverses* the descent of the Word into the world.

[90] See esp. Hom Num 27.5.2.

[91] At several junctures in this homily Origen summarizes the ideal trajectory of this transitory life as the commitment to increasing virtue. For example: "After this let us now strive to go forward and to ascend one by one each of the steps of faith and the virtues. If we dwell for such a

journey in terms of the doctrinal/ethical distinction already discussed above.
"Thus it is necessary for us, when we come forth from Egypt, to have not only
the knowledge of the law and of faith, but also a harvest of works by which one
pleases God." It is necessary, he again remarks, that among Christians be found
"not only the perfection of faith and knowledge, but also that of deeds and
works."[92] When the soul is eventually divested of its earthly body and is
resurrected, it commences the second phase of its journey. Not surprisingly,
Origen has less to say about this journey. His brief accounts of it are consistent
with what we learn elsewhere in his writings: after this life has passed, the soul
embarks upon a path of continual progress in the contemplation of its instructor, the Word, and eventually, of its maker, the Father.[93] Once the soul has left
its life on this earth, he writes, it "constantly gains greater increases in its
enlightenment, until it grows accustomed to endure looking on the 'true light'
itself, 'which enlightens every man [Jn 1:9],' and bears the splendor of its true
majesty."[94] Once this soul has been illumined by "the light of Wisdom," it
"reaches the Father of lights himself [cf. James 1:17]."[95]

As Origen saw it, then, the Hebrew travel itinerary in Numbers 33 allegorically symbolized the soul's quest for salvation in this life and the next. For him,
perceptive readers of Scripture discerned how other passages in the Old and
New Testaments—not simply Numbers 33—narrated different phases of this
quest, though rarely did a passage speak as comprehensively of this journey as
this particular chapter from the Pentateuch. We find, however, an important
exception to this principle in the prologue to Origen's *Commentary on the
Song of Songs*. Here he contends that the three Solomonic writings (Proverbs,
Ecclesiastes, and the Song of Songs) also narrated the three phases of the soul's
journey toward God. What Moses conveyed in one chapter, Solomon conveyed in three books. Origen argues that these three writings propounded the
"threefold structure of divine philosophy"—a philosophy that turns out to be
an itinerary for readers that begins with the cultivation of virtue, progresses

---

long time until we come to perfection, we will be said to have made a stage at each of the steps of
the virtues until, when we reach the height of our instruction and the summit of our progress, the
promised inheritance is fulfilled" (Hom Num 27.3.2/GCS 7, 260.22–27). Or again: the soul will
go "'from virtue to virtue,' (Ps 84:7) until the soul reaches its final end, or rather, the highest
degree of the virtues, and it crosses the river of God and receives the promised inheritance"
(27.5.2/GCS 7, 263.16–18). These references to the soul's increasing commitment to virtue are
tantamount in Origen's thought to its increasing Christ-likeness. For Origen, Christ *is* virtue: see
Hom Num 20.2; Comm Matt 12.14, 14.7; Comm Matt Ser 33; Comm Jn 32.127; Com Rom 9.34;
Comm Eph 19. On this theme, see esp. B. J. M. Bradley, *Arete as a Christian Concept*, 43–52.

[92] Hom Num 27.6.2/GCS 7, 264.19–265.3. Note also the discussion of knowledge and action
in 27.5 where Origen emphasizes the importance of dwelling in a spiritual wilderness where,
alongside a knowledge of God's law, there is also the need to overcome temptation in the pursuit
of virtue.

[93] See the more detailed discussion of Origen's eschatology in the next chapter.

[94] Hom Num 27.5.1/GCS 7, 263.1–4.

[95] Hom Num 27.6.1/GCS 7, 264.11–12—Scheck slightly modified.

through renunciation of the world, and finally arrives at the contemplation and love of God.[96]

Before Origen begins his synopsis of the three books attributed to Solomon, he rehearses for his readers a common ancient division of philosophy: "The basic disciplines through which one attains to the knowledge of things are the three which the Greeks called ethics, physics, and the esoteric discipline; these we may call the moral, natural, and contemplative."[97] He clarifies the scope of each of these disciplines. Moral study imprints a "seemly manner of life" and directs the student along the path of virtue. Natural study concerns "the nature of each single thing" so that nothing is done contrary to nature, "but everything is assigned to the uses for which the Creator brought it into being." Finally, contemplative study calls students to move beyond the visible world and contemplate "divine and heavenly things." Solomon, Origen continues, anticipated these later insights of Greek philosophy and assigned each of his three books to one of these disciplines.[98]

> First, in Proverbs he taught the moral science, putting rules for living into the form of short and pithy maxims, as was fitting. Secondly, he covered the science known as natural in Ecclesiastes; in this, by discussing at length the things of nature, and by distinguishing the useless and vain from the profitable and essential, he counsels us to forsake vanity and cultivate things useful and upright. The contemplative science likewise he has propounded in this little book that we have now in hand—that is, the Song of Songs. In this he instills into the soul the love of things divine and heavenly . . . and teaches us that communion with God must be attained by the paths of charity and love.[99]

A few lines later, Origen revisits Solomon's curriculum, stressing how these three books were not haphazardly arranged. Solomon inculcated his teachings in a planned series, so that readers would move through his curriculum in a sequential manner. The reader begins, thus, with Proverbs, and only after having completed it, "by amending his behavior and keeping the commandments," does he turn to Ecclesiastes where he comes to "renounce the world and all that is therein." After this renunciation has been mastered, the reader reaches the Song of Solomon where he begins to "contemplate and to desire 'the things that are not seen,' and 'that are eternal' [cf. 2 Cor 4:18]."[100]

Here, then, in the *Commentary on the Song of Songs*, is another account of the soul's quest for salvation. Like the quest outlined in Origen's interpretation of Numbers 33, this one traverses familiar moral and contemplative

---

[96] Comm Song of Songs prol./GCS 8, 78.19. Note again how Origen is clear that this three-step itinerary for salvation is not restricted to these Solomonic books—phases of this journey are also indicated throughout the rest of Scripture (Comm Song of Songs prol./GCS 8, 79.9–12).

[97] Comm Song of Songs prol./GCS 8, 75.6–9. Recall the previous discussion of this passage in the section in Chapter 4 entitled "The origins of philology."

[98] Comm Song of Songs prol./GCS 8, 75.17–24.

[99] Comm Song of Songs prol./GCS 8, 76.7–16—Lawson slightly modified.

[100] Comm Song of Songs prol./GCS 8, 79.12–17.

territory.[101] The accent is clearly on the former: living in accordance with commandments, renouncing the world, and striving for communion with God "by the paths of charity and love." At the same time, Origen does not marginalize the intellectual dimensions of this journey: it is, after all, for the "seeker after wisdom."[102] Proverbs teaches its readers to progress both "in understanding and behavior,"[103] and after having learned from Ecclesiastes the distinction between useless and profitable things, readers progress to the Song of Solomon where it advocates not simply knowledge, but the loving contemplation and encounter with God—a "contemplation of the Godhead with pure and spiritual love."[104]

The motif of the soul's journey to God is, then, another way in which Origen configured the scriptural message. As we have seen, there is significant overlap between this synopsis and the two other summaries examined so far: all three point to the Christian life. What is distinctive about this particular summary is that it presents the scriptural message of salvation as a narrative, and not a static snapshot. The Scriptures chronicle the soul's dynamic quest for salvation in the unfolding course of history, where the soul acts ethically and knows theologically, but also encounters in its various stations of life God's Word, and ultimately, God himself.

Jesus Christ

The Scriptures advocated the moral and doctrinal commitments of the Christian faith, its central beliefs, and the soul's journey toward God. They taught, in other words, how Christ's followers ought to pursue salvation. This biographical focus offered one vantage point on Scripture's "saving melody." However, a closer examination of Origen's writings reveals another biographical focus that offered a complementary vantage point on this same saving melody. In Origen's fourth synopsis of the Scriptures, the emphasis no longer rests on how salvation was received and pursued by Christ's followers. It rests, rather, on the person who brought salvation: Jesus Christ. This figure provided Origen a powerful lens for gazing at the one, harmonious message in the Old and New Testaments.

---

[101] Unlike Origen's twenty-seventh *Homily on Numbers*, here there is no explicit reference to the role of Christ in this journey. Perhaps this is because Origen took his point of departure for his interpretation of the three books of Solomon from a common threefold Hellenistic division of philosophy. Nevertheless, elsewhere in this *Commentary*, and indeed throughout his corpus, the Christological focus of this journey, and of Scripture as a whole, is hard to overlook (more on this theme in the next section).

[102] Comm Song of Songs prol./GCS 8, 78.7.

[103] Comm Song of Songs prol./GCS 8, 78.1.

[104] Comm Song of Songs prol./GCS 8, 78.8–10—Lawson modified.

Arguably, none of the aforementioned summaries captured the heart of the scriptural message for Origen as frequently, or perhaps as effectively, as the theme of Christ.[105] The gospels and apostolic writings obviously centered on Jesus. Yet so too, Origen insisted, did the law and prophets. In the opening lines of *On First Principles* he succinctly contends that "Christ the Word of God" inspired Moses and the prophets, but was also their theme:

> By the words of Christ we do not mean only those which formed his teaching when he was made man and dwelt in the flesh [i.e. the gospels], since even before that Christ the Word of God was in Moses and the prophets. For without the Word of God how could they have prophesied about Christ?[106]

In his exegetical writings Origen scours the Old Testament for figures, objects, institutions, and events that referred figuratively to Christ. Jesus is the new Adam,[107] our Noah,[108] the mysterious Joshua.[109] Moses' staff symbolizes Jesus' cross.[110] Jesus is the tabernacle and its high priest,[111] and all sacrifices made in the old covenant point in some way to his sacrifice.[112] A well of water mentioned in the book of Numbers points to Christ,[113] as does the Psalmist's river that gladdens the city of God.[114] And then there are the passages that explicitly prophesy the future Christ: among others, that he would proclaim release to the captives (Isa 61:1), build the city of God (Ps 46:4),[115] be born in Bethlehem (Micah 5:2), be wounded for our transgressions (Isa 53:5), or that his

---

[105] For Origen, the relationship between Jesus Christ and the Scriptures was complex. Christ was far more than the overarching *theme* of these writings. The divine Word also *taught* throughout the Scriptures he helped inspire (see passages in n. 10 above). The Word's inspiration of Scripture also drives an important *analogy* we often see in Origen's writings between Jesus Christ, the Word-made-flesh, and Scripture, the Word-made-page: both Jesus and Scripture are infused and animated by the same divine Word (Hom Lev 1.1.1; Hom Isa 1.5; Hom Jer 9.1.1; Comm Matt 15.3; Comm Matt Ser 27; Phil 15.19). On this analogy between Christ and Scripture, see A. Zöllig, *Die Inspirationslehre*, 17; H. de Lubac, *History and Spirit*, 385–396; R. P. C. Hanson, *Allegory and Event*, 193–194; K. J. Torjesen, *Hermeneutical Procedure*, 113. Recall also the different analogy between Christ and Scripture discussed earlier in this chapter (at n. 52). Finally, it was the Word incarnate, Jesus Christ, who *interpreted* the mysteries of Scripture to his followers, and after his resurrection continued this ministry in the church. There are numerous texts on this theme: see esp. Hom Lev 13.2.1; Hom Josh 9.8; Hom Ez 14.2; PA 4.1.6; Comm Jn 1.32–33; Comm Matt Ser 138–139. For more on Jesus' role in deciphering the Old Testament, see the section in Chapter 7, "Allegorical insight: The exegetical tutelage of Jesus and Paul"; for the Word's role in opening Scripture to the church's interpreters, see the sections on "Divine aid" and "Prayer" in Chapter 8. For another discussion of this multi-faceted relationship between Scripture and the Word, see K. J. Torjesen, *Hermeneutical Procedure*, 108–124.

[106] PA pref.1/GK 82, 7.13–8.2. For other passages where Christ both inspires the ancient writers and is their theme, see Hom Jer 9.1.2 and Comm Jn 1.37. Passages where Origen simply claims the writers of the Old Testament spoke of Christ: Hom Ex 11.2; Comm Jn 1.37, 6.24–25; PA 1.3.1, 4.1.5; CC 1.2, 1.49–57, 5.3.

[107] Hom Gen 9.2.   [108] Hom Gen 2.3–4.

[109] Hom Josh 1.3.   [110] Hom Ex 4.6.

[111] Hom Ex 9.1; Hom Isa 4.2.   [112] Hom Lev 3.5, 4.8.

[113] Hom Num 12.2.5.   [114] Hom Ez 13.4.2.

[115] Both passages at PA 4.2.1.

throne would endure for ever and ever (Ps 44:6).[116] This sort of Christological interpretation of the Old Testament flourishes in Origen's writings (and it is, not surprisingly, often directed polemically against his Gnostic and Jewish exegetical adversaries who, each for their own reasons, sought to unlink the testaments from each other).[117] Put concisely, for Origen, the entire law and prophets pointed to Christ. "[M]ost of the things recorded in the law refer typically and enigmatically to the Christ."[118] And as for the prophets, they "announce Christ in advance,"[119] since they "established the place of his birth, the country where he was raised, the power of his teaching, the working of his marvelous miracles, and his suffering as a man which was brought to an end by his resurrection."[120]

There are two famous texts where Origen steps back from his customary Christological assessment of individual biblical passages to theorize more generally about how Christ was the overarching theme of all of Scripture. In his *Commentary on Matthew* he offers a lengthy allegorical exposition of the transfiguration of Jesus, one of the scenes in this gospel that perhaps more than any other fired his exegetical imagination (Matt 17:1–8). Origen reminds his readers how, in the literal gospel account, Jesus ascended a high mountain with his disciples Peter, James, and John. There he was transfigured before them so that his face shone like the sun and his garments radiated an intense light. As this transpired, Moses and Elijah suddenly appeared beside Jesus and were seen talking with him. In his "mystical" interpretation of this episode,[121] Origen renders Jesus' garments symbolically as the gospels, and Moses and Elijah stand for the law and prophets respectively. The disciples who witnessed the transfiguration become, in turn, the interpreters of all these Scriptures. According to this symbolic interpretation, prior to the coming of Jesus, the law and prophets had no glory in themselves. Their spiritual and mystical sense had not yet been disclosed. How, then, was the Old Testament glorified? Origen returns to the scriptural pericope. He notes that on the mountain where Jesus was transfigured, it was not only he who was illumined, but also Moses and Elijah since they were bathed in his light when they were seen conversing with him. Origen seizes upon the detail of this three-way conversation for his allegorical interpretation. Scripture's interpreters only perceive the law and prophets to be glorious spiritual and mystical documents when they put these into amicable conversation with Jesus Christ. "But if anyone

---

[116] These passages are discussed at CC 1.51–56.

[117] For passages where Origen pointedly critiques his Gnostic opponents when he claims that Moses and the prophets spoke of Jesus Christ, see: Comm Jn 2.199–209, 6.194–197; PA pref.1–2; where the same theme is directed against Jewish scholars, see: PA 4.2.1; CC 1.49–57. For many additional illustrations, see H. de Lubac, *History and Spirit*, 196–199, 296–306.

[118] Comm Jn 13.161/GCS 4, 251.6–7 (the list of passages runs from 13.154–160).

[119] Comm Jn 2.207/GCS 4, 92.24–25.

[120] Comm Jn 2.203/GCS 4, 92.4–7.

[121] Comm Matt 12.43/GCS 10, 168.13.

sees the glory of Moses, having understood the spiritual law as a discourse in harmony with Jesus, and the wisdom in the prophets which is hidden in a mystery, he sees Moses and Elijah in glory when he sees them with Jesus."[122] The spiritual glory of the law and prophets is dependent upon the reader perceiving their harmony with Jesus, as disclosed in the gospels.

A few paragraphs later in the *Commentary*, Origen strengthens this point. He reminds his readers that in the gospel account of the transfiguration, after the terrified disciples averted their gaze from the transfigured Jesus, they looked up and no longer noticed three figures—Moses, Elijah, and Jesus— but rather, only Jesus (Matt 17:8). There is significance in this detail as well for Origen's figurative interpretation. He comments: "Moses—the law—and Elijah—the prophets—became one only with the Gospel of Jesus." While "they were formerly three, did they so abide. But [then] the three became one."[123] After the advent of the Savior, the law and prophets did not simply harmonize with the gospel. They *became* the gospel. For Scripture's interpreters, thus, there is ultimately only one theme in the Bible: Jesus.[124]

Origen's other memorable reflection on the overarching Christological sense of Scripture can be found in the opening pages of his *Commentary on John*. Similar to the passage examined above, here too he argues that "all divine Scripture is capable of being gospel."[125] However, unlike his interpretation of the transfiguration, Origen does not advance his argument through an allegorical reading of an episode in Jesus' life, but rather through an elaborate and extraordinarily rich reflection on the term "gospel." He begins his argument with a definition of "gospel": it is "either a discourse which contains the presence of a good for the believer, or a discourse which announces that an awaited good is present." In either case, the gospel is about good things that "make the hearer glad whenever he accepts what is reported, because they are beneficial."[126] This definition certainly applies to the four gospels with authoritative status in the churches, since each brings "cheer" when their declarations about "good things" are well understood.[127]

Yet what of the rest of divine Scripture, the apostolic writings in the New Testament and the law and prophets in the Old? While Origen is initially hesitant to credit any of these writings with the status of gospel, he quickly

---

[122] Comm Matt 12.38/GCS 10, 155.8–29.

[123] Comm Matt 12.43/GCS 10, 168.8–12 (syntax of English translation modified).

[124] For similar interpretations of the transfiguration, see esp. Hom Lev 6.2.5 and Comm Rom 1.10.3. For additional discussions of the transfiguration in Origen's writings, see CC 2.64, 4.15–16, 6.68, 6.77; Phil 15.19. Also see H. de Lubac, *History and Spirit*, 313–316; J. E. Ménard, "Transfiguration et polymorphie chez Origène," in *Epektasis: Mélanges patristiques offerts au Cardinal J. Daniélou*, ed. J. Fontaine and C. Kannengiesser (Paris: Beauchesne, 1972), 367–374; J. A. McGuckin, "The changing forms of Jesus according to Origen," *Orig IV*: 215–222.

[125] Comm Jn 1.86/GCS 4, 19.15–16.

[126] Comm Jn 1.27/GCS 4, 9.29–30.

[127] Comm Jn 1.12–13, 1.21–22, 1.28–29.

modifies his views.[128] Concerning the apostolic writings, he notices that Paul could write, "according to my gospel" (Rom 2:16). If Paul could claim this for his letters, then so too, Origen concludes, should it hold for the other apostolic writings accepted as sacred by churches.[129] Indeed, the whole New Testament is a gospel.[130] What is especially interesting is how Origen proceeds to elevate the Old Testament to the rank of gospel. The similarities to his allegorical interpretation of the transfiguration are striking: the evangelical status of the law and prophets depends on when, and in whose light, they are read. "Nothing of the ancient [writings] was gospel, then, before that gospel which came into existence because of the coming of Christ." Why? "[B]efore the coming of Christ, the law and the prophets did not contain the proclamation which belongs to the definition of the gospel since he who explained the mysteries in them had not yet come." But now that the Savior has come, and has removed "the antiquity of the letter" (Rom 7:6) from the law and prophets, we can say that, "he has made all things gospel, as it were."[131]

If there is a sense, then, in which all of Scripture is a gospel that proclaims "good things" (in accordance with the definition of gospel), what precisely are these "good things" found throughout Scripture? Here Origen transitions to the Christological theme that runs throughout all of Scripture. "It is the same thing," he answers, "to say that the apostles preach the Savior and that they preach good things."[132] Jesus, in other words, is the "good things," and this plural expression is justified because he is lauded with many names corresponding to his many aspects: Life, Light, Truth, Way, Resurrection, Door, Wisdom, Power, Word, Righteousness, Holiness, and Redemption.[133] Origen continues, strengthening his earlier conclusion that all of Scripture, even the Old Testament, is the gospel. While it is clear that the apostles preached Jesus, as did the evangelists who told of his life and ministry, did the law and prophets ever proclaim Jesus, the heart of the gospel?[134] Origen replies affirmatively. He justifies his sweeping claim by turning to the passage about the suffering servant in the book of Isaiah, which he portrays as

---

[128] See Comm Jn 1.14–17.

[129] Comm Jn 1.25–26/GCS 4, 9.15–22.

[130] Comm Jn 1.36.

[131] These citations come from Comm Jn 1.33/GCS 4, 11.1–7 and 1.36/GCS 4, 11.18–23— Heine modified. For a parallel statement about how only the advent of the Savior discloses the true sense of the law and prophets, see PA 4.1.6.

[132] Comm Jn 1.62/GCS 4, 15.25–26. So also 1.47 and 1.52.

[133] Comm Jn 1.53–59. Note how these forms (μορφαί) or aspects (ἐπίνοιαι) of Christ also imply, for Origen, the soul's journey to salvation (one of the ways he summarizes the message of Scripture, as noted in the previous section). For Origen, the various aspects of Christ are graduated to the differing spiritual capabilities of his followers (see esp. Comm Matt 10.36; Comm Matt Ser 100; Comm Jn 1.119, 19.38–39; CC 2.64–67, 4.16, 6.68, 6.77). Also see n. 52 above.

[134] Comm Jn 1.63–65.

representative of the entire Old Testament. He recollects the encounter between Philip and the Ethiopian eunuch in the Acts of the Apostles. As Philip approached the Ethiopian's chariot, he heard the man reading from this portion of Isaiah. Yet he was puzzled by his reading, and so Philip "told him the gospel about Jesus" (Acts 8:35). "Now how," Origen concludes, "does he preach Jesus, beginning from the prophet, unless Isaiah was some part of the beginning of the gospel?"[135] For Origen, then, all of Scripture was a gospel because of its continual (even if sometimes oblique) reference to the "good things" that made its hearers glad. These good things were, in the end, the many facets of one good thing: Jesus Christ.

In this section I have examined the four leading summaries that captured, for Origen, the sweeping contours of the message in the Christian Scriptures. Each of these summaries had distinctive emphases, yet each also pointed to what Origen envisioned was the one principal message unifying all the Christian Scriptures: the message of salvation. As I have demonstrated, these four summaries clustered around two distinct, yet mutually informing, biographical perspectives: the ministry of Jesus, the bringer of salvation, and the activity of his followers, those who received and pursued this salvation. When the Scriptures taught the elemental distinction between Christianity's moral and doctrinal commitments, or cataloged its essential beliefs, or narrated the soul's journey toward the contemplation of God, they were ultimately conveying the quest for salvation by Jesus' followers. When, on the other hand, they portrayed the giver of salvation, these writings made Jesus Christ their great theme. Viewed from either complementary perspective, the Scriptures ultimately taught the same master theme: the drama of salvation.

SCRIPTURE'S EFFECTS

The Scriptures were composed with the intent of promoting the salvation of their interpreters by making the vast story of salvation their cardinal theme. Yet were these writings actually effective in achieving this end? Origen answered this question affirmatively. These Scriptures often yielded conversions to Christianity and ushered converts further along the path of salvation.[136] When he referred to the salvific potency of these writings in the lives of Christians, scriptural interpreters included, he had in mind a range of salutary effects that corresponded to their message. As the Scriptures spoke broadly of

---

[135] Comm Jn 1.85/GCS 4, 10.10–14.
[136] On the Scriptures helping produce conversions, see esp. PA 4.1.1–7; CC 1.18, 1.26. For other passages on the ability of the Scriptures to achieve their desired ends: Hom Jer 39.1–2; Comm Matt 10.17; CC 3.39, 6.2.

the moral, contemplative and relational dimensions of the Christian life, so they were capable of transforming these dimensions of the interpreter's life. I will conclude this chapter with a brief account of how Origen envisioned Scripture's efficacy.

The scriptural message aimed for moral metamorphosis. Moses' writings are "able to transform [ἐπιστρέψαι δύναται] instantly those who hear them."[137] "The prophets, according to the will of God, said without any obscurity whatever could be at once understood as beneficial to their hearers and helpful towards attaining moral reformation [τῇ τῶν ἠθῶν ἐπανορθώσει]."[138] Over and again Origen evoked the moral efficacy of Scripture. As we have already seen on numerous occasions in this study, he discerned in the figures and events narrated in the Bible a world richly symbolic of some dimension of the exegetical enterprise. To be sure, there were biblical episodes that were also emblematic of the ability of Scripture to usher in moral reform. In his eighth *Homily on Judges,* for instance, Origen ruminates on the symbolism of Jesus commanding his disciples to wash one another's feet (Jn 13:13–14). So too does he, Origen, "wash the feet" of his congregants when he preaches from Scripture: "And I take the feet of those who are present and are prepared to be washed and, as far as I am able, I desire to wash the feet of my brothers and fulfill the Lord's commandment so that the hearers are cleansed from sordid sins by the word of doctrine [*ut in verbo doctrinae purgentur auditores a sordibus peccatorum*]."[139] The exodus from Egypt offered a similar symbolism. Origen contends that Moses wished interpreters to embark not upon a literal exodus, but rather a moral exodus at the prompting of the Scriptures, leaving behind "the activities of the flesh and darkness" and "the confusions and disturbances of the world":

> Do not suppose, therefore, that Moses led the people out of Egypt only at that time. Even now Moses, whom we have with us—"for we have Moses and the prophets" [cf. Lk 16:29]—that is, the Law of God, wishes to lead you out of Egypt. If you would hear it, it wishes to make you "far" from Pharaoh. If only you would hear the Law of God and understand it spiritually, it desires to deliver you from the work of mud and chaff. It does not wish you to remain in the activities of the flesh and darkness, but to go out to the wilderness, to come to the place free from the confusions and disturbances of the world, to come to the rest of silence . . . For that reason, therefore, Moses desires to bring you out of the midst of vacillating daily business and from the midst of noisy people. For that reason he desires you to depart from Egypt . . .[140]

---

[137] CC 1.18/SC 132, 122.5–6.

[138] CC 7.10/SC 150, 36.16–38.19. For other passages where the Scriptures admonish readers who stray from straight paths, as well as exhort them to stay on these paths, see Hom Gen 2.6; Hom Lev 2.4.6, 5.1.2; Hom 3.1 Ps 36; Hom Jer 4.6.3, 5.13.1–3; CC 3.50.

[139] Hom Jd 8.5/GCS 7, 515.9–17—transl. mine.

[140] Hom Ex 3.3/GCS 6, 166.26–167.12.

Of course, this moral transformation did not transpire spontaneously. Those who interpreted Scripture needed to do more than listen to its moral counsel; they needed to actually put it into action. This point is clearly conveyed in Origen's first *Homily on Psalm 38* where he comments autobiographically on "a fire blazing up" (Ps 38:4) when he meditated on God's law. The Scriptures ought to do more than ignite the thoughts of scriptural interpreters like himself, Origen confesses. They ought also to inflame their hearts so that they put these thoughts into action:

> I too meditate on the words of the Lord and repeatedly train myself in them, but I do not know if I am the kind of person in the course of whose meditation fire comes forth from each and every word of God and sets my heart ablaze and inflames my soul to keep those things upon which I am meditating . . . If only now our heart would burn within us, as we open the divine scriptures, and a fire be kindled in our meditation; if only we might be roused to put what we hear and read into action![141]

The Scriptures were capable of transforming the moral lives of their interpreters. They had a similar impact on readers' contemplative and emotional lives. For those who grasped them well, these writings provided intellectual stimulation. When the apostle Paul spoke, for instance, of the continual renewal of the mind in its quest for salvation, he was referring more specifically to the renewal that took place when the interpreter studied Scripture: "Our mind is renewed [cf. Rom 12:1–2] through training in wisdom and meditation upon the Word of God, and the spiritual interpretation of his law. And to the extent that it makes daily progress by reading the Scriptures, to the extent that its understanding goes deeper, to that extent it becomes continuously new and daily new."[142] For Origen, this successful intellectual encounter with Scripture also registered emotionally. The one who interprets the prophetic words "with care and attention," he writes, "will experience from his very reading a trace of enthusiasm [ἴχνος ἐνθουσιασμοῦ]."[143] The joy of intellectual discovery is a continual theme in his writings. In his *Commentary on John*, for instance, he arrives at the Christological title "true vine" (Jn 15:1) and remarks that not simply Jesus, but also the "esoterical and mystical doctrines" in Scripture, are the "true vine." Both have the same effect as wine, "because they cheer and produce enthusiasm [εὐφραίνοντα καὶ ἐνθουσιᾶν ποιοῦντα], residing in those who 'delight in the Lord' [Ps 36:4] and desire not only to be fed [τρέφεσθαι], but also to revel [τρυφᾶν]."[144] Indeed, when Origen

---

[141] Hom 1.7 Ps 38/Prinzivalli, 342.3–344.17. For similar passages, see Hom Lev 6.6.6; Hom 3.6 Ps 36.

[142] Comm Rom 9.1.12/Bammel 717, 130–134. Also see PA 4.2.7.

[143] PA 4.1.6/GK 688, 302.3–5—transl. mine.

[144] Comm Jn 1.208/GCS 4, 37.28–32 (and preceding discussion, beginning at 1.205)—transl. mine. For a similar passage, see Hom Num 27.12 where Origen etymologizes the wilderness station Thara as ἔκστασις, and claims that "ecstasy" or "the contemplation of amazement" occurs when the "mind is struck with amazement by the knowledge of great and marvelous things."

expounds upon this verse in his *Homilies on the Psalms*, he contends in a similar manner that the person who finds "delight in the Lord" (Ps 36:4) is more specifically the student of Scripture who "finds delight in the full attainment of knowledge."[145] The Scriptures sparked the mind on its journey to salvation, and in so doing, the emotions as well.

And yet, for all the ways the Scriptures transformed their readers—exercising their minds with insight into God and God's dealings with the creation, bringing them joy, and challenging them to moral reform—their salvific effect was not fully experienced for Origen if they did not also yield a favorable relationship with the Word and, ultimately, God. As noted above, the Scriptures for Origen narrated the pursuit of salvation. This pursuit required moral action and intellectual growth, yet it was not devoid of a relationship or encounter with God and God's Word. This encounter transpired in a variety of ways and in a variety of venues in the Christian life, but for Origen, arguably the privileged place for this encounter was the interpretation of Scripture. We have already seen this in the previous chapter, where the struggling interpreter occasionally met Scripture's divine authors when searching for insight into a particularly challenging passage. Yet this was not the only encounter with these authors that Origen thought transpired when the Scriptures were studied. It is important to remember that the Scriptures for him were an extension of their divine authors and not some second-hand source of information about them. These writings did not simply talk about God, they *were* "the words of God."[146] Nor was the Word simply one of their themes. They *were* the Word "clothed," not with flesh, but with text.[147] The Scriptures were, in other words, the personal expression of their divine authors, and thus to read them well was not to extract from their pages some viewpoint about these authors. In and through these pages, rather, ideal interpreters had the opportunity to encounter these very divine authors.

Origen occasionally spoke of the growing understanding of Scripture as an encounter with the Word.[148] The soul, he preaches in his *Homilies on Genesis*, is united to the Word when it meditates on the Scriptures: "But it is certain that this union of the soul with the Word cannot come about otherwise than

---

Also see Hom Lev 16.5.2 and Hom 1.2 Ps 36, where Origen again associates the topic of wine with joy in scriptural interpretation.

[145] Hom 1.4 Ps 36/Prinzivalli, 60.43–44. For additional passages on the joy or delight that accompanies insight into Scripture's mystical teachings, see Hom 3.10 Ps 36; Comm Jn 1.27–28; PA 4.3.11. On the consolation and gladness of heart brought about by the Holy Spirit who teaches unspeakable mysteries, see PA 2.7.4.

[146] Hom Num 27.1; Hom Jer 10.1.1; Comm Jn 1.208.

[147] Hom Lev 1.1.1; Hom Isa 1.5; Hom Jer 9.1.1; Comm Matt 15.3; Comm Matt Ser 27; Phil 15.19.

[148] Also see K. J. Torjesen, *Hermeneutical Procedure*, 117–124 on the encounter with Christ through Scripture.

through instruction in the divine books . . ."[149] Or again, in Origen's allegorical account of the transfiguration in the twelfth book of his *Commentary on Matthew*, he contends that Scripture's interpreters meet Jesus when they read the gospels. As the historical disciples encountered Jesus in both his "untransfigured" and "transfigured" forms, so too do his new disciples in the church see him in both of these forms. Yet where do they encounter him? Not on a mountain, but in Scripture, Origen replies: "But if you desire to see the transfiguration of Jesus . . . behold with me Jesus in the gospels."[150]

Ultimately, interpreters encountered God in Scripture. In an important passage from the *Commentary on John*, Origen develops this point at length as he fashions the true interpretation of Scripture as the worship of God. In book thirteen of this monumental (and ultimately incomplete) exegetical project, he arrives at the dialogue between Jesus and the Samaritan woman as their conversation turns to the subject of worship (Jn 4:20–24). The woman remarks that her ancestors worshiped on Mt. Gerizim, while the Jews worshiped in Jerusalem. Jesus responds that she will shortly worship the Father neither on that mountain nor in Jerusalem, but rather with all other true worshipers, will worship the Father "in spirit and in truth" (Jn 4:23).

Origen wonders what it could mean to worship the Father anew in this way. He takes his cues from the prepositional phrase ἐν πνεύματι καὶ ἀληθείᾳ ("in spirit and in truth") and suggests that to worship the Father ἐν πνεύματι is, with Paul, to be ministers "not of letter but of spirit; for the letter kills, but the Spirit gives life" (2 Cor 3:6). To worship "in spirit" is, then, to discern with the help of the Spirit the spiritual meaning of the law. It is opposed to a worship of the "letter": "Now the one who is enslaved to the letter that kills and has not partaken of the life-giving Spirit [cf. 2 Cor 3:6], and who does not follow the spiritual meanings of the law, would be the one who is not a true worshipper and does not worship the Father in Spirit."[151] Origen bolsters this reading by turning to the other noun in the prepositional phrase. To worship the Father ἐν . . . ἀληθείᾳ ("in truth") is not to be wrapped up in the mere figures of Scripture, but rather to search out what the figures figure. Here he is drawing upon a rhetorical distinction familiar in his day, between the figure (τύπος) and that which it figures, its nonliteral referent, the ἀλήθεια. The person who worships God in truth is the person who searches the Scriptures allegorically, whereas the interpreter who is "totally engrossed in the figures and bodily meanings . . . worships God in the figure and not in truth [ἐν τύπῳ καὶ οὐκ ἐν ἀληθείᾳ]."[152] Origen encapsulates his thesis about true worship several

---

[149] Hom Gen 10.5/GCS 6, 99.24–29.

[150] Comm Matt 12.37/GCS 10, 153.8–25—transl. mine. See as well the continued discussion of the transfiguration and biblical interpretation in Comm Matt 12.38, and the parallel passage at Phil 15.19.

[151] Comm Jn 13.110/GCS 4, 242.17–21—Heine modified.

[152] Comm Jn 13.110/GCS 4, 242.21–24—transl. mine.

sections later, identifying the ideal interpreter of Scripture, who searches after its life-giving spiritual sense, with a worshiper of God:

> And let us strive earnestly to worship God in the life-giving Spirit and not in the letter that kills [cf. 2 Cor 3:6], and to honor him in truth and no longer in mere figures, shadows, and examples, just as the angels do not serve God in examples and the shadow of heavenly realities, but in spiritual and heavenly realities, having a high priest of the order of Melchizedech [cf. Heb 5:6] as the guide to worship on behalf of those who need salvation, and as guide in mystical, ineffable contemplation.[153]

Scripture's authors wove the message of salvation into their writings, and this was also their aim: to advance the salvation of those who correctly understood them. As Origen saw it, these writings were often effective in achieving this end. The scriptural message sought continually to reform interpreters by challenging their behavior, deepening their knowledge, eliciting joy, and ultimately, ushering them into a richer encounter with Scripture's divine authors, particularly the Word and God the Father.

In this chapter I have examined the salvific thread that runs through the rich tapestry of Origen's doctrine of Scripture. It was particularly Scripture's divine authors who utilized these writings in a providential manner to advance the salvation of humanity. Their salvific intent found expression in a multi-faceted message that Origen summarized in various ways. Ultimately, however, this message formed a harmonious saving melody that yielded what it described: the continual conversion of interpreters to God. The activity of scriptural interpretation was, then, not simply an opportunity for interpreters to express the commitments of the Christian faith. As we have seen in this chapter, it was also an opportunity to gather resources that strengthened interpreters along their journey in this faith.

---

[153] Comm Jn 13.146/GCS 4, 248.21–27. Also see Comm Jn 13.98–100 and CC 6.70 for a similar association of allegorical interpretation with true worship.

10

Horizons: The Beginning and End of the Drama of Salvation

For Origen, the Christian drama of salvation unfolded in three successive, sweeping acts. The primary focus of this study has been on the scriptural scholar as a participant in the middle act of this drama. Yet it is important to remember that this interpreter also had a past life in the opening act of the drama and would enjoy a future life in its closing act. In this final chapter, I will contend that, when we cast our vision to the horizons of Origen's theology, both to the prelapsarian state of minds in their attentive and loving contemplation of God, as well as to their gradual return to the state from where they fell, we will discover how Origen framed the quest for salvation from Scripture in this life—the middle of the drama—with similar quests at the beginning and end of the drama. Scriptural interpretation both reprised what had fleetingly transpired at the very beginning of the mind's existence, as well as anticipated, and indeed prepared for, what interpreters would be practicing with increasing perfection in the ages to come. The interpreter occupied a place not simply in the middle, but also in the beginning and end, of the Christian drama of salvation.[1]

---

[1] As is well known, Origen's protological and eschatological thought is notoriously difficult to adumbrate. There are several reasons for this. He himself conceded that these topics were "difficult to understand" (PA 1.6.1; also Comm Matt 15.23) and often voiced reticence about delving into these themes (Comm Jn 20.6–7; DH 12–16; CC 4.48, 5.29). When he did touch upon them, his thoughts were rarely comprehensive, but piecemeal and often explicitly provisional (see esp. PA 1.6.1, 2.3.1; at PA 2.3.7 Origen outlines several options for understanding the "end" of all things, and leaves it to his readers to choose which they prefer). Beyond these limitations imposed by Origen, there is the additional problem of the deficient textual status of *On First Principles*, the treatise that, of all of Origen's extant writings, offers us the clearest window onto his ideas about beginnings and endings. The passages that are important for us do not survive in their original Greek, but rather in Rufinus' Latin translation. Moreover, several ancient authors (notably Jerome and Justinian) offered summaries of passages in *On First Principles* that sometimes depart markedly from what Rufinus relays. It is, thus, important to proceed cautiously. The main concern of this chapter—how Origen's protological and eschatological ruminations provide a narrative framework for his understanding of the scriptural interpreter—will allow us to skirt most of the issues that continue to puzzle his modern readers.

IN THE BEGINNING

Two fixed points in Origen's thought provide orientation to the recondite themes of the beginning and the end. The first is a tripartite chronology to which he openly refers in his outline of the church's rule of faith. In the preface to *On First Principles* he writes:

> The Church teaching also includes the doctrine that this world was made and began to exist at a definite time and that by reason of its corruptible nature it must suffer dissolution. But what existed before this world, or what will exist after it, has not yet been made known openly to the many, for no clear statement on the point is set forth in the Church teaching.[2]

Here Origen introduces his readers to the three distinct and successive epochs that constitute all of human existence. He often speaks of these epochs as worlds. There was once an incorporeal "state" or "world" in which God, his Wisdom, and the Holy Spirit, along with a host of lesser rational creatures, resided.[3] This world preceded the world in which we now live, a material and "visible world" that had a distinct beginning and will also have a distinct end.[4] Finally, following the dissolution of our world, another world will emerge, what Origen often terms the "world to come"[5] or "age to come."[6] While this chronological schema was determinate for Origen—it was fixed in the church's rule which itself expressed clear Scriptural teaching—it left unresolved any number of issues that required further inquiry. Most pertinent for Origen was the mysterious topic of how one ought to characterize the worlds that preceded and would follow this life on earth.[7]

To help him negotiate this puzzling topic, Origen proposed a principle around which he could outline the patterns of protological and eschatological existence. On several occasions in *On First Principles* he announced the dictum that what transpired at the beginning would be mirrored at the end: "For the end is always like the beginning."[8] "[T]he world should have

---

[2]   PA pref.7/GK 94, 14.1–5. Origen refers to this article and elaborates on it at PA 2.3.1–7 and 3.5.1–4. In the latter passage he clearly discusses the biblical texts that support this basic tripartite chronology.

[3]   PA 3.5.4/GK 630, 275.1, 5.

[4]   PA 3.5.4/GK 626, 273.2.

[5]   PA 2.1.3/GK 290, 109.7–8.

[6]   PA 1.6.2/GK 222, 82.5. Origen sometimes speaks of this future age (as he does the first age) in the plural: "periods and ages to come" (PA 1.6.4/GK 228, 84.25).

[7]   Recall how for Origen the rule consisted of the clear apostolic teaching, and that this teaching was to serve as a springboard for more inquisitive minds who, having received the higher gifts of God's Spirit, could pursue more deeply the "how or why" behind its individual doctrines (PA pref.3). For passages where Origen raises these very "how or why" questions concerning the basic tripartite chronology, see esp. PA 1.6.1, 2.3, 3.5.

[8]   PA 1.6.2/GK 216, 79.22–23.

a conclusion similar to its beginning."[9] "[A]ll things shall be restored to their original state."[10] With his dictum in hand, Origen often began with the end, and particularly, with Paul's eschatological reflections in 1 Corinthians 15. Christ would rule until he had subjected everything, including his enemies, to himself, whereupon he would hand the kingdom over to God the Father and subject even himself to God, so that God would be "all in all" (1 Cor 15:24–28).[11] God would be "all in all" for rational creatures, humans included, when God finally became the sole object of their desire and thought:

> Now I myself think that when it is said that God is "all in all" [1 Cor 15:28], it means that he is also "all" things in each individual person. And he will be "all" things in each person in such a way that everything which the rational mind, when purified from all the dregs of its vices and utterly cleared from every cloud of wickedness, can feel or understand or think will be all God and that the mind will no longer be conscious of anything besides or other than God, but will think God and see God and hold God and God will be the mode and measure of its every movement; and in this way God will be "all" to it.[12]

In these soaring lines Origen describes the eschaton in which humans would live harmoniously alongside and freely contemplate the everlasting God. Extrapolating from this pattern of eschatological life, Origen insists that life in the first world must somehow have been similar. In the prelapsarian world, he contends, God, with the help of his Wisdom, fashioned incorporeal rational beings, that is, "intelligent natures," "minds," or "souls."[13] These creatures were "equal and alike"[14] and endowed with the power of choice.[15] In response to the gift of their creation, moreover, they directed their loving attention freely and equally toward their supreme Maker and his Son. Thus, in this prelapsarian state of goodness, as in the future eschaton, these minds lived in

---

[9] PA 2.1.3/GK 290, 109.3–4.

[10] PA 2.1.1/GK 284, 107.9–10. For other passages where Origen announces this principle, see PA 3.5.4, 3.6.3, 3.6.8.

[11] For Origen's interpretation of this Pauline passage, see E. Schendel, *Herrschaft und Unterwerfung Christi: 1. Korinther 15, 24–28 in Exegese und Theologie der Väter biz zum Ausgang des 4. Jahrhunderts* (Tübingen: J. C. B. Mohr, 1971), 81–110.

[12] PA 3.6.3/GK 648, 283.14–650, 283.21—slight emendation to Butterworth. For similar statements on the eschatological encounter with God, see PA 2.6.2, 2.11.7, 3.6.1; Comm Jn 20.47.

[13] Following several clear scriptural assertions (esp. Ps 104:24, Jn 1:1–3 and Col 1:16–18), Origen contended that God, with the help of his Son, created and loved all things, including rational minds: see PA 1.7.1, 2.9.1, 2.9.4, 2.9.6, 4.4.3; Comm Jn 1.109–118, etc.

[14] PA 2.9.6/GK 412, 169.25–28.

[15] See, for instance, PA 1.5.3, 1.5.5, 1.6.2, 1.8.3–4, 2.1.2; the major discussion of freedom in *On First Principles* transpires at 3.1.1–24.

an "original unity and harmony,"[16] dwelling in the contemplative love of God and his Word.[17]

The real challenge in Origen's protological thought was not how to portray this ideal, original order. It was, rather, how to explain the diverse, hierarchical and corporeal world that emerged from this pristine state, in such a way as not to implicate the Creator in an act of injustice. "Seeing then that the world contains this great variety, and that even among rational beings there is great diversity... what cause can be given to account for the existence of the world...?"[18] At several junctures in *On First Principles* Origen revisits his answer to this question by excluding the possibility that the hierarchical ranking of rational creatures was the product of some deity's unjust, capricious

---

[16] PA 2.1.1/GK 286, 107.13–14.

[17] Recently P. Tzamalikos has forwarded an unusual position in the Origenian scholarship, insisting that for Origen this "incorporeal creation does not refer to the creation of any individual person" (*Origen: Cosmology and Ontology of Time* [Leiden: Brill, 2006], 42); rather, the "substance of *human nature* (which involves no individuality) was created" in this prelapsarian world, and that "the actual subsistence of individual rational creatures came into being only with the actual creation" (89–90, *passim*). For Tzamalikos, there is no talk of individual souls or minds prior to the fall, but only of what he variously calls reasons, relations, possibilities, or principles (44). Moreover, these reasons or principles that God created were not outside of God or his Wisdom, but rather *in* God's Wisdom: "Therefore, what came into being out of non-being was a 'multitude' of 'wisdom' (σοφίαν), 'reasons' (λόγους), 'forms' (τύπων), and a 'system of conceptions' (συστήματος νοημάτων) and 'objects of contemplation' (θεωρήματα), which were made 'in wisdom,' they were called 'wisdom,' too, and placed, as it were, in the Wisdom of God, the Body of the Son, and they 'embroidered' this Body" (53).
This is a highly unconventional reinterpretation of what has nearly universally been held to be Origen's account of the preexistence of individual, personal minds living prior to their fall. Among the many challenges that Tzamalikos' reading faces, two seem most problematic. First, he diligently excludes many texts in *On First Principles* where Origen clearly claims the existence of these minds or souls. While Rufinus' translations undeniably veer (at times) from Origen's original text, they do so *in the direction of* late fourth-century orthodoxy, not *against it*. It would be highly unusual for Rufinus to foist onto Origen a position such as preexisting minds, if this were not already there in the original.
The other issue facing Tzamalikos is that Origen claims these preexisting minds fell. If they were not individual, personal, rational creatures, but rather something constitutive of and within God's Wisdom, he needs to say—as in fact he does—that "[w]hat fell, therefore, was an 'ornament' from the 'body' of Wisdom. What lived until that moment is pretty clear: it was Wisdom herself, living her divine life" (80). Again, and even more explicitly, Tzamalikos notes that what fell did not have "*its* own life" (thus denying individual existence to these souls) since it already was "the divine life of Wisdom herself" (80). This puzzling position seems to run counter to everything we know of Origen's account of God's Word who is, as Origen says elsewhere, "total virtue [ἡ πᾶσα... ἀρετή]" (Comm Jn 32.127/GCS 4, 444.3). For other texts on Christ as virtue, see Hom Num 20.2; Comm Matt 12.14, 14.7; Comm Matt Ser 33; Comm Jn 32.127; Comm Rom 9.34; Comm Eph 19 (and note esp. the discussion of this theme by B. J. M. Bradley, *Arete as a Christian Concept*, 43–52). For orientation to the complex issue of the preexistence of souls in Origen, see M. Harl, "La preexistence des âmes dans l'oeuvre d'Origène," *Orig IV*: 238–258; M. Edwards, *Origen against Plato*, 89–97.

[18] PA 2.1.1/GK 284, 107.6–9. Origen's customary nomenclature is that of "differences" and "varieties" in this world, of a world "various and diverse" (e.g. PA 1.6.2/GK 216, 80.2–3; 1.8.2/GK 254, 98.19; 2.1.1/GK 284, 106.14, etc.).

decision. His opponents (the Gnostics) think it is "illogical for one and the same creator, quite apart from any reason of merit, to confer on some the authority to rule, while others are subjected to rulers, or to assign principalities to some, while others are made subject to princes." Yet, Origen continues, the true "cause of the diversity and variety among these things is shown to be derived not from any unfairness on the part of the Disposer but from their own actions, which exhibit varying degrees of earnestness or laxity according to the goodness or badness of each."[19] Indeed, he reiterates elsewhere in *On First Principles*, the problem does not lie with God in whom there is "neither variation nor change nor lack of power,"[20] but with creatures: "what other cause can we imagine to account for the great diversity of this world except the variety and diversity of the motions and declensions of those who fell away from that original unity and harmony in which they were at the first created by God?"[21]

To understand how Origen envisioned this falling away, it is instructive to begin with the one soul that did *not* experience this decline: Jesus' soul, which ultimately embarked upon a unique course of action, different from the actions of all other souls in the prelapsarian world. In *On First Principles* Origen writes that Jesus' soul clung to the Word of God "from the beginning of the creation and ever after in a union inseparable and indissoluble, as being the soul of the Wisdom and Word of God and of the Truth and the true Light..."[22] In this unspoiled world, Jesus' soul loved the Word of God to such an extent that it became uniquely one with this Word: "and [this soul] receiving him [the Word of God] wholly, and itself entering into his Light and splendour, was made with him in a preeminent degree one spirit."[23] A few paragraphs later, Origen proposes an analogy to convey the depth of the union between Jesus' soul and God's Word. As an iron is heated so thoroughly in a furnace that it no longer becomes distinguishable from the fire in the furnace, so too is it with Jesus' soul in its relationship with the Word. "In this manner, then, that soul which, like a piece of iron in the fire, was for ever placed in the Word, for ever in the Wisdom, for ever in God, is God in all its acts and feelings and thoughts."[24] The allusions here to the final eschatological state are striking where, as noted above, God would be "all in all" (1 Cor 15:28) when purified rational souls were able only to "feel or understand or think" God.[25] Their *telos* was Christ's beginning.

---

[19] PA 1.8.2/GK 254, 98.13–22.   [20] PA 2.9.6/GK 412, 169.25–28.

[21] PA 2.1.1/GK 286, 107.12–18. For other similar passages where diversity is attributed to rational creatures and not the capricious deity of his opponents, see PA 1.6.2, 1.8.1, esp. 2.9.5–6.

[22] PA 2.6.3/GK 362, 142.5–7—Butterworth emended.

[23] PA 2.6.3/GK 362, 142.7–9—Butterworth emended.

[24] PA 2.6.6/GK 368, 145.17–20—Butterworth emended. A very similar sentiment about the intense union between Christ's soul and the Word of God can be found at PA 2.6.3/GK 364, 143.3–7.

[25] PA 3.6.3 (cited above at n. 12).

Christ's exemplary soul did not fall, but all other souls eventually did. When Origen searched for the cause of the variety of rational creatures in the universe—including angels, celestial bodies, humans, and demons—he did not finger, as noted above, a God who arbitrarily and unfairly assigned these creatures their differing roles. Rather, he located responsibility in the prelapsarian choices these creatures made. One of Origen's clearest, extended statements on the fall of minds occurs in the second book of *On First Principles*. There he identifies the cause of their fall or "withdrawal" from God: "their minds are not rightly and worthily directed." He continues:

> For the Creator granted to the minds created by him the power of free and voluntary movement, in order that the good that was in them might become their own, since it was preserved by their own free will; but sloth and weariness of taking trouble to preserve the good, coupled with disregard and neglect of better things, began the process of withdrawal from the good. Now to withdraw from the good is nothing else than to be immersed in evil; for it is certain that to be evil means to be lacking in good.[26]

Rather than blame God, Origen blames prelapsarian minds. While they had the "power of free and voluntary movement," their choice became corrupted. As he does elsewhere, so here, Origen specifies the deficiencies in these minds: laziness, exhaustion, and neglect for the good steered their gaze awry.[27] By turning away in varying degrees from the loving contemplation of this Good—God and his Word or Wisdom—by definition they immersed themselves in corresponding degrees of evil.[28] Individual minds, thus, once the same in their love and knowledge of God, fell in differing degrees from their Creator so that one could now speak of a diversity of minds.[29]

What ensued was a just, not arbitrary, divine judgment. Using this new postlapsarian heterogeneity of minds as a source, "the Creator of all things obtained certain seeds and causes of variety and diversity, in order that, according to the diversity of minds... he might create a world that was various and diverse."[30] This corporeal world, characterized by a diversity of places or

---

[26] PA 2.9.2/GK 404, 165.23–166.2. Other similar statements on how minds fell: PA 1.6.2, 1.8.2, 2.1.1, 2.6.3, 2.8.3–4, 2.9.6, 3.3.5, 3.5.5; Hom Ex 6.4. On the fall of Satan, see PA 1.5.4; CC 6.44.

[27] There are several other passages where Origen highlights these, or similar, vices that afflicted these primordial minds. On laziness, see: PA 1.4.1, 1.6.2, 1.8.2, 2.9.2; Hom 1.1 Ps 37. On weariness, see PA 2.8.3. On negligence or loss of interest, see: PA 1.4.1, 1.5.4, 1.5.5, 1.6.2, 2.3.6, 2.9.6, 4.4.9. On a diminishing ("cooling") love, see: PA 2.6.3, 2.8.3. Note also the reference to "satiety" retarding the soul's love for God at PA 1.3.8, as well as M. Harl, "Recherches sur l'orgénisme d'Origène: la satiété (koros) de la contemplation comme motif de la chute des âmes," in *SP* 8: 374–405.

[28] PA 1.4.1, 1.6.2, 2.9.2, 2.9.6, 4.4.9.

[29] PA 1.2.2, 1.4.1, 1.6.2, 1.7.1, 2.9.2, 2.9.6, 2.9.8, 3.3.5, 3.6.4.

[30] PA 2.9.2/GK 404, 166.6–10. On God's creation of matter, see esp. PA 2.1.4; on the diverse regions in this world, see PA 2.9.3.

regions, became the new home for fallen minds in which God justly "placed everyone in a position proportionate to his merit."[31] And so the cosmos as we know it emerged, populated by creatures of differing ranks and justly positioned according to the degree by which they fell from their prelapsarian gaze upon God. Angels fell the shortest distance, occupying the highest rank among creatures that fell, whereas demons, including the devil, fell the furthest. Human minds, who fell somewhere in between these two extremes, were placed in bodies and put on this earth. In this embodied state, they were still colored by the habits to which they had variously succumbed in their former state, namely, a distracted and fleeting contemplation of God. This situation was exacerbated, moreover, by the fact that they now had an additional source of distraction from their Maker: their bodies and the vast corporeal universe that surrounded them on all sides. Simply put, these embodied minds were alienated from God and in need of salvation.

Among these embodied minds were, of course, scriptural interpreters. As I have argued in this study, Origen wrote an important part for them in the drama of salvation in which God was actively working to recall all creatures to their one end.[32] Yet the part played by ideal scriptural interpreters in this life was not uninformed by the events that had transpired in the previous world. Rather, their current exegetical project was *patterned* after the original project that they had suspended. The foregoing précis of the opening act in Origen's account of primeval human history strongly suggests that its scenes formed the backstory for his account of the interpreter in this life: ideal scriptural interpreters sought to *reverse* their original fall in an attempt to *reprise*, however fleetingly, their original state, the contemplation of God.

Several of the discussions in foregoing chapters confirm this thesis. Recalling the argument in Chapter 5 (particularly the section entitled "The ordered (and disordered) mind"), Origen painted the life dedicated to scriptural interpretation with one of his leading moral themes: the mind and its divided attention between the corporeal and incorporeal worlds. For him, all human conduct could be dissolved into two antagonistic principles: did the mind attend to the corporeal world, the world into which it fell, or did it lift its gaze beyond that world and begin its quest for the incorporeal God? As we saw in that chapter, the life given to scriptural interpretation signaled the desire to leave behind an inordinate attraction to the flesh and pursue the God it had once lovingly contemplated. The previous chapter extended this argument, since God, our author contended, gathers together the distracted gazes of

---

[31] PA 2.9.6/GK 412, 170.11–14. More passages on minds becoming embodied and justly allocated in this newly fashioned world: PA 1.6.2, 1.7.1, 1.8.4, 2.1.1, 2.9.3; Hom Jer 28.1.1–3.

[32] For a particularly clear statement about how God did not abandon the material cosmos, but rather set to work, providentially transforming and restoring it to a perfect end, see PA 2.1.2. For a more expansive overview of the phases in the history of salvation, see esp. PA 1.3.5–8.

minds in this world with Scripture, the very words of God given for human salvation. It is in the pages of these holy writings that interpreters seek to discern the God whom they once enjoyed. Moreover, as we have also seen in Chapter 8 (particularly the section "Exegetical virtues"), *how* these minds gazed at Scripture became a crucial theme in Origen's writings. The primordial fall was variously characterized by an array of vices, ranging from indolence and neglect, to a lack of interest. Ideal interpreters, however, were committed to a series of remedial habits: when Origen emphasized that interpreters cultivate curiosity, attentiveness, and effort when examining Scripture, seen in light of his account of the fall, it becomes clear that these virtues served as correctives for those particular vices that led to the demise of minds in their primordial state. And finally, just as the original state was characterized by more than contemplation, but also by communion with God and his Word, so too did the exegetical enterprise afford fleeting moments that recalled this pristine state. As we have seen in the two previous chapters (particularly "Divine aid" in Chapter 8 and "Scripture's effects" in Chapter 9), scriptural interpreters were occasionally given moments when they encountered God or the Word. Those who sought to understand these challenging Scriptures were sometimes graced by an illuminating encounter with their divine authors. Moreover, these writings did not simply talk about their divine authors, they were the very personal expression of these authors. Thus in examining them well, interpreters experienced, even if only dimly, the blessed communion that transpired in the original state.

When we examine Origen's account of the mind in the foregoing world, it becomes increasingly clear how the pattern of its prelapsarian life was realized perhaps most profoundly in this world by scriptural scholarship. As he understood it, scriptural interpretation sought to reverse or counteract the original fall, in an attempt to reprise, as best as possible, the prelapsarian communion and contemplation of God. In the next section we will detect how scriptural exegesis was not only linked to the mind's life in the primordial world, but was also remarkably continuous with life in the future eschatological state.

AT THE END

For Origen, scriptural interpretation was a fragmentary anticipation of the more perfect eschatological contemplation of God. "For now in this present life we seek, but there we shall see plainly [cf. 1 Cor 13:12]."[33] In this life, humans were still very much "on the road to perfection" and thus only knew

---

[33]   PA 2.11.5/GK 450, 189.7–8 (an allusion to 1 Cor 13:12).

"in part." It would only be in the eschaton when they would finally reach the perfection of knowledge in the "face to face [cf. 1 Cor 13:9–12]" contemplation of God.[34] Thus even a life wholly devoted to scriptural interpretation, Origen insisted, yielded at best partial knowledge. This was due, in part, to Scripture offering only an incomplete account of the divine mysteries. In his *Commentary on John* Origen claims that "Scripture has not contained some of the more lordly and more divine aspects of the mysteries of God . . ."[35] He notes how many of Jesus' deeds were not recorded in the gospels since "not even the world itself would contain the books that would be written [cf. Jn 21:25]." He also recalls how Paul heard words that could not be spoken (cf. 2 Cor 12:4).[36] Thus, Origen concludes, "all of the Scriptures, even when perceived very accurately, are only very elementary rudiments of and very brief introductions to all knowledge [τῆς ὅλης γνώσεως στοιχεῖά τινα ἐλάχιστα καὶ βραχυτάτας εἶναι εἰσαγωγὰς ὅλας γραφάς]."[37]

  But there was another reason why the study of Scripture offered only a foreshadowing of eschatological knowledge: even its introductory character far transcended what interpreters could grasp. To fully know the mysteries of the Scriptures, Origen preaches in his *Homilies on Numbers*, ultimately "belongs to the same Holy Spirit who inspired these things to be written, and to our Lord Jesus Christ . . . and to the almighty God, whose ancient plan for the human race is not openly indicated, but veiled in the letters."[38] Elsewhere in *On First Principles* he cautions ambitious interpreters eager for an explanation of every detail in the Scripture. Origen reminds them how even the apostle Paul, who searched

> the "depth of the divine wisdom and knowledge" [cf. Rom 11:33], and yet not being able to reach the end and to attain, if I may say so, an innermost knowledge, in his despair and amazement at the task cried out and says, "O the depth of the riches of the wisdom and knowledge of God!" [Rom 11:33] And in what despair of reaching a perfect understanding he uttered this cry, hear him tell us himself: "How unsearchable are his judgments and his ways past finding out!" [Rom 11:33] He did not say that God's judgments were hard to search out, but that they could not be searched out at all; not that his ways were hard to find out, but that they were impossible to find out.[39]

Indeed, Origen continues, no matter how much progress someone has made through the increasingly diligent study of Scripture, "even when aided and

---

[34] PE 25.2/GCS 2, 358.13–17. For other passages on the perfection of humanity only being attained in the eschaton, see Hom Ex 7.5; Hom Lev 7.2; Hom Num 28.3; Hom Josh 6.1; Comm Matt 17.19.

[35] Comm Jn 13.27/GCS 4, 230.3–5.

[36] Comm Jn 13.27–28.

[37] Comm Jn 13.30/GCS 4, 230.13–15. On the incomplete status of Scripture, see Comm Matt Ser 18; Phil 3; also M. Harl, SC 302, 151–153 and H. Crouzel, *Connaissance*, 280ff.

[38] Hom Num 26.3.5/GCS 7, 249.6–10.

[39] PA 4.3.14/GK 774, 345.10–776, 345.20.

enlightened in mind by God's grace, he will never be able to reach the final goal of his inquiries."[40] Why is this so? Because no created mind can by any means possess the capacity to understand all; but as soon as it has discovered a small fragment of what it is seeking, it again sees other things that must be sought for; and if in turn it comes to know these, it will again see arising out of them many more things that demand investigation.[41]

Ultimately, the Scriptures escaped human grasp because God, who helped author these writings, was incomprehensible to created minds. "The creature does not take in what God takes in."[42] "God's wisdom," Origen preaches elsewhere, "is incomprehensible and beyond reckoning," so that "there is no end for those who are energetic in their pursuit of wisdom and knowledge—for what limit will there be to God's wisdom?"[43] Origen often announced some variant of this motif in his writings, that human knowledge of the divine mysteries in this life, including the knowledge to be gleaned from the Scriptures, was woefully incomplete.[44] Given, then, the inability of human minds to plumb the depths of God's wisdom, and the entry-level knowledge conveyed by Scripture, it was to a greater and more complete knowledge in the next life that Origen directed his readers. Life in the world to come would provide opportunities to strengthen what was fleetingly gathered in this life.

What was this future life like?[45] While it was understandably hard to imagine, Origen was quick to dismiss the corporeal dreams entertained by the simpler in the church that the last state would be characterized by bodily pleasures and luxuries.[46] Rather, he envisioned this world in a strongly cognitive manner: it would be a schoolroom where minds found increasing

---

[40] PA 4.3.14/GK 776, 345.21–23.

[41] PA 4.3.14/GK 776, 345.23–346.2. Other passages on the limitations of what Paul knew, or at the least, of what he could communicate, see Hom Num 18.3; Josh 23.4; PA 2.7.4; CC 6.77.

[42] Hom Ez 14.2.4/GCS 8, 453.1.

[43] Hom Num 17.4.2/GCS 7, 160.5–9.

[44] See also Hom Josh 6.1; Hom 5.1 Ps 36; Hom 5.2 Ps 36; Hom 2.2 Ps 38; Comm Matt 17.13; Comm Jn 1.93; PA 2.3.2.

[45] For a concise orientation to Origen's eschatological thought (and its many controversies), see B. E. Daley, *The Hope of the Early Church: A Handbook of Patristic Christology* (Cambridge: Cambridge University Press, 1991), 47–60.

[46] See esp. his critique of the millenarian view of the new Jerusalem as a utopian earthly paradise at Comm Matt 17.35 and PA 2.11.1–2, as well as the discussion by C. E. Hill, *Regnum Caelorum: Patterns of Millennial Thought in Early Christianity*, 2nd edn (Grand Rapids: Eerdmans, 2001), 176–181. The corporeality (or lack thereof) of the eschatological state was closely tied to Origen's debated view of the resurrection of bodies (see esp. PA 2.2.2, 2.10.1–2; CC 5.18–23; Comm Matt 17.29 where he argues for a rarified, spiritual body). Origen wrote a treatise on the resurrection and two dialogues on the theme, though these do not survive intact (PA 2.10.1; CC 6.20; Eusebius, HE 6.24.3). For orientation to this issue, see H. Chadwick, "Origen, Celsus and the resurrection of the body," *HTR* 41 (1948): 83–102; A. Le Boulluec, "De la croissance selon les Stoïciens à la resurrection selon Origène," *Revue des études grecques* 88 (1975): 143–155; H. Crouzel, "La Doctrine origénienne du corps résuscité," *Bulletin de Littérature Ecclésiastique* 81 (1980): 175–200, 241–266.

enlightenment.[47] This proposal is hardly surprising given Origen's dictum that the end would resemble the beginning. If the beginning was characterized by an intellectual activity—minds contemplating God and God's Word—then something similar should transpire at the end. But Origen also advances his schoolroom thesis by reminding his more earthly minded readers that growth in knowledge was the satisfaction of humanity's deepest desire, since "an eager longing for the reality of things is natural to us and implanted in our soul."[48] He draws an analogy to help convey how deeply oriented humans are toward intellectual inquiry. When people encounter a fascinating object crafted by an artisan, they burn with desire to know the "design, the why or how or for what uses a thing is made [*ratio quidem, quid vel qualiter vel ad quos usus fiat*]."[49] All these deeper secrets lie hidden within the mind of the craftsman.

Much more, and beyond all comparison, does the mind burn with unspeakable longing to learn the design of those things which we perceive to have been made by God. This longing, this love has, we believe, undoubtedly been implanted in us by God; and as the eye naturally demands light and vision and our body by its nature desires food and drink, so our mind cherishes a natural and appropriate longing to know God's truth and to learn the causes of things.[50]

This longing, Origen concludes, would never have been given to us if it were not, one day, to be satisfied, "for in that case the 'love of truth' [cf. 2 Thess 2:10] would appear to have been implanted in our mind by God the Creator to no purpose, if its gratification is never to be accomplished."[51] The eschaton will fulfill humanity's deepest intellectual longing.

If the eschatological journey would run through a classroom, what relationship was there between this future scholastic enterprise and the learning that transpired in this life? Origen clearly envisioned a continuum of intellectual

---

[47] PA 2.11.6 (and discussion below). For other passages where Origen closely juxtaposes some facet of eschatological life with education, see PA 1.6.1, 2.3.1, 2.3.7; Hom Ex 6.4; Hom Num 25.6; Hom Ez 1.3; PE 29.15. At the same time, it is important to stress that Origen also envisions the eschaton in relational terms. In that final state, people will not simply know God, they will also live in communion and friendship with God (see esp. Comm Jn 19.24; PA 1.3.8; CC 3.81), so that they will achieve the ultimate aim of resembling God (see PA 2.6.2, 2.11.7, 3.6.1, 3.6.3; Comm Jn 20.47).

[48] PA 2.11.4/GK 444, 186.23–24.

[49] PA 2.11.4/GK 444, 187.2–3.

[50] PA 2.11.4/GK 446, 187.9–15.

[51] PA 2.11.4/GK 446, 187.15–18. In the concluding lines of *On First Principles* Origen revisits this topic, stressing the profoundly intellectual constitution of humans and how they will grow in knowledge in the ages to come. He offers a startlingly vivid image: as minds made in the image of God (who is the supreme Mind), humans "have a kind of blood-relationship with God [*consanguinitatem quandam . . . ad deum*]; and since God knows all things and not a single intellectual truth can escape his notice . . . it is possible that a rational mind also, by advancing from a knowledge of small to a knowledge of greater things and from things visible to things invisible, may attain to an increasingly perfect understanding" (PA 4.4.10/GK 818, 363.29–820, 364.4). Note esp. the discussion of the affinity between our minds and God who is Mind at PA 1.1.6–7.

activity that bridged this life with the next. Since humans were created to quest for knowledge, already "in this life men devote themselves with great labour to sacred and religious studies," among which Origen surely counted scriptural scholarship.[52] What they learn now overlaps with their future curriculum, albeit only partially since "they obtain only some small fragments out of the immeasurable treasures of divine knowledge."[53] Nevertheless, what they learn now prepares them for what they will learn later. From their "sacred and religious" scholarship "they derive much assistance from the fact that by turning their mind to the study and love of truth they render themselves more capable of receiving instruction in the future."[54] Students, and especially students of the Christian Scriptures, have enrolled in a sort of advanced placement course for their future studies in the eschatological schoolroom.[55]

Origen offers a précis of the curriculum in the future schoolroom that further demonstrates how it continues, and deepens, the scriptural message to be discerned in this life. He envisions two eschatological schoolrooms located in the two main places or regions of this world: the earth and the heavens. When people have departed this life and have become sufficiently purified, they will remain on earth and begin their instruction in "Paradise." "This will be a place of instruction and, so to speak, a lecture room or school for souls [*auditorio vel schola animarum*], in which they may be taught about all that they had seen on earth."[56] The curriculum is understandably wide-ranging: it includes humans and their constitution as embodied souls or minds; it concerns nations such as Israel, their twelve tribes, and especially the institutions and activities of the Jewish cult; it also concerns the entire animal and plant kingdoms, as well as the angelic and demonic forces.[57] Origen repeatedly asserts that souls or minds will progress at varying rates through the future classrooms depending on their virtue and intellectual ardor.[58] Once they have qualified to leave their earthly schoolroom they will ascend through the air to the schoolroom in heaven where they will learn about celestial bodies (the stars in particular) and mysterious incorporeal

---

[52] PA 2.11.4/GK 446, 187.18–19.   [53] PA 2.11.4/GK 446, 187.19–20.

[54] PA 2.11.4/GK 446, 187.23–24.

[55] In the subsequent lines Origen develops an interesting analogy to further secure this point. He likens human inquiry in this life and the next to a canvas. An artist will first prepare a canvas with light pencil markings to indicate where the later brush strokes will apply their permanent colors. So it is with people who investigate the cosmos and its Creator in this life. They are more prepared for their eschatological instruction than those who do not make such inquiries since their lives—the canvas—have been prepared with the pencil markings of scholarship in this life. On this passage, and particularly Christ's role in facilitating learning in this life and the next, see B. Studer, "Loving Christ according to Origen and Augustine," *In the Shadow of the Incarnation: Essays on Jesus Christ in the Early Church in Honor of Brian E. Daley, S.J.*, ed. P. W. Martens (Notre Dame: University of Notre Dame Press, 2008), 149–175.

[56] PA 2.11.6/GK 452, 190.1–5.

[57] PA 2.11.5.   [58] See PA 2.11.6; 3.6.6; 3.6.9.

realities.[59] The eschatological curriculum is focused, in short, on all that has transpired on earth and heaven. As such, it is also decidedly focused on the Scriptures to the extent that they narrated many of the aforementioned themes.

Yet there is another, more profound way in which this encyclopedic curriculum touches upon the Scriptural message: it directs pupils to the figure who serves as the overarching theme of Scripture, the Word or Wisdom of God. Origen is insistent that in the aforementioned earthly and heavenly schoolrooms students will receive a "twofold form [*utriusque modi*]" of knowledge.[60] By this expression he means that they will first receive a wide-ranging orientation to all the realities of earth, air, and heaven—to *what* transpires—and thereafter learn about the "reasons" or "causes" that help explain *why* or *how* these realities exist.[61] It is important to stress that for Origen these reasons or causes for the creation were profoundly Christological. Earlier in *On First Principles* he offers an account of Christ's preeminent characteristic or aspect: he is the "Wisdom of God." In this Wisdom, "there was implicit every capacity and form of the creation that was to be." All created things "had been as it were outlined and prefigured" in Wisdom so that it contained within itself "both the beginnings and causes and species of the whole creation."[62] It was in light of this divine blueprint that God, with the help of Wisdom, created the cosmos. Thus, in studying the creation, eschatological students were eventually oriented to the second part of that "twofold form of knowledge": God's Wisdom, who contained the reasons or causes for all things, and through whom all these things came to be. Not surprisingly, Origen identifies God's Word or Wisdom as the eschatological instructor.[63] He teaches pupils his handiwork, and in so doing, grants them through the cosmos an indirect glimpse of himself.[64] In

---

[59] PA 2.11.6–7.   [60] PA 2.11.6/GK 452, 189.21.

[61] PA 2.11.6/GK 452, 189.20–31. For other statements about discerning the deeper causes of things, see PA 2.11.3–5.

[62] PA 1.2.2/GK 124, 30.2–126, 30.9. Note the similar account of Wisdom at Comm Jn 1.109–115, 1.243–246, 19.147; PA 1.4.3–5, 2.6.7; CC 5.39. On this theme, see M. Fédou, *La sagesse et la monde: Essai sur la christologie d'Origène* (Paris: Desclée, 1995).

[63] On God's Word as the eschatological instructor, see PA 1.3.8, 1.6.3, 2.11.4–5, 3.6.8–9, 4.3.14; Comm Matt Ser 51. This pedagogical activity is a continuation of the Word's earthly ministry (see esp. PA 3.5.4–6, 3.5.8) and his continuing ministry in the church (see 2.11.4, and those passages discussed above in Chapter 8 in the sections "Divine aid" and "Prayer" about the interpreter's encounter with the Word).

[64] In this indirect perception of God's Wisdom through the cosmos, Origen occasionally notes that pupils also catch a glimpse of God himself (and in these contexts he will correspondingly refer to God as the eschatological instructor—see PA 2.11.7). When Origen explains what he means by this "twofold form of knowledge" he illustrates his point with the analogy of a craftsman already discussed above. While inquisitive pupils begin superficially with whatever object a craftsman has made, what they are really after is "the design, the why or how or for what uses a thing is made." This design, Origen notes, "lies in the mind" of the craftsman. By implication, a deeper inquiry into the design of the cosmos is an inquiry into God who *is* mind (PA 1.1.6, 2.11.4; note the similar analogy at Comm Jn 1.114). Recall also Origen's

short, in the earthly and heavenly schoolrooms, pupils do not abandon the themes they encountered in scriptural inquiry, but rather deepen their know-ledge of them as they grapple more effectively with the created realities narrated in Scripture and, ultimately through these realities, catch a glimpse of their "cause" or "reason," the Word of God, the master theme in Scripture.[65]

Yet this is an indirect glimpse of the Word since it is a view refracted through his handiwork. Once the mind has passed through the eschatological schoolrooms and achieved a capacity for direct contemplation,[66] it arrives at the climax of this curriculum: direct, personal contemplation, first of the Word, and then of God. In this life, the Word of God is encountered usually as a theme in the pages of Scripture. In the future schoolrooms, the Word will be encountered primarily through his handiwork. Not so in the final stages of the eschaton. Only then will the saints gaze directly upon Christ—something seldom (if ever) experienced by them before. Moreover, they will gaze upon the glorified Christ whom Scripture rarely portrayed.[67] It is one thing to know Christ according to his first coming, when he came in humility and took on the form of a servant (Phil 2:7). It is quite another, Origen insists, to perceive him in his more splendid second coming in which he will be enshrouded in his Father's glory (cf. Matt 16:27).[68] And again, it is one thing to "'know nothing except Jesus Christ, and him crucified' [1 Cor 2:2]," but quite another to

---

references to pupils discerning God's providence when they study the creation in the future schoolroom (PA 2.11.5–7), as well as his discussion earlier at PA 1.1.6 of how God is discerned through creation: "So, too, the works of divine providence and the plan of this universe are as it were rays of God's nature in contrast to his real substance and being, and because our mind is of itself unable to behold God as he is, it understands the parent of the universe from the beauty of his works and the comeliness of his creatures" (GK 108, 21.5–9).

[65] It is interesting to observe that in *On First Principles* Origen offers another, and somewhat different, account of the eschatological curriculum. However, it is just as clear with this account that the future curriculum is an extension of scriptural study in this life. In this different account Origen speculates that the saints will be instructed in the "eternal law" and "eternal gospel" in the eschatological schoolrooms on earth and heaven respectively (PA 3.6.8). In the earthly school-room the focus will be on what the law symbolized, the "true and eternal law," which Origen understands to be the "true and living forms" according to which the Jewish liturgy was patterned. The heavenly schoolroom, in turn, will attend to the "eternal gospel" whose content is here left unspecified, but almost certainly points to the loftier mysteries of Jesus symbolized by his earthly words and deeds (see esp. Comm Jn 1.39–40, and n. 70 below on the eternal gospel). In short, in the earthly and heavenly schoolrooms, the saints will delve into the deeper mysteries symbolized by the law and gospel respectively. By comparison, in his other more developed schema discussed above, the eschatological curriculum is devoted to the realities on earth and in heaven (to which Scripture testifies) and their underlying cause (the theme of Scripture, the Wisdom or Word of God). While there are unmistakable differences in these two versions of the eschatological curriculum, both are strongly oriented in their own ways to deepening pupils' perception of the scriptural message in the afterlife.

[66] PA 2.11.7/GK 456, 191.20–192.1.

[67] The transfiguration scene in the gospels is the notable exception. See the discussions of this scene in the previous chapter.

[68] PA 4.3.13/GK 770, 343.19–21.

contemplate the "Word who returned from being made flesh to what 'he was in the beginning with God' [Jn 1:2]."[69] Corresponding to these two phases in the ministry of the Word were two gospels. Those who know Christ according to his earthly ministry know him as he is portrayed in the "temporal gospel." But this gospel also symbolizes the "eternal gospel" (Rev 14:6) that conveys the deeper mysteries associated with the same Christ in his glorified state, a gospel that is reserved for those who contemplate the Son "face to face."[70] It is this personal encounter with the Son or Word in the eternal gospel to which the saints aspire. Only in the eschaton will Christ fully reveal, and his followers fully perceive, his glorious divinity and highest aspects.[71] Then the "saints shall be counted worthy to behold" Christ, who is "the glory of God and the causes and truth of things."[72] Then will minds encounter and receive Christ's highest aspects: Righteousness, Wisdom, and Knowledge.[73]

The culmination of the curriculum is the direct encounter with God. "There will be one activity for those who come to be with God through the Word who is with him: to perceive God [κατανοεῖν τὸν θεόν]."[74] This is different from perceiving God through the lens of the creation or Scripture. It is also different from perceiving God through the lens of the Son. For indeed, while it is true that the one who sees the Son sees the Father (cf. Jn 14:9),

> there will be a time when one will see the Father and the things with the Father as the Son sees them. Then he will be an eyewitness, as it were, of the Father and of the Father's things in a manner similar to the Son, and will no longer conceive of the things concerning God, of whom the Son is the image, from the image.[75]

This "eyewitness" encounter takes place when Christ advances his pupils to God after they have learned all they can from him and have been adequately

---

[69] Comm Jn 1.43/GCS 4, 13.8–10—Heine modified.

[70] Comm Jn 1.39–40/GCS 4, 12.9–19 (where the implication is that this eternal gospel can be grasped at least partially already now in this life—note esp. 1.44). However, at PA 4.3.13 Origen suggests this eternal gospel is properly eschatological. Only at the second coming of Christ will he "transfer all the saints from the temporal to the eternal gospel" (GK 772, 344.5–6). For the law symbolizing the gospel, and the latter symbolizing realities in the future age to come: Hom Josh 8.4; Hom 2.2 Ps 38; Comm Matt 12.3; Comm Rom 1.4.1. For more on this eternal gospel, see H. de Lubac, *History and Spirit*, 247–259.

[71] For passages on the direct, eschatological gaze upon the Word of God (often with an emphasis on the supremacy of this encounter over what was gleaned beforehand), see Hom Josh 8.4; Comm Matt Ser 18, 86; Comm Jn 19.59; PA 1.3.8, 2.3.2, 2.6.7, 3.6.8–9; CC 2.67, etc.

[72] PA 2.6.7/GK 372, 147.9–12—Butterworth modified. See the related passage at PA 1.1.2.

[73] PA 1.3.8, 2.3.2, 3.6.9. When Origen casts the Son as the object of eschatological knowledge, it is important to perceive how he is drawing a thread through the whole drama of salvation. In the beginning, it was only Jesus' mind that perfectly contemplated God's Word (so much so that it became one with the Word); in the middle of the drama, interpreters are called to contemplate God's written Word; this activity, in turn, leads to the contemplation of the living Word at the end. Here, in the eschaton, minds are at last apprenticed to what Jesus' mind mastered at the beginning.

[74] Comm Jn 1.92/GCS 4, 20.15–16—transl. mine.

[75] Comm Jn 20.47/GCS 4, 334.26–29.

purified.[76] Then they will stand alongside Christ, and not behind him (as it were), gazing upon the everlasting God. Visual imagery gives way to festal imagery when Origen ruminates on the *telos* of human existence. The heavenly banquet promised in Scripture (Prov 9:1–5) is this eschatological contemplation of God. Once the mind has reached the last station on its long journey, it will be nourished by the "food" of this banquet, but not the food that corporeal imaginations think awaits in heaven: "But in all respects this food must be understood to be the contemplation and understanding of God [*theoria et intellectus dei*]."[77] In so contemplating God, minds complete and perfect the instruction from Scripture that transpired in this life, and at last resume their prelapsarian activity: the end finally mirrors the beginning.

In this chapter I have rounded out Origen's profile of the scriptural interpreter by demonstrating how this figure's scholarship in this life was bracketed by similar activities in the worlds that preceded and followed this life. With Origen's dictum again in mind, that "the end is always like the beginning," it is now clear how scriptural scholarship in the "middle" *also* resembled the two epochs that bookended it. The drama of salvation was a threefold act in which the exegetical enterprise occupied privileged space in the middle act. Those who took up scriptural exegesis resumed a flickering version of the primordial activity that they had once abandoned. Indeed, their here-and-now scholarship of the written Word of God served as a remedy for their deficient beginnings, in that they gradually reversed their original fall, the cessation of their contemplation of God's Word. At the same time, the pursuit of biblical scholarship in this life was not an end in itself, since interpreters would never fully plumb the depths of these Scriptures. The final state offered these interpreters an opportunity to resume the scholarship they now practiced in the middle act. Once they left this life behind, they would continue their journey through a series of schoolrooms that extended and deepened the knowledge they gained from Scripture in this life. The culmination of this curriculum would be nothing less than the direct encounter with the overarching theme of the Scriptures, the Word of God, and the supreme author and cause of all things: God. Then, and only then, would interpreters be restored to their original loving and contemplative communion with God, practicing in the end what they had fleetingly experienced in this life when they studied Scripture.

---

[76] See PA 1.3.8, 3.6.9; Comm Jn 1.92, 20.47–48.
[77] PA 2.11.7/GK 456, 192.10–11. For the same imagery, see PA 2.11.3.

11

Epilogue

My principal aim in this study has been to offer a dynamic and composite portrait of the scriptural interpreter as Origen understood this figure. By focusing on the neglected interpreter, the center from which the whole exegetical enterprise emerged, I have contended that we position ourselves well for discerning Origen's sweeping and integrative vision of scriptural exegesis as a distinctive way of life. On the basis of a wide examination of his writings, I have demonstrated that the overarching context in which he situated biblical scholars—himself included—was the Christian drama of salvation. Scholarly competence was certainly an indelible feature of Origen's profile of the ideal scriptural scholar (Part 1). Yet such a profile fails to capture the richness of his portrait of this figure. For Origen, ideal interpreters were more than scholars. Their profile also included a commitment to Christianity from which they gathered a range of loyalties, guidelines, dispositions, relationships, and doctrines that tangibly shaped how they practiced and thought about their biblical scholarship. As I demonstrated in a variety of ways, Origen's ideal interpreters also participated in this drama of salvation by examining it as it was conveyed on Scripture's pages (Part 2). Biblical exegesis afforded Christian philologists an occasion through which to express various facets of their existing Christian commitment. The dispositions, loyalties, and doctrines encouraged by their faith also colored their scriptural exegesis. Moreover, inquiry into Scripture's saving message was one of the privileged means by which these interpreters received divine resources for their continued journey in this faith. In short, the exegetical project for Origen was a way of life, a way of salvation, culminating in the vision of God.

The ancient Christian project of scriptural interpretation remains for many today an irreducibly foreign affair. Whether quaintly exotic or alarmingly alien, much of the approach to Scripture in early Christianity continues to puzzle its modern onlookers. Some responsibility for this cognitive dissonance rests, no doubt, with the long passage of time. Yet primary responsibility rests elsewhere. The emergence of modern professional biblical scholarship in the seventeenth century has probably hindered discernment of the patterns that shaped ancient professional biblical scholarship more than anything else. There can be little doubt that in its formative period, the architects and leading practitioners of modern biblical interpretation explicitly framed their emerging approach to Scripture as, at least in part, a critique and rejection of the centuries-long approach to Scripture that Origen (and many others) helped shape. There emerged an abrupt disjuncture between how Origen (and others) thought about and practiced biblical scholarship, and how biblical scholarship came to be thought about and practiced today. Now, roughly three centuries later, Origen's exegetical enterprise unmistakably resides on the other side of this watershed event. It does not surprise, then, given the training most of us have received in professional scriptural scholarship, that Origen's approach to the Bible appears, at first blush, flatly misguided. Even to those more forbearing, it mystifies. I certainly do not pretend to have defended his view of, or approach to, scriptural interpretation in this study. But I have intended to render this strange intellectual and spiritual exercise intelligible to the modern ear. And if I have succeeded, I hope also to have facilitated a greater appreciation and more thoughtful assessment of Origen's approach to biblical scholarship.

It is also my hope that this study will have implications that reach beyond Origen. He was not simply a prolific practitioner and theoretician of scriptural interpretation. He also exercised remarkable influence over the subsequent exegetical and hermeneutical traditions in Christianity. While his vision of this discipline might not always neatly overlap with how other interpreters thought or went about scriptural interpretation, it stands to reason that, in many cases, it did. Origen cast a long shadow over the history of biblical interpretation. The Greek- and Latin-speaking worlds read, anthologized, translated, and debated his interpretations of Scripture at great length. Despite protests from a handful of (mostly) Antiochene biblical scholars and posthumous ecclesiastical condemnation, he enjoyed a vast and sympathetic reception through the subsequent centuries of Greek and Latin biblical scholarship.[1] In the fourth century, for instance, some of his most important hermeneutical reflections were collected in the *Philocalia*, the first anthology of any Christian author's writings.[2] By the end of that century, Latin Christians clamored for Origen's biblical scholarship and Rufinus and Jerome obliged, translating vast tracts of his exegetical corpus, thereby initiating the Latin world into Christianity's first professional interpreter of Scripture.[3]

---

[1] For orientation to the Antiochene school and its critique of Origen, see S. Hidal, "Exegesis of the Old Testament in the Antiochene School with its prevalent literal and historical method," in M. Saebo, *Hebrew Bible/Old Testament: The History of Its Interpretation*, vol. 1: *From the Beginnings to the Middle Ages (Until 1300)*, part 1: *Antiquity* (Göttingen: Vandenhoeck & Ruprecht, 1996), 543–568 (with bibliography). On the condemnation of Origen, see the literature in Chapter 1, n. 61.

[2] The best overview of this anthology remains M. Harl's introduction to her edition of this work: SC 302, 19–157.

[3] See, for instance, Rufinus' translator's preface to *On First Principles*, 1 (GK 72, 31–35). For a general orientation to this vast issue (with bibliography), see C. Jacob, "The Reception of the

Nor was Origen's influence as a biblical scholar confined to antiquity. P. D. Huet, author of the first modern scholarly treatment of Origen, approvingly passed on the effusive sentiments of the *Suda*, the sprawling tenth-century Byzantine encyclopedia: he expounded Scripture with such erudition that "from him all subsequent teachers of the church have taken their starting-point."[4] Concerning the medieval West, Beryl Smalley insisted similarly that "to write a history of Origenist influence on the west would be tantamount to writing a history of western exegesis."[5] Origen certainly serves as *a* paragon of early Christian biblical scholarship. Thus, to come to terms with scriptural interpretation as he understood and practiced it, we also reacquaint ourselves with a long and influential trajectory of scriptural interpretation within Christianity.[6]

Finally, this study points back to us, should we allow it to do so. There are unquestionably sharp differences between Origen's account of the Christian exegetical enterprise and those that circulate today in professional circles. Some of these are important differences in detail, perhaps none more famous than his assessment of allegory and Scripture's divine authorship. But these incendiary topics can easily become convenient ways to dismiss Origen prematurely, without ever letting him engage us on a more profound level. I have tried to create a space in this study for Origen's modern readers where they can access him on a more fundamental, far-reaching level: his overarching vision of scriptural scholars as participants in the Christian drama of salvation. This thesis throws into sharp relief how Origen's exegetical project appears so foreign, at least to some of us. At the same time, it also holds out a

---

Origenist Tradition in Latin Exegesis," in M. Saebo, ed., *Hebrew Bible/Old Testament: The History of its Interpretation*, 690–700.

[4] P. D. Huet, *Origeniana*, reprinted in *PG* 17.634–1384: II.i.1 (699). Citing *Suidae Lexicon*, ed. A. Adler, vol. 3 (Leipzig: Teubner, 1933), entry 182, 618.37–619.1.

[5] B. Smalley, *The Study of the Bible in the Middle Ages* (Oxford: Basil Blackwell, 1952), 14. Also see H. de Lubac, *Exégèse Médiévale: Les quatre sens de l'Écriture*, 4 vols. (Paris: Aubier, 1959–1964); H. Leclerq, "The exposition and exegesis of Scripture: From Gregory the Great to St. Bernard," in *Cambridge History of the Bible*, vol. 2 (Cambridge: Cambridge University Press, 1969), 183–197; on Origen in the *Glossa Ordinaria*, see A. Siegmund, *Die Überlieferung der griechischen christlichen Literatur in der lateinischen Kirche bis zum zwölften Jahrhundert* (Munich: Filger, 1949), 110–123. Origen's exegesis continued to exercise an influence in the Renaissance. On this theme, see M. Schär, *Das Nachleben des Origenes im Zeitalter des Humanismus* (Basel: Helbing & Lichtenhahn, 1979). For his influence on Erasmus, see A. Godin, *Érasme lecteur d'Origène* (Geneva: Droz, 1982). While M. Luther was famously critical of Origen's approach to Scripture, it is important to note that not all Protestant Reformers were as critical of him. See, for instance, A. Schindler, on U. Zwingli in *Zwingli und die Kirchenväter* (Zurich: Kommissionsverlag Beer, 1984), 27, 48, 96.

[6] For brief overviews of the history of Origen's influence, consult the "Origenismo" articles by B. Studer, G. Lettieri, E. Prinzivalli, and P. Bettiolo in *Origene: Dizionario. La cultura-il pensiero-le opere*, ed. A. M. Castagno (Rome: Città Nuova, 2000), as well as L. Perrone, s.v. "Origenismus," in *Religion in Geschichte und Gegenwart*, 4th edn, vol. 6, ed. H. D. Betz (Tübingen: Mohr Siebeck, 2003), 662–666.

mirror that clearly identifies some of our deepest convictions—or perhaps they are only assumptions?—about the discipline of scriptural scholarship. It seems to me that the challenge Origen presents to Christian theologians and biblical scholars today is whether they wish to join him in contextualizing the project of biblical scholarship within the Christian drama of salvation. If no, then why not? If so, then how? These are difficult questions, but they are also accessible ones, and in asking them we do more than gesture at Christianity's premodern encounter with Scripture—we take this encounter seriously. Whether ancient interpreters of Scripture (like Origen), who reside on the other side of the modern exegetical revolution, will enter into this conversation is a matter for others to decide. Yet should that conversation ever arise in earnest, one can only hope that voices like his will be heard.

Bibliography

Origen: An Orientation

Bibliographies

Crouzel, H. *Bibliographie critique d'Origène*. Instrumenta Patristica 8. The Hague: Nijhoff, 1971.

———. *Bibliographie critique d'Origène: Supplément 1*. Instrumenta Patristica 8a. The Hague: Nijhoff, 1982.

———. *Bibliographie critique d'Origène: Supplément 2*. Instrumenta Patristica 8b. Turnhout: Brepols, 1996.

Farina, R. *Bibliografia origeniana, 1960–1970*. Turin: Società editrice internazionale, 1971.

Overviews of the Literature

Berner, U. *Origenes*. Erträge der Forschung, no. 147. Darmstadt: Wissenschaftliche Buchgesellschaft, 1981.

Crouzel, H. "Les études sur Origène des douze dernières années." *EThR* 58 (1983): 97–107.

———. "The Literature on Origen: 1970–1988." *TS* 49 (1988): 499–516.

———. "Patrologie et renouveau patristique." In *Bilan de la Théologie du XXe Siècle*, ed. R. Vander Gucht and H. Vorgrimler, vol. 2, 661–683. Paris: Casterman, 1971.

Heither, T. "Origenes Als Exeget: Ein Forschungsüberblick." In *Stimuli: Exegese und ihre Hermeneutik in Antike und Christentum. Festschrift für E. Dassmann*, ed. G. Schöllgen and C. Scholten, 141–153. Münster: Aschendorff, 1996.

Lies, L. "Zum Stand heutiger Origenesforschung." *ZKTh* 102 (1980): 61–75, 190–205.

———. "Zum derzeitigen Stand der Origenesforschung." *ZKTh* 115 (1993): 37–62.

Trigg, J. W. "A Decade of Origen Studies." *Religious Studies Review* 7 (1981): 21–27.

———. "Origen and Origenism in the 1990s." *Religious Studies Review* 22 (1996): 301–308.

Additional Aids

Reference Works

Castagno, A. M., ed. *Origene: Dizionario. La cultura-il pensiero-le opere*. Rome: Città Nuova, 2000.

McGuckin, J. A., ed. *The Westminster Handbook to Origen*. Louisville: Westminster John Knox Press, 2004.

Journals

Adamantius: The International Journal of Origen and the Alexandrian Tradition 1 (1995–).

Origeniana Series [Orig I–IX]

Crouzel, H., G. Lomiento, and J. Rius-Camps, eds. *Origeniana: Premier Colloque International des Études Origèniennes (Montserrat, 18–21 septembre 1973)*. Bari: Istituto di letteratura cristiana antica, Università di Bari, 1975.

Crouzel, H. and A. Quacquarelli, eds. *Origeniana Secunda: Second Colloque International des Études Origèniennes (Bari, 20–23 septembre 1979)*. Rome: Edizioni dell'Ateneo, 1980.

Hanson, R. P. C. and H. Crouzel, eds. *Origeniana Tertia: The Third International Colloque for Origen Studies (University of Manchester, September 7–11, 1981)*. Rome: Edizioni dell'Ateneo, 1985.

Lies, L., ed. *Origeniana Quarta: Die Referate des 4. Internationalem Origeneskongresses (Innsbruck, 2–6 September 1984)*. Innsbruck: Tyrolia-Verlag, 1987.

Daly, R. J., ed. *Origeniana Quinta: Papers of the 5th International Origen Congress (Boston College, 14–18 August 1989)*. Louvain: Peeters, 1992.

Dorival, G. and A. Le Boulluec, eds. *Origeniana Sexta: Origène et la Bible. Acts du Colloquium Origenianum Sextum (Chantilly, 30 août – 3 septembre 1993)*. Louvain: Peeters, 1995.

Bienert, W. and U. Kühneweg, eds. *Origeniana Septima: Origenes in den Auseinandersetzungen des 4. Jahrhunderts*. Louvain: Peeters, 1999.

Perrone, L., P. Bernardino, and D. Marchini, eds. *Origeniana Octava: Origen and the Alexandrian tradition = Origene e la tradizione alessandrina : Papers of the 8th International Origen Congress, Pisa, 27–31 August 2001*. Louvain: Peeters, 2003.

Heidl, G. and R. Somos (in collaboration with C. Németh), eds. *Origeniana Nona: Origen and the Religious Practice of his Time (Papers of the 9th International Origen Congress, Pécs, Hungary, 29 August – 2 September 2005)*. Louvain: Peeters, 2009.

Ancient Authors

Origen: Editions and Translations[1]

Homilies on Genesis [Hom Gen]

Baehrens, W. A. *Origenes Werke 6: Homilien zum Hexateuch in Rufins Übersetzung.* Part 1: *Die Homilien zu Genesis, Exodus, Leviticus.* Leipzig: J. C. Hinrichs, 1920, 1–144.

Origen. *Homilies on Genesis and Exodus*, transl. R. E. Heine, FOTC 71. Washington: Catholic University of America Press, 1982, 47–224.

Homilies on Exodus [Hom Ex]

Baehrens, W. A. *Origenes Werke 6: Homilien zum Hexateuch in Rufins Übersetzung.* Part 1: *Die Homilien zu Genesis, Exodus, Leviticus.* Leipzig: J. C. Hinrichs, 1920, 145–279.

Origen. *Homilies on Genesis and Exodus*, transl. R. E. Heine, FOTC 71. Washington: Catholic University of America Press, 1982, 227–387.

Homilies on Leviticus [Hom Lev]

Baehrens, W. A. *Origenes Werke 6: Homilien zum Hexateuch in Rufins Übersetzung.* Part 1: *Die Homilien zu Genesis, Exodus, Leviticus.* Leipzig: J. C. Hinrichs, 1920, 280–507.

---

[1] For a more complete listing of works and editions (esp. fragments from Origen's homilies and commentaries), see M. Geerard, ed., *Clavis Patrum Graecorum*, vol. 1 (Turnhout: Brepols, 1983), 141–186 (nr. 1410–1525).

In keeping with a widespread custom in the Origenian scholarship, I have cited the GCS volumes according to their numeration in the "Origenes Werke" series, and not according to their overall numeration in the GCS series.

Origen. *Homilies on Leviticus*, transl. G. W. Barkley, FOTC 83. Washington: Catholic University of America Press, 1990.

Homilies on Numbers [Hom Num]
Baehrens, W. A. *Origenes Werke 6: Homilien zum Hexateuch in Rufins Übersetzung*. Part 2: *Die Homilien zu Numeri, Josua und Judices*. Leipzig: J. C. Hinrichs, 1921, 3–285.
Origen. *Origen: An Exhortation to Martyrdom, Prayer, First Principles: Book IV, Prologue to the Commentary on the Song of Songs, Homily 27 on Numbers*, transl. and intro. R. A. Greer, pref. H. U. von Balthasar. Mahwah, NJ: Paulist, 1979, 245–269 (used for the translation on the twenty-seventh homily, otherwise used Scheck's translation below).
Origen. *Homilies on Numbers*, transl. T. P. Scheck, ed. C. A. Hall, Ancient Christian Texts. Downers Grove, IL: InterVarsity, 2009.

Homiles on Joshua [Hom Josh]
Baehrens, W. A. *Origenes Werke 6: Homilien zum Hexateuch in Rufins Übersetzung*. Part 2: *Die Homilien zu Numeri, Josua und Judices*. Leipzig: J. C. Hinrichs, 1921, 286–463.
Origen. *Homilies on Joshua*, transl. B. J. Bruce and ed. C. White, FOTC 105. Washington: Catholic University of America Press, 2002.

Homilies on Judges [Hom Jd]
Baehrens, W. A. *Origenes Werke 6: Homilien zum Hexateuch in Rufins Übersetzung*. Part 2: *Die Homilien zu Numeri, Josua und Judices*. Leipzig: J. C. Hinrichs, 1921, 464–522.
Origen. *Homilies on Judges*, transl. E. A. Dively Lauro, FOTC 119. Washington: Catholic University of America Press, 2010.

Homilies on Samuel [Hom Sam]
Nautin, P. and M.-T. Nautin. *Homélies Sur Samuel*. SC 328. Paris: Cerf, 1986.
Trigg, J. W. *Origen*. London: Routledge, 1998, 199–209.

Homilies on Psalms 36–38 [Hom Ps 36–38]
Prinzivalli, E. *Origene, Omelie sui Salmi. Homiliae in Psalmos XXXVI–XXXVII–XXXVIII*. Florence: Nardini, 1991.
Heintz, M. *The Pedagogy of the Soul: Origen's* Homilies on the Psalms. Dissertation. University of Notre Dame. November 2007.

Fragments on Psalm 118 from the Catena
Harl, M. and G. Dorival. *La chaîne palestinienne sur le Psaume 118*. Vol. 1. SC 189. Paris: Cerf, 1972.

Homilies on the Song of Songs [Hom Song of Songs]
Baehrens, W. A. *Origenes Werke 8: Homilien zu Samuel 1, zum Hohelied und zu den Propheten, Kommentar zum Hohelied in Rufins und Hieronymus' Übersetzung*. Leipzig: J. C. Hinrichs, 1925, 27–60.
Origen. *The Song of Songs: Commentary and Homilies*, transl. R. P. Lawson, ACW 26. New York: Newman Press, 1957, 265–305.

Commentary on the Song of Songs [Comm Song of Songs]

Baehrens, W. A. *Origenes Werke 8: Homilien zu Samuel 1, zum Hohelied und zu den Propheten, Kommentar zum Hohelied in Rufins und Hieronymus' Übersetzung.* Leipzig: J. C. Hinrichs, 1925, 61–241.

Origen. *The Song of Songs: Commentary and Homilies*, transl. R. P. Lawson, ACW 26. New York: Newman Press, 1957, 21–263.

Commentary (Short) on the Song of Songs [Phil 7]

Harl, M. *Philocalie, 1–20: Sur les Écritures.* SC 302. Paris: Cerf, 1983, 326 and 328.

Homilies on Isaiah [Hom Isa]

Baehrens, W. A. *Origenes Werke 8: Homilien zu Samuel 1, zum Hohelied und zu den Propheten, Kommentar zum Hohelied in Rufins und Hieronymus' Übersetzung.* Leipzig: J. C. Hinrichs, 1925, 242–289.

Homilies on Jeremiah [Hom Jer]

Nautin, P. *Homélies sur Jérémie.* SC 232, 238. Paris: Cerf, 1976–1977.

Origen. *Homilies on Jeremiah. Homilies on 1 Kings 28*, transl. J. C. Smith, FOTC 97. Washington: Catholic University of America Press, 1998, 3–273.

Homilies on Ezekiel [Hom Ez]

Baehrens, W. A. *Origenes Werke 8: Homilien zu Samuel 1, zum Hohelied und zu den Propheten, Kommentar zum Hohelied in Rufins und Hieronymus' Übersetzung.* Leipzig: J. C. Hinrichs, 1925, 319–454.

Origen. *Homilies 1–14 on Ezekiel*, transl. T. P. Scheck, ACW 62, New York: Paulist Press, 2010.

Commentary on Matthew [Comm Matt]

Klostermann, E. and E. Benz. *Origenes Werke 10: Origenes Matthäuserklärung, 1. Die griechisch erhaltenen Tomoi.* Berlin: Akademie-Verlag, 1935–1937.

Origen. *Commentary on Matthew, books 1, 2 and 10–14.* Transl. J. Patrick. ANF 9, 411–512.

Series of Commentaries (on Matthew) [Comm Matt Ser]

Klostermann, E., E. Benz, and U. Treu. *Origenes Werke 11: Origenes Matthäuserklärung, 2. Die lateinische Übersetzung der Commentariorum Series.* 2nd edn. Berlin: Akademie-Verlag, 1976.

Homilies on Luke [Hom Lk]

Rauer, M. *Origenes Werke 9: Die Homilien zu Lukas in der Übersetzung des Hieronymus und die griechischen Reste der Homilien und des Lukaskommentars.* 2nd edn. Berlin: Akademie-Verlag, 1959, 1–222.

Origen. *Homilies on Luke*, transl. J. T. Lienhardt, FOTC 94. Washington: Catholic University of America Press, 1996.

Commentary on John [Comm Jn]

Preuschen, E. *Origenes Werke 4: Der Johanneskommentar*. Leipzig: J. C. Hinrichs, 1903, 3–480.

Origen. *Commentary on the Gospel of John. Books 1–10*, transl. R. E. Heine, FOTC 80. Washington: Catholic University of America Press, 1989.

Origen. *Commentary on the Gospel of John. Books 13–32*, transl. R. E. Heine, FOTC 89. Washington: Catholic University of America Press, 1993.

Commentary on the Letter to the Romans [Comm Rom]

Hammond Bammel, C. P. *Der Römerbriefkommentar des Origenes: Kritische Ausgabe der Übersetzung Rufins*. Vols. 1–3. Freiburg: Herder, 1990, 1997, 1998.

Origen. *Commentary on the Epistle to the Romans. Books 1–5*, transl. T. P. Scheck, FOTC 103. Washington: Catholic University of America Press, 2001.

Origen. *Commentary on the Epistle to the Romans. Books 6–10*, transl. T. P. Scheck, FOTC 104. Washington: Catholic University of America Press, 2002.

Fragments on Romans [Rom Frg]

Ramsbotham, A. "The Commentary of Origen on the Epistle to the Romans." *JTS* 13 (1912): 209–224; 357–368; 14 (1913): 10–22.

Scherer, J. *Le commentaire d'Origène sur Rom. III.5–V.7 d'après les extraits du Papyrus n. 88748 du Musée du Caire et les fragments de la Philocalie et du Vaticanus gr. 762*. Cairo: L'Institut Français d'archéologie Orientale, 1957.

Commentary on 1 Corinthians [Comm Cor]

Jenkins, C. "Origen on I Corinthians." *JTS* 9 (1908): 232–247; 353–372; 500–514; 10 (1909): 29–51.

Commentary on Ephesians [Comm Eph]

Gregg, J. A. F. "The Commentary of Origen upon the Epistle to the Ephesians." *JTS* 3 (1902): 233–244; 398–420; 554–576.

Heine, R. E. *The Commentaries of Origen and Jerome on St Paul's Epistle to the Ephesians*. Oxford: Oxford University Press, 2002.

Commentary on Titus [Comm Titus]

Amacker, R. and É. Junod, eds. *Apologie pour Origène; suivi de Rufin d'aquilée sur la falsification des livres d'Origène*. SC 464. Paris: Cerf, 2002, 76–90 (sections 31, 33 and 35); 248–250 (sections 163 and 165).

Exhortation to Martyrdom [On Martyr.]

Koetschau, P. *Origenes Werke 1: Die Schrift vom Martyrium, Buch 1–4 gegen Celsus*. Leipzig: J. C. Hinrichs, 1899, 3–47.

Origen. *Origen: An Exhortation to Martyrdom, Prayer, First Principles: Book IV, Prologue to the Commentary on the Song of Songs, Homily 27 on Numbers*, transl. and intro. R. A. Greer, pref. H. U. von Balthasar. Mahwah, NJ: Paulist, 1979, 41–79.

Against Celsus [CC]

Borret, M. *Contre Celse*. SC 132, 136, 147, 150, 227. Paris: Cerf, 1967, 1968, 1969, 1969, 1976.

Origen. *Origen: Contra Celsum*, transl. H. Chadwick. Cambridge: Cambridge University Press, 1953.

On Prayer [PE]

Koetschau, P. *Origenes Werke 2: Buch 5–8 gegen Celsus, die Schrift vom Gebet.* Leipzig: J. C. Hinrichs, 1899, 297–403.

Origen. *Origen: An Exhortation to Martyrdom, Prayer, First Principles: Book IV, Prologue to the Commentary on the Song of Songs, Homily 27 on Numbers*, transl. and intro. R. A. Greer, pref. H. U. von Balthasar. Mahwah, NJ: Paulist, 1979, 81–170.

On Pascha [Pascha]

Guéraud O. and P. Nautin. *Origène: Sur la Pâque. Traité inédit publié d'après un papyrus de Toura.* Paris: Beauchesne, 1979.

Origen. *Treatise on the Passover and Dialogue with Heraclides and His Fellow Bishops on the Father, the Son, and the Soul*, transl. R. J. Daly, ACW 54. New York: Paulist, 1992, 127–156.

Dialogue with Heraclides [DH]

Scherer, J. *Entretien d'Origène avec Héraclide.* SC 67. Paris: Cerf, 1960.

Origen. *Treatise on the Passover and Dialogue with Heraclides and His Fellow Bishops on the Father, the Son, and the Soul*, transl. R. J. Daly. ACW 54. New York: Paulist, 1992, 57–78.

On First Principles [PA]

Görgemanns, H. and H. Karpp. *Origenes. Vier Bücher von den Prinzipien.* 3rd edn. Darmstadt: Wissenschaftliche Buchgesellschaft, 1992.

Origen. *Origen: On First Principles*, transl. G. W. Butterworth. Gloucester, MA: Peter Smith, 1973.

Letter to Gregory [LG]

Crouzel, H. *Grégoire le Thaumaturge: Remerciement à Origène suivi de la lettre d'Origène à Grégoire.* SC 148. Paris: Cerf, 1969, 185–194.

Trigg, J. W. *Origen.* London: Routledge, 1998, 210–213.

Letter to Friends in Alexandria [LF]

From Rufinus', *On the Corruption of Origen's Books*, in *Apologie pour Origène; suivi de Rufin d'aquilée sur la falsification des livres d'Origène*, ed. R. Amacker and É. Junod, SC 464. Paris: Cerf, 2002, 298.6–304.71.

Crouzel, H. "A Letter from Origen 'to Friends in Alexandria,'" transl. J. D. Gauthier. In *The Heritage of the Early Church: Essays in Honor of Georges Vasilievich Florovsky*, ed. D. Neiman and M. Schatkin, 135–150. Rome: Pontifical Institute for Oriental Studies, 1973.

Letter to an Unknown Addressee

Nautin, P. *Lettres et Écrivain Chrétiens des IIe et IIIe Siècles.* Paris: Cerf, 1961, 250–251.

Letter to Julius Africanus [LA]—adapting the paragraph numbering system of the critical edition.

Lange, N. R. M. de. *La lettre d'Origène à Africanus sur l'histoire de Suzanne*. SC 302. Paris: Cerf, 1983, 522–573.

Origen. "A Letter from Origen to Africanus," transl. F. Crombie. ANF 4, 386–392.

Letter to his Disparagers

Schwarz, E. *Eusebius Werke 2.2*. GCS 9.2. Leipzig: J. C. Hinrichs, 1908, 562.8–20.

Hexapla

Field, F. *Origenis Hexaplorum quae supersunt sive veterum interpretum graecorum in totum Vetus Testamentum fragmenta*. 2 Vols. Oxford: Clarendon Press, 1875.

Philocalia [Phil]

Junod, É. *Philocalie 21–27: Sur le Libre Arbitre*. SC 226. Paris: Cerf, 1976.

Harl, M. *Philocalie, 1–20: Sur les Écritures*. SC 302. Paris: Cerf, 1983.

Origen. *The Philocalia of Origen: A Compilation of Selected Passages from Origen's Works made by St. Gregory of Nazianzus and St. Basil of Caesarea*, transl. G. Lewis. Edinburgh: T. & T. Clark, 1911.

Other Ancient Writings

Celsus, True Discourse

Bader, R., ed. *Der Ἀληθὴς Λόγος des Kelsos*. Stuttgart: Kohlhammer, 1940, 39–216.

Decretum Gelasianum

Dobschütz, E. von, ed. *Das Decretum Gelasianum de libris recipiendis et non recipiendis*. Leipzig: J. C. Hinrichs, 1912.

Dionysius Thrax, Art of Philology

Uhlig, G., ed. *Dionysii Thracis: Ars Grammatica*. Grammatici Graeci, 1.1. Leipzig: B. G. Teubner, 1883; reprint, Hildesheim: Georg Olms, 1965.

Kemp, A. "The *Tekhnē Grammatikē* of Dionysius Thrax: English Translation with Introduction and Notes." In *The History of Linguistics in the Classical Period*, ed. Daniel J. Taylor, 169–189. Amsterdam: J. Benjamins, 1987.

Scholia on the Art of Philology

Hilgard, A., ed. *Scholia in Dionysii Thracis Artem Grammaticam*. Grammatici Graeci, 1.3. Leipzig: B. G. Teubner, 1901; reprint, Hildesheim: Georg Olms, 1965.

Epiphanius, Panarion

Holl, K., ed. *Epiphanius I: Panarion (haer. 1–33)*. GCS 25. Leipzig: J. C. Hinrichs, 1915.

Holl, K. and J. Dummer, eds. *Epiphanius II: Panarion (haer. 34–64)*. 2nd edn. GCS 31. Berlin: Akademie-Verlag, 1980.

Holl, K. and J. Dummer, eds. *Epiphanius III: Panarion (haer. 65–80)*. 2nd edn. GCS 37. Berlin: Akademie-Verlag, 1985.

Eusebius, *Ecclesiastical History* [*HE*]
Schwarz, E., ed. *Eusebius Werke 2: Die Kirchengeschichte*. GCS 9.1–3. Leipzig: J. C. Hinrichs, 1903–1909.
Eusebius. *Church History*, transl. A. C. McGiffert, NPNF, vol. 1, 73–387.

Gregory, Address of Thanksgiving to Origen
Crouzel, H., ed. *Grégoire le Thaumaturge: Remerciement a Origène*. SC 148. Paris: Cerf, 1969, 93–183.
Gregory. *St. Gregory Thaumaturgus: Life and Works*, transl. M. Slussler, FOTC 98. Washington, D.C.: Catholic University of America Press, 1998, 91–126.

Jerome, Apology Against Rufinus
Lardet, P., ed. *S. Hieronymi Presbyteri Opera*. Part 3: *Opera Polemica*. Vol. 1: *Contra Rufinum*. CCL 79. Turnhout: Brepols, 1982.

Jerome, On Illustrious Men
Richardson, E. C., ed. *Hieronymus: Liber de Viris Inlustribus*. TU 14, 1a. Leipzig: J. C. Hinrichs, 1896, 1–56.
Jerome. *Saint Jerome: On Illustrious Men*, transl. T. P. Halton, FOTC 100. Washington, D.C.: Catholic University of America Press, 1999.

Jerome, Letters
Hilberg, I., ed. *Sancti Eusebii Hieronymi Epistulae*. Part 1: *Epistulae 1–70*. Part 2: *Epistulae 71–120*. 2nd edn. CSEL 54, 55. Vienna: Verlag der Österreichischen Akademie der Wissenschaften, 1996.

Pamphilus and Eusebius, Apology for Origen
Amacker, R. and É. Junod, eds. *Apologie pour Origène; suivi de Rufin d'aquilée sur la falsification des livres d'Origène*. SC 464. Paris: Cerf, 2002, 22–279.

Photius, Bibliotheca
Henry, R., ed. *Bibliothèque*. 8 vols. Paris: Société d'édition les Belles Lettres, 1959–1977.

Porphyry, Against the Christians
Berchman, R. M., transl. *Porphyry against the Christians*. Leiden: Brill, 2005.

Rufinus, On the Corruption of Origen's Books
Amacker, R. and É. Junod, eds. *Apologie pour Origène; suivi de Rufin d'aquilée sur la falsification des livres d'Origène*. SC 464. Paris: Cerf, 2002, 282–323.

Stoic Fragments
Arnim, H. F. A. von, ed. *Stoicorum Veterum Fragmenta*. 4 vols. Leipzig: B. J. Teubner, 1903–24.

Sextus Julius Africanus, Letter to Origen
Lange, N. R. M. de, ed. *Lettre d'africanus à Origène*. SC 302. Paris: Cerf, 1983, 514–521.

Suda
Adler, A., ed. *Suidae Lexicon*. 5 vols. Leipzig: Teubner, 1928–1938.

Theodore of Mopsuestia, Commentary on the Psalms
Rompay, L. van, ed. and transl. *Théodore de Mopsueste: Fragments syriaques du Commentaire des Psaumes*. Louvain: Peeters, 1982.
McLeod, F. G. *Theodore of Mopsuestia*. London: Routledge, 2009.

Literature

Alviar, J. J. *Klesis: The Theology of the Christian Vocation according to Origen*. Dublin: Four Courts, 1993.
Ameling W. and H.-G. Nesselrath, eds. *Einleitung in die griechische Philologie*. Stuttgart: Teubner, 1997.
Andresen, C. *Logos und Nomos: Die Polemik des Kelsos wider das Christentum*. Berlin: W. de Gruyter, 1955.
Bardy, G. "Faux et fraudes littéraires dans l'Antiquité chrétienne." *RHE* 32 (1936): 5–23; 275–302.
——. "Les idées morales d'Origène." *Mélanges des Science Religieuse* 13 (1956): 23–38.
——. *Recherches sur l'histoire du texte et des versions latines du De Principiis d'Origène*. Paris: É. Champion, 1923.
——. "La Règle de Foi d'Origène." *RSR* 9 (1919): 162–196.
——. "Les traditions juives dans l'oeuvre d'Origène." *RB* 34 (1925): 217–52.
Barthélemy, D. *Critique textuelle de l'Ancien Testament*. Vol. 3. Fribourg: Éditions Universitaires, 1992.
——. "Origène et le texte de l'Ancien Testament." In *Epektasis: Mélanges patristiques offerts au Cardinal Jean Daniélou*, ed. J. Fontaine and C. Kannengiesser, 247–261. Paris: Beauchesne: 1972.
Bate, H. N. "Some Technical Terms of Greek Exegesis." *JTS* 24 (1923): 59–66.
Baud, R. C. "Les 'Règles' de la théologie d'Origène." *RSR* 55 (1967): 161–208.
Beatrice, P. F. "Porphyry's Judgment on Origen." In *Orig V*: 351–367.
Becker, A. H. and A. Y. Reeds, eds. *The Ways that Never Parted: Jews and Christians in Late Antiquity and the Early Middle Ages*. Tübingen: Mohr Siebeck, 2003.
Bertrand, D. "Piété et sagesse dans le *Perì Euchês*." In *Orig V*: 476–480.
Bertrand, F. *Mystique de Jésus chez Origène*. Paris: Aubier, 1951.
Bienert, W. A. *"Allegoria" und "Anagoge" bei Didymos dem Blinden von Alexandria*. Berlin: W. de Gruyter, 1972.
Bietenhard, H. *Caesarea, Origenes und die Juden*. Stuttgart: Kohlhammer, 1974.
Bigg, C. *The Christian Platonists of Alexandria: Being the Bampton Lectures of the Year 1886*. Rev. edn. Oxford: Oxford University Press, 1913.
Blanc, C. "Le Commentaire de Héracléon sur Jean 4 et 8." *Aug* 15 (1975): 81–124.
Blowers, P. M. "Origen, the Rabbis, and the Bible: Toward a Picture of Judaism and Christianity in Third-Century Caesarea." In *Origen of Alexandria: His World and His Legacy*, ed. C. Kannengiesser and W. L. Petersen, 96–116. Notre Dame: University of Notre Dame Press, 1988.
Bludau, A. *Die Schriftsfälschungen der Häretiker: ein Beitrag zur Textkritik der Bibel*. Munster: Aschendorf, 1925.

Bochinger, J. J. *De Origenis allegorica Scripturae Sacrae interpretatione: Dissertatio historico-theologica*. 3 parts. Strasbourg: F. G. Levrault, 1830.

Böhm, T. "Origenes—Theologe und (Neu-) Platoniker? Oder: Wem soll man missvertrauen—Eusebius oder Porphyrius?" *Adamantius* 8 (2002): 7–23.

Bonnefoy, J.-F. "Origène théoricien de la méthode théologique." In *Mélanges offerts au R. P. Ferdinand Cavallera*, 87–145. Toulouse: Bibliothéque de L'Institut Catholique, 1948.

Borret, M. "Celsus: A Pagan Perspective on Scripture." In *The Bible in Greek Christian Antiquity*, ed. and transl. P. Blowers, 259–288. Notre Dame: University of Notre Dame Press, 1997.

Borst, J. *Beiträge zur sprachlich-stilistischen und rhetorischen Würdigung des Origenes*. Freising: Datterer & Cie., 1913.

Boyarin, D. *Border Lines: The Partition of Judaeo-Christianity*. Philadelphia: University of Pennsylvania Press, 2004.

Boys-Stones, G. R. *Post-Hellenistic Philosophy: A Study of its Development from the Stoics to Origen*. Oxford: Oxford University Press, 2001.

Bradley, B. J. M. *Arete as a Christian Concept: The Structural Elements of Origen's Doctrine*. Thesis. University of Cambridge, 1976.

Brock, S. "Origen's aims as a textual critic of the Old Testament." In *SP*, vol. 10, ed. F. L. Cross. Berlin: Akademie-Verlag, 1970: 215–218.

Brox, N. *Falsche Verfasserangaben: zur Erklärung der frühchristlichen Pseudepigraphie*. Stuttgart: KBW, 1975.

Burnyeat, M. "Postscript on Silent Reading." *Classical Quarterly* 47 (1997): 74–76.

Cadiou, R. "Dictionnaires antiques dans l'oeuvre d'Origène." *REG* 45 (1932): 271–285.

——. *La Jeunesse d'Origène*. Paris: Gabriel Beauchesne, 1935. ET: *Origen: His Life at Alexandria*, transl. J. A. Southwell. St. Louis: Herder, 1944.

Campenhausen, H. Frhr. von. *Die Entstehung der christlichen Bibel*. Tübingen: Mohr, 1968. ET: *The Formation of the Christian Bible*, transl. J. A. Baker. Philadelphia: Fortress, 1972.

Capitaine, W. *De Origenis Ethica*. Munster: Aschendorff, 1898.

Carriker, A. J. *The Library of Eusebius of Caesarea*. Leiden: Brill, 2003.

Castagno, A. M., ed. *La biografia di Origene fra storia e agiografia: Atti del VI Convegno di Studi del Gruppo italiano di ricerca su Origene e la tradizione alessandrina*. Villa Verucchio: Pazzini, 2004.

——. *Origene predicatore e il suo pubblico*. Milan: Franco Angeli, 1987.

Castellano, A. *La Exegesis de Origenes y de Heracleon a Los Testimonios del Bautista*. Santiago: Pontificia Universidad Católica de Chile, 1998.

Chadwick, H. "Origen, Celsus and the Resurrection of the Body." *HTR* 41 (1948): 83–102.

Clark, E. A. *The Origenist Controversy: The Cultural Construction of an Early Christian Debate*. Princeton: Princeton University Press, 1992.

——. *Reading Renunciation: Asceticism and Scripture in Early Christianity*. Princeton: Princeton University Press, 1999.

Cocchini, F. *Il Paolo di Origene: Contributo alla storia della recezione delle epistole paoline nel III secolo*. Rome: Edizioni Studium, 1992.

———. "Il progresso spirituale in Origene." In *Spiritual Progress: Studies in the Spirituality of Late Antiquity and Early Monasticism*, ed. M. Sheridan and J. Driscoll, 29–45. Rome: Centro studi S. Anselmo, 1994.

Cornélis, H. "Les Fondements cosmologiques de l'eschatologie d'Origène." *Revue des Sciences philosophiques et théologiques* 43 (1959): 32–80; 201–247.

Cribiore, R. *Gymnastics of the Mind: Greek Education in Hellenistic and Roman Egypt*. Princeton: Princeton University Press, 2001.

———. *Writing, Teachers, and Students in Graeco-Roman Egypt*. Atlanta: Scholars Press, 1996.

Crouzel, H. "Les condemnations subies par Origène et sa doctrine." In *Orig VII*: 311–315.

———. "La Doctrine origénienne du corps résuscité." *Bulletin de Littérature Ecclésiastique* 81 (1980): 175–200; 241–266.

———. "Les doxologie finales des homélies d'Origène selon le texte grec et les versions latines." *Aug* 20 (1980): 95–107.

———. "L'École d'Origène à Césarée: Postscriptum à une édition de Grégoire le Thaumaturge." *Bulletin de littérature ecclésiastique* 71 (1970): 15–27.

———. "L'édition Delarue d'Origène rééditée par J.-P. Migne." In *Migne et le renouveau des études patristiques: Actes du colloque de Saint-Flour (juillet 1975)*, ed. A. Mandouze and J. Fouilheron, 225–253. Paris: Beauchesne, 1985.

———. "Faut-il voir trois personnages en Grégoire le Thaumaturge? A propos du Remerciement à Origène et de la Lettre à Grégoire." *Gregorianum* 60 (1979): 287–320.

———. *Les fins dernières selon Origène*. Aldershot: Variorum, 1990.

———. *Origène et le Philosophie*. Paris: Aubier, 1962.

———. *Origène*. Paris: Lethielleux, 1985. ET: *Origen*, transl. A. S. Worrall. Edinburgh: T. & T. Clark, 1989.

———. *Origène et la "Connaissance Mystique."* Paris: Desclée de Brouwer, 1961.

Curti, C. et al. eds. *La terminologia esegetica nell'Antichità: Atti del Primo Seminario di antichità cristiane*. Bari: Edipuglia, 1987.

Daley, B. E. *The Hope of the Early Church: A Handbook of Patristic Eschatology*. Cambridge: Cambridge University Press, 1991.

———. "Origen's *De Principiis*: A Guide to the Principles of Christian Scriptural Interpretation." In *Nova et Vetera: Patristic Studies in Honor of T. P. Halton*, ed. J. Petruccione, 3–21. Washington: Catholic University of America Press, 1998.

———. "What did Origenism Mean in the Sixth Century?" In *Orig VI*: 627–638.

Daly, R. "The Hermeneutics of Origen: Existential Interpretation in the Third Century." In *The Word in the World: Essays in Honor of Frederick J. Moriarty, S.J.*, ed. R. Clifford and G. MacRae, 135–143. Cambridge, MA: Weston College Press, 1973.

Daniélou, J. *Histoire des doctrines chrétiennes avant Nicée*. Vol. 2, *Message évangélique et culture hellénistique aux IIe et IIIe siècles*. Paris: Desclée, 1961. ET: *A History of Early Christian Doctrine before the Council of Nicaea*. Vol. 2, *Gospel Message and Hellenistic Culture*, transl. J. A. Baker. Philadelphia: Westminster, 1973.

———. *Origène*. Paris: La Table Ronde, 1948. ET: *Origen*, transl. W. Mitchell. New York: Sheed and Ward, 1955.

——. *Sacramentum Futuri: Études sur les Origines de la Typologie biblique*. Paris: Beauchesne, 1950. ET: *From Shadows to Reality: Studies in the Biblical Typology of the Fathers*, transl. W. Hibberd. Westminster: Newmann, 1960.

——. "Traversée de la Mer Rouge et baptême aux premiers siècles." *RSR* 33 (1946): 402–430.

Dawson, D. *Allegorical Readers and Cultural Revision in Ancient Alexandria*. Berkeley: University of California Press, 1992.

——. "Allegorical Reading and the Embodiment of the Soul in Origen." In *Christian Origins: Theology, Rhetoric, and Community*, ed. G. Jones and L. Ayre, 26–43. London: Routledge, 1988.

——. *Christian Figural Reading and the Fashioning of Identity*. Berkeley: University of California Press, 2002.

Delarue, C. *Origenis Opera Omnia*. Vol. 2. Paris: Vincent, 1733.

Devreesse, R. *Introduction à L'étude des manuscrits grecs*. Paris: Librairie C. Klincksieck, 1954.

Dickey, E. *Ancient Greek Scholarship: A Guide to Finding, Reading, and Understanding Scholia, Commentaries, Lexica, and Grammatical Treatises, from Their Beginnings to the Byzantine Period*. Oxford: Oxford University Press, 2007.

Diekamp, F. *Die origenistischen Streitigkeiten im sechsten Jahrhundert und das fünfte allgemeine Concil*. Munster: Aschendorff, 1899.

Dillon, J. "Plotinus, Philo and Origen on the Grades of Virtue." In *Platonismus und Christentum: Festschrift für Heinrich Dörrie*, ed. H.-D. Blume and F. Mann, 92–105. Munster: Aschendorffsche Verlagsbuchhandlung, 1983.

Dively Lauro, E. A. *The Soul and the Spirit of Scripture within Origen's Exegesis*. Leiden: Brill, 2005.

Dorival, G., M. Harl, and O. Munnich. *La Bible grecque des Septante: Du judaïsme hellenistique au christianisme ancien*. Paris: Editions du Cerf, 1988.

Dorival, G. "L'Apport des chaînes exégétiques à une réédition des Hexaples d'Origène." *RHT* 4 (1974): 45–74.

Dörrie, H. "Ammonios der Lehrer Plotins." *Hermes* 83 (1955): 439–77.

——. "Zur Methode antiker Exegesis." *ZNW* 65 (1974): 121–38.

Dräseke, J. "Der Brief des Origenes an Gregorios von Neocäsarea." *Jahrbücher für protestantische Theologie* 7 (1881): 102–26.

Droge, A. J. *Homer or Moses? Early Christian Interpretations of the History of Culture*. Tübingen: Mohr Siebeck, 1989.

Dunn, J. D. G. *The Partings of the Ways: Between Christianity and Judaism and their Significance for the Character of Christianity*. 2nd edn. London: SCM, 2006.

Edwards, M. J. *Origen Against Plato*. Aldershot: Ashgate, 2002.

Ehrman, B. *The Orthodox Corruption of Scripture: The Effect of Early Christological Controversies on the Text of the New Testament*. New York, NY: Oxford University Press, 1993.

Engelhardt, J. G. V. *Bemerkungen über die Exegese des Origenes*. Erlangen: C. H. Kunstmann, 1836.

Ernesti, J. A. *Disputatio historico-critica de Origene interpretationis librorum Sacrae Scripturae grammaticae auctore*. Leipzig: Ex Officina Langenhemiana, 1756.

Ernesti, J. C. G. *Lexicon Technologiae Graecorum Rhetoricae*. Leipzig: C. Fritsch, 1795; reprint, Hildesheim: G. Olms, 1983.

——. *Lexicon Technologiae Latinorum Rhetoricae*. Leipzig: C. Fritsch, 1795; reprint, Hildesheim: G. Olms, 1983.

Etcheverría, R. T. "Orígenes y la regula fidei." In *Orig I*: 327–338.

Fédou, M. *La sagesse et la monde: Essai sur la christologie d'Origène*. Paris: Desclée, 1995.

Festugiere, A. M. J. *Contemplation et vie contemplative selon Platon*. 4th edn. Paris: J. Vrin: 1975.

Fuhrmann, M. *Einführung in die antike Dichtungstheorie*. Darmstadt: Wissenschaftliche Buchgesellschaft, 1973.

——. *Das Systematische Lehrbuch: Ein Beitrag zur Geschichte der Wissenschaften in der Antike*. Gottingen: Vandenhoeck & Ruprecht, 1960.

Gamble, H. Y. *Books and Readers in the Early Church: A History of Early Christian Texts*. New Haven: Yale University Press, 1995.

Gavrilov, A. K. "Reading Techniques in Classical Antiquity." *Classical Quarterly* 47 (1997): 56–73.

Geerlings, W. and H. König, eds. *Origenes, Vir ecclesiasticus*. Bonn: Borengässer, 1995.

Gessel, W. *Die Theologie des Gebetes nach "De oratione" von Origenes*. Munich: Schöningh, 1975.

Gnilka, C. *ΧΡΗΣΙΣ: Die Methode der Kirchenväter im Umgang mit der Antiken Kultur*. Vol. 1, *Der Begriff des "rechten Gebrauchs."* Basel: Schwabe, 1984.

——. *ΧΡΗΣΙΣ: Die Methode der Kirchenväter im Umgang mit der Antiken Kultur*. Vol. 2, *Kultur und Conversion*. Basel: Schwabe, 1993.

Godin, A. *Érasme lecteur d'Origène*. Geneva: Droz, 1982.

Goffinet, E. *L'utilisation d'Origène dans le commentaire des Psaumes de Saint Hilaire de Poitiers*. Louvain: Publications universitairies, 1965.

Gögler, R. *Zur Theologie des Biblischen Wortes bei Origenes*. Dusseldorf: Patmos, 1963.

Goulet, R. "Hypothèses récentes sur le traité de Porphyre 'Contre les chrétiens.'" In *Hellénisme et christianisme*, ed. M. Narcy and É. Rebillard, 61–109. Villeneuve d'ascq: Presses Universitaires du Septentrion, 2004.

Grafton, A. and M. Williams. *Christianity and the Transformation of the Book: Origen, Eusebius, and the Library of Caesarea*. Cambridge, MA: Belknap Press, 2006.

Grant, R. M. *The Earliest Lives of Jesus*. London: SPCK, 1961.

——. *Eusebius as Church Historian*. Oxford: Clarendon Press, 1980.

——. *The Letter and the Spirit*. London: SPCK, 1957.

Greer, R. A. and J. L. Kugel. *Early Biblical Interpretation*. Philadelphia: Westminster, 1986.

Grube, G. M. A. *The Greek and Roman Critics*. Toronto: University of Toronto Press, 1965.

Gruber, G. *ΖΩΗ–Wesen, Stufen und Mitteilung des wahren Lebens bei Origenes*. Munich: M. Hueber, 1962.

Gruber, W. *Die Pneumatische Exegese bei den Alexandrinern: Ein Beitrag zur Noematik der Heiligen Schrift*. Graz: Akademische Druck- und Verlagsanstalt, 1957.

Guillaumont, A. "Évagre et les anathématismes antiorigénistes de 553." In *SP*, vol. 3, ed. F. L. Cross. Berlin: Akademie-Verlag, 1961: 219–226.

——. *Les Képhalaia Gnostica d'Éuagre le Pontique et l'histoire de l'origénisme chez les Grecs et les Syriens*. Paris: Éditions du Seuil, 1962.

Guinot, J. N. "La fortune des Hexaples d'Origèneau IVè et Vè siècles en milieu antiochien." *Orig VI*: 215–225.

Gustafsson, B. "Eusebius' Principle in Handling His Sources, As Found in His 'Church History,' Books I–VII." In *SP*, vol. 4, ed. F. L. Cross. Berlin: Akademie-Verlag, 1961: 429–441.

Hadot, I. *Arts Libéraux et Philosophie dans la Pensée Antique*. Paris: Études Augustiniennes, 1984.

——. "Les introductions aux commentaires exégétiques chez les auteurs néoplatoniciens et les auteurs Chrétiens." In *Les Règles de L'Interprétation*, ed. M. Tardieu, 99–122. Paris: Cerf, 1987.

Hadot, P. "Les Divisions des parties de la philosophie dans l'Antiquité." *MH* 36 (1979): 218–31.

——. "Epopteia." In *HWP*, vol. 2, ed. J. Ritter. Basel: Schwabe, 1972.

——. *Exercices spirituels et philosophie antique*. 2nd edn. Paris: Études Augustiniennes, 1987. ET: *Philosophy as a Way of Life: Spiritual Exercises from Socrates to Foucault*, intro. A. I. Davison and transl. Michael Chase. Oxford: Blackwell, 1995.

——. "La logique, partie ou instrument de la philosophie?" In *Simplicius, Commentaire sur les Catégories*, fasc. 1, transl. and commented I. Hadot, 183–188. Leiden: Brill, 1989.

——. "Philosophie, I.F.: Die Einteilung der Philosophie in der Antike." In *HWP*, vol. 7, ed. J. Ritter and K. Gründer. Basel: Schwabe, 1989.

——. "Philosophie, I.E.: Hellenismus." In *HWP*, vol. 7, ed. J. Ritter and K. Gründer. Basel: Schwabe, 1989.

——. "Théologie, exégèse, révélation, écriture dans la philosophie grecque." In *Les règles de L'Interprétation*, ed. M. Tardieu, 13–34. Paris: Cerf, 1987.

Hagenbach, K. R. *Observationes historico-hermeneuticae circa Origenis Adamanti methodum interpretandae Sacrae Scripturae*. Basel: A. Wieland, 1823.

Hällström, G. af. *Fides Simpliciorum according to Origen of Alexandria*. Helsinki: Societas Scientiarum Fennica: 1984.

Halperin, D. J. "Origen, Ezekiel's Merkabah, and the Ascension of Moses." *CH* 50 (1981): 261–75.

Hanson, R. P. C. *Allegory and Event: A study of the sources and significance of Origen's Interpretation of Scripture*. Richmond: John Knox Press, 1959; reprint, Louisville: Westminster John Knox, 2002.

——. "History and Allegory." *Theology* 59 (1956): 498–503.

——. "Interpretations of Hebrew Names in Origen." *VChr* 10 (1956): 103–123.

——. "Origen's Doctrine of Tradition." *JTS* 49 (1949): 17–27.

——. *Origen's Doctrine of Tradition*. London: SPCK, 1954.

Harl, M. "Le guetteur et la cible: les deux sens de *skopos* dans la langue religieuse des chrétiens." *Revue des études grecques* 74 (1961): 455–456.

——. "La langage de L'expérience religieuse chez les pères grecs." *Rivista di storia e letteratura religiosa* 15 (1977): 5–34.

——. *Origène et la fonction révélatrice du Verbe Incarné*. Paris: Editions du Seuil, 1958.

——. "Origène et la sémantique du langage biblique." *VChr* 26 (1972): 161–187.

——. "Pointes antignostiques d'Origène: le questionnement impie des Écritures." In *Studies in Gnosticism and Hellenistic Religions, presented to Gilles Quispel*, ed. R. Van Den Broek and M. J. Vermaseren, 205–207. Leiden: Brill, 1981.

——. "La preexistence des âmes dans l'oeuvre d'Origène." In *Orig IV*: 238–258.

——. "Recherches sur l'origénisme d'Origène: la satiété (koros) de la contemplation comme motif de la chute des âmes." In *SP*, vol. 8, ed. F. L. Cross. Berlin: Akademie-Verlag, 1966, 374–405.

Harnack, A. *Bible Reading in the Early Church*, transl. J. R. Wilkinson. Eugene, OR: Wipf and Stock, 2005.

——. *Der Kirchengeschichtliche Ertrag der Exegetischen Arbeiten des Origenes*. Vol. 1, *Hexateuch und Richterbuch*. Vol. 2, *Die Beiden Testaments mit Ausschluss des Hexateuchs und des Richterbuchs*. TU 42.3 and 42.4. Leipzig: J. C. Hinrichs: 1918 and 1919.

Harris, W. V. *Ancient Literacy*. Cambridge, MA: Harvard University Press, 1989.

Heine, R. E. *Origen: Scholarship in the Service of the Church*. Oxford: Oxford University Press, 2010.

——. "Reading the Bible with Origen." In *The Bible in Greek Christian Antiquity*, ed. and transl. P. M. Blowers, 131–148. Notre Dame: University of Notre Dame Press, 1997.

Heither, T. "Glaube in der Theologie des Origenes." *Erbe und Auftrag* 67 (1991): 255–265.

Hidal, S. "Exegesis of the Old Testament in the Antiochene School with its Prevalent Literal and Historical Method." In *Hebrew Bible/Old Testament: The History of its Interpretation*, vol. 1, *From the Beginnings to the Middle Ages (Until 1300)*, Part 1: *Antiquity*, ed. M. Saebo, 543–568. Göttingen: Vandenhoeck & Ruprecht, 1996.

Hill, C. E. *Regnum Caelorum: Patterns of Millennial Thought in Early Christianity*. 2nd edn. Grand Rapids: Eerdmans, 2001.

Hoek, A. Van Den. "The 'Catechetical' School of Early Christian Alexandria and Its Philonic Heritage." *HTR* 90 (1997): 59–87.

Hombergen, D. *The Second Origenist Controversy: A New Perspective on Cyril of Scythopolis' Monastic Biographies as Historical Sources for Sixth-Century Origenism*. Rome: Pontificio Ateneo S. Anselmo, 2001.

Hornschuh, M. "Das Leben des Origenes und die Entstehung der alexandrinischen Schule." *ZKG* 71 (1960): 1–25; 193–214.

Hort, F. J. A. *Judaistic Christianity: A Course of Lectures*. Cambridge: Macmillan, 1894.

Huet, P. D. *Origeniana: Tripartitum opus, quo Origenis narratur vita, doctrina excutitur, scripta recensentur*. Rouen: Ioannis Bertholini, 1668.

Humphrey, J. H. ed. *Literacy in the Roman World*. Ann Arbor, MI: Journal of Roman Archeology, 1991.

Jackson-McCabe, M. "What's in a Name? The Problem of 'Jewish Christianity.'" In *Jewish Christianity Reconsidered: Rethinking Ancient Groups and Texts*, ed. M. Jackson-McCabe, 7–38. Minneapolis: Fortress Press, 2007.

Jacob, C. "The Reception of the Origenist Tradition in Latin Exegesis." In *Hebrew Bible/Old Testament: The History of its Interpretation*, vol. 1, *From the Beginnings to the Middle Ages (Until 1300)*, Part 1: *Antiquity*, ed. M. Saebo, 682–700. Göttingen: Vandenhoeck & Ruprecht, 1996.

Jakab, A. *Ecclesia Alexandrina*. Bern: Peter Lang, 2001.

Janssens, Y. "Héracléon: Commentaire sur L'Évangile selon Jean." *Le Muséon* 72 (1959): 101–151; 277–299.

Jellicoe, S. *The Septuagint and Modern Study*. Oxford: Clarendon Press, 1968.

Johann, H.-T., ed. *Erziehung und Bildung in der heidnischen und christlichen Antike*. Darmstadt: Wissenschaftliche Buchgesellschaft, 1976.

Joosen, J. C. and J. H. Waszink. "Allegorese A. III." In *RAC*, vol. 1, ed. T. Klauser. Stuttgart: Hiersemann, 1950.

Junod, E. "Les attitudes d'apelles, disciple de Marcion à l'égard de l'Ancien Testament." *Aug* 22 (1982): 113–133.

——. "En quoi les homélies d'Origène se distinguent-elles de ses commentaires?" In *Le défi homilétique*, ed. H. Mottu and P.-A. Bettex, 137–170. Geneva: Labor et Fides, 1994.

——. "Particularités de la Philocalie," *Orig I*: 181–197.

Kahle, P. E. *The Cairo Geniza*, 2nd edn. Oxford: Basil Blackwell, 1959.

Kalvesmaki, J. *Formation of Early Christian Theology of Arithmetic: Number Symbolism in the Late Second and Early Third Century*. Dissertation. Catholic University of America. 18 April 2006.

Karpp, H. "Viva Vox." In *Mullus: Festschrift Theodor Klauser*, ed. A. Stuiber and A. Hermann, 190–198. Munster: Aschendorff, 1964.

Kaster, R. A. *Guardians of Language: The Grammarian and Society in Late Antiquity*. Berkeley: University of California Press, 1988.

Kattenbusch, D. F. *Das Apostolische Symbol: Seine Entstehung, sein geschichtlicher Sinn, seine urprüngliche Stellung im Kultus und in der Theologie der Kirche*. Vol. 2, *Verbreitung und Bedeutung des Taufsymbols*. Leipzig: J. C. Hinrichs, 1900.

Kennedy, G. A., ed. *Cambridge History of Literary Criticism*. Vol. 1, *Classical Criticism*. Cambridge: Cambridge University Press, 1989.

Kettler, F. H. "War Origenes Schüler des Ammonios Sakkas?" In *Epektasis: Mélanges patristiques offerts au Cardinal Jean Daniélou*, ed. J. Fontaine and C. Kannengiesser, 327–335. Paris: Beauchesne, 1972.

——. *Der ursprüngliche Sinn der Dogmatik des Origenes*. Berlin: A. Töpelmann, 1966.

Kimelman, R. "Rabbi Yohanan and Origen on the Song of Songs: A Third-Century Jewish-Christian Disputation." *HTR* 73 (1980): 567–595.

King, J. C. *Origen on the Song of Songs as the Spirit of Scripture: The Bridegroom's Perfect Marriage-Song*. Oxford: Oxford University Press, 2005.

King, K. L. *What is Gnosticism?* Cambridge: Harvard University Press, 2003.

Kirchmeyer, J. "Origène, commentaire sur le cantique prol." In *SP*, vol. 10, ed. F. L. Cross. Berlin: Akademie-Verlag, 1970: 230–235.

Klein, R. *Oratio prosphonetica ac panegyrica in Origenem: Dankrede an Origenes*, transl. P. Guyot, FC, 24. Freiburg: Herder, 1996.

Klijn, F. J. and G. J. Reininck. *Patristic Evidence for Jewish-Christian Sects*. Leiden: Brill, 1973.

Klijn, F. J. "The Study of Jewish Christianity." *NTS* 20 (1973): 419–431.

Klostermann, E. "Formen der exegetischen Arbeiten des Origenes." *Theologische Literaturzeitung* 72 (1947): 203–8.

——. "Die Schriften des Origenes in Hieronymus' Brief an Paula." *Sitzungsberichte der königlich preussischen Akademie der Wissenschaften* 2 (1897): 855–870.

——. "Überkommene Definitionen im Werke des Origenes." *ZNW* 37 (1938): 54–61.

Koch, H. *Pronoia und Paideusis: Studien über Origenes und sein Verhältnis zum Platonismus*. Berlin: W. de Gruyter, 1932.

Knauber, A. "Das Anliegen der Schule des Origines zu Cäsarea." *MTZ* 19 (1968): 182–203.

Knox, B. M. W. "Silent Reading in Antiquity." *Greek, Roman and Byzantine Studies* 9 (1968): 421–35.

Kraft, R. A. "In Search of 'Jewish Christianity' and Its 'Theology': Problems of definition and methodology." *RSR* 60 (1972): 81–92.

Kühnert, F. *Allgemeinbildung und Fachbildung in der Antike*. Berlin: Akademie-Verlag, 1963.

Kunze, J. *Glaubensregel, Heilige Schrift und Taufbekenntnis*. Leipzig: Dörffling & Franke, 1899.

Labriolle, P. *La réaction païenne: Etude sur la polémique antichrétienne du Ie au VIe siècle*. Paris: l'Artisan du Livre, 1948; reprint, Cerf: 2005.

Lacore, M. "L'homme d'acier-ἀδαμάντινος ἀνήρ de l'Anonyme de Jamblique à Platon." *Revue des études grecques* 110 (1997): 399–419.

Lamberton, R. *Homer the Theologian: Neoplatonist Allegorical Reading and the Growth of the Epic Tradition*. Berkeley: University of California Press, 1986.

Lange, N. R. M. De. "The Letter to Africanus: Origen's Recantation." In *SP*, vol. 16, ed. E. A. Livingstone. Berlin: Akademie-Verlag, 1985, 242–247.

——. *Origen and the Jews: Studies in Jewish-Christian Relations in Third-Century Palestine*. Cambridge: Cambridge University Press, 1976.

Layton, B. "Prolegomena to the Study of Ancient Gnosticism." In *The Social World of the First Christians: Essays in Honor of Wayne A. Meeks*, ed. L. M. White and O. L. Yarbrough, 334–350. Minneapolis: Fortress Press, 1995.

Le Boulluec, A. "De la croissance selon les Stoïciens à la resurrection selon Origène." *Revue des etudes grecques* 88 (1975): 143–155.

——. *La notion d'hérésie dans la littérature grecque IIe-IIIe siècles*. Vol. 2, *Clément d'alexandrie et Origène*. Paris: Études Augustiniennes, 1985.

——. "Aux origines, encore, de L''école' d'alexandrie." *Adamantius* 5 (1999): 8–36.

——. "La place de la polémique antignostique dans le *Peri Archôn*." In *Orig I*: 47–61.

Leanza S. "La classificazione dei libri Salomonici e I suoi riflessi sulla questione dei rapporti tra Bibbia e scienze profane, da Origene agli scrittori medievali." *Aug* 14 (1974): 651–666.

Lebreton, J. "Les degrés de la connaissance religieuse d'après Origène." *RSR* 12 (1922): 265–296.

Lechner, M. *Erziehung und Bildung in der Griechisch-Römischen Antike*. Munich: Max Hueber, 1933.

Leclerq, H. "The Exposition and Exegesis of Scripture: From Gregory the Great to St. Bernard." In *Cambridge History of the Bible*, vol. 2, 183–197. Cambridge: Cambridge University Press, 1969.

Lefeber, P. S. A. *Kreuze en verlangen. Een onderzoek naar zin en functie van het gebed in Origenes' preken en zijn tractaat Over het gebed*. Gorinchem: Narratio, 1997.

——. "The Same View on Prayer in Origen's Sermons and his Treatise *On Prayer*. In *Orig VII*: 33–38.

Levieils, X. *Contra Christianos: Le critique sociale et religieuse du christianisme des origines au concile de Nicée (45–325)*. Berlin: W. de Gruyter, 2007.

Lienhard, J. T. "Origen as Homilist." In *Preaching in the Patristic Age: Studies in Honor of Walter J. Burghardt, S.J.*, ed. D. G. Hunter, 36–52. New York: Paulist Press, 1989.

Lies, L. *Wort und Eucharistie bei Origenes: Zur Spiritualisierungstendenz des Eucharistieverständnisses*. Innsbruck: Tyrolia-Verlag, 1978.

Lieske, A. *Die Theologie der Logosmystik bei Origenes*. Munster: Aschendorff, 1938.

Lobkowicz, N. *Theory and Practice: History of a Concept from Aristotle to Marx*. Notre Dame: University of Notre Dame Press, 1967.

Lomiento, G. "Note sulla traduzione Geronimiana delle omelie su Geremia di Origene." In *Orig I*: 139–162.

Lona, H. E., transl. and ed. *Die* Wahre Lehre *des Kelsos*. Freiburg: Herder, 2005.

Louth, A. "The Date of Eusebius' *Historia ecclesiastica*." *JTS* 41 (1990): 111–123.

——. *The Origins of the Christian Mystical Tradition*. 2nd edn. Oxford: Oxford University Press, 2007.

Lubac, H. De. *Exégèse Médiévale: Les quatre sens de L'Écriture*. 4 vols. Paris: Aubier, 1959–64. ET: *Medieval Exegesis*. Vol. 1, *The Four Senses of Scripture*, transl. M. Sebanc. Grand Rapids: Eerdmans, 1998. *Medieval Exegesis*. Vol. 2, *The Four Senses of Scripture*, transl. E. M. Macierowski. Grand Rapids: Eerdmans, 2002.

——. *Histoire et Esprit: L'Intelligence de L'Écriture d'après Origène*. Paris: Aubier, 1950. ET: *History and Spirit: The Understanding of Scripture according to Origen*, transl. A. E. Nash and J. Merriell. San Francisco: Ignatius Press, 2007.

——. "Typologie et allégorisme." *RSR* 34 (1947): 180–226.

Lührmann, D. "Glaube." In *RAC*, vol. 11, ed. T. Klauser. Stuttgart: Hiersemann, 1981.

MacLeod, C. W. "Allegory and Mysticism in Origen and Gregory of Nyssa." *JTS* 22 (1971): 362–379.

Malingrey, A. M. *"Philosophia": Étude d'un groupe de mots dans la littérature grecque, des Présocratiques au IVe siècle ap. J.-C.* Paris: C. Klincksieck, 1961.

Marcos, N. F. *The Septuagint in Context: Introduction to the Greek Versions of the Bible*, transl. W. G. E. Watson. Leiden: Brill, 2001.

Margerie, B. De. *An Introduction to the History of Exegesis*. Vol. 1, *The Greek Fathers*, transl. L. Maluf. Petersham: Saint Bede's Publications, 1993.

Marjanen, A. and P. Luomanen, eds. *A Companion to Second-Century Christian "Heretics."* Leiden: Brill, 2005.

Markschies, C. *Gnosis: An Introduction*, transl. J. Bowden. London: T. & T. Clark, 2003.

——. *Kaiserzeitliche christliche Theologie und ihre Institutionen: Prolegomena zu einer Geschichte der antiken christlichen Theologie*. Tübingen: Mohr Siebeck, 2007.

——. "Origenes in Berlin und Heidelberg." *Adamantius* 8 (2002): 135–145.

Marrou, H. I. *Histoire de L'Education dans l'Antiquité*. 3rd edn. Paris: Editions du Seuil, 1955. ET: *A History of Education in Antiquity*, transl. G. Lamb. New York: Sheed and Ward, 1956.

Martens, P. W. "Revisiting the Allegory/Typology Distinction: The Case of Origen." *JECS* 16 (2008): 283–317.

——. "Scripture." In *Routledge Companion to Early Christian Thought*, ed. D. J. Bingham, 288–312. London: Routledge, 2009.

——. "Why Does Origen Accuse the Jews of 'Literalism'? A Case Study of Christian Identity and Biblical Exegesis in Antiquity." *Adamantius* 13 (2007): 218–230.

——. "Why Does Origen Introduce the Trinitarian Authorship of Scripture in Book 4 of *Peri Archon*?" *Vigiliae Christianae* 60 (2006): 1–8.

Marti, H. *Übersetzer der Augustin-Zeit: Interpretation von Selbstzeugnissen.* Munich: Fink, 1974.

Martin, J.-P. P. *Origène et la critique textuelle du Nouveau Testament.* Paris: V. Palmé, 1885.

Masi, G. *Origène o della riconciliazione universale.* Bologna: Cooperativa Libraria Universitaria Editrice Bologna, 1997.

McDonald, L. M. and J. A. Sanders, eds. *The Canon Debate.* Peabody, MA: Hendrickson, 2002.

McGinn, B. *The Presence of God: A History of Western Christian Mysticism.* Vol. 1, *Foundations of Western Mysticism.* New York: Crossroad, 1991.

McGuckin, J. A. "Caesarea Maritima as Origen Knew It." *Orig V*: 3–25.

——. "The Changing Forms of Jesus According to Origen." *Orig IV*: 215–222.

——. "Origen on the Jews." In *Christianity and Judaism*, ed. D. Wood, 1–13. Oxford: Blackwell, 1992.

Ménard, J. E. "Transfiguration et polymorphie chez Origène." In *Epektasis: Mélanges patristiques offerts au Cardinal J. Daniélou*, ed. J. Fontaine and C. Kannengiesser, 367–374. Paris: Beauchesne, 1972.

Metzger, B. M. "Explicit References in the Works of Origen to Variant Readings in New Testament Manuscripts." In *Biblical and Patristic Studies in Memory of Robert Pierce Casey*, ed. J. N. Birdsall and R. W. Thomson, 78–95. Freiburg: Herder, 1963.

Mimouni, S. C. *Le judéo-christianisme ancien: essais historiques.* Paris: Cerf, 1998.

Mimouni, S. C. and F. Stanley Jones, eds. *Le judéo-christianisme dans tous ses états.* Paris: Cerf, 2001.

Miura-Stange, A. *Celsus und Origenes: Das Gemeinsame ihrer Weltanschauung.* Giessen: Töpelmann, 1926.

Molland, E. *The Conception of the Gospel in the Alexandrian Theology.* Oslo: I Kommisjon Hos Jacob Dybwad, 1938.

Morgan, T. *Literate Education in the Hellenistic and Roman Worlds.* Cambridge: Cambridge University Press, 1998.

Nardoni, E. "Origen's Concept of Biblical Inspiration." *The Second Century* 4 (1984): 9–23.

Nautin, P. *Lettres et Écrivains Chrétiens des IIe et IIIe Siècles.* Paris: Cerf, 1961.

——. *Origène: Sa vie et son oeuvre.* Paris: Beauchesne, 1977.

Nemeshegyi, P. "La morale d'Origène." *Revue d'ascétique et de mystique* 37 (1961): 409–428.

Neuschäfer, B. *Origenes als Philologe.* 2 Vols. Basel: Friedrich Reinhard, 1987.

Norelli, E. "Marcione e gli gnostici sul libero arbitrio, e la polemica di Origene." In *Il cuore indurito del faraone: Origene e il problema del libero arbitrio*, ed. L. Perrone, 1–30. Geneva: Marietti, 1992.

Ohme, H. *Kanon ekklesiastikos: Die Bedeutung des altkirchlichen Kanonbegriffs*. Berlin: W. de Gruyter, 1998.

Oppel, H. "Κανών. Zur Bedeutungsgeschichte des Wortes und seiner lateinischen Entsprechungen (Regula-Norma)." *Philologus*, Supplement vol. 30.4 (1937).

Outler, A. C. "Origen and the 'Regula fidei.'" *CH* 8 (1939): 212–221. Revised version in *Second Century* 4 (1984): 133–147.

Pagels, E. H. *The Johannine Gospel in Gnostic Exegesis: Heracleon's* Commentary on John. Nashville: Abingdon, 1973.

Paget, J. C. "Jewish Christianity." In *Cambridge History of Judaism*, vol. 3, eds. W. Horbury, W. D. Davies, and J. Sturdy, 733–742. Cambridge: Cambridge University Press, 1999.

——. "The Definition of the Terms 'Jewish Christian' and 'Jewish Christianity,'" 30–48. In *Jewish Believers in Jesus: The Early Centuries*, eds. O. Skarsaune and R. Hvalvik. Peabody, MA: Hendrickson, 2007.

Papanikolaou, D. "The allegorical exegetical method of Origen." *Theologia* 45 (1974): 347–359.

Pépin, J. *Mythe et Allégorie: Les origines grecques et les contestations judéo-chrétiennes.* 2nd edn. Paris: Études Augustiniennes, 1976.

Perrone, L. "Christianity as 'Practice' in Origen's *Contra Celsum*." In *Orig IX*: 293–317.

——. "Il discorso protrettico di Origene sulla preghiera. Introduzione al ΠΕΡΙ ΕΥΧΗΣ." In *Il dono e la sua ombra: Ricerche sul ΠΕΡΙ ΕΥΧΗΣ di Origene*, ed. F. Cocchini, 7–32. Rome: Institutum Patristicum Augustinianum, 1997.

——. "Fede/Ragione." In *Origene: Dizionario. La cultura-il pensiero-le opere*, ed. A. M. Castagno. Rome: Città Nuova, 2000.

——. "I paradigmi biblici della preghiera nel *Peri Euchês* di Origene: Aspetti formali e problematiche ermeneutiche." *Aug* 33 (1993): 339–368.

——. "Origenismus." In *Religion in Geschichte und Gegewart*, 4th edn, vol. 6, ed. H. D. Betz, 662–666. Tübingen: Mohr Siebeck, 2003.

——. "Prayer in Origen's *Contra Celsum*: The knowledge of God and the truth of Christianity." *VigChr* 55 (2001): 1–19.

Pfeiffer, R. *History of Classical Scholarship*. Vol. 1, *From the Beginnings to the End of the Hellenistic Age*. Oxford: Clarendon, 1968.

Philippou, A. J. "Origen and the early Jewish-Christian debate." *GOTR* 15 (1970): 140–152.

Pichler, K. *Streit um das Christentum: Der Angriff des Kelsos und die Antwort des Origenes*. Frankfurt am Main: Lang, 1980.

Pizzolato, L. F. *La "Explanatio Psalmorum XII": Studio letterario sulla esegesi di Sant' Ambrogio*. Milan: Viboldone S. Giuliano Milanese, 1965.

Pizzolato, L. F. and M. Rizzi, eds. *Origene maestro di vita spirituale/Origen: Master of Spiritual Life (Milano, 13–15 Settembre 1999)*. Milan: Vita e Pensiero, 2001.

Poffet, J.-M. *La Méthode exégétique d'Héracléon et d'Origène: commentateurs de Jn 4: Jésus, la Samaritaine et les Samaritains*. Fribourg: Éditions Universitaires, 1985.

Rajak, T. *Translation and Survival: The Greek Bible and the Ancient Jewish Diaspora.* Oxford: Oxford University Press, 2009.

Redepenning, E. R. *Origenes: Eine Darstellung seines Lebens und seiner Lehre.* 2 vols. Bonn: E. Weber, 1841–1846.

Reemts, C. *Vernunftsgemässer Glaube: Die Begründung des Christentums in der Schrift des Origenes gegen Celsus.* Bonn: Borengässer, 1998.

Ridings, D. *The Attic Moses: The Dependency Theme in Some Early Christian Writers.* Göteborg: Acta Universitatis Gothoburgensis, 1995.

Riedweg, C. *Mysterien Terminologie bei Platon, Philon, und Klemens von Alexandrian.* Berlin: W. de Gruyter, 1987.

Rius-Camps, J. "Origenes y Marción: Caracter preferentemente antimarcionita del Prefacio y del segundo ciclo del Peri archôn." In *Orig I*: 297–313.

Robins, R. H. "Linguistics, ancient." In *OCD*, 3rd edn, ed. S. Hornblower and A. Spawforth. Oxford: Oxford University Press, 1996.

Rondeau, M.-J. *Les Commentaires patristiques du Psautier (IIIe-Ve siècles).* Vol. 2. Rome: Pontificium Institutum Studiorum Orientalium, 1985.

Rosenmüller, J. G. *Historia interpretationis librorum sacrorum in ecclesia christiana, inde ab Apostolorum aetate usque ad Origenem.* Vol. 3. Leipzig: Fleischer: 1807.

Rossi, G. E. *Bibel und Gebet in den Predigtepilogen bei Origenes.* Dissertation. Friedrich-Schiller-Universität Jena. 2003.

Rougier, L. *Celse ou le conflit de la civilisation antique et du monde chrétien.* Paris: Editions du Siècle, 1926.

Runia, D. T. *Philo in Early Christian Literature: A Survey.* Minneapolis: Fortress, 1993.

Russell, D. A. *Criticism in Antiquity.* Berkeley: University of California Press, 1981.

Salvesen, A., ed. *Origen's Hexapla and Fragments: Papers presented at the Rich Seminar on the Hexapla.* Tübingen: Mohr Siebeck, 1998.

Sandys, J. E. *A History of Classical Scholarship.* Vol. 1, *From the Sixth Century BC to the end of the Middle* Ages. 3rd edn. New York: Hafner, 1967.

Schäfer, T. *Das Priester-Bild im Leben und Werk des Origenes.* Frankfurt am Maine: P. Lang, 1977.

Schär, M. *Das Nachleben des Origenes im Zeitalter des Humanismus.* Basel: Helbing & Lichtenhahn, 1979.

Schäublin, C. "Μήτε προσθεῖναι μήτ᾽ ἀφελεῖν." *MH* 31 (1974): 144–149.

——. "Homerum ex Homero." *MH* 34 (1977): 221–227.

——. *Untersuchungen zu Methode und Herkunft der Antiochenischen Exegese.* Cologne: Peter Hanstein, 1974.

Schendel, E. *Herrschaft und Unterwerfung Christi: 1. Korinther 15, 24–28 in Exegese und Theologie der Väter biz zum Ausgang des 4. Jahrhunderts.* Tübingen: J. C. B. Mohr, 1971.

Schenker, A. *Hexaplarische Psalmenbruchstücke: die hexaplarischen Psalmenfragmente der Handschriften Vaticanus graecus 752 und Canonicianus graecus 62.* Freiburg: Universitätsverlag, 1975.

Schindler, A. *Zwingli und die Kirchenväter.* Zurich: Kommissionsverlag Beer, 1984.

Schockenhoff, E. *Zum Fest der Freiheit: Theologie des christlichen Handelns bei Origenes.* Mainz: Matthias-Grünewald, 1990.

Schoeps, H. J. "Ebionite Christianity." *JTS* 4 (1953): 219–224.

Scholten, C. "Die alexandrinische Katechetenschule." *JAC* 38 (1995): 16–37.

Scott, A. B. *Origen and the Life of the Stars: A History of An Idea.* Oxford: Oxford University Press, 1991.

Sgherri, G. *Chiesa e Sinagoga nelle opere di Origene.* Milan: Vita e Pensiero, 1982.

Sheerin, D. "The role of prayer in Origen's homilies." In *Origen of Alexandria: His World and His Legacy,* ed. C. Kannengieser and W. L. Petersen, 200–214. Notre Dame: University of Notre Dame Press, 1988.

Sieger, F. "Selbstbezeichnungen der Gnostiker in den Nag-Hammadi-Texten." *ZNW* 71 (1980): 129–132.

Siegmund, A. *Die Überlieferung der griechischen christlichen Literatur in der lateinischen Kirche bis zum zwölften Jahrhundert.* Munich: Filger, 1949.

Simon, M. "Problèmes du Judéo-Christianisme." In *Aspects du judéo-christianisme. Colloque de Strasbourg, 22–25 avril 1964,* 1–17. Paris: Presses Universitaires de France, 1965.

——. *Verus Israel: A Study of the Relations between Christians and Jews in the Roman Empire (132–425).* Oxford: Oxford University Press, 1986.

Simonetti, M. "Eracleone e Origene." *VetChr* 3 (1966): 111–141; 4 (1967): 23–64.

——. "Eresia ed eretici in Origene." *Aug* 25 (1985): 735–748.

——. *Lettera e/o allegoria: Un contributo alla storia del L'esegesi patristica.* Rome: Institutum Patristicum Augustinianum, 1985.

——. "Il Millenarismo in Oriente a Origine a Metodio." In *Corona Gratiarum: Miscellanea Patristica, Historica et Liturgica Eligio Dekkers O.S.B. XII Lustra Complenti Oblata,* vol. 1, ed. A. J. De Smedt, et al., 37–58. Brugge: Sint Pietersabdij, 1965.

——. "Una nuova ipotesi su Gregorio il Taumaturgo." *Rivista di storia e letteratura religiosa* 24 (1988): 17–41.

——. *Profilo Storico del L'Esegesi Patristica.* Rome: Institutum Patristicum Augustinianum, 1981. ET: *Biblical Interpretation in the Early Church: An Historical Introduction to Patristic Exegesis,* transl. J. A. Hughes. Edinburgh: T. & T. Clark, 1994.

——. "La Sacra Scrittura nel *Contro Celso.*" In *Discorsi di Verità: Paganesimo, Giudaismo e Christianesimo a Confronto nel* Contro Celso *di Origene,* ed. L. Perrone, 97–114. Rome: Institutum Patristicum Augustinianum, 1998.

——. "Sul significato di alcuni termini technici nella letteratura esegetica greca." In *La terminologia esegetica nell'Antichità,* ed. C. Curti, 36–42. Bari: Edipuglia, 1987.

Skarsaune, O. and R. Hvalvik, eds. *Jewish Believers in Jesus: The Early Centuries.* Peabody, MA: Hendrickson, 2007.

Skarsaune, O. "Jewish Believers in Jesus in Antiquity—Problems of Definition, Method, and Sources," 3–21. In *Jewish Believers in Jesus: The Early Centuries.* Peabody, MA: Hendrickson, 2007.

Smalley, B. *The Study of the Bible in the Middle Ages.* Oxford: Basil Blackwell, 1952.

Smith, M. "The History of the Term Gnostikos." In *The Rediscovery of Gnosticism: Proceedings of the International Conference on Gnosticism at Yale, New Haven, Connecticut, March 28–31, 1978,* ed. B. Layton, vol. 2, 796–807. Leiden: Brill, 1981.

Soisalon-Soininen, I. *Der Charakter der asterisierten Zusätze in der Septuaginta.* Helsinki: Suomalainen Tiedeakatemia, 1959.

Somos, R. "Christianity as Practical Philosophy in Origen." In *Orig IX*: 327–335.

Speyer, W. *Die literarische Fälschung im heidnischen und christlichen Altertum: ein Versuch ihrer Deutung.* Munich: Beck, 1971.

Stroumsa, G. "Clement, Origen, and Jewish Esoteric Traditions." *Orig VI*: 61–80.

Strutwolf, H. *Gnosis als System: Zur Rezeption der valentinianischen Gnosis bei Origenes.* Göttingen: Vandenhoeck & Ruprecht, 1993.

Studer, B. "Zur Frage der dogmatischen Terminologie in der lateinischen Überset-zung von Origenes' De Principiis." In *Epektasis: Mélanges patristiques offerts au Cardinal J. Daniélou,* eds. J. Fontaine and C. Kannengiesser, 403–414. Paris: Beauchesne, 1972.

——. "Zur Frage des westlichen Origenismus." In *SP*, vol. 9, ed. F. L. Cross, 270–287. Berlin: Akademie-Verlag 9.

——. "Loving Christ According to Origen and Augustine." In *In the Shadow of the Incarnation: Essays on Jesus Christ in the Early Church in Honor of Brian E. Daley, S.J.,* ed. P. W. Martens, 149–175. Notre Dame: University of Notre Dame Press, 2008.

——. "Die patristische Exegese, eine Aktualisierung der Heiligen Schrift." *Revue des Etudes Augustiniennes* 42 (1996): 72–95.

——. "À propos des traductions d'Origène par Jérome et Rufin." *VetChr* 5 (1968): 137–154.

——. *Schola Christiana: Die Theologie zwischen Nizäa und Chalcedon.* Paderborn: Ferdinand Schöningh, 1998.

Studer, B., et al. "Origenismo." In *Origene: Dizionario. La cultura-il pensiero-le opere,* ed. A. M. Castagno. Rome: Città Nuova, 2000.

Stuiber, E. "Einiges zur Schriftauffassung des Origenes." *IKZ* 13 (1923): 145–169.

Swete, H. B. *Introduction to the Old Testament in Greek,* rev. R. R. Ottley. Cambridge: Cambridge University Press, 1914.

Taylor, C. *Hebrew-Greek Cairo Genizah Palimpsests from the Taylor-Schechter Collec-tion: Including a Fragment of the Twenty-Second Psalm According to Origen's Hexapla.* Cambridge: Cambridge University Press, 1900.

Taylor, J. E. "The Phenomenon of Early Jewish-Christianity: Reality or Scholarly Invention?" *VC* 44 (1990): 313–334.

Tomson, P. J. and D. Lambers-Petry, eds. *The Image of the Judaeo-Christians in Ancient Jewish and Christian Literature.* Tübingen: Mohr Siebeck, 2003.

Torjesen, K. J. "'Body,' 'Soul,' and 'Spirit' in Origen's Theory of Exegesis." *ATR* 67 (1985): 17–30.

——. *Hermeneutical Procedure and Theological Method in Origen's Exegesis.* Berlin: W. de Gruyter, 1986.

——. "Hermeneutics and Soteriology in Origen's *Peri Archon*." In *SP*, vol. 21, ed. E. A. Livingstone, 333–348. Leuven: Peeters, 1989.

Trigg, J. W. *Origen.* London: Routledge, 1998.

——. *Origen: The Bible and Philosophy in the Third-Century Church.* Atlanta: John Knox, 1983.

Tzamalikos, P. *Origen: Cosmology and Ontology of Time.* Leiden: Brill, 2006.

——. *Origen: Philosophy of History and Eschatology.* Leiden: Brill, 2007.

Urbach, E. "Homiletical Interpretations of the Sages and the Expositions of Origen on the Canticles, and the Jewish-Christian Disputation." *Scripta Hierosolymitana* 22 (1971): 247–275.

——. "Rabbinic exegesis and Origen's commentary on the Song of Songs and Jewish-Christian polemics." *Tarbiz* 30 (1960): 148–170.

Van Den Eynde, D. *Les normes de L'enseignement chrétien dans la littérature patristique des trois premiers siècles.* Paris: Gabalda & Fils, 1933.

Van Unnik, W. C. "De la règle Μήτε προσθεῖναι μήτε ἀφελεῖν dans l'histoire du canon." *VChr* 3 (1949): 1–36.

Vogt, H. J. *Das Kirchenverständnis des Origenes.* Cologne: Böhlar, 1974.

——, intro., transl., and notes. *Der Kommentar zum Evangelium nach Mattäus.* 3 parts. Stuttgart: Anton Hiersemann, 1983–1993.

——. "Die Lehre des Origenes von der Inspiration der Heiligen Schrift: Ein Vergleich zwischen der Grundlagenschrift und der Antwort auf Kelsos." *ThQ* 170 (1990): 97–103.

——. *Origenes als Exeget*, ed. W. Geerlings. Paderborn: Ferdinand Schöningh, 1999.

Völker, W. "Paulus bei Origenes." *Theologische Studien und Kritiken* 102 (1930): 258–279.

——. *Das Vollkommenheitsideal des Origenes: Eine Untersuchung zur Geschichte der Frömmigkeit und zu den Anfängen christlicher Mystik.* Tübingen: J. C. B. Mohr, 1931.

Wasserstein, A. "A Rabbinic Midrash as a Source of Origen's Homily on Ezekiel." *Tel Aviv* 46 (1977): 317–318.

Whitman, J. *Allegory: The Dynamics of an Ancient and Medieval Technique.* Cambridge, MA: Harvard University Press, 1987.

Wickert, U. "Glauben und Denken bei Tertullian und Origenes." *ZTK* 62 (1965): 153–177.

Wiles, M. "Origen as a Biblical Scholar." In *The Cambridge History of the Bible*, vol. 1, ed. C. F. Evans and P. R. Ackroyd, 468–470. Cambridge: Cambridge University Press, 1970.

——. *The Spiritual Gospel: The Interpretation of the Fourth Gospel in the Early Church.* Cambridge: Cambridge University Press, 1960.

Wilken, R. "Alexandria: A School for Training in Virtue." In *Schools of Thought in the Christian Tradition*, ed. P. Henry, 15–30. Philadelphia: Fortress Press, 1984.

——. *The Christians as the Romans Saw Them.* New Haven: Yale University Press, 1984.

——. *Judaism and the Early Christian Mind: A Study of Cyril of Alexandria's Exegesis and Theology.* New Haven: Yale University Press, 1971.

Williams, M. A. *Rethinking "Gnosticism": An Argument for Dismantling a Dubious Category.* Princeton: Princeton University Press, 1996.

Williams, R. "Regola di Fede." In *Origene: Dizionario. La cultura-il pensiero-le opere*, ed. A. M. Castagno. Rome: Città Nuova, 2000.

Winkelmann, F. "Einige Bemerkungen zu den Aussagen des Rufinus von Aquileia und des Hieronymus über ihre Übersetzungstheorie und –methode." In *Kyriakon, Festschrift J. Quasten*, eds. P. Granfield and J. A. Jungmann, vol. 2, 534–538. Munster: Aschendorff, 1970.

Wucherpfennig, A. *Heracleon Philologus: Gnostische Johannesexegese im zweiten Jahrhundert.* Tübingen: Mohr Siebeck, 2002.

Wutz, F. *Onomastica Sacra: Untersuchungen zum Liber Interpretationis Nominum Hebraicorum des hl. Hieronymus.* TU 11.1–2. Leipzig: J. C. Hinrichs, 1914–1915.

Young, F. M. *Biblical Exegesis and the Formation of Christian Culture.* Cambridge: Cambridge University Press, 1997.

——. "The Rhetorical Schools and their Influence on Patristic Exegesis." In *The Making of Orthodoxy: Essays in Honour of Henry Chadwick,* ed. R. Williams, 182–199. Cambridge: Cambridge University Press, 1989.

Ziebritzki, H. *Heiliger Geist und Weltseele: Das Problem der dritten Hypostase bei Origenes, Plotin und ihren Vorläufern.* Tübingen: Mohr Siebeck, 1994.

Zöllig, A. *Die Inspirationslehre des Origenes: Ein Beitrag zur Dogmengeschichte.* Freiburg: Herder, 1902.

Index of Ancient Passages Cited
Origen

Other Ancient Authors

Index of Names, Places and Concepts